I0890231

FUNDAMENTAL ISSUES IN THE ROMANCE LANGUAGES

CSLI Lecture Notess Number 195

Fundamental Issues in

THE ROMANCE LANGUAGES

EDITED BY

Danièle Godard

CSLI PUBLICATIONS

Center for the Study of
Language and Information
Stanford, California

Center for the Study of Language and Information
Leland Stanford Junior University
Printed in the United States
14 13 12 11 10   1 2 3 4 5

Library of Congress Cataloging-in-Publication Data

Fundamental issues in the Romance languages /
edited by Danièle Godard.

p. cm. – (CSLI lecture notes ; no. 195)

Includes bibliographical references and index.
ISBN 978-1-57586-587-4 (cloth) – ISBN 978-1-57586-586-7 (pbk.)
1. Romance languages–Grammar. I. Godard, Danile. II. Title. III. Series.

PC61.F86 2009
440′.045–dc22 2009031916

CIP

∞ The acid-free paper used in this book meets the minimum requirements of the American National Standard for Information Sciences—Permanence of Paper for Printed Library Materials, ANSI Z39.48-1984.

CSLI was founded in 1983 by researchers from Stanford University, SRI International, and Xerox PARC to further the research and development of integrated theories of language, information, and computation. CSLI headquarters and CSLI Publications are located on the campus of Stanford University.

CSLI Publications reports new developments in the study of language, information, and computation. Please visit our web site at
http://cslipublications.stanford.edu/
for comments on this and other titles, as well as for changes and corrections by the author and publisher.

Acknowledgments

This book is a revised version of *Les Langues Romanes ; Problèmes de la phrase simple* (2003, Paris: CNRS Editions). I thank CNRS Editions for giving permission for this English publication.
I gratefully acknowledge the financial support of the University Paris 7-Diderot, and the CNRS (Fédération de Typologie et des Universaux Linguistiques) regarding the translation.
Special thanks go to Jesse Tseng, for his manifold help.

Contents

Contributors

ANNE ABEILLÉ: Professeur des Universités, Université Paris-Diderot, UFR Linguistique, Laboratoire de Linguistique Formelle, Case 7003
9 rue Thomas Mann, 75205 Paris cedex 13, France.
anne.abeille@linguist.jussieu.fr

FRANCIS CORBLIN: Professeur des Universités, Université Paris 4-La Sorbonne, UFR Langue Française,
8 Boulevard Malesherbes, 75850 Paris Cedex 17, France.
Francis.Corblin@paris4.sorbonne.fr

CARMEN DOBROVIE-SORIN: Directeur de Recherches, CNRS et Université Paris-Diderot, UFR, Linguistique, Laboratoire de Linguistique Formelle, Case 7003
9 rue Thomas Mann, 75205 Paris cedex 13, France.
Carmen.sorin@linguist.jussieu.fr

DANIÈLE GODARD: Directeur de Recherches émérite, CNRS et Université Paris 7-Diderot, UFR Linguistique, Laboratoire de Linguistique Formelle, Case 7003
9 rue Thomas Mann, 75205 Paris cedex 13, France.
daniele.godard@linguist.jussieu.fr

BRENDA LACA: Professeur des Universités, Université Paris 8, Département de sciences du langage, Laboratoire SFL,
2 rue de la liberté, 93526 Saint-Denis Cedex, France.
laca@linguist.jussieu.fr

GÉRALDINE LEGENDRE: Professor of Cognitive Science, John Hopkins University, Department of Cognitive Science,
237 Krieger hall, 3400 N. Charles Street, Baltimore, MD 21218-2685, USA.
legendre@cogsci.jhu.edu

JEAN-MARIE MARANDIN: Directeur de Recherches, Université Paris 7-Diderot, CNRS et UFR Linguistique, Laboratoire de Linguistique Formelle,
Case 7003
9 rue Thomas Mann, 75205 Paris cedex 13, France.
Jean-marie.marandin@linguist.jussieu.fr

PHILIP MILLER: Professeur des Universités, Université Paris 7-Diderot, UFR Etudes anglophones,
10 rue Charles V, 75004, France.
philip.miller@univ-paris-diderot.fr

PAOLA MONACHESI: Utrecht University, Utrecht Institute of Linguistics-OTS,
Trans 10, NL-3512 JK Utrecht, The Netherlands.
Paola.Monachesi@phil.uu.nl

SANDA REINHEIMER: Professor, Universitatea Bucureşti, Facultatea de Limbi străine,
Edgar Quinet, 5-7, 010017, Bucharest, Romania.
ripeanus@gmail.com

ANTONELLA SORACE: Professor of Developmental Linguistics, The University of Edinburgh, Department of linguistics and English Language,
Dugald Stewart Building, 3 Charles Street, Edinburgh EH8 9AD, Scotland, UK.
antonell@ling.ed.ac.uk

LILIANE TASMOWSKI: Professeur émérite à l'Université d'Anvers, membre de l'Académie Royale flamande de Belgique pour les arts et les sciences / Koninklije Vlaamse Academie van België voor Wetenschappen en Kunschen,
De Pintelaan 287, 9000 Gent, Belgium
Liliane.tasmowski@ua.ac.be

LUCIA TOVENA: Professeur des Universités, Université Paris-Diderot, UFR Linguistique, Laboratoire de Linguistique Formelle,
Case 7003
9 rue Thomas Mann, 75205 Paris cedex 13, France.
Lucia.tovena@linguist.jussieu.fr

1

Introduction

DANIÈLE GODARD

The field of Romance studies has seen a revival over the last thirty years within various linguistic traditions: historical, typological, and structural. These traditions are no longer viewed as being in competition, but rather as being mutually beneficial to one another. Annual conferences dedicated to Romance linguistics, for example, are held in Europe and the United States. Also, there have been several recent books which offer general overviews of the Romance languages, from different perspectives. For instance, Harris and Vincent (1988) give a comprehensive presentation of the current geographical distribution of the Romance languages and their history, which is then followed by monographs treating individual languages; these are not just limited to the major standard languages, but include (in addition to Latin) creoles and the Romansch and Sardinian 'dialects'. By contrast, Agard (1984), Reinheimer and Tasmowski (1997, 2005), and Posner (1996) adopt a deliberately comparativist point of view. The first two are reference books, focusing either on syntax or on phonology and morphology. Teyssier (2004) also belongs to the category of reference books, with a practical end in view. Posner (1996) is more of a discussion of what constitutes or defines a Romance language, discussing a certain number of features from a quite general diachronic and typological perspective. We felt there was room for a book which, while adopting a comparative or typological perspective, would study certain issues raised by the Romance languages in more detail.

Firstly, we decided to give cross linguistic studies the kind of attention to detail which is usually reserved for specific studies in a given language. For every problem, we provide the relevant data in the different languages

Fundamental Issues in the Romance Languages.
Danièle Godard (ed.).

under consideration. The first objective of the studies here, then, is to provide a more complete knowledge of the facts than was available.

Because of the multiplicity of grammatical formalisms today, certain descriptive and theoretical advances can be obscured by issues and terminology which only make sense internally to a particular formalism. Romance linguistics is no exception. However, there are concepts and theoretical proposals of a general kind, which are relatively independent of any particular formalism. It is with this level of analysis that the studies in this book are concerned. The central issues are driven by the concerns of formal linguistics, without being dependent on any particular grammatical formalism. Thus, the second objective of the book is to present problems and analyses in a way which is accessible to the entire linguistic community.

We do not claim here to be an exhaustive reference work. Firstly, the authors have restricted themselves to the major standard Romance languages: Catalan, French, Italian, Portuguese, Romanian and Spanish. Clearly, there is no theoretical reason for this choice. Extending the studies to other languages and dialects would of course be interesting, but the collection of the data is a piece of work in itself. Secondly, we have selected a number of topics which are recognized as being characteristic of simple sentence constructions in Romance, but do not cover the totality. The chapters focus on different aspects of the grammar (excluding phonology): morphology, syntax, semantics, information and discourse structure, and the syntax-morphology and syntax-semantics interfaces. With the possible exception of the first chapter (on verbal morphology), the areas discussed have already been well-researched: the status and precise position of clitic pronouns, complex predicates, unaccusativity, negative concord, noun phrases without determiners (or 'bare nouns'), and subject inversion.

Giving an overview of **verbal inflection** in the Romance languages is a daunting task given the sheer diversity of forms which language change has engendered; this is the case both between different languages, and even just within a language. Liliane Tasmowski and Sandra Reinheimer have taken up this challenge. They show that there is a common tendency among the Romance languages which underpins the evolution of each of them. While phonetic changes depend on the variable position of the accent in Latin verbs (which falls either on the stem or on the inflexion) and apply independently of morphological paradigms, destroying the lexical base stem, each language reacts against this evolution by recreating the lexical base stem. A transparent morphology (the authors speak of an idealized schema of the form: lexical base + thematic element + tense / mood + endings) is not accomplished in the same way in the different conjugations; it is very advanced in the productive conjugations and less advanced in the unproductive ones. In fact, there is a clear relationship between productivity of the conjugation type and the unicity of the lexical base stem for the whole of a conjugation. But even among irregular verbs, it is possible to discern subregularities.

By illustrating the present tense in detail (which is a prototypical instance of tenses with the Latin *infectum* stem), the authors show the different ways in which the languages they consider (Spanish, French, Italian, Portuguese and Romanian) have reacted to the destruction of the lexical base stem: the elimination of variants due to phonetic evolution, the creation of forms by integrating suffixes into a conjugation in order to avoid the effects of accent variation, or the creation of morpho-phonological alternations not specific to verbs. In addition to a parallel problem (which is dealt with by similar means), the forms of the simple past and the past participle (which come from the *perfectum* and *supinum* stems in Latin) show another form of regularization. While in Latin, one cannot predict the formation of one stem on the basis of another (one has to learn the three stems for each lexeme separately), the Romance languages generally ensure that all verbal forms can be calculated from those belonging to the *infectum* tenses. Where a purely synchronic approach would not allow these cross-linguistic regularities to appear, this study, at once diachronic and synchronic, shows that precisely the same kind of development is involved in each of the languages studied; that of associating a single base stem with each verbal lexeme.

Without doubt the single most-studied property of the Romance languages (notably since the work of Richard Kayne 1975) are the **pronouns known as 'clitics' (pronominal clitics** or **clitic pronouns)**, pronouns that do not appear in their usual argument positions, and are not separated from the verb. Theoretical issues have generally focused on defining the exact status of these elements (whether they are syntactically autonomous elements, or verbal morphemes), and explaining their position pre- or post-verbally, the exact conditions for which vary between languages. It is still unclear to what extent this variation is related to syntactic, semantic, or morphological factors. The chapter by Philip Miller and Paola Monachesi is a precise and systematic description of the data in the different Romance languages. No such description has previously been available, yet it is surely necessary to have one in order to evaluate the answers to the theoretical questions.

The authors identify two sets of properties: syntactic properties on the one hand, and morphological and phonological ones, on the other. The syntactic properties have to do with the positions clitics occupy according to type of sentence and type of language; with the problem of clitic doubling (the co-occurrence of a clitic and a full NP or PP), and the interactions between clitics and coordination (governing whether clitics can be coordinated with each other, or whether a clitic can have 'wide scope' over coordinated verbs). With the categorial status of clitics in mind, the authors tackle the other (morphological and phonological) properties. What is the degree of prosodic integration of clitics with verbs? What are the morphophonological interactions between verbs and clitics? What are the constraints upon sequences of clitics (the realization of a sequence is not always predictable from the elements which it is composed of)?

By the end of the chapter, it is clear that the behavior of clitics is more complex than had previously been thought; it fails to be totally consistent, not only between languages, but even sometimes internally to one language. The different empirical properties pose problems for different theoretical approaches, which appear to give priority either to the syntactic properties, or the morpho-phonological ones. Because clitics are at the interface between syntax, morphology and phonology, they constitute a challenge for every linguistic theory.

Complex predicates, which have monoclausal properties while containing two or more predicates, have also been studied a great deal in the Romance languages, since the pioneering works of Kayne (1975), Rizzi (1982) and Aissen and Perlmutter (1976/83). However, there was still no work which systematically compared the languages in terms of the properties which had been identified for them individually. Furthermore, there continues to be no agreement on which aspect of the syntax the phenomenon relates to. Some believe the properties of complex predicates are linked to a special structure (which contrasts with that of ordinary verbs), while others contend that they are due to the head verb inheriting the arguments subcategorized by the embedded predicate. By systematically laying out the properties of different Romance languages, Anne Abeillé and Danièle Godard suggest an answer: complex predicates may have a specific complementation structure, but they all have properties which follow from the inheritance (or sharing) of arguments.

The head of a complex predicate is either a tense auxiliary verb, a 'restructuring' verb (modal, aspectual, or movement verb), a causative verb, a predicative verb (e.g. copulas), or a 'support' verb. Support verbs, which take a nominal complement are left aside. Complex predicates can be identified by two properties: clitic-climbing (a clitic pronoun is attached to the head of the construction rather than to the verb which sub-categorizes for it), and the non-finiteness of the complement. Certain properties are clearly correlated with clitic climbing: the occurrence of complex predicates in bounded dependencies, the middle passive *se* formation and long periphrastic passives. This behavior follows from the inheritance of arguments by the head verb. In certain other respects (which have not been systematically compared until now), complex predicates differ among themselves: the possibility of conjoining sequences of complement predicates with their complements, and the possibility of inserting elements (adverbs, inverted lexical subjects) between the two predicates. These differences follow from the following analysis. There is a contrast between Spanish complex predicates at least for certain speakers, as well as tense auxiliaries in Romanian, on the one hand, and the other cases on the other one. The first involve a verbal complex structure (where the head verb and the complement verb form a sub-constituent); in other cases, we have a 'flat structure', a VP where the head verb and the bare (or lexical) complement verb are both at the same level as the complements that the complement verb sub-categorizes for. However, copulas and copular verbs behave identically in all languages, but pattern differently from the other heads of complex predicates: they do not head a verbal complex or a flat structure, but take a phrasal complement with variable saturation (the complements may be inherited by the head, but do not have to). Moreover, languages differ according to their ordering rules.

This suggests the following conclusions: (i) The formation of a complex predicate is the result of the lexical properties of the head verbs. Thus, while these verbs belong to the same semantic classes cross-linguistically, this is not enough to predict the behavior of any given verb. Furthermore, it is (family of) lexemes which specify whether the embedded predicate is a phrase or a bare word (not dominated by a phrase): copular verbs in all languages require a phrasal complement, while the others do not. (ii) While it is possible for a bare word to enter directly into the syntax, this is a 'marked option', in the sense that either a specific structure is created (verbal complex), or specific ordering rules are used (in the flat structure). Languages differ in the choice they make between these two options.

Italian was one of the first languages which was used to demonstrate the distinction between **two types of intransitive verb**, 'unaccusatives' and 'unergatives' (see, in particular, Perlmutter 1978). This distinction results from both lexical semantic and syntactic factors. However, there is not a total correspondence whereby all the lexical semantic factors coincide with the syntactic ones. Furthermore, different tests which have been used to identify unaccusatives and unergatives do not define the exact same classes, either between languages or within one and the same language. It is not at all obvious what the regularities are which underpin the correlation between the syntax and lexical semantics of these verbs. It is precisely this problem which Géraldine Legendre and Antonella Sorace take on, particularly in relation to French and the comparison with Italian.

The authors discuss two criteria for the unaccusative / unergative distinction: the choice of tense auxiliary and the occurrence of the participle in a related range of contexts. Grounding the distinction on these criteria encounters difficulties: In Italian, which like French has a choice of two auxiliaries (unlike the other main Romance languages), there are many more verbs which combine with *essere* than there are verbs in French which combine with *être*. Furthermore, there are a certain number of verbs which exhibit variation between the two auxiliaries. The authors make sense of this data by using two particular tools of analysis: firstly, the semantic classes of the verbs can be organized according to a particular gradient (or hierarchy), with – at each extreme – verbs which are prototypically associated with one or the other auxiliary; the verbs in the centre of the hierarchy exhibit variation between and within languages. The second tool of analysis is the decomposition of the lexical semantics of a verb into semantic features, which makes it possible to identify the relevant semantic classes for each test, and also to establish a foundation for the hierarchy of auxiliary-selection. French differs from Italian in terms of the (higher) position in the hierarchy which separates the two auxiliaries. The other fundamental aspect of the distinction between unaccusative and unergative verbs, is the properties of the participle form: only certain (active) participles can be heads of a phrase adjoined to the sentence, or act as a predicative complement to verbs like *croire* ('believe'). The overall presentation of the data here brings to light certain inclusive relations: all the verbs in French which take *être* are included in the set of Italian verbs which take *essere*, which are themselves included in the set of verbs where the participles behave in the manner just mentioned. Thus the authors' analysis of the situation is the following: it is the behavior of their participles which allows verbs to be classified as unaccusative or unergative. The selection of the auxiliary *être / essere* is thus considered as a sufficient but not a necessary condition of belonging to the class of unaccusative verbs.

The data are interpreted in the following way: the authors agree with the syntactic representation of the intransitive dichotomy, according to which the argument of unergatives is always a subject, while that of an unaccusative may be an object or a subject. At the same time, they rely on optimality theory to 'align' this syntactic dichotomy with the semantic properties of the verbs, which the hierarchy of auxiliary-selection is built upon. According to this theory, the properties of an utterance result from the competition among non-rigid constraints, which form a universal set. The constraints in question pertain to the way an argument is projected onto a syntactic grammatical function. The differences between languages and constructions regarding unaccusativity are a consequence of the variable place in the hierarchy of a non-lexical constraint, which says 'avoid projecting the first argument onto the object function'.

As in the Germanic languages, the Romance languages in general allow **NPs without determiners, or 'bare nouns'**, with an interpretation close to that of NPs with indefinite determiners. Carmen-Dobrovie-Sorin and Brenda Laca pose the following questions: how do we describe and represent the interpretation of bare nouns, how do we account for their distributional constraints, and how do we account for interpretative and distributional differences between languages? Spanish, Catalan (which is not distinct from Spanish in this respect), Italian and Romanian present the same properties for bare NPs based on a mass or plural N; these languages contrast with French which, with the same usage, does not have NPs without determiners; they also contrast with Portuguese, especially Brazilian Portuguese, where bare nouns can be used more extensively.

Bare nouns do not have exactly the same properties as NPs with indefinite determiners (see Carlson 1977); despite appearances, their interpretations are not identical. The analysis proposed by Carlson for English, according to which bare nouns are kind nouns does not apply to the Romance languages where bare nouns generally do not have the generic interpretation which is associated with the kind denotation of nominals. The authors' proposal is to extend to NPs without determiners the interpretation associated with the N when it is accompanied by a determiner or when it is predicative: bare nouns are predicates, or expressions which denote 'properties'. Their anaphoric and aspectual properties are related to the lack of boundedness of predicates, in contrast with expressions denoting individuals. Their absence of wide scope comes from the facts of compositionality: the particular lexical items which select bare nouns permit them as a co-predicate of one of their arguments, and supply it with an existential quantifier with narrow scope.

NPs with so-called 'partitive articles' in French (*du, de la, des*) have the same uses as bare NPs in the other Romance languages: it is surely therefore due to syntactic constraints that French fails to use bare nouns the way the other Romance languages do. In contrast, Portuguese has a more extended use of bare nouns, especially Brazilian Portuguese, where they have generic interpretations (Schmitt and Munn 1999). The semantic mechanism responsible for the shifting of the property-interpretation to a kind interpretation therefore depends on the presence of an explicit operator (the definite article) in the Romance languages generally, though not in Brazilian Portuguese (or English). Finally, Brazilian Portuguese allows bare nouns with a singular count N: unlike the other Romance languages, the morphological singular is not semantically specified as being singular; it can denote not only in the domain of atomic entities, but also in the domains structured by the 'part-of' relation, reserved for plurals and mass Ns in the other Romance languages (as well as the Germanic languages).

Another well-known characteristic of the Romance languages is **negative concord** (on negative concord in English, see, notably, Labov 1972), or the possibility of a sentence being interpreted as only containing one semantic negation while containing several words which, independently, are associated with negation. How do we construct such an interpretation? Studies dedicated to this phenomenon usually try to find a solution in the specific properties of the negative words. However, for Francis Corblin and Lucia Tovena, this somewhat misses the essential aspects of the problem: How is it that this phenomenon is at once widespread across languages, and yet has no equivalent in the rest of the grammar? How do we explain the fact that the phenomenon essentially characterizes the elements of a predicative domain, which are the constituents of one event, being participants or a localization?

Building on some of their previous work, the authors suggest that the expression of negation follows from the interaction of three principles which affect the relation between a predicate and its arguments. Semantic arguments are obligatory, and include spatio-temporal referents as well as what are usually taken to be arguments (see Corblin and Derzhanski 1997). According to the first principle, natural languages have specialized lexical expressions (negative polarity items or negative words) for those arguments which must be interpreted in the domain of a negation. The second principle says that for any given verbal predicate, there is only normally one (semantic) negation associated with it, two negations being the 'maximal permitted complexity'. The third principle is a tendency, at work in the Romance languages: a negative (verbal) clause includes a preverbal negative element.

After having surveyed the occurrence of negative words in negative polarity contexts (an unstable phenomenon in Romance languages, only found these days in formal styles), the authors describe the syntactic and interpretive constraints on the co-occurrence of negative words. The languages in question fall into three groups. In Romanian, it is the obligatory negative marker *nu* which satisfies the third principle. In Spanish, Italian, and Portuguese, all negations satisfy this principle, which should be strengthened to 'a negative clause contains one and only one pre-verbal negation'. In contrast, French is largely unconstrained by this third principle, since it reduces to the presence of *ne* in the formal and / or written form of the language. The second principle holds absolutely in Romanian, and almost absolutely in Spanish, Italian, and Portuguese, where double negative interpretation requires strong prosodic and discourse conditions; French allows this interpretation more widely, even rendering it obligatory (in the standard French spoken in France) if the negative argument and *pas* are both present. In their analysis, negative argument words are semantically ambiguous, as they correspond either to a negative indefinite or a variable in the context of the negation; such a variation or semantic 'degrading' is not open to negative adverbs.

The conditions under which **subject inversion** can take place in the Romance languages, has been the topic of numerous studies, within different approaches. Jean-Marie Marandin's study casts new light on this topic, by shifting the focus of inquiry from the properties which characterize (the referent of) the subject to those which characterize the predicate. The most generally accepted analysis of subject inversion is based on an information structure partition (focus / ground), and makes the following generalization: the subject is obligatorily post-verbal if it is a narrow focus. A narrow focus characterizes the constituent which represents the new information carried by the sentence. Jean-Marie Marandin straightforwardly shows that this analysis cannot account for all the data. In particular, it does not account for French, a language which, while distinguishing itself from the other Romance languages by not having so-called 'free' inversion, does still have subject inversion. The standard analysis also fails to account for the inversion in subordinate clauses, since the focus / ground partition characterizes the utterance as a whole, and subordinate clauses do not have their own.

The chapter by Jean-Marie Marandin aims to cover all the cases of subject inversion that have been identified in the Romance languages, although they are not structurally identical. At the same time, the author shows that inversion does not constitute a unified phenomenon, but is determined by two distinct conditions. The first, which he refers to as 'the Given Predicate Condition' pertains to discourse grammar. In the modelization of Büring (1997), the theme of a discourse is defined as the set of propositions which can resolve the question posed at a given point in the discourse. The given content is what is common to this set of propositions. The condition says that inversion is appropriate if the predicate is given, that is, belongs to the given content. The second condition, the 'Presupposed Disposition condition', is pragmatic, and liable to be satisfied in several configurations. Inversion is appropriate if the predicate denotes a disposition of (the referent of) the subject, which is present in the cognitive state of the speaker. This condition is satisfied if the predicate denotes a property stereotypically associated with the class of objects denoted by the head N of the subject (as in *The bells ring*), or associated with the class to which the referent of the subject belongs, according to knowledge shared by the speakers (Proust is a writer, and writers have a disposition to write and read books, so Proust has a disposition to read and write). According to the author, it is this condition that subject inversion in presentative constructions must satisfy: in the narrative genre, participants have the disposition to appear or disappear. Crucially, these two conditions are autonomous: they cannot be defined in terms of lexical class, they do not depend on the focus / ground partition, and are indifferent to the various syntactic conditions which govern the possibility of the post-verbal occurrence of the subject in the various languages. These conditions are among the properties determining the linearization of constituents, which emerges today as a specific component of the grammar.

The chapters here are essentially independent from each other, except for two pairs. The first is the chapter on clitics and the one on complex predicates. In the chapter on complex predicates, clitics are analyzed as verbal affixes rather than syntactically autonomous elements. In the chapter on clitics, it is shown that the data are more complex than is usually acknowledged. Nevertheless, the authors conclude that there is a tendency towards the treatment of pronominal clitics as affixes in the Romance Languages. The analysis of complex predicates, according to which the phenomenon rests essentially on the inheritance of the arguments of one predicate by a higher predicate, is in fact compatible with other analyses of clitics. In contrast, the affixal analysis of clitics is rendered more difficult if complex predicates are claimed to rely on having a specific syntactic structure instead of a particular argumental structure. Indeed, to account for clitic climbing in the absence of the general inheritance of arguments, one would have to appeal to the 'movement' of these elements. Now, if these elements are affixes, that leads to a conception according to which the units taken into account by the syntax can be sub-parts of words rather than inflected words. It seems clear that a grammar which assumes a leafing-through of the morphology and the syntax, is more complex than a grammar which conceives each of them as (relatively) independent components.

There is also some intersection between the chapters on unaccusativity and subject inversion. Both raise the question of the definition of unaccusativity. Broadly, there are two possible approaches, semantic and syntactic. They have in common the observation that, in some cases, the first argument of a verb is or can be realized as an object. However, in the first approach, this is correlated with semantic properties of the verb, as well as some formal properties (such as the occurrence in participials, and the selection of auxiliary). In the alternative view, one looks at the actual realization of the first argument as an object, correlated with its being possibly realized as the indefinite clitic *en/ne*. Thus, unaccusativity defines either a lexical semantic class (with formal reflexes), or a syntactic realization of arguments. Legendre and Sorace adopt the first approach in chapter 5, while Marandin adopts the second in chapter 8. Although Marandin concentrates on the semantico-discursive conditions on 'subject inversion' rather than on the syntactic analysis, he accepts the hypothesis that, among the post-verbal occurrences of the first argument there is one in which it is an object (see also Marandin 2001). The two views do not coincide either in Italian or in French (*contra* Burzio 1986). Saccon (1995) shows that, in Italian, object realization and *ne*-clitization are perfectly compatible with the selection of auxiliary *avere* (see the following sentence where the auxiliary and *ne* are underlined, *Ieri hanno parlato cinque linguisti alla TV, anche oggi ne parleranno tre al Convegno*, 'Yesterday five linguists spoke on TV; also today three of them will speak at the meeting'), and goes on to suggest that all intransitive verbs can give rise to such argument realization, subject to semantico-discursive constraints rather than lexical ones. Similarly, there are two constructions in French where one finds a first argument realized as an object: the narrative root sentence (*Ont alors surgi trois policiers*, 'Just at that moment did three policemen appear'), and the subjunctive complement sentence (*Je voudrais qu'en soient achetés plusieurs*, 'I would like that several of them be bought', see Kampers-Manhe 1998). The sets of data defined by the lexico-semantic and the syntactic approaches are different. There are verbs whose first argument is an object and which are not semantically unaccusative. In fact, the two approaches manifest a tension between two ways of tackling the intransitivity split, whose unification is still a topic of ongoing research.

These studies provide detailed and systematic presentations and discussions of data, which, in certain cases at least, appear more complex than had previously been thought. They also propose a certain number of analyses which are empirically testable. We therefore believe that this book makes a contribution to the understanding of the grammar of Romance languages, and to the knowledge of the general linguistic problems which have been tackled.

2

Verb Stem Variations in Romance

LILIANE TASMOWSKI AND SANDA REINHEIMER

1 Introduction[1]

Studies of verbal inflection in the Romance languages are generally fragmentary, focusing on individual languages instead of attempting a global comparison. This is understandable, given the extraordinary synchronic diversity resulting on the one hand from divergent phonetic developments that have brought all of the languages away from their common origin, and on the other hand from the specific analogical restructuring processes operating within each individual language. In each and every one of them, the joint action of these two forces has given rise to a significant number of residual irregular verbs that on the whole resist systematization.

Indeed, each of the Romance languages (we will consider only Portuguese, Spanish, French, Italian and Romanian)[2] reacts differently to the newly generated state of affairs. In what follows, we will nevertheless try to show that an overall general tendency towards restructuring can be identified across the languages, with the same endpoint in every case: a unitary verb stem. From this perspective, even the so-called irregular verbs have developed subregularities (albeit of a local nature) in the very same direction.

[1] We thank Jean Lowenstamm and Jean-Marie Marandin for their judicious comments. This study was carried out as part of a research project funded by the FWO (Flemish Foundation for Scientific Research), to which we express our gratitude.

[2] The term 'Romance languages' should be understood here as referring to these five languages; such a restriction is of course motivated by purely practical considerations.

Fundamental Issues in the Romance Languages.
Danièle Godard (ed.).

In section 2, we present the situation in Latin and the transformations that Latin verbal forms underwent in their evolution towards the Romance languages. Section 3 is devoted to the reorganization of the *present* stem, which can be characterized as a reaction to phonetic developments. Section 4 examines the reorganization of the Romance *preterite* and *participle*, comparing their stems to that of the present, and taking into account the surviving vestiges of the phonetic structure of the Latin etymon.

2 Presentation of the Facts

2.1 Latin

2.1.1 The conjugations

Latin verbs are divided into four classes, according to the vowel in the infinitive:[3]

conjugation I	-a-	*am**a**re, laud**a**re*	'love, praise'
conjugation II	-ē-	*uid**ē**re, hab**ē**re*	'see, have'
conjugation III	-ĕ-	*scr**i**bĕre, f**a**cĕre*	'write, make'
conjugation IV	-i-	*aud**i**re, sent**i**re*	'hear, feel'

In vulgar and late Latin, new verbs were created by adding the inchoative suffix *-esc(ĕre)* or *-isc(ĕre)* to the stem of conjugation II verbs: *florescĕre* 'flourish' < *florēre* 'be in bloom', *putrescĕre* 'rot' < *putrēre* 'be rotten', *putescĕre* 'begin to stink' < *putēre* 'stink'. This set the stage for the emergence of a new conjugational group in French, Italian, and Romanian, characterized by the presence of this suffix in certain forms. In the languages mentioned, this group is incorporated into the *-i-* conjugation.[4] In our representations (see Table 1 below), the verbs whose stem is extended by an inflectional suffix are marked by the subscript '$_S$'.

2.1.2 Stem and themes

In Latin, the verbal stem corresponding to a base lexeme is realized concretely as one of three different themes — the *infectum*, for present tenses, the *perfectum*, for past tenses, and the *supinum*[5], from which the Romance past participle is derived. The three themes are related more or less systematically according to the conjugation. The degree of systematicity can be judged in terms of:

---

[3] Boldface characters indicate accent placement.

[4] In Portuguese and Spanish by contrast, the suffix appears with verbs of the *-er* conjugation. In these languages, the suffix is not inflectional but derivational (and productive), and it is found in all forms of the verb.

[5] For example *crescere* (stem *cre-*: infectum *cre+sc-*, perfectum *cre+u-*, supinum *cre+t-*).

(a) the existence of a single derivational process *vs* the existence of multiple derivations for the three themes starting from the base stem;

(b) (for the preterite and past participle) the existence of a single stem form, always unaccented (weak) *vs* an alternation between an unaccented (weak) form and an accented (strong) form of the same stem.

According to these two criteria, conjugations I and IV (the more recent conjugations in Latin) show more uniformity in their themes:

I *laudare*: ***laud**o – **laud**aui – **laud**atum* 'praise, I praise, I praised, praised'
(but also rare cases like *crepare*: *crepo – crepui – crepitum* 'burst')
IV *audire*: ***aud**io – **aud**iui – **aud**itum* 'hear'
(but also rare cases like *sentire*: *sentio – sensi – sensum* 'feel')

whereas conjugations II et III (the older conjugations) generally exhibit an alternation of themes:

II *uidēre: uideo – uidi – uisum* 'see'
(but also, more rarely, *implēre*: *impleo – impleui – impletum* 'fill')
III *uiuĕre*: *uiuo – uixi* – ∅ 'live'
(but also, rarely, *petĕre*: *petio – petiui – petitum* 'ask')

A given theme, however, does not show any phonetic alternations. In other words, there are no vowel or consonant alternations within the *infectum*, *perfectum*, or *supinum* themselves.

2.2 Towards the Romance Languages

2.2.1 The conjugations

Table 1 gives a rough presentation[6] of the Romance counterparts of the four Latin conjugations:[7]

[6] We will not address the issue of class switching in Latin or in Romance. Table 1 simply indicates that a significant number of Latin verbs in *-ĕre* gave rise to (for example) Portuguese and Spanish verbs in *-ir*.

[7] The suffix *-ez-*, which extends the stem of conjugation I verbs in Romanian, comes from *-idiare*. For example: pres. ind. 1. *lucr-ez* (*-ez* < *-idio*, from *a lucra* 'work' < Lat. *lucrare/lucubrare*) vs 1. *cânt* < *canto* (from *a cânta* 'sing' < Lat. *cantare*). The suffix *-idiare* is also found in the other Romance languages (Pt. *-ejar*, Sp. *-ear*, Fr. *-oyer*, It. *-eggiare*), where it has a purely derivational function.

<table>
<tr><th></th><th>Latin</th><th>Portuguese</th><th>Spanish</th><th>French</th><th>Italian</th><th>Romanian</th></tr>
<tr><td>conj. I</td><td>-are</td><td>-ar</td><td>-ar</td><td>-er</td><td>-are</td><td>-a / -a$_S$</td></tr>
<tr><td>conj. II</td><td>-ēre</td><td rowspan="2">-er</td><td rowspan="2">-er</td><td rowspan="3">-oir
-re</td><td rowspan="3">-ere
-ere</td><td>-ea</td></tr>
<tr><td rowspan="2">conj. III</td><td rowspan="2">-ĕre</td><td rowspan="2">-e</td></tr>
<tr><td rowspan="2">-ir</td><td rowspan="2">-ir</td></tr>
<tr><td>conj. IV</td><td>-ire</td><td>-ir / -ir$_S$</td><td>-ire / -ire$_S$</td><td>-i / -i$_S$</td></tr>
</table>

Table 1

Among these, the *productive* conjugations are those in *-a-* for Spanish and Portuguese, those in *-a-* and *-i*$_S$*-* for French and Italian, and those in *-a*$_S$*-* and *-i*$_S$*-* for Romanian. For our purposes, the productive conjugations are interesting for the variations — not found in Latin (see section 2.1.2 above) — that emerged in the present tense (i.e. in the old *infectum*), and for the way in which these variations were undone in the course of time.

The *non-productive* conjugations, deriving from Latin ***-ē-*** and *-ĕ-* verbs, will be of concern to us because of the way in which the past tense stem (which goes back to the old *perfectum* and *supinum*) is becoming linked to the present stem, a relationship that in most cases could not have been detected in Latin.

2.2.2 The verb stem

The phonetic evolution from Latin to the Romance languages is largely a context-dependent process: for vowels, it is conditioned above all by the placement of the accent, whereas for consonants, it is conditioned by the position of the consonant in the word and the nature of the following vowel. As such, the process necessarily disrupts the intra-stem morpho-phonetic uniformity found in Latin, and in the transition from Latin to Romance, it gives rise to a series of variants whose phonetic relationship is sometimes quite obscure. But this fragmentation due to phonetic developments is counterbalanced by analogical tendencies that (i) block certain phonetic phenomena and (ii) favor the emergence of a single stem per base lexeme. All forms of the verb can then be derived from this stem, in accordance with the ideal schema:

invariant base lexeme + thematic element + tense/mood + endings

For all of the Romance languages, in the productive conjugations, the degree of invariability of the base lexeme reaches 100% for verbs marked '$_S$' (see section 2.2.1), and decreases progressively as we enter the non-productive conjugations, with the lowest degree of uniformity observed for verbs deriving from the old conjugation III in Latin. We will now proceed to the description of this evolution from an invariant Latin stem to a set of stem variants in Romance, followed by the re-emergence of an invariant stem.

2.2.3 Phonetic modifications leading to divergence

2.2.3.1 Phonetic erosion

In the transition from Latin to the Romance languages, the ends of words are targeted by a phonetic erosion that works its way towards the accented vowel (which is preserved). Several distinct phases can be identified in the course of this process; we focus on the following, which have a direct impact on verbal development:

(i) Final consonants disappear. Some consonants, however, resist this process, the most notorious case being that of final *-s* in Western Romance.

(ii) Unstressed vowels in final syllables undergo modification or disappear altogether.[8]

Lat. {o, u}	⇒	[o] (written *o*) in Spanish and Italian [u] (written *o*) in Portuguese {∅, [u] (written *u*) after muta cum liquida} in Romanian {∅, [ə] (written *e*) after muta cum liquida} in French
Lat. a	⇒	[a] (written *a*) in Spanish and Italian [ɐ] (written *a*) in Portuguese [ə] (written *ă*) in Romanian [ə] (written *e*) in French
Lat. {e, i}	⇒	{[e] (written *e*), ∅} in Spanish {[^{ə}] (written *e*), ∅} in Portuguese {Ø, [ə] (written *e*) after muta cum liquida} in French
Lat. e	⇒	[e] (written *e*) in Italian and Romanian
Lat. i	⇒	[i] (written *i*) in Italian {[^{i}], [i] after muta cum liquida (written *i*)} in Romanian

[8] The symbol ∅ here means 'disappears'.

(iii) Phase (iii), not observed in the other Romance languages, is a phonetic phenomenon in the history of French. We will refer to it as the '(Rule of) Truncation':[9]

> A morpheme-final consonant – primary or secondary (i.e. final as a result of (ii)) – other than *l* or *r*, reduces to ∅ phonetically if it is in absolute final position or if it is followed by a consonant-initial morpheme.

This is what we observe in the evolution of words like *ceruum* in the nominal domain and *battit* in the verbal domain:

ceruu(m) ⇒ Pt. *cervo*, Sp. *ciervo*, It. *cervo*, Rom. *cerb*, Fr. *cerf* ⇒ Fr. [sɛr]
batti(t) ⇒ **batte(t)* ⇒ Pt., Sp. *bate*, It. *batte*, Rom. *bate*, Fr. *bat* ⇒ Fr. [ba]

2.2.3.2 Consonant palatalization

The palatalization over time of the original Latin consonants, more precisely the palatalization of velar consonants under the influence of a following palatal vowel, is a particularly complex problem. Here we will consider only what is relevant for our study: the fate of final consonants in verb stems.

		{[s], [z] intervocalically, [ʃ] finally} (written *s* or *z*) in Portuguese
k / __ e, i	⇒	[θ] (written *z* or *c*) in Spanish
		{[s], [z] intervocalically, ∅ finally} in French
		[tʃ] (written *c(i)* or *c(e)*) in Italian and Romanian

uicinu(m) ⇒ **vecinu* ⇒ Pt. *vizinho*, Sp. *vecino*, Fr. *voisin*, It. *vicino*, Rom. *vecin*
dicit ⇒ **dice(t)* ⇒ Pt. *diz*, Sp. *dice*, Fr. *dit*, It. *dice*, Rom. *zice*

Compare this with:

k / __ a ⇒ Pt., Sp. [g], Fr. [j] or ∅, It. [k] or [g], Rom. [k]

lactuca(m) ⇒ Pt. *leituga*, Sp. *lechuga*, Fr. *laitue*, It. *lattuga*, Rom. *lăptucă*
pacat ⇒ Pt., Sp. *paga*, Fr. *paie*, It. *paga*, Rom. *(îm)pacă*

---

[9] We adopt this term because (iii) corresponds to part of the phenomenon that Dell (1973: 182) describes from a synchronic point of view with his 'Rule of Truncation', applying to occlusives and fricatives:

> A morpheme-final [–RESONANT] segment is deleted in all contexts other than {__ + Vowel, __ # Vowel}

('+' represents a morpheme boundary and '#' a morpheme or word boundary in a tight syntactic group). For the sake of convenience, the formulation of (iii) also includes nasals, which Dell accounts for with a separate Rule of Nasalization ordered before Truncation. For an overview of the problems particular to the analysis of nasals, see Dell (*op.cit.*:192 and *passim*).

In the transition from Latin to Romanian, the presence of an adjacent morpheme *ī* in Latin[10] also triggers palatalization of dentals. This phenomenon is not observed in the other languages. Thus, for Romanian only:

t / __ + ī ⇒ [ts] (written *ţ*)
d / __ + ī ⇒ [z] (written *z*)
s / __ + ī ⇒ [ʃ] (written *ş*)

**mentire* ⇒ Pt., Sp., Fr. *mentir*, It. *mentire* but Rom. *a minţi* [mintsi]
**ordire* ⇒ Pt., Sp. *urdir*, Fr. *ourdir*, It. *ordire* but Rom. *a urzi*
tussire ⇒ Pt. *tossir*, Sp. *toser*, Fr. *tousser*, It. *tossire* but Rom. *a tuşi* [tuʃi]

2.2.3.3 Modifications affecting vowel quality in the verb stem

It is well known that [ɛ] and [ɔ] in vulgar Latin evolved into other phonemes depending on whether or not they are accented. When accented (and only then), these vowels became diphthongs, except in Portuguese. Diphthongization did not proceed in the same way throughout Romance, however. In French and Italian, it only occurred with vowels appearing in open syllables in Latin, for Spanish it applied to both free and checked vowels, and in Romanian it only involved [ɛ] (free or checked).[11] Romanian also displays metaphonic diphthongization, conditioned by the nature of the final vowel. These modifications are summarized in Table 2.[12]

Accent	Latin	Port.	Spanish	French	Italian	Romanian
+acc	ɛ[	ɛ	**ie**	**ie**	**ie**	**ie**
	ɛ]			ɛ	ɛ	**ie** ⇒ **ia** / __ ə
−acc	ɛ	ə	e	ə, e	e	e
+acc	ɔ[	ɔ	**ue**	**œ, ø**	**uo**	**o**
	ɔ]			ɔ	ɔ	**o** ⇒ **oa** / __ e, ə
−acc	ɔ	u	o	o, u	o	o, u

Table 2

On the other hand, the vowels [e], [o], and [a] in vulgar Latin evolved as shown in Table 3.

[10] An indicator of conjugation or a personal marker in verbal morphology, or a plural marker in nominal morphology.

[11] [ɔ] was not part of the phonological system of Eastern Latin.

[12] The symbol [indicates an open syllable,] a closed syllable (e.g. *quae*[-*ro* with **ɛ**[, *per*]-*do* with **ɛ**]).

Accent	Latin	Port.	Spanish	French	Italian	Romanian
+acc	**e[**	**e**	**e**	**wa**	**e**	**e** **e ⇒ ea** / __ ə
	e]			**e, ɛ**		
–acc	e	ə	e	ə, e	e	e
+acc	**o[**	**o**	**o**	**œ, ø**	**o**	**o** **o ⇒ oa** / __ e, ə
	o]			**u**		
–acc	o	u	o	o, u	o	o, u
+acc	**a[**	**a**	**a**	**ɛ**	**a**	**a**
	a]			**a**		
–acc	a	ɐ	a	a, ə	a	ə

Table 3

3 The Present Tenses in the Romance Languages

Let us see how these general evolutionary principles are realized in Romance verb forms.

3.1 Variation and Regularization of the Stem-final Consonant

3.1.1 Phonetic erosion

The application of the principles outlined in section 2.2.3 allows us to derive the regular present indicative stem for first conjugation verbs.

Note that these principles do not predict the disappearance of the final consonant of the Latin stem. A consonant final Latin stem should (and does) develop into a consonant-final stem in Romance, in all persons. French, however, is an exception. In the development of French and Romanian, Latin final *-o* disappeared (see section 2.2.3.1 (ii)). The consequence of this loss of final *-o* — characteristic of person 1. in Latin — is that the final consonant of the stem is now in final position, and can thus undergo the Rule of Truncation (see section 2.2.3.1 (iii)). This corresponds to the situation in old French described by Fouché (1981: 182), where person 1. of a verb like *chanter*, *chant*, can be reduced to [ʃɑ̃]. In persons 2. and 3., on the other hand, the Latin ending begins with *-a* (vowel characteristic of conjugation I). This *a* appears in an unaccented position and develops into schwa (see sections 2.2.3.1 (ii) and 2.2.3.2), and schwas do not disappear. So the final consonant of the stem is now protected and is consequently maintained; in this case the stem takes the expected phonetic form [ʃɑ̃t]. In short, the application of the principles of phonetic evolution to old French creates contexts where a conjugation I verb stem should be realized with two phonetically distinct forms, one vowel-final and one consonant-final. At this point, a new 'anti-phonetic' tendency appears: schwa, derived from the characteristic vowel of conjugation I, found in *chantes* and *chante*, is introduced also in person 1., so that the stem in this case also takes the form [ʃɑ̃t]. The result of this analogical *tour de force* is that the French stem has a unique phonetic form for all persons (Table 4).

Latin *cant-are*	Portuguese *cant-ar*	Spanish *cant-ar*	French *chant-er*	Italian *cant-are*	Rom. *a cânt-a*
cant-o	cant-o	cant-o	(chant >) chante [ʃɑ̃t]	cant-o	cânt
cant-as	cant-as	cant-as	chant-es [ʃɑ̃t]	cant-i	cânț-i
cant-at	cant-a	cant-a	chant-e [ʃɑ̃t]	cant-a	cânt-ă
cant-amus	cant-amos	cant-amos	chant-ons [ʃɑ̃t]	cant-iamo	cânt-ăm
cant-atis	cant-ais	cant-áis	chant-ez [ʃɑ̃t]	cant-ate	cânt-ați
cant-ant	cant-am	cant-an	chant-ent [ʃɑ̃t]	cant-ano	cânt- ă

Table 4

This regularizing tendency is not observed, however, in the paradigms resulting from the Latin conjugations II, III, and IV. For example, Table 5 shows the development of verbs deriving from conjugation IV.

Latin *sentire*	Portuguese *sentir*	Spanish *sentir*	French *sentir*	Italian *sentire*	Romanian *a simți*
sentio	sento	siento	sens [sɑ̃]	sento	simt
sentis	sentes	sientes	sens [sɑ̃]	senti	simți
sentit	sente	siente	sent [sɑ̃]	sente	simte
sentimus	sentimos	sentimos	sentons [sɑ̃t]	sentiamo	simțim
sentitis	sentis	sentís	sentez [sɑ̃t]	sentite	simțiți
sentiunt	sentem	sienten	sentent [sɑ̃t]	sentono	simt

Table 5

According to the Rule of Truncation, the present stem of a verb like *sentir*, /sɑ̃t/, is realized as [sɑ̃t] if the ending begins with a vowel, and as [sɑ̃] otherwise. In contrast to conjugation I, the endings for persons 2. and 3. in Latin (and for person 1., as above), do not contain a vowel capable of protecting the final consonant of the stem from Truncation: The characteristic vowel is *i* for conjugation IV, and *e* for conjugations II and III, vowels that are doomed to disappear in French (see section 2.2.3.1 (ii)). The final consonant of the stem, unprotected, is thus subject to Truncation and is lost.

In contrast to the productive conjugation I, where analogy gives rise to a stem invariant with respect to the final consonant, the non-productive

French conjugations, with origins in the Latin conjugations II, III, and IV, present two different phonetic realizations in the present.[13]

3.1.2 Palatalization

In principle, the phenomenon of palatalization described in section 2.2.3.2 should have affected all forms of verbs with velar-final stems in the presence of an ending beginning with a palatal vowel. For conjugation I, we expect that the opposition between present indicative (with characteristic vowel *a*) and present subjunctive (with vowel *e*) should be marked by two different phonetic realizations of a velar-final stem, the first preserving the original form of the consonant and the second containing its palatalized variant. For a verb like Lat. *plicare* 'fold', we should obtain the subjunctive forms Pt. **cheze*, Sp. **llece*, It. **piege*, Rom. *plece*. But as Table 6 shows, this is not at all what we observe.

	Latin	Portuguese	Spanish	French	Italian	Romanian
ind.3.	plicat	chega	llega	plie	piega	pleacă [pleakə]
subj.3.	plicet	chegue	llegue	plie	pieghi	plece [pletʃe]

Table 6

It is clear that for conjugation I, all of the Romance languages (aside from Romanian), resisted the palatalization of final velars, and the result of this opposition is again the existence of a single consonant-final stem for this productive conjugation.

For Romanian, recall from section 2.2.3.2 that not only velars, but also dentals, are influenced by a following palatal vowel. In this language, the palatalization of velar and dental consonants has acquired the status of a synchronic rule of combinatorial (morpho-)phonetics: Whenever a velar or dental consonant occurs before a palatal vowel (but separated from it by a morpheme boundary), palatalization takes place systematically — for example, even within the present tense paradigm of conjugation I.[14] But in conjugation I_S, with a suffixed stem (fn. 7), the suffix *-ez* begins with a palatal vowel and should therefore palatalize a preceding velar. For instance, *a parca* should have a present indicative present 1. form *[partʃez]. This is not

13 In section 4 below, devoted to stem regularization in the past tenses of irregular verbs, of these two phonetic realizations, we will always take as base form the unaccented stem (characteristically appearing in the imperfect tense).

14 The present indicative of *a pleca* is thus phonetically realized as [plek, pletʃⁱ, pleakə, plekəm, plekatsⁱ, pleakə] and that of *a muta* 'change' as [mut, mutsⁱ, mutə, mutəm, mutatsⁱ, mutə]}. Note that in person 2., the final consonant of the stem is modified under the influence of the personal ending *-i* (see the paradigms presented in section 3.1.1). The synchronic palatalization rule is transcategorial and applies also in the nominal domain (see e.g. Tasmowski 2001).

the case. In the productive conjugation I_S, the suffix has no effect on the quality of the final consonant of the stem, which is realized as [park] across the entire verbal paradigm. In this respect Romanian patterns with the other languages.

3.2 Variation and Regularization of the Stem-final Vowel

3.2.1 The effect of accent

In the Romance languages, in the present indicative (and subjunctive), the accent falls on the stem in persons 1., 2., 3., and 6., whereas forms in persons 4. and 5. are accented on the ending.[15] We therefore expect that vulgar Latin verb stems ending in [ɛ] or [ɔ] should not remain phonetically constant in Romance: with the exception of Portuguese, and with some further conditions, an accented Latin stem vowel should become a diphthong (see Table 2) while in unaccented position, the original Latin vowel can become closed (Tables 2 and 3). If we apply the correspondences given in Tables 2 and 3, the pair *[jɔcat] / *[jɔcamus] (< Lat. *jocare* 'play') for example, are expected to develop as shown in Table 7.

	Latin	Portuguese	Spanish	Old French	Italian	Romanian
pers.3	jɔcat	j**o**ga [ʒɔɣɐ]	j**ue**ga	j**oe** ?[dʒueə]	gi**uo**ca	j**oa**că
pers.4	jɔc**a**mus	jog**a**mos [ʒuɣɐmuʃ]	jug**a**mos	jo**on**s ?[dʒuɔ̃]	gio-chi**a**mo	juc**ă**m

Table 7

3.2.2 Loss of the diphthong/vowel alternation

In French and Italian, where diphthongization only applied in cases where the accented vowel was in an open syllable in Latin, verbs of the productive conjugation I undergo an anti-phonetic reconstruction that leads to the complete neutralization of these alternations triggered by the oscillation of the accent:[16] The original diphthong/vowel alternations are eliminated (purely and simply in French, more hesitantly in Italian) and one of the two forms of the stem is generalized to all persons. The form chosen is either that of the unaccented stem (the most frequent case in French, e.g. verbs like *laver*, *crever*, *lever*, *peser*, *jouer*, *labourer*, *nouer*, *trouver*, and

---

[15] This is true for all of the conjugations, except for the *-e* conjugation in Romanian, the only real descendant of the *-ĕre* conjugation in Latin. In this case, the accent falls on the stem not only in the infinitive, but also in all persons in the present indicative and subjunctive. In the imperfect, on the other hand, the stem is always unaccented.

[16] This does not imply that uniformization of the stem is *not* found in the non-productive conjugations (e.g., the verbs in *-ir*: *ouvrir* or *courir*), but the process is not systematic as it is in the productive conjugation.

for Italian *giocare*) or that of the accented stem (e.g. French *aimer* and *pleurer*, and Italian *tuonare*).

Fr. *laver*	(OFr. *l**e**f, l**e**ves, l**e**ve, l**e**vent*) > *l**a**ve, l**a**ves, l**a**ve, l**a**vent*	*lav**ons**, lav**ez***
Fr. *aimer*	(OFr. ***aim*** [ɛ̃]) > ***ai**me, **ai**mes, **ai**me, **ai**ment* [ɛm]	(OFr. *am**ons**, am**ez*** >) *aim**ons**, aim**ez***
It. *gioc**a**re*	(*gi**uo**co, gi**uo**chi, gi**uo**ca, gi**uo**cano*) > *gi**o**co, gi**o**chi, gi**o**ca, gi**o**cano*	*gioch**ia**mo, gioc**a**te*
It. *tuon**a**re*	***tuo**no, **tuo**ni, **tuo**na, **tuo**nano*	*ton**ia**mo, ton**a**te* > *tuon**ia**mo, tuon**a**te*

For Romanian, on the contrary, the path of phonetic evolution leading from Latin, in particular the metaphonic diphthongization described in Tables 2 and 3, has resulted in a set of alternations that are still very much alive and that apply to both verbal and nominal paradigms. It should be said, however, that these alternations are characteristic of the older lexical core of the language, in particular verbs inherited from Latin. Thus:

Lat. *plic**a**re*	Rom. *a plec**a*** 'leave' 3. *pl**ea**că*, 6. *pl**ea**că*	 1. *pl**e**c*, 2. *pl**e**ci*, 4. *plec**ă**m*, 5. *plec**a**ți*
Lat. *rog**a**re*	Rom. *a rug**a*** 'ask' 3. ***roa**gă*, 6. ***roa**gă*	 1. *r**o**g*, 2. *r**o**gi*, 4. *rug**ă**m*, 5. *rug**a**ți*

In general, they do not apply to Latino-Romance borrowings. For these verbs, the stem remains invariant:

Rom. *a costa* 'cost': pres.ind.3. *c**o**stă* (**c**oa**stă*)
a repeta 'repeat': pres.ind.3. *rep**e**tă* (**rep**ea**tă*)

3.2.3 The stem-extending suffix and the stabilization of the accent

We now turn to verbs of the productive conjugation in 's' (i.e. verbs whose stem is extended by a suffix — recall section 2.2.1). In Eastern Romance (Italian and Romanian), the stem-extending suffix appears in those present tense forms where the stem is accented, that is in persons 1., 2., 3., and 6. in the indicative and subjunctive, and it attracts the accent. In French, the only Western Romance language where the suffix is not derivational, the suffix has the same effect, but it is present for all persons in tenses that are not in *-r*.[17] The result of this process is that the verb stem becomes unaccented in all persons, and so phonetic alternations conditioned by accent shift can no longer operate.[18]

---

[17] French thus recreates the exact counterpart of the non-suffixed conjugation: persons 1., 2., and 3. continue to contrast with persons 4., 5., and 6., but not in terms of stem variation, as is the case with non-suffixed verbs (e.g. [par] *vs* [part], [syfi] *vs* [syfiz], etc.) but by means of the suffix ([i] *vs* [is]). The stem itself stays invariant.

[18] For example, suffixed forms such as pres.ind.3. *ferist* or pres.ind.6. *ferissent* (< *férir*), used by Rabelais instead of OFr. *fiert, fierent*

The consequences of the presence of the suffix (the stem is uniformly unaccented and therefore shows no variation in vowel quality) are particularly striking in Romanian. In this language (recall section 3.2.2), the core verbs inherited from Latin continue to show a systematic alternation between accented diphthong and unaccented vowel:

Rom. *a ieşi* 'exit': pres.subj.3. *să **ia**să* *a pieri* 'perish': pres.subj.3. *să pia**ră***
a dormi 'sleep': pres.ind.3. ***doa**rme* *a sorbi* 'sip': pres.ind.3. ***soa**rbe*

However, for lexemes borrowed from Old Slavic, for example, the stem is most often suffixed, which prevents variations in the stem vowel:[19]

Rom. *a trezi* 'awaken': pres.ind.3. *trezeşte*
a lovi 'strike': pres.ind.3. *loveşte* *a obosi* 'tire': pres.ind.3. *oboseşte*

In Romanian (and only in Romanian), suffixation applies also to verbs deriving from conjugation I (see Table 1), with the same effect. The subset of verbs in -a_S comprises above all Latino-Romance borrowings whose stems are *ipso facto* exempt from the vowel modifications characteristic of verbs inherited directly from Latin:

Rom. *a purta* 'carry': pres.ind.1. *port*, 3. ***poa**rtă*, 4. *purtăm*, vs
a raporta 'report': pres.ind.1. *raportez*, 3. *raportează*, 4. *raportăm*

In the three languages with conjugations in '$_S$' (exhibiting no stem vowel variation), if it is productive, the corresponding conjugations without '$_S$' are not.

3.3 Non-unified Stems

The facts described in sections 3.1 and 3.2 suggest that the Romance languages tend to develop invariant present tense stems, in terms of both vowel and consonant alternation, and this stem invariability is (in part) what makes the conjugation productive. Although we have seen many examples of this generalization, it must nevertheless be noted that in some cases the tendency is not fully realized.

3.3.1 Preservation of the diphthong/vowel alternation

For Spanish, diphthongization of an accented stem vowel [ɛ] ou [ɔ] does not depend on the Latin syllable structure (see Table 2) and it applies more freely than in French and Italian.[20] Here are some examples:

---

19 *-esc-* + *-e* (the pres.ind.3. ending) > *-eşte* [eʃte].

20 Vowel alternation in verb stems is also found in French and Italian, but it is restricted to the non-productive conjugations. We simply give two examples of such idiosyncratic residual cases (*moviamo, movete* are dialectal):

Lat. *debere* > Fr. *devoir*: 1. *dois*, 2. *dois*, 3. *doit*, 6. *doivent*, 4. *devons*, 5. *devez*
Lat. *mouere* > *mouere* > It. *muovere*: 1. *muovo*, 2. *muovi*, 3. *muove*, 6. *muovono*,
4. *moviamo*, 5. *movete* (standard It. *muoviamo*, *muovete*)

Lat. *negare* > Sp. *negar* 'deny'
  1. *niego*, 2. *niegas*, 3. *niega*, 6. *niegan* — 4. *negamos*, 5. *negáis*
Lat. *errare* > Sp. *errar* 'wander'
  1. *yerro*, 2. *yerras*, 3. *yerra*, 6. *yerran* — 4. *erramos*, 5. *erráis*
Lat. *rogare* > Sp. *rogar* 'pray'
  1. *ruego*, 2. *ruegas*, 3. *ruega*, 6. *ruegan* — 4. *rogamos*, 5. *rogáis*
Lat. *computare* > Sp. *contar* 'count'
  1. *cuento*, 2. *cuentas*, 3. *cuenta*, 6. *cuentan* — 4. *contamos*, 5. *contáis*

Here, diphthongization occurs with a subset of verbs that has grown larger through time by the integration of verbs with stems in *-e-* and *-o-*, alongside those in [ɛ] and [ɔ]:

Lat. *pensare* > Sp. *pensar* 'think'
  pienso, *piensas*, *piensa*, *piensan* — *pensamos*, *pensáis*
Lat. *consolare* > Sp. *consolar* 'console'
  consuelo, *consuelas*, *consuela*, *consuelan* — *consolamos*, *consoláis*

The stem variation in this last group cannot be explained by historical phonetic considerations and is synchronically unmotivated. In the current stage of the language, this group is closed to new verbs. In fact, the original group, where diphthongization is etymologically justified, is also closed, and has lost several of its members over time (e.g. *aportar*, *confortar*, *entregar*, *prestar*).[21]

In Romanian, as already mentioned in sections 3.2.2 and 3.2.3, a similar set of alternations of phonetic origin (*e*/*ea*, *o*/*oa*) are still active synchronically as morpho-phonetic combination rules. They apply to the old core lexicon of the language — both nominal and verbal elements — and are in fact largely restricted to this domain.

3.3.2 Vowel$_1$/vowel$_2$ alternations

Portuguese, which does not have stem diphthongization (see Table 2), nevertheless displays an alternation in the quality of the stem vowels *a*, *o*, *e* depending on accent placement: in unaccented positions, these vowels are closed (see Tables 2, 3 and 5), in all conjugations. The alternation, completely conditioned by variation in accent placement, is independent of the (non-)productivity of the conjugation.

An analogous situation can be observed in Romanian, where stems in *a* and *o* participate in an alternation between open accented vowels and closed unaccented vowels. But here, as for the diphthong/vowel alternation discussed above, the phenomenon remains limited to verbs inherited from Latin, and does not apply to Latino-Romance borrowings:

21 See Penny (1993:176).

Lat. *crepare* > Rom. *a crăpa* 'burst'
pres.ind.3. *crapă* [krapə], pres.ind.4. *crăpăm* [krəpəm]
(vs *a repara* 'repair': pres.ind.3. *repară* [reparə], pres.ind.4. *reparăm* [reparəm]

Finally, we need to say something about the totally paradoxical situation in French. All of the stem variations caused by the phonetic developments in the transition from Latin to French were eliminated from the productive conjugations, but then a new one was introduced, apparently less conditioned by accent placement than by syntagmatic context. The phenomenon in question is the realization of an open vowel in the place of [ə] and [e] in conjugation I before [ə]:[22]

Fr. *lever* 'raise': *lève* [lɛv] vs *levons* [ləv]
céder 'yield': *cède* [sɛd] vs *cédons* [sed]

Note that the three phenomena described in this section are not restricted to the verbal domain.

3.4 The Romance Verb Stem in the Present Tenses: Conclusions

In the evolution from Latin to the Romance languages, the present tense base form — the *infectum* theme — was exposed to a series of phonetic modifications that threaten to disrupt its uniformity. Nevertheless, nowadays verb stems in Romance do not present the fragmented set of stems that phonetic evolution should have produced. The languages reacted against the processes that would have destroyed the integrity of the stem. This happened in several different ways:

1. One of the variants generated by phonetic evolution is generalized to the whole paradigm. French and Italian eliminate the diphthong/vowel alternations in conjugation I. In this same conjugation all of the languages (besides Romanian) eliminate the palatalized variants of velar-final stems.
2. The effects of phonetic evolution are eliminated by introducing a morpheme that attracts the accent away from the stem, thereby blocking the creation of stem variants based on accent placement. This is what happened in the suffixed conjugations in '$_S$'
3. The results of phonetic evolution are redistributed, and a set of transcategorial morpho-phonetic rules develops. This is the case for Portuguese and Romanian with their vowel alternations conditioned by accent placement. Romanian also has consonant alternation effects in palatal contexts, and context-dependent alternation of diphthongs and accented

[22] This is a special case of the Schwa Adjustment Rule, formulated by Dell (1973:210) as follows:

/E/ > ɛ / __ C] {#, C, ə [–SEG]}

vowels. Finally, French falls into this category for its conjugation I verbs with stem vowel /ɛ/.[23]

The only subset of verbs belonging to conjugation I that did not adopt one of these 'remedies' is that of Spanish verbs showing diphthong/vowel alternation, but as we have seen, this group has restricted membership.

We conclude therefore that the evolution of the present indicative in Romance can be characterized in the vast majority of cases by the emergence of a unitary form, with the elimination of certain variations that cannot be brought into line synchronically.

4 The Preterite and the Past Participle

4.1 Latin

For the past tenses, the situation is complicated by the existence of 'strong' paradigms alongside 'weak' ones, and by the existence of specific stem forms for the past tenses, distinct from those used for the present tenses.

4.1.1 The position of the accent

For past tense forms, the question of accent placement must be addressed with care. Verbs can be divided into two groups, 'strong' and 'weak', which cut across the conjugations: each conjugation has strong verbs and weak verbs, although the majority of conjugation II verbs and practically all conjugation III verbs are strong. For weak verbs, the accent is always after the stem, but not always on the same syllable. In persons 1., 3., and 4., it falls on the characteristic vowel of the conjugation (**a** for I, **e** for II, **i** for III and IV), and in persons 2. and 5., it falls on the following vowel. In person 6., the accent fluctuates. This produces the following:

Lat. *am**a**ui, amau**i**sti, am**a**uit, am**a**uimus, amau**i**stis, am**a**uerunt / amau**e**runt*
*del**e**ui, deleu**i**sti, del**e**uit, del**e**uimus, deleu**i**stis, del**e**uerunt / deleu**e**runt*
*aud**i**ui, audiu**i**sti, aud**i**uit, aud**i**uimus, audiu**i**stis, aud**i**uerunt / audiu**e**runt*

For strong verbs, we find the same pattern of accent shift, but moved over one step. That is, in persons 1., 3., 4. (and 6.), the accent is on the stem. The preterite of strong verbs therefore includes both strong forms (persons 1., 3.,

[23] Solutions 1 and 3 are also relevant for members of the non-productive conjugations, but not systematically: These conjugations continue to manifest forms not reconstructed by analogy, whose status is that of etymological residues (see for example the descendants of the Latin verbs *venire*, *sapere*, *facere*, etc.).

4., (6.)) and weak forms (persons 2., 5., (6.)). Thus, for *dicere*, which has a sigmatic perfect (type (d) in Table 8 in section 4.1.2):[24]

Lat. *dixi, dixisti, dixit, diximus, dixistis, dixerunt / dixerunt*

The same problem arises for the participle: Depending on the verb, the accent falls either on a vowel after the stem (weak), or on the stem vowel (strong).

In the development of the Romance languages, this should of course in principle lead to phonetic effects analogous to those seen in sections 2 and 3.

4.1.2 Formal relationships between *infectum*, *perfectum*, and *supinum*

As already mentioned in section 2.1.2, in Latin, the relationships between the *infectum*, *perfectum*, and *supinum* themes are not generally codifiable. In the general case, knowing the *infectum* of a verb, particularly in conjugations II and III, does not allow one to generate the *perfectum* or *supinum*, and for a very large number of verbs, none of the three forms can be used to derive the two others. In short, the formal relationships linking the three themes (all related to a common base) are largely unpredictable. Even verbs with identical or nearly identical forms can have totally divergent preterite and past participle forms.

Strong verbs in Latin show four ways of forming the preterite (which can sometimes be applied cumulatively).[25] Table 8 describes these patterns in relation to the *infectum*.

(a) modif. of stem V	(b) cons. reduplication	(c) suffixation of -*u*	(d) suffixation of -*s*
feci (vs. facio) bibi (vs. bibo)	momordi (vs. mordo) cecidi (vs. cado)	tacui (vs. taceo)	dixi [diksi] (vs. dico)

Table 8

Furthermore, there are three ways of forming the past participle: (a′) with -*tu*: *factu*, (b′) with -*su*: *morsu*, and (c′) with -*ĭtu*: *tacitu*.[26]

---

[24] Type (a) in Table 8 follows the same pattern, for example *feci, fecisti, fecit, fecimus, fecistis, fecerunt*. Type (c) is somewhat more complex, e.g. *habui, habuisti, habuit, habuimus, habuistis, habuerunt*.

[25] The four preterite patterns are not equally represented in the Latin inflectional system: out of 133 verbs that have survived in the Romance languages, 47% have a sigmatic preterite (type (d) of Table 8), 28% have a strong preterite with or without vowel modification (type (a)), 17% have a preterite in -*u* (type (c)), and 8% show reduplication (type (b)). It should be noted, however, that the least common inflectional types occur with highly frequent verb tokens.

[26] To give an idea of the relative proportions of the three patterns: out of 118 verbs found in the Romance languages, 52% have participles in -*t*-, 44% have participles in -*s*- (sigmatic), and

4.2 From Latin to the Romance Languages

Just as happens with the present tense, then, the conjugation paradigm has to be 'normalized' by neutralizing the phonetic alternations triggered by accent shift, and moreover the problem of the unpredictable relationships between *infectum*, *perfectum*, and *supinum* must be resolved.[27] By conjecture, there are three possible options:

1. fixing the position of the accent
2. generalizing the weak paradigms at the expense of the strong ones
3. substituting new anti-phonetic forms.

4.2.1 Accent placement

In the transition to Romance, the accent in Latin weak preterites becomes fixed, eventually falling systematically on the thematic vowel.[28] This vowel is also systematically accented in the past participle.

Table 9 gives the list of forms for verbs deriving from the Latin *-are* and *-ire* conjugations. The corresponding past participles are given in Table 10.

Portuguese		Spanish		French	
I	III	I	III	I	III
cant**e**i	part**i**	cant**é**	sal**í**	chant**ai**	sort**is**
cant**a**ste	part**i**ste	cant**a**ste	sal**i**ste	chant**a**s	sort**is**
cant**o**u	part**i**u	cant**ó**	sal**ió**[29]	chant**a**	sort**it**
cant**á**mos	part**i**mos	cant**a**mos	sal**i**mos	chant**â**mes	sort**î**mes
cant**a**stes	part**i**stes	cant**a**steis	sal**i**steis	chant**â**tes	sort**î**tes
cant**a**ram	part**i**ram	cant**a**ron	sal**ie**ron	chant**è**rent	sort**i**rent

Italian		Romanian	
I	III	I	IV
cant**a**i	sent**i**i	cânt**a**i	fug**i**i
cant**a**sti	sent**i**sti	cânt**a**și	fug**i**și
cant**ò**	sent**ì**	cânt**ă**	fug**í**
cant**a**mmo	sent**i**mmo	cânt**a**răm	fug**i**răm
cant**a**ste	sent**i**ste	cânt**a**răți	fug**i**răți
cant**a**rono	sent**i**rono	cânt**a**ră	fug**i**ră

Table 9

3% have participles in *-itu-*; 7% of these verbs have variant forms or forms that combine two patterns of formation.

[27] See in particular Mourin (1974, 1975) and Reinheimer and Tasmowski (1999a, 2000).

[28] Or on the result of syncretism of the thematic and the ending vowels.

[29] The current Spanish forms *salió* / *salieron* did also go through a phase **salío* / **salíeron*.

Portuguese I	Portuguese III	Spanish I	Spanish III	French I	French III	Italian I	Italian III	Romanian I	Romanian IV
cantado	partido	cantado	salido	chanté	sorti	cantato	sentito	cântat	fugit

Table 10

For strong preterites, on the other hand, the phenomenon of accent oscillation described in section 4.1.2 is not neutralized in Romance. None of the languages introduces a past tense suffix that attracts the accent, for example.[30] The variation in accent placement is therefore maintained, but it has different manifestations, depending on the language; a full description is provided in Table 11.

	accent position				
person	Latin	Portuguese	Spanish	Italian	Romanian
1.	stem	stem	stem	stem	ending
2.	ending	ending	ending	ending	ending
3.	stem	stem	stem	stem	stem
4.	stem	ending	ending	ending	stem
5.	ending	ending	ending	ending	stem
6.	ending/stem	ending	ending	stem	stem

Table 11

Table 12 gives an example.

Latin	Port.	Spanish	French	Italian	Rom.
dixi	disse	dije	dis	dissi	zisei
dixisti	disseste	dijiste	dis	dicesti	ziseși
dixit	disse	dijo	dit	disse	zise
diximus	dissemos	dijimos	dîmes	dicemmo	ziserăm
dixistis	dissestes	dijisteis	dîtes	diceste	ziserăți
dixerunt / dixerunt	disseram	dijeron	dirent	dissero	ziseră

Table 12

As we can see, in the Romance languages, the position of the accent is not linked in any systematic way to the adoption of a particular form of the stem, except in Italian. In Italian, we observe a rather dramatic interaction between accent shift and the choice of one of two distinct stem forms corresponding to the opposition between strong (persons 1., 3., 6.) and weak (persons 2., 4., 5.) forms. A special stem is used for the strong persons,

[30] See however fn. 61.

while the stem in the weak persons is identical to the unstressed stem used in the present tenses—more precisely, the imperfect.[31]

In modern French, the position of the accent does not oscillate in the preterite.[32]

4.2.2 Extension of weak paradigms for the preterite

4.2.2.1 Extension of existing weak paradigms

As demonstrated by the Romance forms, the strong verbs that belonged to the Latin *-are* and *-ire* conjugations but that had a strong preterite and/or past participle were incorporated into the normal paradigm by the vulgar Latin period:

crepare	pret.: *crepui* > **crepaui* > Pt. *quebrei*, Sp. *quebré*, Fr. *crevai*, It. *crepai*, Rom. *crăpai*
lauare	pret.: *laui* > **lauaui* > Pt. *lavei*, Sp. *lavé*, Fr. *lavai*, It. *lavai*
sentire	pret.: *sensi* > **sentiui* > Pt. *senti*, Sp. *sentí*, Fr. *sentis*, It. *sentii*, Rom. *simţii*
crepare	pp: *crepitum* > **crepatum* > Pt., Sp. *quebrado*, Fr. *crevé*, It. *crepato*, Rom. *crăpat*
lauare	pp: *lautum* > **lauatum* > Pt., Sp. *lavado*, Fr. *lavé*, It. *lavato*
sentire	pp: *sensum* > **sentitum* > Pt., Sp. *sentido*, Fr. *senti*, It. *sentito*, Rom. *simţit*

4.2.2.2 Creation of new weak paradigms

The weak preterite in *-ēui*, found in Latin conjugation II, disappeared. New patterns of weak inflection developed in vulgar Latin and incorporated some originally strong verbs, for which we observe (i) a uniform placement of the accent on the ending, and (ii) an alignment of the preterite stem with that of the present.

These verbs thus take on the two characteristics of Romance verbs belonging to conjugations in *-a-* and *-i-*, which are weak conjugations in all of the Romance languages.

[31] This last specification is needed because in Italian a certain number of verbs belonging to conjugation II and III employ several distinct stems in the present tenses (e.g. *sapere* 'know', present: *so*, *sai*, *sa*, *sappiamo*, *sapete*, *sanno*; imperfect: *sapevo*, *sapevi*...; *fare* 'make', present: *faccio*, *fai*, *fa*, *facciamo*, *fate*, *fanno*; imperfect: *facevo*...).

[32] The situation was different in Old French, where the pattern of accentuation was the same as that given for Italian in Table 12, with stem alternation (e.g. *dis*, *desis*, *dist*, *desimes*, *desistes*, *distrent*).

4.2.2.2.1 Preterite in *-éi

Vulgar Latin introduced a weak preterite in **-é(d)i*, accented on the ending, based on a group of strong preterites in Latin with stems in *-d-*:[33]

vendere 'sell': pret.1. *vendĭdi* > **vendedi* > **vendei*

We can recognize the effects of this operation in conjugation II in Portuguese, Spanish, French, and Italian:

Pt. *vendi, vendeste, vendeu, vendemos, vendestes, venderam*
Sp. *vendí, vendiste, vendió, vendimos, vendisteis, vendieron*
Fr. *vendis, vendis, vendit, vendîmes, vendîtes, vendirent*
It. *vendei, vendesti, vendé, vendemmo, vendeste, venderono*

As we can see, a specific preterite form developed in Portuguese for *-er* verbs, distinct from that of *-ar* and *-ir* verbs. In Spanish, on the other hand, a series of analogical re-formations led to the assimilation of the preterites of the new conjugation in *-er* with those of the conjugation in *-ir*. For these two languages, only very few verbs remain outside of the weak patterns.

In Italian, the type extends to verbs of both the conjugation in *-ere* (*potere*: *potei*, *dovere*: *dovei*) and the conjugation in *-ere* (*credere*: *credei*, *cedere*: *cedei*), but in spite of this, strong preterites are still very much in evidence in the language.[34]

In French, the new weak model was at first limited to stems ending in a voiced dental. These verbs took on a form in *-dedi* (e.g., *perdre*, Lat. preterite *perdidi* > **perdedi* > **perdei*). They were joined later on by other verbs in –C[35] + *d-* such as *attendre*, *défendre*, *descendre*, *répondre*, and some verbs with stems ending in a consonant cluster with no voiced dental: *battre*, *rompre*, *vaincre*.[36] For all of these verbs, the preterite stem ended up coinciding with the unaccented present stem. The same thing happened to verbs with epenthetic *-d-* in the infinitive (*jungere* > *joindre*, *plangere* > *plaindre*) and to verbs with infinitives in *-uire* (*cuire*, *conduire*).[37]

---

[33] We can think of this mechanism as a transition to a weak form via the strong type (b) in Table 8, based on the most frequently used verb of the series, *dedi* (preterite of *dare* 'give'): *vendidi* > **vendedi*.

[34] As we will see later (see section 4.3.2.1), these strong preterites correspond mostly to type (d) and (to a much lesser extent) type (c) in Table 8.

[35] A nasal consonant nasalizes the preceding vowel and is no longer pronounced.

[36] Also *vêtir*: *vêtis* (p.p. *vêtu*) and *coudre*: *cousis* (p.p. *cousu*). However, *prendre* does not enter into this system, despite its classical preterite *prehendi*. The Romance languages show that *prehendi* was replaced by **prehensi*, most likely influenced by the past participle *prehensum*.

[37] But for these verbs, the participle is formed in a different way from that shown below in Table 13.

4.2.2.2.2 Preterite in *-úi

In Romanian, the suffixal extension *-u-* was used to create the typical weak preterite of all verbs in **-ea** (< Latin conjugation II) and some verbs in *-e* (< Latin conjugation III).[38] The suffixal extension *-u-* attracts the accent. Thus:

Rom. *a tăc**ea*** 'be silent' *tăc**ui**, tăc**uși**, tăc**u**, tăc**urăm**, tăc**urăți**, tăc**ură***
*a **vinde*** 'sell' *vând**ui**, vând**uși**, vând**u**, vând**urăm**, vând**urăți**, vând**ură***

But alongside this new weak type, for some of the verbs in conjugation III, the strong preterite[39] is still very actively attested.

4.2.3 The past participle

The participles of all of these verbs, if they became weak, were remodeled to have a stem either in **-i-** (Pt., Sp. *vend**i**do*), or in **-u-** (Fr. *vend**u*** with palatalization to [y], It. *vend**u**to*, Rom. *tăc**u**t*, *vând**u**t*). This is summarized in Table 13.

	Portuguese	Spanish	French	Italian	Romanian
preterites	vend**i**, vend**este**…	vend**í**, vend**iste**…	vend**is**, vend**is**…	vend**ei**, vend**esti**…	vând**ui**, vând**uși**…
participles	vend**i**do	vend**i**do	vend**u**	vend**u**to	vând**u**t

Table 13

4.3 Strong Preterites and Past Participles in Romance: Synchronic View

The processes described in section 4.2 did not lead to the complete elimination of strong verbs in the Romance languages. A significant number of verbs — the great majority of which trace back one way or another to the Latin *-ēre* or *-ĕre* conjugations — were not integrated into the weak paradigms and continue to exhibit the accent alternation typical of strong verbs. The facts show, however, that these survivors have also migrated into mini-systems. Our description will highlight the extent to which they have entered into a more or less identifiable relationship with the present and past stems. This relationship is either vowel-based or consonant-based, or both, and it divides the Romance languages into three groups: (1) Portuguese and Spanish, (2) Italian and Romanian, and (3) French.[40] In the following, we provide an overview of the current situation in each of the three groups.

---

[38] This process constitutes a transition to a weak form via the strong type (c) in Table 8, based on the most frequently used verb in the series, *fui* (preterite of *esse* 'be').

[39] This form is always sigmatic; see section 4.3.2.2 below.

[40] In our presentation we will abstract away from a certain number of rarely-used forms, and obviously we will not discuss totally irregular verbs, which cannot be organized into any (mini-)system.

4.3.1 Portuguese and Spanish

Portuguese and Spanish have almost totally eliminated their strong preterites. Moreover, for the ten or so surviving forms, there is rarely a corresponding strong past participle:[41]

	Portuguese	Spanish
pres.stem {e,i}	dizer: disse / *dito*; querer: quis / querido; vir: vim (vieste, veio) / *vindo*; ter: tive / tido	decir: dije / *dicho*; querer: quise / querido; venir: vine (viniste, vino) / venido; [tener: tuve / tenido]
pres.stem {o,u}	poder: pude / podido; pôr: pus / *posto*	poder: pude / podido; poner: puse / *puesto*; -ducir: -duje / -ducido
pres.stem {a}	caber: coube / cabido; saber: soube / sabido; haver: houve / havido; prazer: prouve; trazer: trouxe / trazido; [fazer: fiz / *feito*]	caber: cupe / cabido; saber: supe / sabido; haber: hube / habido; [traer: traje / traido; hacer: hice / *hecho*]

Table 14

The stem vowel in these preterites characterizes the group. It is always either a closed palatal vowel [i][42], or a non-palatal vowel, closed or half-closed in Portuguese {[u], [o]}, closed in Spanish [u]. The correlation with the present tense stem vowel is analogous for the two languages:

(i) An unstressed stem[43] in *-e-* or *-i-* is correlated with a Portuguese preterite in *-i-* (/*-e-*[44]), with a Spanish preterite in *-i-*;

(ii) An unstressed stem in *-o-* or *-u-* is correlated with a Portuguese preterite in *-u-* (/*-o-*), with a Spanish preterite in *-u-*;

(iii) An unstressed stem in *-a-* is correlated with a Portuguese preterite in *-o-* (written *ou*), with a Spanish preterite in *-u-*.[45]

41 These are indicated in italics in Table 14.

42 There is a single exception to this: Spanish *traje* (*traer* 'bring'). The form *traje* is anomalous from a diachronic perspective also. According to Lloyd (1993: 485), who refers to Malkiel (1969) for further details, *traxi* should have resulted in **trexi*. Note that the form *truje*, which must derive from **traxui*, is found in dialects (Penny 1993:208).

43 Recall fn. 13.

44 A stem with a closed vowel is generally used for all strong forms of the preterite. In Portuguese, however, the vowel of the person 3. form is sometimes less closed (*fiz* / *fez*, *pude* / *pôde*, *pus* / *pôs*, *tive* / *teve*).

45 Diachronically, the closed quality of the stem vowel is the result of the metaphonic action of final *-i* for stems in -i- (e.g. *feci* > Pt. *fiz*, Sp. *hice*) and the result of metathesis of the suffixal extension *-u* in the other cases (e.g *habui* > *haubi* > Pt. *houve*, Sp. *hube*), followed by analogical reorganization.

A number of forms are exceptional in terms of vowel quality (but not closedness): Pt. *fazer*, Sp. *hacer*, with preterites *fiz*, *hice*, and in Spanish only, *tener*, with preterite *tuve*.[46]

The consonants of these preterite stems are mostly the result of phonetic evolution of the Latin form (preterite or participle). Synchronically, they cannot be deduced from the present tense stem. For the small number of strong forms still found in Portuguese and Spanish, the relationship that exists between the present and past stems involves only the stem vowel.

4.3.2 Italian and Romanian

4.3.2.1 Italian

In Italian, the strong preterite is either sigmatic or formed by reduplication of the final stem consonant. These processes are sometimes accompanied by modification of the stem vowel, or (in very rare cases) the preterite is formed by vowel modification alone.[47]

The formation of the sigmatic *preterite* of a conjugation II verb accented on the stem (*ridere* type) proceeds as follows, taking the unaccented present tense stem as reference.

The final consonant of the stem disappears or assimilates to *-s-* in accordance with the following conditions:

(i) a voiced dental disappears before *-s-* taking with it a preceding nasal:

It. *decidere* 'decide': *decid-*, *decisi*; *difendere* 'defend': *difend-*, *difesi*

(ii) all other consonants become *-s-* by assimilation, resulting in a sequence *-ss-*, unless preceded by a resonant, in which case the sequence is reduced to RESONANT + *s*:

It. *dire* 'say': *dic-*, *dissi*; *vincere* 'conquer': *vinc-*, *vinsi*[48]

The formation of the *past participle* is also based on the present stem. If the final consonant of this stem is a dental, the past participle is in *-s-*; otherwise, it is in -t-. We observe the following context-dependent phenomena:

---

[46] The forms *fiz* and *hice* are justified etymologically (see the preceding footnote), but *tuve* was created by analogy.

[47] These three options correspond historically to types (d), (c) et (a) in Table 8, respectively.

[48] Six verbs show exceptional behavior: two with a labial nasal (*redimere* 'redeem': *redensi*, *assumere* 'assume': *assunsi*) and four with a dental (*scindere* 'split': *scissi*, {*con*/*suc*}*cedere* 'concede, succeed': {*con*/*suc*}*cessi*, *mettere* 'put': *misi*).

(i) A voiceless dental (simple or geminate) assimilates to *-s*, giving rise to *-ss-*. A voiced dental disappears (along with a preceding *-n-*), giving rise to -V*s*-:

It. *discutere* 'discuss': *discut-*, *discusso*; *mettere* 'put': *mett-*, *messo*
perdere 'lose': *perd-*, *perso*; *difendere* 'defend': *difend-*, *difeso*

(ii) a non-dental consonant (simple or geminate) assimilates to *-t*, giving rise to *-tt-*, unless preceded by a resonant, in which case the sequence is reduced to RESONANT + *t*:

It. *dire* 'say': *dic-*, *detto*; *leggere* 'read': *legg-*, *letto*
cogliere 'gather': *cogl-*, *colto*; *vincere* 'conquer': *vinc-*, *vinto*[49]

Abstracting away from the distinction between simple and geminate consonants, we can say that a sigmatic preterite in Italian is associated with a past participle in *-s-* if the present tense stem ends in a dental, and a past participle in -t- otherwise.[50]

Alongside this dominant system combining a sigmatic preterite and a past participle {s, t}, there is a subsystem involving around 20 verbs that have a preterite ending in a geminate consonant.[51] This group includes most of the strong verbs in *-ere* (*cadere* 'fall', *volere* 'want', *tenere* 'hold', *sapere* 'know', etc.), some verbs with a strong infinitive in *-ere* (*crescere* 'grow', *conoscere* 'know', etc.), and one conjugation III verb (*venire* 'come'). The past participles corresponding to these preterites with a gemi-

---

[49] Among the 100 or so non-derived participles that fall into this category in Italian, fifteen or so show divergent behavior. First we can mention four participles in *-st-*: *chiedere* 'ask': *chiesto*, *rispondere* 'respond': *risposto*, *nascondere* 'hide': *nascosto*, *porre* 'put': *posto*. Furthermore, we find:

(i) NASAL + *t* for *redimere*: *redento*, *assumere*: *assunto*;

(ii) *-tt-* for *stringere* 'tighten': *stretto*;

(iii) *-(s)s-* for *emergere* 'emerge': *emerso*, *spargere* 'spread': *sparso*, *tergere* 'clean': *terso*, *-vergere* (*convergere* 'converge'): *-verso*; *rifulgere* 'shine': *rifulso*; *{af,in}figgere* 'fix': *{af,in}fisso*, *imprimere* 'print' : *impresso*, *muovere* 'move': *mosso*;

(iv) *-ss-* for *scindere*: *scisso*, *{con/suc}cedere*: *{con/suc}cesso*.

Finally, one verb with a strong preterite takes a weak past participle (*vivere* 'live': *vissuto*).

[50] Remember, however, that these observations hold for strong sigmatic verbs with accent on the stem. There are a few cases (three, in fact) of conjugation II verbs with unstressed stems that also form a sigmatic preterite. For these verbs, the correlation with the past participle is unstable (*dolere* 'regret': *dolsi*, *doluto*; *valere* 'be worth': *valsi*, *valso* (or *valuto*); *rimanere* 'remain': *rimasi*, *rimasto*).

[51] From the historical phonetic perspective, the gemination of the consonant was triggered by the suffixal extension *-u* (type (c) in Table 8), which was only preserved after *k* (e.g. *giacqui* < *iacui*, *nacqui* < **nascui*, *nocqui* < *nocui*, *piacqui* < *placui*, *tacqui* < *tacui*). For several of these verbs, the link between the stem vowels in the present and past tenses is now opaque.

nate consonant are almost always weak. The list of forms is given in Table 15.[52]

	preterite with geminate
weak p.p.	cad-: caddi / caduto; vol-: volli / voluto; ten-: tenni / tenuto; ven-: venni / venuto ; bev-: bevvi / bevuto ; piov-: piovve / piovuto; sap-: seppi / saputo; av-: ebbi / avuto; cresc-: crebbi / cresciuto; conosc-: conobbi / conosciuto; giac-: giacqui / giaciuto; piac-: piacqui / piaciuto; noc-: nocqui / nociuto; tac-: tacqui / taciuto
p.p. in *-t*	romp-: ruppi / rotto; nasc-: nacqui / nato

Table 15

This subsystem is not characterizable, in that nothing in the modern language marks the fact that these verbs form their preterite by consonant reduplication.

In the dominant sigmatic system and also quite generally in the secondary geminate consonant system, the preterite and past participle stems can be related to the present stem only in terms of the final stem consonant. The vowel correspondences are not systematic.

4.3.2.2 Romanian

The number of non-derived strong verbs (or more precisely, verbs not perceived as derived) is around fifty in Romanian. All of them belong to conjugation III, with accent on the stem in the infinitive. In the present, these verbs have a velar or dental stem, with very few exceptions: two labial stems, one voiceless (*rup-* 'break') and one voiced (*fierb-* 'boil'), and one vocalic stem (*scri-* 'write').

The formation of the preterite (all of these verbs take the mark *-s*, corresponding to type (d) in Table 8) and of the (almost always sigmatic) past participle on the basis of the present stem can be characterized as follows:

preterite stem = present stem – final stem CONS + *s*
p.p. stem = present stem – final stem CONS + *s*

So for example:

Rom. *a duce* 'lead' — *duc-*, pret. (**duc-s-ei* >) *dusei*[53], p.p. (**duc-s* >) *dus*
a arde 'burn' — *ard-*, pret. (**ard-s-ei* >) *arsei*, etc.[54], p.p. (**ard-s* >) *ars*, etc.[55]

---

[52] Three verbs whose preterite does not end in a geminate might also be added to this list: *vedere* 'see': *ved-*, *vidi* / {*veduto*, *visto*}; *parere* 'seem': *par-*, *parvi* / *parso* (*paruto*); *fare* 'make': *fac-*, *feci* / *fatto*.

[53] But in Romanian (see Table 11), the person 1. (and person 2.) form of the strong preterite has an unaccented stem. So in fact, only persons 3. to 6. can be considered strong.

In other words, in Romanian, the correlation 'present – strong preterite – strong past participle' has become structural. It is totally predictable in more than 80% of cases.

If we compare Romanian and Italian, we basically find the same situation in both languages, except that Italian systematically distinguishes different stem-final consonants while Romanian hardly ever does. This is shown schematically in Table 16.

stem-final cons.	Italian		Romanian
present	DENTAL	≠ DENTAL	CONS
preterite	$\varnothing + s$ / $s + s$		$\varnothing + s$
participle	$\varnothing + s$ / $s + s$	$\varnothing + t$ / $t + t$	$\varnothing + s$

Table 16

In words: the strong preterites and participles in the two languages are generally marked by *s*. A sigmatic/non-sigmatic contrast appears for Italian past participles, conditioned by the final consonant of the present stem.

4.3.3 The case of French

French no longer has strong preterite forms in the way the other Romance languages do. For the other languages, the diagnostic is the placement of accent on the stem or on the ending depending on the person. Applying this criterion from a purely etymological point of view, the past participle *pris* 'taken' would be a strong form because it comes from **prens-u* (< Lat. *prehens-um*), while the participle *tu* 'kept silent' would be weak because it derives from **tac-**utum**. In fact, one of the consequences of the phonetic evolution of French is the elimination of any criterion based on the position of the accent, which now always falls on the last syllable. From a synchronic perspective, the distinction between strong and weak forms is no longer pertinent. Instead of maintaining the terminology based on etymological considerations, for French we refer not to strong verbs, but to *irregular* verbs.

[54] For four verbs, the final consonant of the stem is replaced by *-p-* before *-s-* (*a coace* 'cook': *copsei*, *a frige* 'roast': *fripsei*, *a înfige* 'stick in': *înfipsei*, *a suge* 'suck': *supsei*). This situation reflects the evolution of the Latin consonant cluster *-ks-* > Romanian *-ps-* and these preterites are thus the counterparts of the Italian preterites in *-ss-*. But in Romanian verbs the expected cluster *-ps-* is quite often reduced to *-s-* (e.g. *a duce* 'lead': *dusei*, *a trage* 'pull': *trăsei*).

[55] For the four verbs of the preceding footnote, the mark of the past participle is *-t* preceded by *p-* (*a coace*: *copt*, *a frige*: *fript*, *a înfige*: *înfipt*, *a suge*: *supt*). The sequence *-pt-* (cf. *-tt-* in Italian) reflects the transformation of Latin *-kt-*. We can also add *a rupe* 'break': *rupt*, *a frânge* 'break': *frânt* (with participles in *-kt-* in Latin), and *a sparge* 'break': *spart*, *a fierbe* 'boil': *fiert* (non-etymological).

4.3.3.1 The regular 'irregulars'

The first series of verbs that we will consider is remarkable for having a past participle in *-t*, while the preterite follows the regular model with a stem identical to the unaccented present tense stem — the one found, for example, in the imperfect. This type includes verbs like *conduire* 'lead': *conduisis* (cf. *conduis-ais*), *conduit*; *joindre* 'join': *joignis* (cf. *joign-ais*), *joint*. The participles of these verbs are formed from the present stem after application of Truncation before the mark *-t*.[56] This series, whose weak preterite is formed exactly like that of *dormir* 'sleep', *finir* 'finish', or *vendre* 'sell', can be considered to fit into a regular paradigm including the past participle, which we can formulate as follows, taking the infinitive as the base form:

-[ɛ̃]dre / -[ɥi]re (+ *écrire*) → preterite in *-i-* & past participle in *-t*

A complete presentation of the regular-irregular verbs is provided in Table 17, which also gives the classical Latin etymon for the preterite in person 1.

preterite → past participle ↓	imperfect indicative stem + *i*		
	(a)	(b)	(c)
imperfect stem + *i*	(dormiui) dormis,[57] dormi… (finiui) finis, fini…		
imperfect stem + [y]		(tendi) tendis, tendu (fudi) fondis, fondu (rupi) rompis, rompu…	
imperfect stem + *t* (and Trunc.)			(pinxi) peignis, peint … (-duxi) conduisis, conduit … (scripsi) écrivis, écrit

Table 17

Series (a) is etymological, series (b) is built on the new *-ei* preterite (recall section 4.2.2.2.1), and the (c) preterites are formed by analogy. They show

56 To take just one example: *conduis-* + *t* ⇒ *conduit*. We do not take into account the fact that some of these verbs introduce an epenthetic dental in the *-r-* tenses (but see section 4.4.1.1 below).

57 The first person mark *-s* is not etymologically derived, of course.

in a striking way how Latin strong verbs gave rise to regular irregular verbs in French — verbs whose past stem can be deduced from their present stem.

4.3.3.2 The irregulars

Taking into account both the preterite and the past participle, the subsystems that French irregular verbs fall into can be presented as in Table 18.[58]

preterite → past participle ↓	(a) -[y]	(b) -i-
(a′) -[y]	aperçus / aperçu, eus / eu, dus / dû, mus / mu, plut / plu, pus / pu, reçus / reçu, sus / su valus / valu, voulus / voulu bus / bu, résolus / résolu, conclus / conclu, crus / cru moulus / moulu, courus / couru connus / connu, crûs / crû, parus / paru lus / lu, plus / plu, tus / tu	vis / vu
(b′) -*i*(*s*)		assis / assis ; {ac/con/re}quis / {ac/con/re}quis, mis / mis ; pris / pris ris / ri, suffis / suffi
(c) + *t* (and Trunc.)	mourus / mort	dis / dit, fis / fait

Table 18

The verbs in (a) constitute a relatively large group, while (b) has fewer than ten members. If we compare them, we observe that the series fall into two types: In (a) the forms have as characteristic vowel a closed palatal labial [y], while in (b) they have as characteristic vowel a closed non-labial palatal [i]. Furthermore, we note that the stem of these preterite forms is contained within the stem of the imperfect indicative. We can say that the preterite stem is an 'amputated' variant of the imperfect stem.[59]

58 Four verbs resist classification: *naître* 'be born' (*naquis / né*), *vivre* 'live' (*vécus / vécu*), *tenir* 'hold' (*tins / tenu*), *venir* 'come' (*vins / venu*).

59 An amputated preterite stem never corresponds to a non-amputated past participle stem, or vice versa (except perhaps for the examples *luire* 'shine': *luisis*/*lui* and *nuire* 'harm': *nuisis*/*nui*, which are not represented in the tables, and whose participles might result from Amputation).

Amputation is an operation on the unaccented present tense stem (the one appearing in the imperfect tense) from right to left, first deleting all final non-liquid consonants (if any). A liquid stops the process. If no *-l* or *-r* appears, the vowel preceding any deleted consonants is also deleted. In the following discussion, the loss of consonants and vowels is indicated by the notations '– C' (minus C) and '– V' (minus V), respectively:

imperfect stem	– C	– V
lis-	li-	l-
mett-	me-	m-
recev-	rece-	reç-
résolv-	résol-	résol-
conclu-	conclu-	concl-
ri-	ri-	r-
val-	val-	val-

Thus, for irregular verbs in general:[60]

preterite stem = imperfect stem – C (C ≠ *l*/*r*) – V

The form produced by Amputation is followed by the vowel [i] or [y], characteristic of the preterite/past participle. In short, the two series (a) and (b) can be analyzed as follows:[61]

60 It should be noted that the condition "C ≠ *l*/*r*" is not always active: We would expect to find the preterites **{ac/con/re}quéris* instead of *acquis*, *conquis*, *requis*. In fact, when the condition holds, it has a historical basis in Latin weak verbs (*parui* > *paru*, *valui* > *valu*, etc.)

61 To a large extent, this analysis echoes van den Eynde and Blanche-Benveniste (1970), although for these authors, preterites of the *finis* type (Table 17, section (a)) are also the result of Amputation (e.g. imperf. stem *finis* with deletion of the sequence 'vowel + final consonant' = pret. stem *fin-*). This amounts to saying that the stem suffix is introduced not only in the present tenses (see section 3.2.3), but also in the past, a hypothesis that we do not adopt for the moment in this comparative study, given that no other Romance language exhibits any such suffix in the past tenses. But if the conditions for Amputation could be defined in this way, the following generalizations could be proposed:

suffix	present throughout paradigm	present in part of paradigm
derivational	Portuguese, Spanish	*
inflectional	French	Italian, Romanian

To go one step further, if a specific element of meaning can be identified for verbs taking *-iss-*, it can be considered to be a derivational suffix in Western Romance, and an inflectional suffix in Eastern Romance.

It should perhaps be pointed out that the synchronic analysis proposed here is at odds with certain historical facts. From a diachronic point of view, the stem that we derive by Amputation of the unaccented present tense stem is in fact the result of one of two processes:

(i) the adoption of the strong form of the Latin preterite and/or participle (*pris* 'taken' < **prensi*/*pris* < **prensu-*, *mis* 'put' < Lat. *misi*/*mis* < Lat. *missu-*, etc.). The vowel in this case — in general *i* — corresponds to the stem vowel of the Latin preterite. So etymol-

amputated imperfect stem + {i, y} + ending

As for the choice between [i] and [y], Table 18 shows that in most cases, Amputation supposes [y]. This vowel is found with verbs having infinitives in *-oir* or in epenthetic -t-.[62]

From the preceding discussion, we conclude that in modern French, irregular verbs are verbs for which the relationship between the present forms and the irregular, originally strong, past forms involves both consonant and vowel alternations. The position of the accent, always on the final syllable, plays no role.

4.3.4 Synchronic overview

Table 19 gives a combined view of the most important ways of forming strong preterites and past participles. At first sight, it suggests great disparities across the three groups of languages.

---

ogically we have *pris-*, *mis-*, but synchronically, according to our analysis, we have *pr+i+s*, *m+i+s*;

(ii) the extension of the weak form of the Latin preterite. The vowel in this case represents the coalescence of the unaccented stem vowel and the accented non-stem vowel, triggered by the loss of the intervocalic consonant. According to Fouché (1969: 317) and Lanly (1977: *passim)*, in person 2. (where the stem is unaccented) -[y]- derives from the labialization of the ending vowel *-i-* under the influence of *-ww-*: *habuisti* ⇒ **awwusti* ⇒ **owüs* ⇒ *eus* [y] 'had', **creduisti* ⇒ ... ⇒ **crewüs* ⇒ *crus* [kry] 'believed', **leguisti* ⇒ ... ⇒ **lewüs* ⇒ *lus* [ly] 'read', **crevuisti* 'grew' (from *crescere*) ⇒ ... ⇒ **crewüs* ⇒ *crûs* [kry], etc. Unaccented, the stem vowel weakens and is absorbed by the adjacent accented [y]. The vowel [y] is then extended to the entire paradigm. So, for example, etymological [y] + s corresponds to synchronic ∅ + [y] + s.

Similar proposals can be found in Plénat (1981: 55) and Tasmowski (1980).

62 Broadly speaking, we can capture the cases of [y] as follows:

[y] if the imperfect stem ends in [non-*i* VOWEL + non-nasal FRICATIVE]

(Plénat 1981: 56). But this says nothing about stems with no final consonant like *rire* 'laugh', exceptions like *résolus* 'resolved' and *lus* 'read' are not accounted for, and amputated stems that take [i] must be marked in the lexicon.

	Pt./Sp.		French		Italian		Rom.
pret.→ part. ↓	palat. stem V	non-palat. stem V	amput. + palat. V	amput. + labial V	redupl. of stem C	± delet. of C + *s*	delet. of C + *s*
weak part.	+	+			+		
amp. + palat.			+				
amp. + velar				+			
cons. + *s* / *t*						+	+

Table 19

We will argue that these disparities are in part illusory, but it is striking that there is only one verb that is strong in all of the languages under consideration, and that is *dire* 'say'.

Still, if we consider the most representative schemas for irregular and strong preterites and past participles (for the moment leaving aside Portuguese and Spanish, which have largely eliminated these forms), we arrive at the following generalizations:

Fr.	past stem of irreg verb	=	imperfect stem – V	– C	
Rom.	past stem of strong verb	=	imperfect stem	– C	+ *s*-
It.	past stem of strong verb	=	imperfect stem	– C	+ *(s)s*-

Table 20 summarizes the situation for the preterite in all of the languages.

pret. marked by:	Portuguese	Spanish	French	Italian	Rom.
closed V	+ (stem V)	+ (stem V)	+	–	–
inflect. C	–	–	–	+	+
– imperf. stem C			+	+	+
– imperf. stem V			+	–	–

Table 20

It is clear that in French, Italian, and Romanian too, the relationship between the past and the present tense stems has become largely regular, and that in all three of these languages, the relevant process is the reduction of the final consonant of the unaccented present tense stem. We can also see that with Amputation, just as with Truncation (see section 2.2.3.1 (iii)), French goes one step further than the other languages, in this case targeting a consonant and a vowel at the same time.

4.4 Preterites and Participles: Diachronic View

The facts described in sections 4.2 and 4.3 reveal that Romance verbal paradigms have been restructured on the basis on the present tense stem, either by adopting weak preterites and past participles, or by establishing a set of codifiable links between present and past tense forms.

But what determines the choice of one solution over the other, when both are equally possible in principle? We will attempt to demonstrate that this choice depends at least partially on the phonological structure of the *infectum* of the Latin etymon itself. This hypothesis, if true, is surprising, because as we have mentioned several times, the relationships among the three themes of a Latin verb are unpredictable, and they cannot be organized hierarchically (recall section 4.1.2). Table 21 gives some further examples of verbs with the same phonetic structure in the present, but diverging forms in the preterite.

	reduplication	V modified or unmodified	sigmatic	-ui
prete-rite	totondi < tondere fefelli < fallere	respondi < respondere fudi < fundere scidi < scindere -puli < -pellere	uulsi < uellere	dolui < dolere
	-tu	-itu	-su	
parti-ciple	tentu- < tendere[63]	absconditu- < abscondere dolitu- < dolere	tonsu- < tondere fusu- < fundere scissu- < scindere falsu- < fallere	

Table 21

In order to test the proposed link between the phonological structure of the *infectum* of the Latin verbal etymon and the type of morphological restructuring adopted in Romance, we will assemble a corpus of the Latin verbs that are best represented in the Romance languages, that is the two large subsets characterized by the final consonant of the *infectum* theme:

(i) verbs with a final velar (most often voiced);
(ii) verbs with a final dental (most often voiced).

Within these groups, the verb stems ending in a velar or dental in combination with a nasal constitute a particularly rewarding base for our study, because the nasal offers protection against the phonetic disruptions that inter-

[63] There is a sigmatic variant *tensu-*.

vocalic occlusives are subject to in the evolution towards the modern languages. The presence of a consonant cluster is particularly important in the development of French forms because phonetic processes must normally lead to the deletion of the simple intervocalic consonant, a deletion that corresponds to the first phase of Amputation in our synchronic analysis. But the final velar or dental consonant of the infectum stem is most likely to be preserved in the simple past and the past participle if protected by a preceding consonant.

4.4.1 Verbs with stem accent in the Latin infinitive

4.4.1.1 *Infectum* with final voiced velar preceded by nasal (*tingere* type)

Strong Latin verbs in *-ng-* most often formed a sigmatic preterite. They acquired weak forms in Ibero-Romance (Lat. *tingere* 'soak' > Pt. *tingir*, Sp. *teñir*; Lat. *cingere* 'gird' > Pt. *cingir*, Sp. *ceñir*). In the transition to French, these develop into a set of weak verbs in *-i-*, at least as far as the simple past is concerned. Italian and Romanian retain a sigmatic preterite.

These verbs had a past participle in *-t-*. This was maintained in Italian and French, but it became sigmatic in Romanian.

French weak preterite + participle in -t-	Italian sigmatic preterite + participle in -t-	Romanian sigmatic preterite + participle in *-s-*
atteignis, ceignis, enfreignis, éteignis, feignis, joignis, oignis, peignis, plaignis, teignis... + empreignis, geignis, craignis[64]	aggiunsi, attinsi, cinsi, distinsi, finsi, fransi, funsi, giunsi, minsi, munsi, piansi, pinsi, punsi, respinsi, (s)tinsi, strinsi, unsi, vinsi	ajunsei, atinsei, distinsei, împunsei, încinsei, învinsei, plânsei, respinsei, stinsei, strânsei, unsei
atteint, ceint, enfreint, éteint, feint, joint, oint, peint, plaint, teint... + empreint, geint, craint	aggiunto, attinto, cinto, distinto, finto, franto, funto, giunto, minto, munto, pianto, pinto, punto, respinto, (s)tinto, stretto, unto, vinto	ajuns, atins, distins, împuns, încins, învins, plâns, respins, stins, strâns, uns

Table 22

4.4.1.2 *Infectum* with final intervocalic voiced velar (*protegere* type)

This group — also taking mostly a sigmatic preterite and a past participle in *-t-* in Latin — disappeared as a whole in Ibero-Romance, where only a sin-

64 Latin infinitives in *-emere* were incorporated into this group.

gle verb with an old sigmatic preterite remains (Pt. *trouxe*, Sp. *traje* 'bring'). Apart from some isolated past participles (*frit* 'fried', *extrait* 'extracted'), French did not preserve this group either, and the inherited verbs migrated towards other models (e.g. Latin *colligere* vs French *cueillir* 'gather').[65] In contrast, Italian shows preterites that have become uniformly sigmatic, while the participles still end in *-t-*. As for Romanian, not only the preterites but also most of the participles derive from sigmatic forms.

Italian preterite in *-ss-* + participle in *-tt-*	Romanian preterite in *-(p)s-* + participle in *-s-* or *-(p)t-*
afflissi, diressi, elessi, fissi, frissi, lessi, neglessi, protessi, redassi, ressi, trassi	alesei, culesei, trăsei înfipsei, fripsei, supsei
afflitto, diretto, eletto, fitto, fritto, letto, negletto, protetto, redatto, retto, tratto	ales, cules, tras înfipt, fript, supt

Table 23

4.4.1.3 *Infectum* with final voiced dental preceded by nasal (*tendere* type)

In Latin, among the verbs falling into this category, we find no sigmatic preterites. In Ibero-Romance, the descendants of these Latin verbs are weak (Lat. *pendere* > Pt., Sp. *pender* 'hang'; Lat. *tendere* > Pt., Sp. *tender* 'tend'). The situation in French is identical, with a characteristic vowel *-i-* in the simple past and -[y]- in the past participle. But in Eastern Romance, the preterites of this group are now systematically sigmatic, with variation only in the presence or absence of the original nasal. Romanian always preserves the cluster *-ns-*, while Italian reduces *-ns-* to *-s-*. The participles are also sigmatic.

French	Italian	Romanian
défendis, descendis, entendis, fondis, pendis, rendis, répondis, tendis, tondis	difesi, {ap/di}pesi, fusi, incisi, intesi, presi, resi, scesi, tesi	ascunsei, depinsei, încinsei, întinsei, prinsei, răspunsei, tinsei, tunsei
défendu, descendu, entendu, fondu, pendu, rendu, répondu, tendu, tondu	difeso, {ap/di}peso, fuso, inciso, inteso, preso, reso, sceso, teso	ascuns, depins, încins, întins, prins, răspuns, tins, tuns

Table 24

[65] Cf. also *legere* > Fr. *lire* 'read'.

4.4.1.4 *Infectum* with final intervocalic voiced dental (*claudere* type)

Verbs of this type had a sigmatic preterite and past participle in Latin.[66] Here again, we find only weak verbs in Portuguese and Spanish (Lat. *comedere* > Pt., Sp. *comer* 'eat'). The sigmatic perfect forms, on the other hand, are maintained in Eastern Romance, both in the simple past and in the past participle — and the *claudere* type has superceded the *tendere* type (see section 4.4.1.3).

Italian	Romanian
chiusi, conclusi, decisi, divisi, elisi, esclusi, esplosi, rasi, risi, uccisi	decisei, {în/des}chisei, inclusei, răsei, râsei, ucisei
chiuso, concluso, deciso, diviso, eliso, escluso, esploso, raso, riso, ucciso	decis, {în/des}chis, inclus, ras, râs, ucis

Table 25

In French, the inherited verb *rire* 'laugh' < *ridere* (classical *ridere*) and the semi-learned borrowing *conclure* 'conclude' < *concludere*, which take sigmatic preterites (*risi*, *conclusi*) developed the simple past forms *ris* and *conclus*. The vowels *-i-* and -[y]- and the consonant *s-* in these forms belong to the stem etymologically, but since they are identical to the characteristic vowels and endings of other verb groups, we can conjecture that the forms were reanalyzed in terms of the structure 'Stem + Thematic vowel {*i*, [y]} + Ending'.[67]

4.4.2 Verbs with unaccented stem in the Latin infinitive

In this section we will consider only verbs of Latin conjugation II that have survived as such, leaving aside those that shifted into other groups in Latin or in Romance. This leaves us with around fifteen verbs. The ones in *-ere* most often formed their perfect in *-ui* and their past participle in *-itu*.[68] Sigmatic perfects and participles are much less widespread.

In the development of the Romance languages, the perfect in *-ui* became the prototype for the group and is responsible for:

---

[66] Except for *credere* 'believe', which gave rise to a weak verb in the Romance languages.

[67] The same remark applies to the forms *assis* 'sat', *dis* 'said', *mis* 'put', *pris* 'took ', *-quis*, and *fis* 'made' in Table 18, forms that we analyzed synchronically in section 4.3.3 as *ass+i+s*, *d+i+s*, etc. Note that in the phonetic evolution of person 2., the only stem-final intervocalic consonant that had to disappear systematically was *-d-* (*vis* < *veis* < *vedis* < *vidisti*). The fact that other consonants disappeared in these forms (*assis* < *asses-is* < *assess-isti*, *dis* < *des-is* < *dix-isti*, *mis* < *mes-is* < *mis-isti*, etc.) supports the reanalysis proposal.

[68] Only one of these verbs still has a strong participle in Italian (*solere*: *solito*); there is no preterite form.

(i) the development in Italian of simple past forms with geminate consonants (*ebbi*, *giacqui*, *piacqui*, *seppi*, *tacqui*, *tenni*, *volli*), with a weak participle in *-u-* (see section 4.3.2.1);

(ii) the set of Ibero-Romance preterites with a (semi-)closed velar stem vowel (Pt. *coube*, *houve*, *pude*, *prouve*, *soube*, Sp. *cupe*, *hube*, *pude*, *supe*, see section 4.3.1), with a corresponding weak past participle in *-i-*;

(iii) a set of French verbs containing the vowel -[y]- in the simple past and in the past participle (*eus*, *eu*; *sus*, *su*, see section 4);

(iv) the development of preterites and participles in *-u-* in Romanian, where the vast majority of ***-e*** verbs became weak (*avui*, *avut*, see section 4.2.2.2.2).

Preterites in *-ui* thus gave rise to strong preterites in Portuguese, Spanish, and Italian, and weak preterites in Romanian, with the accent always on *-u*, and irregular preterites in French, with the accent always on -[y]-. Paradoxically, the French verbs in -[y]- are just like the Romanian verbs in *-u-*, the descendants of a paradigm with the accent on the ending. But in contrast to Romanian (for which the relevant process must date back to vulgar Latin), in French the phenomenon is particular to French itself, and the resulting verbs are not regular.[69]

4.4.3 Other verbs

The evolution of verbs not satisfying any of the criteria adopted up to now can generally be characterized by the one of the following two options: integration into an existing category, or (in a very small proportion of cases) preservation of a Latin paradigm.[70]

4.4.4 Summary

Table 26 presents the groups of strong or irregular verbs in Romance, (re)structured according to the final consonant of the Latin stem, abstracting away from some marginal cases (for Portuguese and Spanish, the empty slots correspond to forms that were incorporated into weak paradigms).

4.5 The Romance Verb Stem in the Past Tenses: Conclusions

We have seen how, in the evolution of the Romance languages, the three themes corresponding to one verbal base in Latin tend to become unified. The paths to this unification are essentially of two types:

---

[69] See fn. 61.

[70] In the case of verbs borrowed (not inherited) from Latin, only Italian perpetuates the original model in this way. In the other languages, these borrowed verbs behave like regular weak verbs (with a few exceptions).

1. The *infectum* theme is extended to the entire verbal paradigm. The verb, originally strong, becomes weak.
2. The results of phonetic evolution are re-interpreted synchronically, allowing the establishment of a predictable relationship between the past tense and the present tense stems. Either the final consonant or the sequence V + final C undergoes modifications specific to each language, according to principles that, in the end, continue to be influenced by the phonetic structure of the Latin etymon.[71]

Latin *infec-tum*	Portuguese		Spanish		French		Italian		Romanian	
	pret.	prt.	pret.	prt.	pret.	part.	pret.	part.	pret.	part.
III: -ng-					i plai- gnis	t plaint	ns piansi	nt pianto	ns plân- sei	ns plâns
III: -g-							ss trassi frissi	tt tratto fritto	s (ps) trăsei fripsei	s (pt) tras fript
III: -nd-					i tendis	[y] tendu	s tesi	s teso	ns tinsei	ns tins
III: -d-					{i,[y]} ris crus	{i,[y]} ri cru	s risi	s riso	s râsei	s râs
II	closed V houve		closed V hube		[y] eus voulus	[y] eu voulu	CC ebbi volli			

Table 26

5 General Conclusions

1. The phonetic evolution from Latin to the Romance languages should normally have given rise to a series of allomorphs for the present stem.

71 This is not meant to suggest that the paradigm-unifying phenomena observed in the modern languages are necessarily of the same type (for example, in French, the re-formation *croivent* instead of *croient* 'believe' by analogy with *doivent, boivent, reçoivent*). This question calls for a separate study, for which a comparative Romance perspective would be invaluable.

The morphological evolution of the verb reveals a process of paradigm reconstruction resulting in a stem with an invariant form.

2. Latin used three distinct themes for various tenses: *infectum*, *perfectum*, and *supinum*. In the development of the Romance languages, this situation is eliminated in favor of another system, where the stems of the preterite and of the participle are calculated from that of the present.

3. The regularization strategies observed are the same for the present and past tenses.

   (i). replacement of forms with accented stem with forms accented on the thematic vowel or on the ending;
   (ii). vowel uniformization;
   (iii). constraints on the consonantal structure of the stem.

4. Interestingly, these regularization strategies amount to a partial return to the original situation, given that:

   (i). in Latin, the present tense stem did not exhibit any variation, and
   (ii). for new preterites (weak and strong), the sub-classes of verbs that emerge can be closely correlated with the phonological structure of the *infectum* of the Latin etymon.

3

Clitic Pronouns in the Romance Languages

PHILIP MILLER AND PAOLA MONACHESI

1 Introduction[1]

In the vast majority of the world's languages, there are certain elements whose status is problematic because their behavior apparently lies somewhere between that of an independent word and that of a normal affix. Even if they seem to enjoy greater autonomy than affixes, these elements are phonologically dependent upon a *host*, unlike normal words, and form a single prosodic word with this host. Such elements were called 'clitics' by the comparative linguists of the 19th century and the structuralists, who distinguished 'proclitics' from 'enclitics' according to whether the clitic is attached prosodically to the word which follows it (proclitics), or the word which precedes it (enclitics).

[1] The authors wish to thank Anne Abeillé, Julie Auger, Sabrina Bendjaballah, Berthold Crysmann, Elisabeth Delais-Roussarie, Paul Hirschbühler, Marie Labelle, Bernard Laks, Yves-Charles Morin, Marc Plénat and Marleen Van Peteghem for their help while writing this chapter. We also thank Anne-Marie Berthonneau and Anne Zribi-Hertz who re-read a draft version and made many comments about it; thanks also to Danièle Godard for many comments and her unfailing support. Finally, we wish to thank especially those of our colleagues who provided native speaker judgements: Ileana Comorovski, Donka Farkaş, Josep Fontana, Rafael Marín, Alexandra Popescu, Liliane Santos, Lucia Tovena, Enric Vallduví and Marina Vigário, who sacrificed so much of their time to help clarify the often complex data. However, none of the above mentioned can be held responsible for any errors of fact or interpretation which remain.

Fundamental Issues in the Romance Languages
Danièle Godard (ed.).

The interest in clitics within the generative tradition (in the broad sense) is linked to two key works: firstly the analysis of French clitic pronouns (traditionally referred to as 'weak pronouns' or 'pronoms conjoints') by Kayne (1975), a book based on his unpublished 1969 doctoral thesis; secondly, the typological study of different sorts of clitics by Zwicky (1977). In this work, Zwicky looked at what kinds of elements can be called clitics and the problems such elements raise for syntax, morphology, phonology and the interfaces between them. One of the most important distinctions he proposed was that between 'simple clitics' and 'special clitics'. Simple clitics are the result of a word which is not stressed, being phonologically reduced and attached prosodically to an adjacent word. This means that a simple clitic will occupy the same surface syntactic position as a corresponding unreduced morpheme. In contrast, special clitics are elements which are prosodically dependent on a host, and which appear as variants of independent forms with which they share a meaning and, usually, a similar phonology; however, their surface syntactic distribution is different. In the framework of this dichotomy, elements like articles or monosyllabic prepositions in the Romance languages can be classed as simple clitics, while clitic pronouns[2] are classed among the special clitics.

Indeed it is well-known that personal pronouns in the Romance languages are divided into two main types:[3] clitic pronouns, and what have traditionally been called the 'strong', 'tonic' or 'disjoint' forms, which have the same distribution as normal NPs.[4]

(1) F a. Pierre te le donnera. *Peter will give it to you*
I b. Pietro te lo darà.

[2] We adopt the term 'clitic pronoun' in this chapter, because it is the most widespread term nowadays. As we will see below however, it is not at all clear that all the elements that have been referred to as 'clitic pronouns' in the study of the Romance languages should be analyzed as clitics in the technical sense of the term that we discuss in this introduction. Where there is no ambiguity, we omit 'pronouns' and refer to the elements in question simply as 'clitics'.

[3] See, however, Cardinaletti and Starke (1999) who distinguish three classes, clitics, weak pronouns and strong pronouns.

[4] Where possible, for each example we give corresponding sentences for each of the different Romance languages we are dealing with, along with a translation into English or a morpheme-by-morpheme gloss if we feel it is more useful. Each example is preceded by the initial letter of the language which it is in: F(rench), P(ortuguese), S(panish), C(atalan), I(talian), R(omanian), QF (Quebec French). We indicate the old, standard, and spoken forms of a language with O, St, Sp respectively, preceding the initial of the language: OF = Old French, StF = Standard French, SpF = spoken French. Except for certain specific remarks, we only discuss the European versions of Spanish and Portuguese, which is what S and P will refer to here. In addition, we use the following abbreviations: pres = present, subj = subjunctive, psp = past participle, acc = accusative, dat= dative, pl = plural, sg = singular, m = masculine, f = feminine, S = Sentence (in the sense of an IP in generative grammar, see Haegeman 1991).

(2) F a. Pierre lira un livre pour Marie / pour elle.
Peter will read a book for Mary / for her
b. Pierre donnera le livre à Marie.
I c. Pietro darà il libro a Maria.
Peter will give the book to Mary

From (1), we see that clitic pronouns can appear in front of a finite verb, unlike the strong form *elle* in (2a) and the full NPs and PPs in (2a,b,c). We also notice that the dative pronoun *te* precedes the accusative pronoun in (1); the inverse order would be ungrammatical, while the accusative-dative order is possible for the corresponding full forms in (2). So we can see that clitic pronouns are special clitics.

In this study, we will adopt the 'lexicalist' hypothesis, according to which morphologically complex words are created in the lexicon by morphological rules and subsequently inserted into syntactic structures (see for example Lapointe 1980, Anderson 1992). A sentence is thus a sequence of syntactic words linked to a sequence of prosodic words by post-lexical prosodic principles. However, there is not a one-to-one relation between these two structures; the prosodic rules can form one prosodic word from two syntactic words, by joining them together (see e.g. Kaisse 1985, Nespor and Vogel 1986).[5]

In this framework, simple clitics have an entirely natural status: they are independent words syntactically, which are attached post-lexically to an adjacent word (the 'host') to form a single prosodic word; simple clitics are therefore 'post-lexical' clitics. We follow Kaisse (1985) and many others in adopting the hypothesis that phonological and morpho-phonological interactions between post-lexical clitics and hosts can be different to the interactions between affixes and roots. In particular, we assume that the internal morphological structure of a syntactic word (the morphemes it is composed of) is not accessible to post-lexical rules, but only its phonological and prosodic structure. If one takes them seriously, these hypotheses encounter a number of apparent and well-known counter-examples for which different solutions have been proposed (see e.g. Inkelas and Zec 1990 and particularly the article of Hayes 1990 included in that volume). Every theoretical framework adopts, in one way or another, a difference between lexical and post-lexical processes and it is this distinction which will be crucial and problematic in our discussion of clitic pronouns in Romance.

Special clitics are more difficult to deal with in a strictly lexicalist framework. As they do not appear in the same syntactic position as their

[5] Different types of attachments (of syntactic words by prosodic rules) have been suggested in the literature, see e.g. Peperkamp (1997), Delais-Roussarie (2000) for recent discussions.

corresponding full phrases would, the analysis we have suggested for simple clitics would seem, *a priori*, not to apply. Anderson (1992), Halpern (1995), and Fontana (1993, 1996), building on the work of Klavans (1985), have proposed that the position of special clitics can be explained via a combination of syntactic and prosodic constraints. Syntax determines the type of constituent with respect to which the clitic is positioned (e.g. S, NP), whether the clitic is placed next to the initial or final element of the constituent in question, and finally whether it is positioned in front of or behind this (initial or final) element. For example, a clitic could be positioned *in front of* the *first* element of S (where fronted constituents or complementizers which precede the verb, do not count as the first element of S). Then, depending on whether the clitic is a proclitic or enclitic, prosodic constraints determine the particular item to which the clitic attaches itself. Continuing the previous example, if the clitic is prosodically an enclitic, it would attach itself leftward to a fronted constituent or complementizer. In the absence of hosts of this sort to its left, there are two possible solutions. Exceptionally, the clitic may stay in its normal position and be attached as a proclitic (this is essentially the analysis proposed by Fontana 1993, 1996 for clitic pronouns in Old Spanish); or a post-lexical operation called 'prosodic inversion' may allow the clitic to attach itself as an enclitic to the first word of the S domain. Essentially therefore, this means that prosodic constraints on the attachment of clitics can take precedence over the syntactic constraints on their position which we just mentioned. This analysis has been proposed by Halpern (1995) for several languages and is very close to the analysis of clitic pronouns in the first stages of Old French, by Hirschbühler and Labelle (2000, 2001b). We will consider these issues in section 2.1.6 below; as we will see, an analysis of this kind (using mixed syntactic and prosodic constraints) can partially account for the data from Portuguese and Romanian. A consequence of this kind of analysis is that the syntactic category of the host of a special clitic is very variable.

However, for the majority of modern Romance languages, and notably French, Italian, Catalan and Spanish, a different analysis of clitic pronouns can be considered, whereby they are seen as inflectional affixes which are lexically attached to a base.[6] Several arguments will be put forward in sup-

[6] This analysis has been supported by, among others, Miller (1992), Fontana (1993), Auger (1994), and Monachesi (1999). It has also been proposed for Romanian by Monachesi (1998, 2000) and for Portuguese by Crysmann (2000a,b), although for these two languages the theory needs to be extended, in order to explain certain apparent counter-examples, specifically the cases where the clitic is not contiguous to the verb. However, in view of the impossibility of maintaining an analysis strictly in terms of post-lexical clitics, we might suppose that these languages are in a transitional phase; similar hypotheses have been proposed in slightly differ-

port of this theory below, specifically the fact that in these languages the position of the clitic pronouns is not determined in relation to the first word of a given phrase, but in relation to the verb, to which they are always contiguous. Furthermore, we notice phonological and morphological interactions of a lexical kind, between clitic pronouns and the verb.

Our purpose in sketching the broad outlines of this theoretical position is to clarify the descriptive presentation in the rest of the chapter and not to argue in favor of one theoretical framework or another.[7] In adopting this model as a framework, we are nonetheless entirely aware of the problems which it might encounter and we will try to stick as closely as possible to the data without avoiding data which appear problematic for this position, and which is – precisely for this reason – very important. Indeed we attempt, in this chapter, to bring together what is currently known about clitic pronouns, while insisting more on empirical adequacy than on the analyses. Clearly we cannot cover all the data, far from it, but we hope to make the problems clear and to present the results of previous research that seem the most relevant to us. We will try to supply a detailed presentation of specific aspects of the behavior of clitic pronouns at the syntactic, morphological, and phonological levels, in a certain number of Romance languages and dialects.

Due to their numerous noteworthy properties, clitic pronouns have been the object of a great deal of research in linguistics (see for example Benveniste 1965 for an early synthesis of the central properties of clitic pronouns in French). Over the last thirty years, they have been studied in the framework of generative grammar in a broad sense, particularly since the publication of the influential works by Perlmutter (1970) and Kayne (1975), which focused on Spanish and French, and which placed clitic pronouns at the centre of important theoretical issues. The studies since have been characterized on one side by the increasing number of languages and dialects studied, with recognized national languages being considered initially, and afterwards several more geographically limited varieties. Concurrently, there has been more detailed analysis of the phenomena at work in each of these languages, whether it is at the level of the syntax or at the level of the phonology and morphology. These studies have made it clear that the details of the behavior of clitic pronouns across different languages, and often even within the same language, is far from being uniform, even if certain

ent frameworks by, among others, Rivas (1977), Jaeggli (1982) and Enrique-Arias (2000) for Spanish, by Cummins and Roberge (1994) for French, and by Bonet (1991, 1995) for Catalan.

[7] For an overview of recent and varied points of view on the problem of clitics in general, see the collections of van Riemsdijk (1999), Gerlach and Grijzenhout (2000) and Muller (2001), as well as the very useful thesis of Gerlach (2002).

properties are shared. The studies have also brought to light a variety of properties spread across the data, apparently demonstrating all the possible intermediate cases between a normal full word and a normal inflectional affix. In view of their position at the interface between syntax, morphology and phonology, and the complexity of the data, clitic pronouns in the Romance languages constitute a particularly relevant domain for testing out any linguistic theory.

2 Syntactic properties of clitic pronouns

The first generative studies of clitics, such as Perlmutter (1970) and especially Kayne (1975), mainly looked into their syntactic status. Their problematic status from the point of view of the interaction between syntax, morphology and phonology was not really taken into account until Zwicky (1977). Basing himself on French, Kayne (1975) highlighted a series of syntactic properties of clitic pronouns which were subsequently shown to be typical of the situation in the majority of Romance languages, even though there is a great deal of variation in the details. We are going to review these properties below mentioning certain interesting cases as we go along.

2.1 Position of clitics in the sentence

2.1.1 Clitics positioned in relation to a finite verb

The most immediately distinctive property of clitic pronouns in the Romance languages is that they do not appear in the same positions as the corresponding full NPs or PPs. They are therefore special clitics in the sense of Zwicky (1977). This is particularly clear in the case where the sentence contains a finite verb. Indeed, in this case, pronouns generally appear in front of the verb, while the usual position of the corresponding full phrases is behind.[8]

(3) I a. Martina legge il libro. *Martina reads the book*
F b. Martine lit le livre.

(4) I a. Martina lo legge. *Martina reads it*
F b. Martine le lit.

[8] The finite verb in question here is either the lexical verb, or an auxiliary verb in the sense of Abeillé and Godard (this volume). When the finite verb is restructuring in the sense of Abeillé and Godard, the clitics can equally appear on the non-finite complement verb, see sections 2.1.2 and 2.1.5.

(5) I a. *Martina legge lo.
F b. *Martine lit le.

The data are identical in this respect in French, Catalan, Spanish and Italian (except the exceptional case of *loro* in Italian, which has been discussed in detail in Monachesi 1999a:119-133, and which we do not have space to discuss here). In Romanian, pronouns are proclitics with finite verbs (6a), except for certain configurations with the feminine accusative pronoun *o*: in the case of verbs with tense auxiliaries (where clitics are generally on the auxiliary (6b), see section 2.1.5), the clitic *o* is on the past participle with the past auxiliary (6c), and on the infinitive with a conditional auxiliary (6e). *o* is however a proclitic on the future auxiliary (6d).

(6) R a. Marina îl/o citeşte. [*citeşte-l / o] *Marina reads it(m)/it(f).*
b. Marina l-a citit. [*a citit-îl] *Marina read it(m).*
c. Marina a citit-o. [*o a citit]
Marina AUX.PST read-it.fem *Marina read it.*
d. Marina o va citi. [*va citi-o]
Marina it(f) AUX.FUT read *Marina will read it.*
e. Marina ar citi-o. [*o ar citi]
Marina AUX.COND read-it.fem *Marina would read it.*

Portuguese, in this respect, is exceptional in the Romance languages. Indeed, in this language enclisis is the default position (7a,b). The choice between enclisis and proclisis here is not linked to the finite or non-finite status of the verb, but is determined by the presence of a series of elements which force proclisis when they appear in front of the verb (see Barbosa 1996, Rouveret 1999, Crysmann 2000a). Specifically, they are complementizers, *wh*-expressions, negation, certain quantifiers and certain adverbs (7c,d,e). In the absence of such elements in preverbal position, the clitics are enclitics (7a,f). The common properties of these different proclisis triggers are not very clear.

(7) P a. A Marina lê-o. *Marina reads it.*
the Marina reads-it
b. *A Marina o lê.
the Marina it reads
c. A Marina não o lê. *Marina doesn't read it.*
d. *A Marina não lê-o.
e. A Marina raramente o lê / *lê-o. *Marina rarely reads it.*
f. A Marina lê-o / *o lê raramente. 'Marina reads it rarely.'

Finally, in finite sentences the order of clitics in relation to other clitics is not the same as the order between the corresponding full phrases. Indeed, as we will see below in section 3.4, the order of clitics is fixed, contrary to what is the case for complement phrases (for them, discourse factors can favor one or the other order, but the order is not syntactically constrained).

(8) F a. Martine donnera le livre à Jean / à Jean le livre.
I b. Martina darà il libro a Gianni / a Gianni il libro.
Martina will give the book to John / to John the book.
F c. Martine le lui / *lui le donnera.
Martina it to him / *to him it will give *M. will give it to him.*
I d. Martina glielo / *logli darà. *M. will give it to him.*
Martina to him it/ *it to him will give

The order between the corresponding clitics in French (8c) and Italian (8d) is the opposite. Furthermore, in French, if you have a dative other than *lui, leur,* you get the opposite order to that of the example in (8c): dative followed by the accusative (9a); the corresponding Italian sentence is (9b), consistent with (8d).

(9) F a. Martine me le / *le me donnera.
I b. Martina me lo / *lo me darà.
Martina to.me it / *it to.me will give *M. will give it to me.*

So there are complex factors regulating the order of clitics in relation to each other, with variation between languages and within the same language. We will come back to this issue in detail in section 3.4.

2.1.2 Clitics positioned in relation to a non-finite verb

In the case where a clitic combines with a verb in the infinitive or a participle, Italian, Spanish, Catalan, and Romanian require enclisis, as we see in the examples in (10) (also (6c,e) above). Only Italian allows cliticization to the past participle as in (10b), the corresponding forms being impossible in the other Romance languages studied here (10e,i) (see for example, Fernández Soriano 1999:1261 for Spanish, Crysmann 2000a:78 for Portuguese).

(10) I a. Martina vuole leggerlo.
Martina wants to.read-it.
b. Lettolo, fu facile decidere.
read(PSP)-it, was easy to decide
Having read it, it was easy to decide.
c. Avendolo letto, fu facile decidere.
Having-it read, it was easy to decide
S d. Martina quiere leerlo.
e. *Leídolo, fue fácil decidir.
f. Habiéndolo leído, fue fácil decidir.

C g. Martina vol llegir-lo.
h. Martina vol vendre'l.
Martina wants to sell-it.
i. *Llegit-lo, va ser fàcil decidir.
j. Havent-lo llegit, va ser fàcil decidir.
P k. Tendo-o lido, foi fácil decider.
R l. văzîndu-mă *seeing me*

We notice that the standard spelling attaches the enclitics to the verb in all the languages (directly in Italian and Spanish, by a hyphen or apostrophe in Catalan, and by a hyphen in Romanian and Portuguese). These spelling conventions reflect the fact that, despite appearances, the clitics in these sentences are not in the same position as the corresponding full phrase. Indeed, in contrast with the full phrases, enclitics can never be separated from the verb, a fact which holds in all the Romance languages (see below section 2.1.4).

In French however, there is proclisis with the infinitive and the present participle (the past participle being incompatible with clitic pronouns), just as with the finite verbs.

(11) F a. Martine veut le lire. [vs. *lire-le]
Martine wants it to.read *Martine wants to read it.*
b. En l'ayant lu / En le lisant, il fut facile de décider.
[vs. *ayant-le lu / *lisant-le]
In it-having read / In it reading, it was easy to decide
Having read it / Reading it, it was easy to decide.
c. *Lu-le / *Le-lu, il fut facile de decider.
Read it / It read, it was easy to decide

In Portuguese, the factors governing the choice between proclisis and enclisis function the same way as they do in finite sentences; it is thus the only language to have a choice between the enclitic and proclitic position which is not governed solely by the inflectional properties of the verb (see Rouveret 1999, Crysmann 2000a,b, Duarte and Matos 2000). Thus we get cases of proclitics on infinitives if they are preceded by a proclisis trigger within the infinitival clause as in (12a), which contrasts with (12b).[9]

(12) P a. Marina lamentava não o conhecer.
Marina regretted not him to.know
Marina regretted not knowing him.

[9] The situation is the same with inflected infinitives in Portuguese. See Crysmann (2000a: 83) on the locality requirements upon the trigger of proclisis (which has no effect if it is in the main clause).

b. Marina lamentava conhecê-lo.
Marina regretted knowing him.

2.1.3 Clitics positioned in relation to an imperative verb

In standard French, clitics appear as enclitics with positive imperative verbs, but as proclitics with negative imperatives (13a,b). In spoken French, with negative imperatives without *ne*, there is a choice according to dialects between keeping proclisis as in (13c) or an innovative enclisis variant which generalizes to all the uses of the imperative (13d) (see Hirschbühler and Labelle 2001a for a detailed study).

(13)	F	a.	Lis-le!	*Read it!*
		b.	Ne le lis pas!	*Don't read it!*
	SpF	c.	Le lis pas !	*Don't read it !*
	SpF	d.	Lis-le pas !	*Don't read it !*

In Spanish (Fernández Soriano 1999:1261), Catalan (Wheeler *et al.* 1999, sections 12.2.2, 16.5.11) and Portuguese the situation is quite similar to that of standard French, but for these languages, we must bear in mind that the imperative (which exists only in 2sg and 2pl) is only possible in positive imperative clauses. In negative imperatives, the subjunctive is used (without a *que*-like element introducing it). Despite the different forms, one principle governs the position of clitics; they are enclitics in positive imperatives (14a,c,e) and proclitics in negative imperatives (14b,d,f).[10] The same positioning principles apply in Romanian (14g,h).[11]

(14)	S	a. ¡Léelo! (imp)	b. ¡No lo leas! (subj)
	C	c. Llegeix-lo! (imp)	d. No el llegeixis! (subj)

---

10 Note that in Spanish and Catalan, with the usual uses of the subjunctive (preceded by *que*), clitics precede the verb, whether negation is present or not. One can therefore contrast C *Llegim-lo!* 'Let's read it!' with *És possible que el llegim* 'It is possible that we read it', and notice that when one uses a subjunctive with *que* in the main clause in order to express an order, there is also proclisis: C *Que el llegeixi!* 'He must read it!'.

11 (14g,h) are 2pl because for 2sg (*Citeşte-l!*) the infinitive is used when the imperative is negated (*Nu-l citi!*). In the 2pl, the form of the imperative is identical to that of the present subjunctive. It is possible, in Romanian, to express an order using the subjunctive, without a governing clause or the particle *să*, in which case enclitics are used: *Bată-l Dumnezeu!* 'God punish him!' (see Lombard 1974:130, who says that such subjunctives are limited to set expressions expressing imprecations or wishes). With *să*, pronouns are proclitics: *Să-l bată!* (this last form is commonly used). The fact that examples like (14g) are not fixed expressions suggests that the use of the form is imperative and not subjunctive. Lombard (1974:131) mentions that, in a coordination of imperatives, the second coordinate can receive proclisis like in 17th century French (Haase 1930: 417, for example *Faites-en faire des informations, et me les envoyez le plus tôt que vous pourriez* 'Have inquiries carried out about this, and send them to me as soon as you can.').

P e. Lê-o! (imp) f. Não o leias! (subj)
R g. Citiţi-l! (imp) h. Nu-l citiţi! (imp)

In Italian (Cordin and Calabrese 1988:552; Vogel and Napoli 1995), we find specific imperative forms in the 2sg, 1pl and 2pl. These forms are compatible with negation, except the 2sg which is replaced by the infinitive with negation, as in Romanian. Otherwise, the subjunctive forms are possible with every person with the meaning of an exhortation, but are of a more formal register. As regards clitic placement, the situation in Italian is more complex than the other languages. With the specific forms of the imperative, and in the absence of negation, only enclisis is possible (15a,d). On the other hand, with negation, both proclisis and enclisis are possible (15b,c,e,f). Finally, with the subjunctive forms (15g,h,i), proclisis is always obligatory, even with negation.

(15) I a. Leggilo! b. Non lo leggere! c. Non leggerlo!
d. Leggetelo! e. Non lo leggete! f. Non leggetelo!
g. Lo legga! h. Non lo legga! i.*Non leggalo!

The same kind of rigid constraints on the order between clitics, which we noted in the case of proclisis on finite forms, is also present in the case of enclisis on non-finite and imperative forms, although the order between clitics is not always the same in enclisis and proclisis. The imperatives corresponding to (9a,b) are given in (16). The order is preserved in Italian, but inverted in standard French (see section 3.4 for more details).

(16) I a. Dammelo!
F b. Donne-le-moi. *Give it to me !*

2.1.4 Clitics must be adjacent to the verb

Beyond their particular linear position, clitic pronouns in modern Romance languages must be adjacent to the verb, except in a few limited cases. This constraint is respected in all Romance languages with respect to enclitics.[12]

(17) I a.*Leggi-bene-lo! a'. *Voglio leggere-bene-lo.
Read well it I want to read well it

[12] The infinitive *ler* reduces to *lê* in front of an accusative clitic in Portuguese (see section 3.2 below), but the choice of *lê* or *ler* in front of *bem* in (17c') makes no difference to the ungrammaticality of the sentence. In (17c,c'), the chosen form for the clitic pronoun is the one expected after the verb (which it is separated from by *bem*) (*lê-o; lê-lo*). However, after a verbal form which ends in [m], the 3m.sg.acc clitic is realized as *–no* (see below section 3.2) and thus one might wonder whether the problem with the examples has to do with the choice of *–o* and *–lo* behind a word ending in [m]. But this is not the right explanation, as substituting *–no* in these examples doesn't improve their acceptability at all: **Lê / Ler-bem-no!*

S b. *¡Lée-bien-lo! b'. *Quiero leer-bien-lo.
P c. *Lê-bem-o! c'. *Quero lê / ler-bem-lo.
R d. *Citeşte-bine-o! d'. *Marina ar citi-bine-o.

For proclitics, the examples in (18) illustrate the general case.

(18) F a. *Martine le souvent lit. Martine it often reads
I b. *Martina lo non legge.
S c. *Martina lo no lee.

The French example (18a) may not seem like a very useful one because it is not generally normal to put an adverb in front of a finite verb in any case, and also because the inversion of the adverb and the clitic pronoun does not lead to an entirely acceptable sentence (*?Martine souvent le lit*) either. However, the sentence where the clitic is separated from the verb is of a far more extreme degree of unacceptability than the variant where the adverb appears in front of the clitic pronoun, to the point of being completely uninterpretable. Elsewhere in French, where the clitics are proclitics to infinitives, we can show the distinction much more clearly; infinitives generally can be preceded by adverbs.[13]

(19) F a. Je veux bien le regarder. b. *Je veux le bien regarder.
I want (to) well it look.at

However, while enclitics can never be separated from the verb, the situation is a little more complex for proclitics. Indeed, Portuguese and Romanian allow a few cases (traditionally referred to as 'interpolations') where the clitics can be separated from the verb by a limited number of elements, typically 'light' adverbs. In Portuguese, it is mainly the negation *não*;[14] (20a) is borrowed from Barbosa (1996:7). Note however that the inverse order (20b) is the natural one in ordinary speech. In Romanian, there are a limited number of adverbials of quantity, *mai* 'again', *cam* 'a little', *prea* 'too much', *şi* 'already', *tot* 'still', as shown in (20c). Yet these ele-

---

[13] In 17th century French, it was possible to violate the usual adjacency constraint when the verb was in the infinitive, as is also marginally the case today in an archaic style, as in *Il a delibérément choisi de n'en pas tenir compte* 'He deliberately chose not to take account of it'; *Puis j'avais découvert le moyen infaillible de ne les plus jamais confondre* 'Then I had discovered the infallible means of no longer ever confusing them'. These two examples are borrowed from Togeby (1982, I:398). In present day French, the construction is a little less marked with the adverbial clitics *y* and *en*, however no example of this type is attested in everyday French.

[14] On this point, see also Vigário (2003) and Crysmann (2000a: 85). Barbosa (1996:7) gives examples of acceptable sentences with interpolation by a strong subject pronoun, which come from conservative Portuguese dialects from the north, and Galician. But Sánchez-Rei (1999) states that interpolation is generally ungrammatical in contemporary Galician. According to the Portuguese informants we consulted, the forms with interpolations are not at all natural in contemporary Portuguese. It would seem therefore that they are on the verge of disappearing.

ments themselves must without doubt be analyzed as adverbial clitics (see Dobrovie-Sorin 1994:10ff; 63ff, Monachesi 2000).

(20) P a. Ela prometeu que lhe não diria nada.
She promised that she would say nothing to him.
b. Ela prometeu que não lhe diria nada.
R c. Îl mai văd.
him still see.1sg
I still seem him.

In conclusion, even if in a few very limited cases clitic pronouns can be separated from the verb, they can never appear in a sentence where the verb which they depend on is absent. This is shown by the ungrammaticality of the elliptical responses in examples (21) and of the sentences with gapping in (22). This is equally true in Portuguese and Romanian where clitics can appear non-adjacent to the verb in the few cases that we have just discussed.[15] The contrast with the English glosses is striking.

(21) F a. Que voit Martine? – *Le. / *Me.
What does Martina see? Him. / Me.
I b. Che vede Martina? – *Lo. / * Mi.
P c. Que vê a Marina? – *O. / *Me.
R d. Ce vede Marina? – *O. / *Îl. / *Mă.
e. Cui îi vorbeşte Marina? – *Îşi. / *Îmi.
Who did Marina speak to?' To them. / To me.

(22) F a. *Jean la voit, et Martine le / me.
John sees her, and Martina him / me.
I b. *Gianni la vede e Martina lo / mi.
P c. *O João vê-a e a Martina o / me.
R d. *Radu îl vede şi Marina o / îl / mă.

Similarly, clitics cannot be directly cliticized to a category other than a verb, even if this category can govern a full PP which corresponds to the clitic. The following examples show this, where, as indicated in (23a), the clitic is semantically the dative complement of the predicative adjective, but must however take the copula verb as a host (see also examples (66), (67), (68) and (70) in section 4.2 for examples where *en* and *y* are semantically

[15] In section 3.1 we will look at a few cases where the clitic pronouns in Romanian are phonologically enclitics to the word which precedes the verb in front of which they are placed (see (14h) and *nu-l citi!*, *să-l bată!* in note 10). But such forms are not exceptions to the general rule of clitic-verb adjacency, because they must always be followed by a verb.

arguments of an adjective or of a complement noun of a verb, yet are still attached to the verb).

(23) F a. L'article semble incompréhensible à Paul.
The article seems incomprehensible to Paul
b. L'article lui semble incompréhensible. / *semble lui incompréhensible.
The article seems incomprehensible to him.
I c. L'articolo gli sembra incomprensibile. / *sembra gli incomprensibile.
S d. El artículo le parece incomprensible. / *parece le incomprensible.

Finally, even in the absence of the verb, an attributive adjective cannot govern a dative clitic (24a,b,c). One must use a strong form introduced by a preposition (24d,e,f).

(24) F a. *un article lui incompréhensible
I b. *un articolo gli incomprensibile
S c. *un artículo le incomprensible
F d. un article incompréhensible pour lui
I e. un articolo incomprensibile per lui
S f. un artículo incomprensible para él
an article incomprehensible to him

2.1.5 Clitic climbing

In all the Romance languages, there are classes of verbs which govern non-finite VPs, and which allow or require that the complements of the governed verb are cliticized on the governing verb and not on the verb of which they are the semantic arguments. In the examples in (25a,b), the pronoun is the argument of the embedded verb *lire* / *leggere* but it must cliticize onto the governing verb *avoir* / *avere*. In (25c), the pronoun argument of the embedded verb can cliticize either onto the embedded verb or onto the governing *volere*. This phenomenon is usually called 'clitic climbing'.

(25) F a. Jean a lu le livre. / *a le lu. / l'a lu.
I b. Gianni ha letto il libro. / *ha lettolo. / l'ha letto.
John read the book. / John read it.
c. Gianni vuole leggere il libro. / vuole leggerlo. / lo vuole leggere.
Gianni wants (to) read the book / wants to read-it / it-wants to read

It is particularly interesting to contrast (25b) and (10b). Indeed, (10b) shows that at least in Italian, in the tenses constructed with the past participle, the impossibility of keeping clitics on the participle cannot be explained by the incompatibility of the clitic pronoun with the verbal form of the past participle.[16] The chapter by Abeillé and Godard in this volume contains a detailed analysis of clitic climbing in Romance languages. They show that the special position of clitics in these structures is a consequence of a more general phenomenon which has to do with the inheritance of the arguments of a non-finite verb by a governing verb.

Finally, when there are several clitic arguments of the same verb, they are not free to raise independently from each other. If one of the clitics climbs the others must follow it ('the bandwagon effect'), as illustrated in the Italian examples in (26).[17]

(26) I a. Gianni vuole darglielo. Gianni wants (to) give-to.him-it.
b. Gianni glielo vuole dare.
c. *Gianni gli vuole darlo.
d. *Gianni lo vuole dargli.

2.1.6 Conclusion

The data discussed here taken as a whole clearly shows that clitic pronouns in the Romance languages are special clitics in the sense of Zwicky (1977), since they do not appear in the same positions as their corresponding full phrases. However, the rules governing the positioning of the clitics refer to syntactic properties (adjacency to the verb) and morphosyntactic properties (finite, non-finite, or imperative verb form) and do not refer to prosodic properties. This therefore gives us a first argument for viewing clitic pronouns, at least in modern Romance languages, as inflectional affixes on the verb.[18] Furthermore, the fact that clitics must be adjacent to the verb (ex-

---

16 However, this argument can be made for the other Romance languages, where we have seen that it is impossible to attach a clitic pronoun to a past participle.

17 Note however that the 3f.sg clitic *o* in Romanian stays on the participle, even if another clitic raises: *Le-am dat-o* '(I) it to gave'. Also note the classic examples like *%Je l'en ai fait se souvenir* 'I made him remember it' (Martinon 1927:302) where the reflexive clitic *se* stays on the infinitive while *en* raises (see Kayne 1975:427–8, Kayne 199:661). Finally, Kayne (1991: 661) mentions examples (taken from Chenal 1986) like (i), which show clitic separation in Franco-Provençal dialects. However, this kind of example is extremely marginal in the Romance languages.

(i) T'an-të deut-lo ?
2.sg.dat-have-3.pl.subject said.3sg.acc?
To you-have-they said-it? *Have they said it to you?*

18 The fact that clitics sometimes appear as prefixes and at other times as suffixes, according to the morphosyntactic properties of the verb, is not a valid counterargument against an

cept for the very limited exceptions we noted for Portuguese and Romanian) shows that they are very selective about the syntactic category of the element to which they attach themselves, a characteristic which is typical of affixes but not of clitics according to the criteria of Zwicky and Pullum (1983).[19]

In the older variants of the languages, by contrast, one might say that clitic pronouns really were special clitics (following Fontana 1993,1996 and Hirschbühler and Labelle 2000, 2001b). Fontana proposes that in Old Spanish, clitics are placed in front of the first element of S according to a syntactic constraint, but they are enclitics prosodically. He also proposes that Old Spanish was a V2 language (similar to modern Dutch and German), the verb being the first element of S, preceded by a constituent in an initial position, outside the S domain. Thus one obtains examples like the following, taken from Fontana (1996:55, 1993:20).[20]

(27) OS a. mas que=l diessen a los freyres del Temple
but that=it they.give to the brothers of.the Temple
but that they give it to the brothers of the Temple.

b. Esto=t lidiare aqui antel Rey don Alfonso
this=you I.challenge here in.front.of.the King don Alfonso
I challenge you about this here in front of the King…

c. tomo=l consigo por compannero
he.took=him with.him as.a companion

d. por que=las vos dexastes
because=them you abandoned
because you abandoned them.

In (27a), there is a subordinate clause and the element in its initial position is the subordinator *que*, the verb *diessen* being the first element of S. In (27b), the NP object is in the initial position, and in (27c) it is the verb itself which is in this position. Example (27d) is interesting because it is a case of interpolation, which would be impossible in contemporary Spanish. Such

affixal analysis. Indeed, on the one hand we can find languages where morphemes which are clearly affixes have the same property of 'mobility' in relation to the base (see for example Noyer 1994 and Bendjaballah 2002); on the other hand, the form of the clitic pronoun is not always the same depending on whether it is a proclitic or an enclitic, contrary to what one might expect if it was a true postlexical clitic with variable attachment (see for example Morin 1979b for data from spoken French, notably the fact that *y* and *en* appear as /zi/ and /zã/ when they are behind the verb in a number varieties of spoken French: *donne-z-en* 'Give it': *donne-moi-z-en* 'Give it to me').

[19] But see Monachesi (1998, 2000) and Crysmann (2000a,b) for affixal analyses of the non-adjacency cases (illustrated in (20)) in Romanian and Portuguese respectively.

[20] The '=' sign is used here to separate the clitic from the verb to which it is phonologically and orthographically attached, clearly showing that it is an enclitic in each case.

examples were possible at the time because the syntactic structure of subordinate clauses provided a preverbal position in the S domain, where the subject *vos* (which separates the clitic *las* from the verb) can appear. The disappearance of this possibility in Spanish (and more generally in all the Romance languages, except for the exceptional Portuguese and Romanian cases in section 2.1.4) eliminated the only case where clitics were not adjacent to the verb.

This analysis of Old Spanish, presented here in a very simplified way, can be extended to all the other old forms of the Romance languages (even though no attested examples of interpolation in Old French have survived, see Hirschbühler and Labelle 2000). In a highly schematic way, we can understand the change that took place in Spanish, Catalan, Italian, Romanian, and French in the following way: these languages lost their V2 status, which led to a considerable increase in the number of sentences where the finite verb is in the initial position in S, preceded by no other element (V1 structure). Recall that in these languages, which include Old French, a subject which is anaphorically recoverable from the context of the sentence is simply not expressed, so that in this case the verb is in the initial position in an (S)VO main clause. Given these conditions, clitics frequently ended up in front of a finite verb in the initial position of the sentence, forcing them to attach as proclitics.[21] This proclitic attachment then extended to the cases where the finite verb was not in the initial position, leading to the systematic proclisis on the finite verb that we have seen for the modern languages. (P. Hirschbühler (p.c.) has pointed out to us that Old French, in particular, is *a priori* problematic for this explanation, because V1 clauses are observed mainly before the 13th century and, at this time, the clitics were enclitics to a verb in initial position).

For imperatives, in the V2 stage, Fontana hypothesizes that the verb itself is in the initial position in front of S, unless it is accompanied by negation (which occupies this initial position itself). It follows that clitics were enclitics to the verb unless negation was present, in which case they were enclitics to the negation. The order of clitics in modern imperatives, described in section 2.1.3, can be seen as a fixing of the typical order of positive imperatives, accompanied by a reanalysis of the clitics in the negative imperatives as proclitics to the verb, and not enclitics to the negation (except in Romanian, see (14h)).

In Portuguese, by contrast, the system evolved very differently. Here, it is possible to hypothesize that the phonological status of enclisis was privi-

---

21 Fontana shows that proclitic attachment exists even in the oldest variants of Spanish, but that it is very rare since the syntactic structure of the language is such that there is normally an element in the initial position in front of S.

leged, leading to an enclisis on the verb by prosodic inversion (Halpern 1995) in verb-initial sentences.[22] With the increasing frequency of this type of construction, this position became the default position, proclisis no longer being triggered by prosodic constraints, but rather by a very restricted set of types of initial phrases. See also Vigário (2003:309-314) for a more detailed analysis of the emergence of enclisis in European Portuguese, based on prosodic factors.

We can therefore hypothesize that in the old Romance languages, clitic pronouns were post-lexical clitics and that their distribution was defined by a combination of syntactic and prosodic constraints, typical of special clitics. However, a process of morphologization of these elements has taken place (and has perhaps finished in languages like French, Spanish, Catalan, and Italian) by which the clitics are reanalyzed as inflectional affixes on the verb.

2.2 The doubling of full NPs and PPs by clitic pronouns

In standard French and in Italian, there is a complementary distribution between clitic pronouns and the corresponding full phrases, which is illustrated in (28) and (29).

(28) F a. Martine lit le livre. *Martina reads the book.*
b. Martine le lit. *Martina reads it.*
Martina it reads
c. %Martine le_i lit le $livre_i$.
Martina it reads the book Martina reads (it) the book.
d. Martine le_i lit, le $livre_i$.

(29) I a. Martina legge il libro.
b. Martine lo legge.
c. *Martina lo_i legge il $libro_i$.
d. Martina lo_i legge, il $libro_i$.

Sentence (28c) is a case where the NP direct object *le livre* is 'doubled' by a coreferential clitic *le*; (29c) shows the same thing for Italian. It is necessary to distinguish these cases from those of right dislocation, given in (28d) and (29d). The difference between these examples is indicated by the comma, which marks an intonation break between the sentence and the dislocated phrase, a break which is absent in (28c) and (29c). The sentences with doubling by a clitic are considered unacceptable in standard prescriptive French and in Italian. The dislocation examples are perfectly grammatical, although their use in discourse is subject to certain conditions (Ashby

22 See the end of section 3.1 below.

1988, Lambrecht 1994). However, in spoken French, as well as in the other Romance languages, the doubling sentence (28c) is entirely natural in certain situations where it can be preferred to (28a).[23] The data relating to this issue are extremely complex, on the one hand because each language is subject to strong variations according to dialects and registers, and on the other hand because the possibility of doubling is linked in part to complex pragmatic and discourse factors, which make judgments out of context rather difficult. This explains a number of inconsistencies in the data which has been presented in various previous studies of the subject.

It is clearly beyond the scope of this chapter to deal with this complex problem. However, one should note the importance of this domain of variation for typological studies on the origin of agreement markers. Indeed, since the works of Moravcsik (1974) and Givón (1976), we can, on the basis of typological analyses, speculate that agreement systems between the verb and its arguments result from the morphologization of pronouns that double the arguments in question, and that the development of this process is subject to certain universal principles. Givón proposes that agreement developed initially with the arguments that are most likely to be topics. Furthermore, he noticed that agreement appeared sooner with pronouns than with full NPs, with definite NPs rather than indefinite ones, datives rather than accusatives, NPs with human referents rather than inanimate ones, etc. A systematic study of the variation within this development – in the Romance languages – would be extremely interesting, in order to develop and verify hypotheses such as Givón's, particularly by comparing them with Bantu languages where there has been a similar development (see Givón 1976, and for example, Bresnan and Mchombo 1987, Creissels 2001).

Indeed the data we have for Romance languages is largely compatible with Givón's hypotheses. The first works which discussed the conditions for doubling, such as Farkas (1978) for Romanian and Jaeggli (1982:12-14) for Spanish, proposed that the relevant parameters were the pronominal/non-pronominal status of the NP object, and whether it is dative or accusative, animate/inanimate, specific/non-specific. Farkas also noted the relevance of factors which have to do with discourse information structure.

In all Spanish dialects (see Jaeggli 1982:12-14, Suñer 1988:394, Fernández Soriano 1999, Franco 2000) doubling by a clitic pronoun is obligatory if the direct or indirect object is a strong pronoun (30a,b). For non-pronoun objects, the situation varies according to different syntactic, semantic, and pragmatic constraints, and according to the different dialects. In standard Spanish, if the objects are behind the verb in an unmarked posi-

[23] We will return to the case of subject-clitic doubling in French in section 4.1 below.

tion, doubling is possible with full dative objects (30c) but impossible with direct objects (30d,e). It is, however, obligatory with certain verbs which take a dative experiencer (the clitic can only be omitted if the experiencer is not expressed and is interpreted as generic).

(30) S a. Lo veo a él. / *Veo a él. I *(him) see him.
b. Le hablo a él. / *Hablo a él. I *(to him) speak to him.
c. Le hablo a Juan. / Hablo a Juan. I (to him) speak to John.
d. *Lo veo a Juan. / Veo a Juan. I (*him) see Juan.
e. *La veo la mesa. / Veo la mesa. I (*it) see the table.

Certain dialects, however, notably Latin-American ones, have a quasi-systematic doubling of full datives, and a strong preference for doubling animate and specific direct objects. In these dialects, the variants with the clitics in (30c,d) are strongly preferred.[24] Similarly, doubling is obligatory when a dative or accusative complement marked by *a* is placed in front of the verb, and it is obligatory for accusatives without *a* which are placed in front of the verb, if they are definite. Various arguments have been put forward to show that doubled NPs are not dislocated to non-argumental positions. Jaeggli (1986:34) shows that doubling is subject to the subjacency condition; Suñer (1988) observes that the doubled constituent is not separated by an intonation break. According to the informants we consulted, Portuguese seems quite close to standard Spanish, but we have found very little published data.

The data in Catalan (Wheeler *et al.* 1999:462-4) are also quite similar. Strong pronouns in direct and indirect object position must be doubled by a clitic. In informal registers, there is doubling in relative clauses and *wh*-questions, and even when a full dative NP is present after the verb (this is considered as non-standard by some grammarians). There are certain verbs with dative experiencer complements like *plaure* 'plaire' and *convenir* 'to agree' where clitic-doubling is always necessary, whether the dative is a normal phrase, a *wh*-expression, or a relative pronoun.

Finally, there is an abundant literature about doubling in Romanian (see Lombard 1974:150-151, Farkas 1978, Dobrovie-Sorin 1990, 1994), which shows that similar factors are at work. According to Farkas (1978), when a direct object is a strong definite pronoun and follows the verb, doubling is obligatory for a [+human] pronoun, optional for [±human] pronouns when they refer to non-humans, and impossible for strictly non-human pronouns.

---

24 See Suñer (1988), Fernández Soriano (1999), Villada Moirón (2001:36sq) for a detailed discussion of the dialectal variation and the syntactic and semantic conditions on doubling. In certain constructions with inalienable possession, doubling of the indirect object is obligatory, for example **(Le) duele la cabeza a Mafalda* (to her$_i$ hurts the head to Mafalda$_i$ *Mafalda has a headache*, Jaeggli 1982:13).

For indefinite direct object pronouns after the verb, doubling is impossible except in the case of partitive referents extracted from a given set, for which it is optional. For a full NP direct object after the verb, doubling is optional if it is definite and human (31a) or if it is indefinite and has a human referent extracted from a specific set. When the direct object is in front of the verb, doubling is more common in all cases (as Givón's generalizations would lead us to expect, since such objects are typically discourse old); doubling is obligatory when the object is definite, and optional if the direct object is indefinite and human (31b), or an indefinite non-human which has been extracted from a specific set (31c) (these examples are borrowed from Farkas 1978:88, 94).

(31) R a. L-am văzut pe Ion. 'I saw Ion'
[I] 3m.sg.acc-have.seen PE Ion
b. Pe un argat l-a mînat la cîmp.
PE a worker 3m.sg.acc-has.sent to.the field
He sent one of the workers to the field.
[=extraction from an already known group]
c. O parte din pîine am mîncat-o eu.
A bit of.the bread [I] have eaten-3f.sg.acc me
I ate a bit of the bread.

With indirect objects, doubling is common. It is always possible and is obligatory with definite pronouns and full preverbal NPs. Even full NPs with inanimate reference, which are placed behind the verb can be doubled. The studies of Dobrovie-Sorin (1990, 1994) put forward detailed analyses of the doubling phenomena of Romanian, especially their interaction with *wh*-movement, within the 'principles and parameters' framework.

2.3 Clitic pronouns and coordination

Kayne (1975:83, 97) noticed that French clitic pronouns do not behave like their corresponding full phrases with respect to coordination. To begin with, it is impossible to coordinate clitics with each other.[25] This is true in all

[25] Morin (1981:19n) noticed that examples with coordination of subject clitics, such as the following, are acceptable:

(i) F Le candidat doit s'adresser au surveillant lorsqu'il ou elle veut quitter la salle.
The candidate must go to the invigilator when he or she wishes to leave the room.

Uses of this kind are very restricted though, and are only acceptable in a metalinguistic use (see Miller 1992:150-151) where they allow the speaker to avoid referring to the specific sex of the referent. (ii) has exactly the same syntactic structure as (i), but does not receive the same sort of interpretation (with plural – rather than singular *candidats*), and is unacceptable:

(ii) F *Les candidats doivent s'adresser au surveillant lorsqu'il et elle veulent quitter la salle.

Romance languages whether they are proclitics or enclitics, except for certain very limited cases in Romanian.

(32) F a. *Martine le et la voit. *Martina sees him and her*
I b. *Martina lo e la vede.
S c. *Martina lo y la ve.
C d. *La Martina el i la veu.
P e. *A Marina não o e a vê. *Marina doesn't see him and her*

(33) I b. *Martina vuole vederlo e – la. *M. wants to see him and her*
S c. *Martina quiere verlo y – la.
C d. *La Martina vol veure'l i – la.
P e. *A Marina quer vê-lo e – la.

(34) F a. *Prends-le et –la ! *Take him and her!*
I b. *Prendilo e –la!
S c. *Tómalo y –la!
C d. *Pren-lo i –la!
P e. *A Marina vê-o e –a. *Marina sees-him and her*
f. *Olha-o e -a! *Look.at-him and her!*

In Romanian, the situation is more complex. The coordination of enclitics is impossible in every case, but the coordination of proclitics is sometimes possible, at least for certain speakers. Ileana Comorovski (p.c.) suggests that this may have to do with whether the pronouns in question can form an autonomous prosodic word or not. Indeed, the lexical verb *a scrie* 'écrire', which has an initial consonant, can combine with the syllabic forms of the 1st and 2nd person dative clitics, *îmi* and *îţi*, which can be coordinated with each other (35a) (at least for certain speakers); these clitics can form autonomous phonological words. In contrast, the past auxiliary *a* must com-

---

These types of examples with metalinguistic interpretation are very marginally acceptable with object pronouns, in similar instances to (i).

(iii) F ??Dans ce cas, le surveillant le ou la fera sortir.
In this case, the invigilator will escort him or her
(iv) *Dans ce cas, le surveillant le et la fera sortir.
In this case, the invigilator will escort him and her

The metalinguistic type of interpretation illustrated in (iii) is equally marginally available in proclisis examples in Italian, Spanish, and Catalan. As in French, cases like (iv) are excluded in all languages. In the case of enclisis, even the metalinguistic interpretation is unacceptable. The convergence of the data between the languages is surprising for such an *a priori* marginal point and would merit a deeper investigation.

bine with the non-syllabic forms *mi* and *ţi*, which, themselves, cannot form an autonomous phonological word and cannot be coordinated (35b).[26]

(35) R a. %Îmi şi îţi scrie. [he] to.me and to.you writes
b. *Îmi / mi şi ţi-a scris. [he] to.me and to.you-has written

In view of the prosodically deficient status of the clitic pronouns, the impossibility of coordinating them is not *a priori* surprising. However, this explanation cannot be wholly sufficient as there are exceptional cases where clitics can be coordinated such as the Romanian examples in (35a) above, as well as the examples with a metalinguistic interpretation mentioned in note 24. Such exceptional cases show that it is not the prosodic properties of clitics *per se* which make coordinating them impossible, nor their status as special clitics in the sense of Zwicky (1977). From the perspective of an affixal analysis of clitic pronouns, this constraint finds a natural explanation to the extent that it is normally impossible to coordinate inflectional affixes.

Kayne (1975) also noticed a second interesting property of object clitics in French: they cannot take wide scope over a coordination of verbs, as shown in (36a). The data are similar in Italian, as indicated in (36b).[27,28]

---

26 These data would be worth examining more closely, because the precise nature of the conditions allowing coordination is not clear. Indeed, for other syllabic clitics, coordination is impossible.

(i) R *Mă şi te vede. me and you he.sees
(ii) R *Te şi îl văd. you and him I.see

27 Kayne (1975:97n) notices however that with pairs of verbs of the type *V et re-V*, wide scope is possible: *Paul les lit et relit sans cesse* 'Paul reads and re-reads them incessantly'. Similarly for Italian, Spanish and Catalan: I *Paolo lo legge e rilegge continuamente;* S *Pedro los lee y relee sin parar;* C *En Per els llegeix i rellegeix sense parar*. As Josep Fontana noticed (p.c.), from a pragmatic point of view this is not particularly surprising, since the action 'V and re-V' is conceived of as a single complex event. The question remains however of knowing how this pragmatic property can make it possible to escape what is apparently a morphosyntactic impossibility (see note 28 on this point). Also, sentences like (36a) seem to have been possible in French until the 17th century at least. Haase (1930:401) gives attested examples of this type (however, all the examples except one come from verse works and the repetition of the pronoun leads to the addition of a syllable in each case, so the naturalness of these data remains somewhat uncertain).

28 It is important to notice that the impossibility only appears if the coordinate structure is at the level of the verbs to which the clitic would be attached in the absence of coordination. Examples like *Martine l'a vu et écouté* ('Martine saw and heard it') are perfectly well-formed because the clitic is not attached to the coordinated elements *vu* and *écouté*, but to the auxiliary *a*, which itself has scope over the coordination of the two verbs. Ignoring this crucial distinction, Vigário (2003:133), citing Matos, gives (i) as a counter-example.

(i) P Ele estava-lhe sempre a telefonar e a comprar livros.
He was-to.him always to telephone and to buy books
He was always phoning him and buying him books.

(36) F a. *Martine la voit et écoute.
Martina her sees and hears.
[vs. voit et écoute Marie *sees and hears Marie*]
I b. *Martina la vede e ascolta. [vs. vede e ascolta Maria]

In the other Romance languages, however, the facts are more complex. In the case of enclisis, wide scope is always impossible. In order to save examples like (37), the clitic must be repeated on each verb.[29]

(37) I a. *Voglio vedere e ascoltarla. [I] want to see and hear-it
S b. *Quiero ver y escucharla.
C c. *Vull veure i escoltar-la.
P d. *Posso aplaudir e festejá-lo. [I] can applaud and celebrate-it
e. *Ele viu-me e cumprimentou. He saw-me and greeted
f. *Ele viu e cumprimentou-me. He saw and greeted-me

However, in the case of proclisis, the results seem acceptable in Portuguese and Romanian (in certain cases). For Spanish and Catalan, the data are marginal, but not totally excluded.[30, 31]

(38) P a. Afirmo que ele me viu e cumprimentou.
I maintain that he saw and complimented me.
b. Todos o aplaudiram e festejaram.
Everyone applauded and congratulated him.
R c. Marina îmi scria şi telefona zilnic.
Marina was writing to me and telephoning me every day.
S e. ??Martina la ve y escucha. M. her-sees and hears
[cf. Martina ve y escucha a Maria]
C f. ??La Martina la veu i escolta. M. her-sees and hears

This example is not relevant for the reasons given, such examples being grammatical in all the Romance languages.

29 Examples (37e,f) and (38a) are borrowed from Rouveret (1999:648). Wide scope for enclitics is excluded even in coordinations of the type 'V and re-V' discussed in note 26 (I **Voglio leggere e rileggerlo continuamente*; F **Lis et relis-le sans cesse!*, see Benincà and Cinque 1993), which shows clearly that the pragmatic explanation suggested is not sufficient.

30 The marginal possibility of wide scope here seems to correspond to a earlier system in the history of Spanish and Catalan, which is still partially accessible to modern speakers. For example, Uriagereka (1995:105) gives the following example of a proclitic with wide scope, which he judges to be well-formed: S *Juan les hablará y perdonará*. (John to.them will speak and will.forgive; 'John will speak to them and forgive them') but this kind of example is not considered natural by native speakers. Furthermore, it seems that the situation is similar in Italian where, in the same conditions, certain speakers marginally accept the examples of wide scope of a proclitic like (36b).

31 According to our informants, the R sentence seems less acceptable with *o* (feminine accusative) or *îl* (masc. accusative): *?Marina o / îl cunoaşte şi admiră*. ('M. knows and admires her / him').

[cf. La Martina veu i escolta la Maria]

The difficulties posed by wide scope over a coordination of host verbs cannot be explained in the framework of an analysis of Romance clitic pronouns as post-lexical clitics on the basis of the prosodically deficient status of clitics. Indeed, there is no universal restriction against cliticization of a prosodically weak element onto one of the members of a coordinated structure (see Miller 1992:155ff). As one would expect, prosodic attachment of a clitic is an operation which cannot normally be subjected to the syntactic condition on coordinated structures (the 'coordinate structure constraint') where syntactic phenonomena must apply in a parallel way to both conjuncts. Indeed, only the prosodic structure, and not the syntactic structure, can constrain post-lexical operations and the coordinate status of the structure is not visible at the prosodic level. In contrast, it is well-known that affixes are typically repeated on each member of a coordination of words, although certain exceptions exist.[32] The fact that one must obligatorily repeat an element on a coordination of hosts can thus be considered as a particularly strong argument in favor of the affixal (rather than postlexical clitic) status of this element. In contrast, to the extent that there *are* affixes which can have wide scope over a coordination of bases, the possibility of wide scope noticed for proclitics in several Romance languages in e.g. (38), does not actually tell us anything about their status as affixes or post-lexical clitics (Miller 1992:155ff).

2.4 Syntactic Rules affecting a verb and the clitics attached to it

Italian and Catalan exhibit a particular syntactic construction, typical of the spoken register, which is sometimes called 'verb left dislocation' (see Benincà 1988, Monachesi 1999a:31, Vallduví 2001). This is a construction where the infinitive is dislocated to the left, and doubled in the sentence by the same verb in the indicative, as in (39a,b). This construction is available for bare infinitives as in (39a,b), and also for infinitives with clitics attached to them, as in (39c,d). In contrast, it is impossible to dislocate an infinitive verb with a full phrase complement in the same way, as the ungrammaticality of (39e,f) show.

(39) I a. Dormire, dormo benissimo. *[As for] sleep, I sleep very well.*
C b. Dormir, dormo molt bé.

[32] For example wide scope for the ordinal suffix *–ième* in French, as in *à la cinq ou sixième entrevue* (in the five or sixth ('fifth or sixth') meeting) (Stendhal, cited in Grevisse 1980: § 892).

I c. Vederla, la vedo ogni giorno.
[As for] seeing her, I see her every day.

C d. Veure-la, la veig cada dia.

I e. *Vedere Martina, la vedo ogni giorno.
[As for] seeing Martina, I see her every day.

C f. *Veure la Martina, la veig cada dia.

So with respect to this construction, bare verbs and verbs with clitics attached to them are treated in the same way, in contrast to the combination of a verb and another phrase. This can be easily explained by assuming that left dislocation of the verb applies to an X^0 constituent and not a phrase; this also provides an argument for saying that the unit formed by a verb and the clitics which are attached to it becomes a lexical unit at the syntactic level. In the lexicalist framework adopted here, this implies an affixal analysis of clitic pronouns in Italian and Catalan (Zwicky and Pullum 1983). Otherwise it would be necessary to assume that the results of post-lexical cliticization are "visible" for a syntactic rule, which would contradict the principle of the inaccessibility of phonology by syntax (see Miller, Pullum, and Zwicky 1997).[33]

---

[33] A similar argument has been made for French on the basis of the alternation between *Ils m'ont vu* ('They saw me') and *M'ont-ils vu?* ('Did they see me?') Kayne (1975: 92ff) analyzes this last sentence as resulting from the inversion with the subject pronoun, of a V node dominating *m'ont*; he then develops an argument based on this which analyzes the object clitic as being adjoined to the verb. However, this argument loses a great deal of force due to the fact that the inversion of the verb is only possible with a subject clitic, and not with a full NP: **M'ont les garcons vu?* To the extent that there are good reasons for thinking that subject clitics are themselves affixes (see section 4.1), one can have doubts about the fact that we are dealing with a syntactic inversion operation here and consider this case simply as a problem of the position of morphemes within the word.

2.5 The obligatory status of cliticization

In French, it is generally impossible to use a strong form of a pronoun in the complement position if there is a corresponding clitic, as can be seen in (40a,b,c,d). We can therefore say that the cliticization of object pronouns is obligatory. There are however two cases which escape this constraint: (i) modification, for example, in a sentence where *que* is used to focus the pronoun (40e,f), or where a strong pronoun is coordinated (40g,h); (ii) in cases where an illicit sequence of clitics must be avoided (40i,j, see section 3.4 below). In the case of coordination, it is much more natural, at least in spontaneous spoken French, to double the coordinate strong forms with a clitic pronoun as in (40g′,g″).[34]

(40) F a. *Marie voit moi / toi / elle / lui / nous / vous / eux.
b. Marie me / te / le / la / nous / vous / les voit.
Marie sees me / you(sg) / him / her / us / you(pl) / them.
c. *Marie parle à moi / toi / elle / lui / nous / vous / eux.
d. Marie me / te / lui / nous / vous / leur parle.
Marie speaks to me / you(sg) / him / us / you(pl) / them.
e. Marie ne voit que moi / toi / elle / lui / nous / vous / eux.
f. *Marie ne me / te / le / la / nous / vous / les voit que.
Marie NE sees only me / you(sg) / her / him / us / you(pl) / them
g. Marie voit Pierre et moi / toi et lui /...
Marie sees Pierre and me / you and him ...
g′. Marie nous voit$_{(,)}$ Pierre et moi.
Marie us sees, Pierre and me
g″. Marie vous voit$_{(,)}$ toi et lui.
Marie you sees, you and him
h. *Marie me voit Pierre et.
i. *Marie me te présente.
Marie me to.you presents
j. Marie me présente à toi.
Marie me presents to you
Marie presents me to you

---

[34] In written French, one would hesitate to write (40g′,g″) without a comma separating the coordinate NP, thus making it a right dislocation structure. See section 2.2 on doubling. Anne Zribi-Hertz (p.c.) suggests that one of the differences between the versions with and without doubling is that the absence of doubling is only possible in the uses where the reference of the pronoun is given ostensively. When it is an anaphoric reference to topicalized elements, doubling would be necessary. This becomes more apparent with a pair of examples like *Pierre (les) connaît elle et lui*. The variant without doubling is only compatible with ostensive reference to the two people mentioned.

The other Romance languages,[35] except Italian, appear similar in this respect at first sight, but it turns out that the facts must almost certainly be analyzed differently to standard French[36] (spoken French, on the other hand, is very similar to the other Romance languages). This variation is a result of the obligatory/non-obligatory doubling of strong pronouns, discussed in section 2.2. Indeed, we see that, contrary to French and Italian, when one has a modified strong pronoun or a coordination of pronouns as in (40e,g), they are normally doubled by a clitic. This is illustrated in the following examples:

(41)	S	a.	*Veo solo a él.	[I] see only (to) him
		b.	Lo veo solo a él.	[I] him see only (to) him
		c.	*Hablo solo a él.	[I] speak only to him
		d.	Le hablo solo a él.	[I] to.him speak only to him

(42)	R	a.	*Maria nu vede decît pe mine.	*Maria only sees me.*
		b.	Maria nu mă vede decît pe mine.	Maria only (me) sees me
		c.	*Maria nu vorbeşte decît mie.	*Maria only speaks to me.*
		d.	Maria nu-mi vorbeşte decît mie. Maria only (to.me) speaks to me'	
		e.	*Văd pe tine şi pe el. [I] see PE you and PE him	
		f.	Vă văd pe tine şi pe el. [I] you(pl) see PE you and PE him	

(43)	P	a.	??Vejo a ele e a ela.	I.see (to) him and (to) her
		b.	Vejo-os a ele e a ela.	I.see-them (to) him and (to) her
		c.	??Vê a mim e a ela.	He.sees (to) me and (to) her
		d.	Vê-nos a mim e a ela.	He.sees-us (to) me and (to) her

Thus in these languages, it is not so much the cliticization of pronouns which is obligatory, as the doubling. Italian, on the other hand, seems to lie at the other extreme. It is difficult to say that cliticization of pronouns is obligatory in this language. Non-cliticization (without doubling) is possible even without modification of the object pronoun or coordination, in cases of contrastive focus for example.

[35] Brazilian Portuguese is completely exceptional in this respect. Indeed, the use of strong pronouns without doubling is entirely normal, see Galves (1997).

[36] It is possible that even standard French is closer to the other Romance languages than we are suggesting. Indeed, as Anne Zribi-Hertz (p.c.) has pointed out to us, with certain pronoun modifiers, the absence of doubling is only possible in cases of ostensive reference: *Je vois seulement lui* vs *Je le vois seulement lui*. (see also note 34).

2.6 Conclusion

The set of syntactic properties discussed in this section suggest, as we have already said, that clitic pronouns in the Romance languages are actually inflectional affixes on the verb, or are at least involved in a process of grammaticalization leading to this status. We should mention here – in order to refute it – an objection which has often been raised against such an analysis, namely the fact that clitics are regularly attached to a word of which they are semantically not the argument. This is what we see in the clitic-raising examples like (25), but also in examples like (23) where the clitic is the semantic argument of the predicative adjective, while still appearing on the copula verb.[37] Even if it is true that these phenomena make the most simple affixal analysis impossible, grammatical formalisms based on feature systems like Head driven Phrase Structure Grammar (HPSG) or Lexical Functional Grammar (LFG) still allow strictly lexicalist analyses of the problematic raising phenomena. The central idea is that the governing element which triggers raising, can receive – as markers of inflection in the morphological component – all possible combinations of clitics. Thus inflected, it will select as a complement a constituent which could have been combined with the clitics in question. This type of analysis has been proposed in a detailed way in various works, notably Miller (1992), Miller and Sag (1997), Monachesi (1999a), Crysmann (2000a,b).

3 Specific phonological and morphological properties of clitic pronouns

We saw in the preceding sections that clitic pronouns in the Romance languages have properties which, at first sight, seem to be intermediate between those of words and those of affixes. In this section, we will examine to what extent the phonological and morphological data on the behavior of clitic pronouns throws light on their status at the interface between syntax, morphology and phonology.[38] We will see once again that the details of behavior are far from uniform, both between languages and even within the

---

[37] See also the examples with *en* and *y* in section 4.2. One finds examples where, as with the dative clitics in (23), *en* and *y* are semantically the arguments of a complement of the verb which hosts them e.g. (66),(67),(68),(70), as well as the examples where they correspond to complements which are not subcategorized by the verb (see note 65), and where they are therefore not, strictly speaking, arguments of the verb.

[38] On this issue, see among others Auger (1994, 1995), Bonet (1995), Delais-Roussarie (1999), Gerlach (2002), Halpern (1995), Labelle (1985), van de Leeuw (1997), Miller (1992), Monachesi (1999), Peperkamp (1997), Popescu (2000), Vigário (1999, 2003), Watson (1997), Zwicky (1987).

same language. The complexity of the observed data and the variety of the intermediary situations that one notices is such that it is difficult to establish uniform answers, which are simple and totally convincing, on the status of clitic pronouns across the different languages or even within one of them. None of the various specific solutions which have been advanced in the literature achieve obviously superior coverage with respect to the data. Thus, in the current state of knowledge, any firm general answer on the status of clitic pronouns can only be obtained on the basis of major theoretical assumptions. Though such assumptions can be very interesting, they should not lead one to conceal the degree of real complexity of the data; that would lead us to over-simplify a field of empirical data the complexity of which should, in contrast, lead us to further develop our theories on the interfaces between the different grammatical components.

3.1 Clitics and prosody

To begin this discussion, we will turn to the prosodic interactions between clitics and their hosts, and more precisely to the prosodic behavior of the unit which is the result of the cliticization of pronouns to the verb which hosts them. We will see that, according to the languages, the behavior of clitic pronouns is more or less identical to the behavior of affixes, though not identical, particularly with respect to proclitics.

In French, the effect of enclitics upon stress-placement is identical to that of suffixes, that is, stress switches to the final syllable, as long as this syllable does not have a schwa as a nucleus. *Re'garde!* alternates with *Re-garde-'les!* which is itself entirely comparable to the result of adding an inflectional suffix: *Regar'dez!* (Delais-Roussarie 1999:22).[39] For proclitics the situation is less clear; Delais-Roussarie (1999:21) suggests that they have a different status from prefixes with respect to the stress that one can optionally find on the initial syllable of the word. This stress can, according to Delais-Roussarie, fall on the prefix *re-*, but not on the clitic *le* in *Paul le reverra demain*. However, the facts themselves are not as clearly established as she suggests: contrastive stress on *me* in *Il me le donnera* does not appear to be impossible in an appropriate context.[40] It seems that in French

[39] We use an apostrophe in front of a syllable to mark that it bears the main stress. We will not dwell here upon the enclitic *le*, which is exceptional if it is analyzed phonologically as /lə/, because it belongs to a small group of cases (among them the use of *Parce que!* as an elliptic response) where a final syllable with /ə/ for a nucleus would be stressed in French (*Regarde-'le!* vs. **Re'garde-le!*). Various solutions have been suggested in the literature on this point, one of them considering that the vowel is not really /ə/ but /ø/.

[40] These facts run counter the usual claim that clitics cannot be stressed. In French, final clitics are always stressed, and proclitics can carry a contrastive stress when they establish a contrast. However, clitics can never carry focal stress (that is, the stress that normally appears

therefore, the behavior of clitic pronouns from this point of view is at least very similar to the behavior of affixes.

In Italian, the presence of variable word stress makes the data more interesting. In fact, this variable word stress cannot normally fall before the antepenultimate syllable. Adding a suffix which would lead to a violation of this constraint generally leads to the stress shifting to the right. But adding an enclitic never leads to stress-shifting, even when that means stressing a syllable before the antepenult: *Te-'le-fo-na-mi* 'telephone-me', *Pren-'de-te-ve-lo* 'take it for yourself'.[41] This kind of data has been used by Nespor and Vogel (1986), for example, to underline that clitic pronouns do not form part of the prosodic word. However, the inflectional suffix of the 3rd person plural *–no* also does not produce any stress-shifting even when it leads to a stress before the antepenult: *te-'le-fo-na-no* 'they telephone', *in-'ter-ro-ga-no* 'they interrogate'. Nespor and Vogel (1986:148, 163n.2) consider that these cases do not invalidate the general rule because they represent a small set of predictable cases. However, as Monachesi (1999a) points out, the case of enclitic pronouns also constitutes a small set of predictable cases and it is not clear what would justify treating them differently. Monachesi proposes that the 3pl inflection and clitics in Italian are adjoined to the prosodic word, and that it is the minimal prosodic word which constitutes the assignment domain of the stress.

Furthermore, the behavior of clitics in Italian dialects exhibits complex situations. In Napolitan (Bafile 1993, Monachesi 1999a), for example, the situation is similar overall to that of Italian (stress can generally not appear before the antepenult; the distribution of clitics in relation to the verb is the same). However, when one finds two clitics (notably in the imperative), word stress falls on the first of the clitics, as would be expected if the verb and the clitic formed a single prosodic word. For example, in /pɔrta'tillə/ ('carry+2sg+3sg.acc'), the stress is carried on the first of the two clitics. Monachesi shows that the most appropriate analysis of the phenomenon is to consider that the group of clitics is attached to the verb by a composition-type operation, that is, a lexical operation.

In Catalan, Spanish and Portuguese, the presence of clitics can also lead to the stress being placed before the antepenultimate syllable (e.g. P *di'z-iamo-no-lo* 'say.impft.1pl-1pl-3sg.acc'), where the clitic falls on the fifth syllable before the end (Vigário 1999:224, 2003:134). Contrary to Italian, there seems to be no case where an inflectional or derivational suffix leads to the same result, which suggests that clitics are not part of the domain in

---

on the stressed syllable of a word when it is used as an answer to a *wh*-question), see Bolinger (1961). We thank Anne Zribi-Hertz for bringing this reference to our attention.

41 We use the hyphen here to mark the syllable boundaries.

which lexical stress is defined. However, in view of the various types of prosodic attachment operations which have been proposed in the literature (see e.g. the references given in note 4), it is difficult to consider this as a totally conclusive objection against the lexical attachment of clitics. One could for example invoke an analysis similar to that of Monachesi for Italian, with adjunction of the clitic to a prosodic word (see however Vigário 2003:186-195 for arguments against this position).

To conclude this section, let us briefly look at two cases, in Romanian and Portuguese, where the prosodic properties of clitics lead to prosodically attaching them as enclitics to a word which precedes the verb, a property which seems to have survived from the properties of clitics in older Romance languages discussed in section 2.1.6. First, let us consider the Romanian examples in (44) (see also the examples in note 10).

(44) R a. Mama-l place. Mother-him likes (Popescu 2000:784)
b. Nu-l / N-o / Nu-i aştept. (I) not-him / not-her / not-them wait.for (Dobrovie-Sorin 1994:74)
c. Nu ştie că-l / c-o / că-i aşteaptă mama. (S/He) not knows that-him / that-her / that-them his / her mother is.waiting.for (Dobrovie-Sorin 1994:70)

In these examples though the clitic is positioned in front of the verb, it is an enclitic to the word which precedes it, a noun in (44a), negation in (44b), a complementizer in (44c). The enclitic status conforms with the intuition of the speakers, as the hyphen (which is orthographic) indicates. Furthermore, it is confirmed by the phonological interactions with the preceding word, for example the disappearance of the vowel of *nu* and *că* when followed by the accusative pronoun *o* in (44b) and (44c). According to Dobrovie-Sorin (1994:71) and Popescu (2000:784), Romanian clitics can attach optionally to the left or to the right in these kinds of cases.

However, it is crucial to note that the clitic cannot appear in configurations like those in (44), if it is not followed by a verb. Thus (45a,b) are ungrammatical elliptical responses to the questions *Who loves him?* and *Who is he waiting for?* Furthermore, it is impossible to coordinate the element which the enclitic has attached to, repeating the clitic in (45c). In contrast, without repetition of the clitic, the sentence is possible (45d).

(45) R a. *Mama-l.
b. *Nu-l.
c. *Tata-l şi mama-l plac. Father-him and mother-him love
d. Tata şi mama-l plac. Father and mother-him love

These two factors suggest that the attachment of the clitic to the preceding element cannot be lexical.[42] The analysis which seems most plausible, in view of these phenomena, is that clitics in Romanian can still be post-lexical clitics (cf. section 2.1.6). In this case, they position themselves in front of the first element of S (which is, given the syntactic properties of Romanian, either the verb, or one of the adverbs which can separate the clitic from the verb in the cases of interpolation discussed in section 2.1.4) and they tend to attach enclitically.[43] It is possible that this analysis is synchronically in competition with an affixal analysis; this would account for the possibility of a choice between enclisis and proclisis.

For European Portuguese, it has been proposed by Carvalho (1989) that clitics are always prosodically enclitic. Thus, the cases that we have treated as proclitics in the section 2 would also need to be analyzed as cases of post-lexical clitics preceding the verb but attaching themselves prosodically to the element which precedes them. See however Vigário (2003: 54-5, 184-203) who supports a position opposed to that of Carvalho. In the framework of these observations, it is interesting to recall that it is precisely Romanian and Portuguese which still allow (restricted) cases of interpolation.

3.2 Arbitrary morpho-phonological interactions between clitics and their hosts

A second way of investigating the status of clitics consists in studying the kinds of morpho-phonological interactions that they have with their hosts in order to see if their behavior more closely resembles that of normal affixes or that of independent, albeit prosodically deficient, words. However, these interactions, the theoretical importance of which was initially noticed by Zwicky and Pullum (1983), present certain interpretation problems: morpho-phonological interactions are not always identical for different classes of affixes which are clearly lexically attached (hence the idea of a level-ordered morphology where the affixes are divided into groups which are attached at successive levels and where the application of phonological rules is defined for each level, see Kiparsky 1982). From this perspective, the fact that a clitic pronoun does not present the same phonological interactions with its host as an affix with the same phonological properties, means

[42] It would be necessary though to check in detail that this in not in contradiction with the type of phonological interaction attested in these contexts, for example the missing final vowel before the clitic *o* as in (44b,c). Note however that even if it is a typically lexical interaction, the precompiled phonological strategies proposed by Hayes (1990) allow us to account for such cases, on condition that only a limited number of grammatical words are concerned, which would without doubt be the case here.

[43] This analysis is close in spirit to the one proposed by Dobrovie-Sorin (1994).

either that it is not lexically attached, or that it *is* lexically attached, but to a stratum where the type of interaction in question is not applicable. This difficulty in interpreting the data is even more problematic with Romance clitic pronouns: if they are indeed affixes, they will inevitably be among the most recently morphologized affixes in the Romance languages. Consequently, we can expect that they will be attached at a higher level than older affixes. Indeed, to the extent that the degree of morpho-phonological idiosyncrasy tends to increase over time, we expect that there will be relatively few specific interactions between clitics and hosts, and in any case many fewer than between the bases and oldest affixes.

In this section, we will review a range of specific morpho-phonological interactions that are found between clitics and their hosts[44] in different Romance languages as well as cases where the clitics diverge in their behavior with respect to standardly recognized affixes. For detailed studies on these issues, see among others Vigário (2003) for Portuguese; Miller (1992), Auger (1994), Delais-Roussarie (1999), for French; Peperkamp (1997), Monachesi (1999a), for Italian; Monachesi (2000), Popescu (2000), for Romanian; Gerlach (2002) provides a general, less language-specific, discussion. Following these studies, we distinguish two kinds of morpho-phonological idiosyncrasies, those which are linked to a specific host, and those which are phonologically conditioned.

The first kind of idiosyncrasy (that which is linked to a specific host), can be exemplified with the French verb *aller* ('to go'), where the clitic *y* (see section 4.2) is never realized phonologically before the *ir-* allomorph (of *aller*). So we get *Pierre y va* ('Pierre goes there'), *Pierre y allait* ('Pierre was going there'), but **Pierre y ira* ('Pierre will go there') which must be realized simply as *Pierre ira*; yet this elision of an /i/ in front of a root beginning with an /i/ is not a productive rule in the phonology of French (*y illustrera* 'will illustrate there' is never elided to *illustrera*).[45] Another similar example is the realization of the sequence *je suis* ('I am') as *chuis* [ʃɥi] and of *je sais* ('I know') as *chais* [ʃe] in spoken French. The phenomenon is idiosyncratic to these two verbs and cannot be attributed to a productive phonological rule, since the homonymous sequence *je suis* (1sg of the verb *suivre* 'to follow') cannot reduce to [ʃɥi] in most varieties of spoken French.

For the second kind of idiosyncrasy (that which is phonologically conditioned), there is in French a phenomenon of semi-vocalization or yod in-

---

[44] We do not consider here specific interactions between clitics (see section 3.4), but only those between a clitic and the host verb.

[45] See Miller (1992:176-7) which shows that *ira* must be interpreted as the realization of *y*+ *ira*, and that it is impossible to deal with all the relevant data if the *y* is assumed to be absent.

sertion, between the proclitic *y* and a verb with an initial vowel which follows it (*ils y allaient* 'they were going there' is thus realized as [izjalɛ] or [izijalɛ]). Johnson (1987) sees this as an exceptional application, at the phrasal level, of a rule which applies – according to her system of stratified morphology – at level 1 and 2 (e.g. *colonie* + *-al* → [kolonjal]) but not at level 3 (e.g. the prefix *anti-* is attached at stratum 3, thus there is no semi-vocalization in words like *antiaérien*). On the contrary, one could conclude, as Miller (1992:180) does, that the behavior of *y* here suggests that it is attached lexically before level 3.[46] However, this phenomenon is problematic because of the uncertainty about the data, particularly given the extensive interspeaker variation (see in particular Delais-Roussarie 1999:21 who comes to the opposite conclusion). Similarly, the reduction of *la* to [l] (*Martine l'accepte*) and of *tu* to [t] (*t'es prêt*) in front of hosts with initial vowels cannot be the result of a productive phonological rule either (see Morin 1979b:4, 24; Miller 1992:176ff).

There are similar phenomena in the other Romance languages, and we give a few examples here. In Italian, there is an optional reduction of the accusative clitics *lo* and *la* to [l] before a host with an initial verb (*Martina l'elegge* ou *lo elegge* 'Martina chooses him / it'). This cannot be the result of a productive phonological rule (see Monachesi 1999a), particularly if you consider the predicative clitic *lo* – a homonym of the accusative clitic – which cannot reduce at all in the same environments (*Martina lo è* vs. **Martina l'è* 'Martina is it' [*it* = e.g. *happy*]).

In Romanian there are also certain idiosyncrasies in the realization of clitics (see Lombard 1974: 134ff and Monachesi 2000; see also Popescu 2000 and Gerlach 2002 for a different interpretation of the facts). For example, the vowel of clitics which end in [ă] in front of a verb beginning with an unstressed [a] or an [o] can be elided, as shown in (46a,b). If the verb is an auxiliary, however, elision is obligatory (47a,b), while for non-auxiliary uses of *a avea* 'to have', elision is impossible, although the phonetic form is identical to that of the auxiliary (48a,b). This all clearly shows that elision here cannot be the result of a productive phonological rule.

(46) R a. Mă aşteaptă. *He is waiting for me.*
b. M-aşteaptă. *He is waiting for me.*

(47) R a. M-a invitat. *He invited me.*
b. *Mă a invitat.

[46] Another argument in favor of this position would be the fact that *ni* 'nor' (which is monosyllabic and unstressed) does not behave like *y*: *ni en courant* ('nor while running') doesn't undergo semi-vocalization: *[njãkurã]. There is therefore a difference in status between prosodically weak words like *ni* and the clitic *y*.

(48) R a. *M-ai acolo. *You have me there.*
b. Mă ai acolo. *You have me there.*

Similarly, the reflexive clitic *se* is optionally elided in front of a verb which has an unstressed initial [a] or [o], as in (49a,b). In contrast, the elision is impossible for the clitics *te, ne,* or *le* in the same contexts (50a,b).

(49) R a. Se aşează. *He sits.*
b. S-aşează. *He sits.*

(50) R a. Te aşteaptă. *He is waiting for you.*
b. *T-aşteaptă. *He is waiting for you.*

In Portuguese, the 3m.sg accusative clitic can be realized with the forms *o, lo* and *no* (the pattern is the same for the other accusative clitics *os* (3m.pl), *a* (3f.sg) and *as* (3f.pl)). The choice between these forms (see Vigário 1999: 228-9, 2003: 141-143) depends on the phonology of the host. If the preceding verb (or the preceding clitic) ends in a consonant, the consonant of this preceding verb is elided and the clitic appears as *lo* (e.g. *dás* [give.pres.2sg] + 3m.sg.acc → *dá-lo*). If the preceding verb ends with a nasal diphthong, the clitic is realized as *no* (e.g. *comem* 'eat-pres.3pl' + 3m.sg.acc → *comem-no*). (For certain speakers, *no* is limited to nasal diphthongs which are 3pl suffixes.) In all other cases, *o* appears (e.g. *como* 'eat-pres.1sg' + 3m.sg.acc → *como-o*). Vigário shows that these variations clearly cannot be due to productive phonological rules in Portuguese.

Also in Portuguese, the presence of certain other clitics behind a final consonant leads to the consonant being elided; this is productive for the accusative clitics, but for the others it only applies to specific combinations. For example, the final consonant is deleted if it is part of the 1pl marker and if the following clitic is a 1st or 2nd person plural dative (*nos* or *vos*), but not any of the other dative clitics (*me, te, lhe, lhes*). Thus, *damos* 'give-pres.1pl' + 1pl.dat → *damo-nos,* but *damos* + 3pl.dat → *damos-lhes*. Likewise, if the final *–s* is not the 1pl marker, there is no elision, even in front of *nos* and *vos*, e.g. *dás* 'give-pres.2sg' + 1pl.dat → *dás-nos*.

In contrast, continuing with Portuguese, Vigário (1999: 224ff, 2003: 314ff) highlights certain lexical phonological processes which apply between affixes and bases but not between clitic pronouns and host verbs. For example, according to Vigário, nasal diphthongization is a lexical rule which only applies to the final position of a word. Furthermore, this rule is not blocked by adding an enclitic, which suggests that such an enclitic is added post-lexically.

(51) P a. bat*en*te [ẽ] / *[ɐ̃j̃] *door knocker*
b. bat*em* *[ẽ] / [ɐ̃j̃] They.are beating

c. bat*em*-te *[ẽ] / [ɐ̃j] They.are beating you'

Similarly, according to Vigário, there is a lexical rule whereby /e/ is centralized when it is followed by a heterosyllabic palatal segment, e.g. the *e* in *abelha* 'bee' is realized as /ɐ/ and not /e/. However, this rule does not apply in a similar example where the palatal segment is part of an enclitic, e.g. *dê-lha* 'give-it-to him' where the *e* is realized as /e/ and not /ɐ/. But there are different sorts of exceptions to this rule (Vigário 2003: 78-82) and the interpretation of the data turns out to be complex for several reasons. Firstly, there is significant dialectal variation, rendering the collection of uniform data difficult. Secondly, the proposed analyses are not obvious *a priori* and need to be looked at more carefully. Finally, even if we accept that the characterization of the data and the basic analysis of them is right, differing conclusions can be drawn according to different hypotheses. Indeed, certain researchers have suggested that there is a "pre-compiled" phrasal morphology (see e.g. Hayes 1990), which makes it possible to explain, at the level of phonology and lexical morphology, morpho-phonological alternations depending on the syntactic environment; Vigário (2003) adopts the mechanisms of Hayes, in order to be able to treat Portuguese clitics as post-lexical clitics while accounting for their idiosyncratic morpho-phonological properties. Likewise, as we saw in section 3.1, various extensions of the theory of the hierarchy of prosodic constituents (and in particular the possibility of prosodic adjunction) allow us to predict various interactions among affixes according to whether they are part of the minimal prosodic word, or prosodically adjoined to it; Crysmann (2002), in particular, makes proposals of this sort. Finally, if one adopts the principles of distributed morphology (Harley and Noyer 1999, Harris 1997a,b), the whole debate over the status of Romance clitic pronouns as affixes or clitics loses much of its interest. Indeed, at the level of syntax, affixes and clitics are treated in the same way, as feature matrices without phonological substance, while at the morphological and phonological level, the distinction between lexical and post-lexical processes is not considered to be relevant.[47]

3.3 Gaps in the paradigms

Another property identified by Zwicky and Pullum (1983) as being characteristic of affixes are gaps in the paradigms (*defective* paradigms in traditional terminology). In constrast, they believe post-lexical clitics should not exhibit gaps in their paradigms of combination (unless they are due to gen-

[47] See for example Harley and Noyer (1999:4) "In D[istributed] M[orphology] the distinction between two types of phonology – 'lexical' and 'post-lexical' – is abandoned."

eral phonological principles); indeed, if cliticization is a truly post-lexical phenomenon, it cannot be constrained, in a lexicalist model, by specific properties of the host to which the clitic is attached. Yet there are gaps in the paradigms of clitic pronouns. As with morpho-phonological idiosyncrasies, one can distinguish between cases where the gaps concern the combination of clitics with their hosts, and those where the gaps concern the combination of clitics with other clitics. We will only look at the first case in this section, and come back to the second in section 3.4, which deals more generally with constraints on sequences of clitics.

In French, one finds with the vast majority of verbs, a gap in the paradigm of subject clitics which have undergone subject-clitic inversion, for the 1sg indicative present tense of the verb: **Chante-je* 'sing-I' ('Am I singing') vs. *Chantes-tu? Chante-t-il?* etc. ('Are you/he etc. singing').[48] Some verbs have a form with the clitic *je* inversed (e.g. *suis-je, puis-je, dois-je,...*) but French speakers vary in the precise list of verbs allowing an enclitic *je*.[49] Likewise, Miller (1992:175-6) notes that, among the so called compound tenses in French, the past imperative is exceptional in that it is impossible to have clitic objects with it: *Aie mangé ton potage avant mon retour!* 'Eat your soup before my return!' and **Aie-le mangé avant mon retour!* Note that the full non-auxiliary use of the verb *avoir* in the imperative does not exclude object clitics: *Aie-le toujours present à l'esprit !* 'Have it always present in mind!' Finally, reflexive clitics are impossible on *avoir* when it is a main verb, in any form (**Heureusement qu'on s'a / que nous nous avons* 'Fortunately that one oneself has / that we ourselves have').[50]

In Italian , Benincà and Cinque (1991) note that present participles can be followed by any dative clitic, e.g. (52a); for accusative clitics, first and second person clitics are possible (52b), while third person ones are not, except the masculine plural clitic *li*, when the participle is plural (52c). If, however, the participle is singular, even the masculine plural is excluded (52d).

---

[48] We ignore here the form *chanté-je* which is no longer commonly used except in an archaic written style. Note, furthermore, that no pragmatic explanation can be given to explain the unacceptability of forms like **Chante-je?* since sentences like *Est-ce que je chante ce soir?* are unproblematic.

[49] Note that *puis-je* ('can I') is a case of morpho-phonological idiosyncrasy, since the enclitic *–je* selects the form /pɥi/ of *pouvoir*, while excluding the allomorphic /pø/ (**peux-je*) while they are both acceptable (though with register variations) when *je* is a proclitic (*je peux, je puis*).

[50] Notice that the meanings of these sentences, if they were well-formed, would be perfectly coherent (roughly, 'It is lucky that we are there for one another'). It should also be remarked that there is some variation about the judgments here; certain speakers find *nous nous avons* less unacceptable than *on s'a* (on this property of *avoir*, see Morin 1984, Abeillé and Godard 2002).

(52) I a. I compensi spettanti-mi/-ti/-gli/-le/-ci/-vi
The compensations belonging to me/you/him/her/us/you(pl)
b. Gli argomenti riguardanti-mi/-ti/-ci/vi
The arguments concerning me/you/us/you(pl)
c. Gli argomenti riguardanti*-lo/*-la/*-le/ ?-li
The arguments concerning him/her/them(fem)/them(masc)
d. *L'argomento riguardante-li
The argument concerning them

Finally in this section, Romanian examples like (6), repeated here as (53), can be considered a gap in the paradigm. Indeed, the necessity of using the accusative feminine pronoun *o* as an enclitic on the non-finite form of the verb, and not as a proclitic on the auxiliary verb, when the auxiliary begins with a vowel, can be seen as a mechanism of suppletion for the missing forms with proclitics of type **o a* and **o ar*.[51]

(53) R a. Marina o citeşte. *Marina reads it.*
b. Marina a citit-o. *Marina has read it.*
c. Marina o va citi. *Marina will read it.*
Marina it.fem AUX.FUT read
d. Marina ar citi-o. *Marina would read it.*
Marina AUX.COND read-it.fem

3.4 Constraints on the order and realization of sequences of clitics

The constraints upon the order and realization of sequences of clitics constitute one of their most intriguing properties. Perlmutter (1970), in the first major generative work on the issue, set out to describe these constraints for Spanish and French. He concluded that it was impossible to provide a purely syntactic explanation of them, and offered an analysis whereby a matrix of possible sequences filtered the (surface structure) results of the syntactic combination of the clitics. Despite certain attempts to account for these sequences syntactically,[52] the vast majority of linguists working on this question have accepted Perlmutter's conclusions, even if they have not adopted his filtering analysis.

There are three main features which characterize these constraints. Firstly, the order between clitics is fixed for each dialect and seemingly cannot be explained by usual syntactic principles. Secondly, there are many

---

[51] This impossibility is sometimes explained by the fact that the verb begins with a vowel (see Lombard 1974:128-129). This explanation cannot be sufficient, though, seeing as *o* climbs to the modal *a avea de* + supine.

[52] e.g. Fiengo and Gitterman (1978) (see Morin 1979a for a detailed critique of their proposals). Laenzlinger (1993) offers a more recent and interesting analysis.

possible orders of clitic sequences which are impossible, despite not being *a priori* excluded on syntactic or semantic grounds. Thirdly, the morphophonology of the clitic sequences clearly involves lexical phonology: the phonological realization of the sequences is often not predictable on the basis of the forms of the individual clitics when they stand alone. Consider (54) and (55), in contrast to the unacceptable variants (56) to (58):[53]

(54) F a. Martine {le lui / lui} envoie. *Martine sends it to him.*
Martina it to.him / to.him sends
I b. Martina glielo spedisce.
R c. Marina i-l trimite.
S d. Martina se lo envía. [cf. *Martina le lo envía.]
Martina to.him it sends

(55) F a. Martine me l'envoie. *Martina sends it to me.*
I b. Martina me lo spedisce.
R c. Marina mi-l trimite.
S d. Martina me lo envía.
Martina to.me it sends

(56) F a. *Martine lui l'envoie. *Martina sends it to him*
Martina to.him it sends
I b. *Martina lo gli spedisce.
R c. *Marina l-i trimite.
S d. *Martina lo se / le envía.
Martina it to.him sends

(57) F a. *Martine le m'envoie.
I b. *Martina lo me spedisce.
R c. *Marina îl-mi trimite.
S d. *Martina lo me envía.
Martina it to.me sends

(58) F a. *Martine me lui / lui me présente.
[vs. Martine me présente à lui.]
I b. *Martina mi gli / gli mi presenta.
[vs. Martina mi presenta a lui.]
R c. *Marina mă îi prezintă.
[vs. Marina mă prezintă lui.]
S d. *Martina me le / le me presenta.
Martina me to.him / to.him me presents

[53] Note that (58d) is an acceptable form in the North and Center of Spain, where *le* is an accusative clitic referring to humans; the interpretation is 'Marina introduces him to me'.

[vs. Martina me presenta a él.]
[Martina me presents to him]

To start with, we notice that in French, the order between the accusative and dative clitics depends on the person of the clitics in question. If the two clitics are third person, the accusative precedes the dative, (54a) *vs* (56a). However, if the dative clitic is first or second person and the accusative clitic is third person, the dative must precede the accusative, (55a) *vs* (57a). No such constraint has ever been noted for the full phrases corresponding to the clitics.

Likewise, these examples show that the order between 3rd person accusative and dative clitics is the opposite of French (dative following accusative) in Italian, Romanian, and Spanish (accusative following dative), see (54) and (56). Yet it seems impossible to correlate this difference to other more general syntactic contrasts which hold between French, on the one hand, and Italian, Spanish, and Romanian, on the other (this is all the more true as the sequence *lui le* in an enclitic position (and also, more rarely, in a proclitic position, as in (56)) is attested in certain regional varieties of French which otherwise do not have any notable syntactic differences with standard French; see among others Morin 1979a:306-308, and Morin 1979b:34).

Next we notice in (54) to (58) that certain clitic combinations are impossible, and thus we have another example of a paradigm gap (see section 3.3). For example, (58) shows that it is impossible to combine accusative *me* and dative *lui*. This is the case in all the Romance languages (and apparently in other language families) and has received various explanations (see e.g. Haspelmath 2001 for a recent discussion). But the majority of constraints of this type are much more idiosyncratic. For example, the sequence *me te* ('me to-you / to-me you') is generally excluded in the Romance languages. However, it is possible in Romanian, as long as the first person pronoun is dative, and the second person pronoun accusative: *Marina mi te trimite* ('Marina sends you to me'). Elsewhere in French, the sequence *me te* is acceptable for some speakers as long as the two pronouns are dative, such as one finds in constructions like *%Pierre me te semble fidèle* (Pierre to-me to-you seems faithful 'Pierre seems to me to be faithful to you'), where *me* must be interpreted as the complement of *semble* and *te* as the complement of *fidèle*. Finally, it is generally difficult to have sequences of more than two clitics. Once again, it is hard to see how the usual syntactic principles could explain this kind of constraint, since the strong pronominal forms and the corresponding full phrases are not subject to them at all.

The examples also reflect the very many morpho-phonological idiosyncrasies in the realization of sequences of clitics in Romance. In Spanish, the combination of the 3rd person dative (*le, les*) and accusative clitics (*lo, la, los, las*), causes the dative clitic to be replaced by the clitic *se*, as (54d) shows (Perlmutter 1970). In French, it is normal (even in writing, see Grevisse 1980, section1070.2) for the sequences *le/la/les* + *lui/leur* to be realized as *lui/leur*, as in the second variant of (54a) (see e.g. Morin 1979b, Auger 1994, Miller 1992 for numerous examples of this kind in French). Likewise, in Portuguese (see Hutchinson and Lloyd 1996: 39, Vigário 1999, 2003: 141ff) sequences corresponding to the combination of the 3rd person dative (*lhe, lhes*) and accusative (*o, a, os, as*) are realized as *lho, lha, lhos, lhas,* where the marker of number *–s* is the accusative's, the dative's being neutralized. Similarly, the dative clitics of the first and second person (*me, te, nos, vos*) merge with the accusatives of the third person (so e.g. with *o*, you get *mo, to, no-lo* and *vo-lo*). In Italian, with the combination of 3rd person dative clitics and 3rd person accusative clitics (like *lo*), the distinction between the dative singular masculine clitic *gli*, and the feminine *le* is neutralized, and results in *glielo* in both cases, **lelo* being impossible. Likewise, in a situation where you would expect to have a sequence consisting of the reflexive *si* and the impersonal *si*, the result is not the anticipated *si si* sequence, but rather *ci si*. Thus, in (59a), there is a reflexive *si* and in (59b) a *si* marking the impersonal. If you transform (59a) into an impersonal too, as in (59c), then instead of adding a second *si*, you get *ci si*.

(59)	I	a.	Si veste pesante.	*He dresses himself warmly.*
		b.	Si mangia bene.	*One eats well.*
		c.	Ci si / *Si si veste pesanti.	*One dresses oneself warmly.*

It is interesting to note here that the idea often used to explain this phenomenon – a constraint against the repetition of two clitics with an identical form – is not sufficient, even if it is partly true. Indeed, a sequence like *se se* is possible if the first *se* is the conjunction 'if' and the second one the impersonal clitic, e.g. *Se se la sente* 'If he wants to' (litt. if (he) to.himself it feels). The clitic *si* (like all the clitics ending in *-i*) always appears as *se* in front of clitics beginning with *l* and *n*, another morpho-phonological idiosyncrasy. Likewise, in situations where you might expect the combination of the locative clitic *vi* and the homonymous 2nd person plural clitic, you get *vi ci*, not *vi vi* (see e.g. Monachesi 1999a: 28ff).

This kind of phenomenon appears in all the Romance languages, especially Romanian (Monachesi 1998, Popescu 2000) and Catalan (Bonet 1991, 1995, Harris 1997a,b, Wheeler *et al.* 1999: 202ff). In the spoken Catalan of Barcelona (just to take one of many examples of the kind), combining the neuter clitic *ho* and the locative clitic *hi* leads to the completely unexpected form *li*, as the following examples from Bonet (1995:662) demonstrate:

(60) C a. Això, ho portaré a Sabadell demà.
this, 3.neut I.will.bring to Sabadell tomorrow
b. A Sabadell, hi portaré això demà.
to Sabadell there I.will.bring this tomorrow
c. Això, a Sabadell, li portaré demà. (**ho hi* / **hi ho*)
this, to Sabadell, it-there I.will.bring tomorrow

Though some cases such as these might be amenable to some deeper explanation, it is implausible that all of the complex morpho-phonological irregularities that we have seen in the preceding paragraphs should be the result of productive post-lexical phonological rules. Consequently, it appears that it is impossible for sequences of clitics to be constructed post-lexically.[54] For this reason, all those who have studied sequences of clitics since Simpson and Withgott (1986) have concluded that they must be constructed in the morphology, even if certain authors who support this position do not agree with the affixal analysis proposed here for attaching the sequence of clitics to the verb (e.g. Popescu 2000, Gerlach 2002).

In order to account for the constraints on the order and compatibility of clitics, we analyze them in terms of morphological templates, such as the ones in tables 1 and 2. In these tables, the successive columns indicate the order in which the clitics can appear. Clitics appearing in the same column cannot be combined with each other. Table 1 represents the template of positions for Italian.[55] Except for very exceptional cases the sequence can contain a maximum of two elements.

---

[54] This is admitted even by opponents of the affixal status of clitics e.g. Vigário (1999, 2003), who assumes that the lexically constructed clitic sequence is syntactically combined with the verb.

[55] See Monachesi (1999:203ff) for an inventory of all the attested clitic sequences in an Italian corpus of 13 million words. Table 1 accounts for all of these sequences. Cordin and Calabrese (1988:589) suggest a different version where columns I and II are separated in five: (i) *mi*; (ii) *gli, le* (dative); (iii) *vi*; (iv) *ti*; (v) *ci*. This allows them to account for certain marginal combinations (unattested in Monachesi's corpus) which table 1 cannot account for (e.g. ?*mi gli*, ?*gli ti*); however, their version requires certain unacceptable combinations to be separately stipulated (e.g. (i) and (iv) **mi ti* and (iii) and (iv) **vi ti*); such impossible combinations fall out automatically in table 1. Furthermore, it is not completely clear that these marginal combinations depend on ordering restrictions, since the order ?*gli mi* is not judged to be any worse than the order ?*mi gli* which Cordin and Calabrese's system accounts for.

Position	I	II	III	IV	V	VI
	mi *ti* *gli* *le* (dat) *ci* *vi*	*ci* (adv)	*si* (refl)	*lo* *la* *li* *le* (acc)	*si* (imp)	*ne*

Table 1: Template for clitics in Italian (Monachesi 1999a:23)

For French, the following table has been proposed by Perlmutter 1970: 226. It covers proclitics, and includes positions for subject clitics (in column I) and for the negative clitic *ne* (column II), which does not exist in standard Italian. For enclitics, columns III and IV must be switched round in standard French. Furthermore, there is a great deal more variation in the ordering of enclitics, in relation to different varieties of French (this is also true in a more limited fashion for proclisis), but also in certain configurations for the same speaker, who might alternate between e.g. *Donne-moi-le !* and *Donne-le-moi !* 'Give it to me!'

Position	I	II	III	IV	V	VI	VII
	je *tu* *il, elle* *on* *etc.*	*ne*	*me* *te* *nous* *vous* *se*	*le* *la* *les*	*lui* *leur*	*y*	*en*

Table 2: Template for clitics in French (Perlmutter 1970:226)

On top of the constraints that the table (by its very nature) imposes, the impossibility of combining elements from columns III and V must be stipulated, in order to exclude examples such as in (58a); the problem (similar to the one noted above for *me te* in *%Pierre me te semble fidèle*) remains that sequences like *me lui/leur* are acceptable for certain French speakers when the two clitics are dative (*%Pierre me lui semble fidèle*). It is also often claimed that a sequence of clitics can only have a maximum of two complement clitics (coming from columns III to VII in the table above).[56] Fur-

[56] But note the perfect acceptability of examples like *Pierre me la lui a fait raconter* 'Pierre made me tell it to him', discussed by Tasmowski (1985), where one has a sequence of three clitic complements on the one hand, and members of columns III and V on the other (separated however in this case by an element from IV, without which the sequence becomes unacceptable). The clear and uniform acceptability of these examples is all the more surprising, given

thermore, various other co-occurrence difficulties must be stipulated which do not always involve the entire set of a column (see e.g. Morin 1979b, 1981), above all for enclisis (e.g. **Menons-l'y* 'let's take him there'; **lui y parler* 'to talk to him there' vs. *m'y parler* 'to talk to me there'). Finally, it is well-known that in all the Romance languages, ethical datives largely escape the constraints imposed by matrices of this type, which is possibly related to the acceptability for certain speakers of sequences with *te lui*, where *te* is dative (e.g. *%Paul te lui a donné une de ces gifle,* 'Paul gave me (you) a slap in the face', Leclère 1976:93).

Beyond the problems already mentioned, these templates can be criticized for the fact that they lack explanatory power, since nothing really independently motivates the classing of clitics into the columns, nor the order of the columns, nor the compatibility constraints. Some people have tried to propose syntactic and/or semantic and/or phonological explanations for these phenomena. For example, Watson (1997) who, while admitting that the sequential ordering of clitics is built morphologically, explains the order and co-occurrence in terms of the features ±ACCUSATIVE and ±INDIVIDUATION, combined to certain phonological constraints; similarly, Laenzlinger (1993) proposes a syntactic explanation of the order and the co-occurrence constraints, based on morphosyntactic and semantic features. The question remains open, however, as to how far the explanations proposed can be generalized to all cases in all languages and dialects in a coherent manner.

Other recent studies have tried to explain the phenomena of order, co-occurrence and idiosyncrasy in terms of optimality theory, which allows a great deal of flexibility in the explanation thanks to the possibility of organizing the same constraints into different hierarchies according to languages or dialects (see e.g. Grimshaw 1997, Popescu 2000, Legendre 2000, Gerlach 2002). However, in this type of framework, one might say that there is an explanatory gap at the level of the choice and hierarchical organization of the constraints.

In these two kinds of explanations, the motivation of the constraints proposed is of varying plausibility. For example, the animacy hierarchy of Siewierska (1988) (1> 2> 3> human> higher animals> other organisms> inorganic matter> abstracts) and a hierarchy of arguments (subject> indirect object> direct object) have been used to suggest that clitics tend to be ordered as a function of these (Watson (1997) and Gerlach (2002)) which appears interesting *a priori*. However, such general principles are clearly

---

that it cannot have to do with frequency effects (i.e. the combination and order are not frequently observed).

not sufficient. For example, the sequence *le lui* of (54a) — where *le* is the object and refers to something inanimate, and *lui* is the dative and refers to something animate – contradicts the animacy hierarchy and the hierarchy of arguments. Watson and Gerlach suggest explanations for this sequence based on auxiliary principles, but this makes things seem much less convincing.

A different hypothesis might be put forward to account for the status of the partial regularities we have just observed, i.e. that they have to do with morphological freezing of formerly motivated orderings, which have been modified by the phenomena of morphological metathesis and syncretism between morphemes (see Hyman and Mchombo 1992 for an argument of this type in favor of the lexicalization of a series of affixes en Chichewa).

3.5 Mesoclisis and interactions between clitics and affixes

In a lexicalist model, a post-lexical clitic must *a priori* be positioned outside affixes attached to the same base. Zwicky and Pullum (1983) capture this with a constraint whereby clitics, but not affixes, can be attached to a host which already contains a clitic. There are two cases in Romance languages where a clitic pronoun is apparently in a position between a verbal base and a suffix, a phenomenon sometimes referred to as *mesoclisis*.

The best-known such cases are Portuguese future and conditional verb forms where, instead of the expected enclitics, there are clitic pronouns between the verbal base and the tense and person suffixes.[57] However, if there is a proclisis trigger in the sentence, the suffix is directly attached to the verbal base.

(61) P a. Falaremos. *We will speak.*
b. Falar-lhe-emos. *We will speak to him.*
c. Não lhe falaremos. *We will not speak to him.*

On the basis of these facts, Zwicky (1987) and Halpern (1995) have suggested that Portuguese clitic pronouns must be analyzed as affixes. However, several authors have disputed the validity of this analysis. Leeuw (1997: 139ff) proposes a detailed analysis of the phenomenon, in the framework of optimality theory, in terms which somewhat negate the relevance of the distinction between affixes and clitics in such cases, and Vigário (1999, 2003: 147ff) suggests that the marking of tense and person here (which, in Portuguese as in all the other Romance languages, derives from the Latin verb *habere*) has a double status; on the one hand, as in examples like (61a,c), the marking functions like a wholly morphological inflectional affix. In contrast, as in the mesoclisis examples like (61b), the

[57] There are similar examples in archaic Romanian, see Lombard (1974).

marking functions like a verb, serving to host clitics, and combining with the infinitive via composition. Vigário gives different arguments in favor of this analysis, notably showing that the forms with mesoclisis behave like two phonological words and have two primary stresses. She additionally mentions the fact that certain Portuguese speakers use a novel form *falaremos-lhe* instead of (61b), where the clitic is behind the tense and person marking. According to her, in such variants the analysis of the marking of tense and person as a verb disappears, and thus the marking receives normal suffix status. It is worth pointing out however, that the data collected here is not necessarily incompatible with a wholly morphological analysis of the forms in question.

The second case where it appears that there is a suffix after a clitic, involves forms in certain varieties of spoken Spanish, where the third person plural suffix *-n* can be found after an enclitic, and not in front of it, as is required in the standard variant of the language. One thus obtains, instead of *siéntense!* 'Sit down!' (sentar-subj.pres-3.pl.refl), forms like *siéntesen* (Fernandez Soriano 1999: 1257) where the 3rd person plural marking *-n* does not appear on the verbal base, but rather after the reflexive clitic *se*. This type of example seems to be a very strong argument in favor of the affixal status of clitic pronouns (or more precisely of enclitics) in the varieties of Spanish in question, at least to the extent that it would seem to be very difficult to attribute a non-affixal status to the morpheme *-n*.

4 Subject clitics and adverbial clitics

4.1 Subject clitics

In the majority of Romance languages, a subject which is anaphorically or deictically recoverable is not expressed by a pronoun, but simply by a suffix indicating person inflection (certain theories however suggest there is a phonologically empty pronoun 'pro' in the subject position, see e.g. Haegeman 1991). Thus, (62a) is well-formed in Italian. In French and in the majority of the dialects of northern Italy,[58] in contrast, there are obligatory subject clitics in the same contexts, as we see in (62b,c).

(62)	I	a.	Mangia.	*He eats.*
	Tr	b.	El magna. / *Magna.	*He eats.* (Trentino, Rizzi 1986: 391)
	F	c.	Il mange. / *Mange.	*He eats.*

Kayne (1975) proposed an analysis for the subject clitics of French which is essentially the same as that of complement clitics, in terms of the

[58] We will take our examples for this chapter from Rizzi (1986); see also Poletto (1999)

movement of the pronoun from the normal syntactic position of the subject to a position adjoined to the verb. This analysis in terms of movement allows one to account for the complementary distribution between subject clitics and full NPs in standard formal French (StF), parallel to the situation described in (28c) for complement clitics. However, in most varieties of spoken French (SpF), one notices a very systematic presence of the subject clitic which doubles the full NP when it is present. It is the same with the Italian dialects discussed by Rizzi (1986). This doubling even extends, in the Italian dialects and certain varieties of French, to indefinite quantified NPs like *un enfant* 'a child', *quelqu'un* 'someone' or *personne* 'anybody/nobody'.

(63) StF a. *Personne il ne mange.
Nobody he (not) eats.
QF b. en campagne, quand quelqu'un il dansait (Auger 1994: 97)
in countryside, when someone he danced...
SpF c. Ben oui mais alors personne il a une table exhaustive ?
well yes but well nobody he has a table exhaustive ?
Sure, but does anybody have an exhaustive table?
(example found in a discussion forum on the web)
TI d. Gnun l'a dit gnent. *Nobody said anything.*
(Turinese, Rizzi 1986: 396).

These phenomena led Rizzi (1986) for Italian dialects (TI= Turinese), Auger (1994) for spoken Quebecois French (QF), and Zribi-Hertz (1994) for the variety of spoken French sometimes called "advanced" French, to conclude that the subject clitic pronouns were in fact subject-agreement markers. In contrast, Auger (1994) noticed that one does not find, in spoken French, doubling of quantified indefinite NPs in complement position and concluded that complement clitics are therefore not (yet) agreement markers in spoken French.[59] This asymmetry between subject and object, as well as the historical order in which different types of NPs were able to be systematically doubled, is entirely compatible with the hierarchy of the agreement markings of Givón (1976), discussed in section 2.2 above, according to which subject pronouns grammaticalize themselves into agreement markers before complement pronouns and definite NPs trigger agreement sooner than the indefinite NPs.

We dealt in sections 3.2 and 3.3 with morpho-phonological idiosyncrasies and paradigm gaps for French subject clitics, suggesting that they are at once agreement markers and lexically attached affixes. The same arguments

[59] Following Givón (1976), one might say that object clitics are already agreement markers in spoken French, but that agreement is not triggered by all types of NP.

carry over to show that complement pronouns can be analyzed as affixes in all current varieties of spoken French; however, as we have just mentioned, it is not at all clear that complement pronouns function as agreement markers in French.[60] This fact led Miller (1992) and Auger (1994) to contest the fairly common notion that agreement-marker status is a precondition of affix status in Romance languages. This position brings a language like French in line with certain Bantu languages where the subject and object markers are indisputably lexically attached affixes, but only the subject is an agreement marker (see e.g. Givón 1976, Bresnan and Mchombo 1987 and Creissels 2001).

Another indicator of the lexically attached affix status of subject pronouns in spoken French is the fact, noted by Miller (1992: 158) and Zribi-Hertz (1994: 138), that one must repeat the subject pronoun with a coordination of hosts, unlike in standard French (see section 2.3 above). Thus, *Elle chante et elle danse* ('She sings and she dances') is very clearly preferred to *Elle chante et danse* ('She sings and dances') in spoken French. Rizzi (1986: 403) shows that the same thing is true in Trentino where only *La canta e la balla* with repetition of the subject clitic *la* is acceptable.

In section 2.5 above, we dealt with the obligatory status of the cliticization of complement pronouns in French. In this respect, subject pronouns are more complex. Doubling strong subject forms (e.g. *Moi je viendrai*, *Lui il viendra*) is the norm in all the usual variants of spoken French, but standard French allows non-doubled strong subject forms, but only in the third person (*Lui viendra* 'He will come'; Eux *viendront* 'They will come'; but **Moi viendrai* 'I will come'; **Toi viendras* 'You will come'). This asymmetry, previously studied by Benveniste (1965: 201), has still not been explained in a satisfactory manner.

4.2 'Adverbial' clitics

We will conclude this fourth section with a few words about "adverbial" clitics (an unfortunate title, as in many cases they correspond to full phrases which are not adverbs) in French (*en* and *y*), Italian (*ne, ci* and *vi*), and Catalan (*en, hi*).[61] In terms of morphology and phonology, these elements clearly have the same status as normal complement pronoun clitics. However, their potential functions in a sentence are much more varied (see e.g.

---

[60] In certain theoretical frameworks, one might call them "incorporated" pronouns e.g. Baker (1988).

[61] To make the text more readable, where the languages show the same behavior pattern, we will use *EN* to represent the *en* in Catalan and French and the *ne* in Italian, and *Y* to represent *y* in French, *ci* and *vi* in Italian, and *hi* in Catalan. We will not take into account any differences between *ci* and *vi* in Italian.

Sandfeld 1970: 134-168 and Pinchon 1972 for French; Wheeler *et al.* 1997: 186-196 for Catalan; Cordin and Calabrese 1988: 559-565 and 633-644 for Italian).[62]

To start with, one function of *EN* is as an anaphor of a PP with DE (F *de*, I *di, da*; C *de*). The clitic *Y* is similar in this respect and can be anaphoric for PPs with every kind of locative preposition like *à, dans, sur, sous,...*(I *a, in,...*; C *a, en, ...*).[63,64] This is illustrated in examples (64) and (65).[65]

(64) a. F Les étudiants n'en sont pas sortis. [*en* = de cet amphi]
The students not-from.it are not exited [*en* = from this hall]
I Gli studenti non ne sono usciti. [*ne* = da questo anfiteatro]
C Els estudiants no n'han sortit. [*n'* = d'aquesta aula]
The students haven't exited it.
b. F Il en a parlé. [*en* = de ce cas]
He of.it has spoken [*en* = of this case]
I Ne ha parlato. [*ne* = di questo caso]
C N'ha parlat. [*n'* = d'aquest cas]
He has spoken of it.

(65) a. F Il y allait souvent. [*y* = à Paris]
He there went often [*y* = to Paris]
I Ci andava spesso. [*ci* = a Parigi]
C Hi anava sovint. [*hi* = a París]
He went there often.
b. F Tu n'y étais pas. [*y* = dans ta maison]

---

62 For more detailed studies of these clitics, see among others Belletti and Rizzi (1981), Haverkort (1999), Milner (1978), Ruwet (1990).

63 In all three languages there is a particularly significant restriction concerning the pronominalization with *Y* of PPs introduced by *à*,namely that these PPs cannot in general be pronominalized by dative clitics. We will see however that this constraint is less obvious in certain varieties of spoken French (considered non-standard) where *y* can replace *lui*: *%J'y ai dit.* ('I have told him). Cordin and Calabrese (1988:562) report a similar phenomenon among regional spoken varieties in Italy, North and South: *%A Maria, ce l'ho ditto ieri* (to Maria, to.her it I.have told yesterday 'I told it to her, Maria, yesterday').

64 In Catalan (Wheeler *et al* 1999:191ff), *hi* allows a greater variety of PPs to be pronominalized, including non-locatives, e.g. *Sortia amb en Terenci, però ja no hi surt.* (she. was.going.out with Terenci, but already not-*Y* she.goes.out 'She was going out with Terenci, but she's no longer going out with him').

65 In all three languages, *EN* and *Y* generally have non-human antecedents but this is far from always being the case, see e.g. Herslund (1988), Ruwet (1990), Sandfeld (1970), as well as the Catalan example of the preceding note; similarly, the verb *penser* 'to think' (65d,e,f) allows *y* with a human antecedent. In all three languages, there is, with certain verbs, an alternation between the dative and *Y* according to whether the antecedent is human or not, e.g. *Il lui / y a dédié l'après-midi* [*à son ami / à son travail*] 'He dedicated the afternoon to him (his friend) / it (his work)'.

You not-there were not [*y* = in your house]
I Non c'eri. [*ci* = a casa tua]
C No hi eres. [*hi* = a casa teva]
You were not there.
c. F Il y pense. [*y* = à son examen]
He about.it is.thinking [*y* = about his exam]
I Ci pensa. [*ci* = al suo esame]
C Hi pensa. [*hi* = en el seu examen]
He thinks about it.

These examples show that the pronominalized PP can be a locative complement (64a, 65a,b).[66] It can equally be a non-locative complement introduced by a preposition (64b) and (65c). Furthermore, as we saw with the examples of dative clitics governed by adjectives in (23), adverbial clitics can appear on a verb while being semantically governed by a predicative adjectival complement of the verb, as illustrated in (66) and (67).[67]

(66) F a. Il en est très content. [*en* = de sa voiture]
I b. Ne è molto contento. [*ne* = della sua macchina]
C c. N'està molt content. [*n'* = del seu cotxe]
He is very happy with it (his car).

(67) F a. Il s'y sent attaché. [*y* = à ce laboratoire]
I b. Egli ci si sente legato. [*ci* = a questo laboratorio]
C c. Ell s'hi sent vinculat. [*hi* = al seu laboratori]
He feels attached to it (this laboratory).

---

[66] In all three languages, the examples are less natural when the locative PP is not an argument subcategorized by the verb. However, with Y, if the context sets up a relation between the place and the activity, the sentences are acceptable.

(i) F J'aimais aller à cette discothèque. Je savais que Marc y dansait chaque nuit.
I Mi piaceva andare a quella discoteca. Sapevo che Marco ci ballava ogni notte.
C M'agradava anar a aquella discoteca. Sabia que en Marc hi ballava cada nit.
'I used to like going to that disco. I knew that Mark used to dance there every night'.

In contrast, it seems impossible in the three languages to pronominalize with EN a locative PP introduced by *de*, under the same conditions: **Marc en a plongé* [du dessus de la falaise]; **Marco se ne è tuffato; *En Marc se n'ha capbussat* 'Marc dived from.there' [from the top of the cliff]'.

[67] These constructions are subject to certain constraints which remain to be elucidated in detail. For example, while a sentence like *Il y est fidèle* [*y* = à ses principes] 'He is faithful to them (his principles)', similar to (67a), is accepted by French speakers, the Italian and Catalan variants of this example are rejected by our informants, despite the apparent parallelism with (67b,c): I **Ci è fedele* [*ci* = ai suoi principi]; C **Hi és fidel* [*hi* = als seus principis]. For some observations on the construction, see Abeillé and Godard, this volume, section 2.4.

Elsewhere, the clitic *EN* can correspond with the complement of a noun which is the object of the verb, as in (68). The parallel examples with *Y* are not possible however, as (69) shows, even though the noun governs a complement introduced by *à* in all three languages. Furthermore, with a limited class of verbs in French and Italian, though not in Catalan,[68] *EN* can correspond with a complement of a subject noun, as in (70).

(68) F a. Je n'en connais pas le nom. [*en* = de l'auteur de ce livre]
I don't know the name of him/her.
I b. Non ne conosco il nome. [*ne* = dell'autore di questo libro]
C c. No en conec el nom. [*en* = de l'autor d'aquest libre]

(69) F a. *Je ne m'y rappelle pas le voyage.
[*vs* Je ne me rappelle pas le voyage à Paris]
I don't recall the voyage there.
I b. *Non ci ricordo il viaggio. [*vs* Non ricordo il viaggio a Parigi]
C c. *No hi recordo el viatge. [*vs* No recordo el viatge a Paris]

(70) F a. L'auteur en est célèbre. [*en* = de ce livre]
The author of it is famous.
I b. L'autore ne è celebre. [*ne* = di questo libro]
C c. *L'autor n'és cèlebre. [*n'* = d'aquest llibre]

Notice that Catalan is exceptional in that it allows *hi* to be used to pronominalize certain predicative complements (AdjP or NP).[69] Finally, *EN* and *Y* appear in numerous idiomatic expressions in all three languages. In French, one has for example *en avoir marre* 'to be fed up', *il y a* 'there is/are' etc. See Wheeler *et al.* (1999: 195) and Cordin and Calabrese (1988 : 640) for similar examples in Catalan and Italian.

The second main use of *EN* is the *partitive* (or *quantitative*) use, see e.g. Milner 1978, in which it serves as an anaphor for a non-specific nominal antecedent. For example, in (71), the antecedent could be *livres, livres anglais, livres de grammaire,* etc.

---

[68] The precise nature of the class of verbs allowing *EN* pronominalization of a subject's complement, as in (70) has been the object of some debate, and is often claimed to be the class of unaccusatives (see Belletti and Rizzi 1981, for example, but see also Tasmowski 1990 for a different point of view).

[69] Wheeler *et al.* (1999:193-4) give the following examples: *Digué que el ferro es tornaria or, però no s'hi va tornar.* 'He said that the iron should turn into gold, but it didn't turn into it'; *És gaire salat aquest arròs? – Sí que l'hi trobo.* ' Is this risotto very salty? – I find it is'. Wheeler *et al.* also note that this use of *hi* (as well as a similar use of *en*) appears in the spoken form of the language for complements of the verbs *ser, estar, semblar, esdevenir* and *aparentar*, although the standard form demands that these verbs pronominalize their complement with the neuter pronoun *ho*.

(71) F a. Il en veut (trois) [, de livres]. *He wants three of them (books).*
I b. Ne vuole (tre) [, di libri].
C c. En vol (tres) [, de libres]

On the basis of the contrast between (72) and (73), it is often claimed (e.g. Belletti and Rizzi 1981) that this use is limited to the object of transitive verbs and to the postverbal subject of unaccusative verbs. These data have been used as an argument in favor of a syntactic representation of unaccusativity, the preverbal subject of the unaccusative verb being in the object position in deep structure and behaving like an object in this position from the point of view of a quantitative EN.[70]

(72) F a. *Trois en sont venus. [*en* = de clients]
I b. *Tre ne sono venuti. [*ne* = di clienti]
C c. *Tres n'han vingut. [*n'* = de clients]
Three of them are / have come

(73) F a. Il en est venu trois. [*en* = de clients]
I b. Ne sono venuti tre. [*ne* = di clienti]
C c. N'han vingut tres. [*n'* = de clients]
There are / have come three of them

However, in Italian and in Catalan, many speakers have the same contrast with verbs which are clearly unergative like *dormir* and *téléphoner*, which seriously undermines the claims of Belletti and Rizzi.[71]

(74) I a. *Tre ne hanno telefonato. [*ne* = di clienti]
C b. *Tres n'han telefonat. [*n'* = de clients]
Three of them have called

(75) I a. %Ne hanno telefonato tre. [*ne* = di clienti]
C b. %N'han telefonat tres. [*n'* = de clients]
There have called three of them

It appears then that the clitics EN and Y function in a very complex way, and yet this functioning is surprisingly uniform across the three languages discussed here.

[70] (72b) and (74b) are acceptable in Italian with focal stress on *Tre*.

[71] On this point, see Centineo (1996:230-231), Saccon (1995) for Italian and Cortès and Gavarró (1997) for Catalan. For a discussion of the criteria for unaccusativity, see the chapter by Legendre and Sorace, and the introduction, this volume.

5 Conclusion

Clitic pronouns in the Romance languages have been the subject of many studies, yet the key role they play for the understanding of the properties of the interfaces between the different components of the language faculty has not yet always been made sufficiently clear. Thus far, studies have generally focused on only one aspect of cliticization – most often the syntactic side – neglecting morphological and phonological properties.

In this chapter, we have tried to give an idea of the complexity of the data, taking into account at once the syntactic, morphological, and phonological properties of clitic pronouns in various Romance languages. This overview has highlighted the difficulties posed by clitic pronouns for grammatical theories. Their morpho-phonological properties must be reconciled with their syntactic characteristics. Thus, clitics are crucially relevant for understanding interactions between different modules of the grammar and their internal organization.

The data we have examined has brought to light a large amount of behavioral variation among clitics both internal to one language and cross-linguistically. Clitics therefore constitute a particularly rich field of investigation for the problems of both synchronic and diachronic variation among a group of very closely related languages. In view of the variation we have seen, it would seem difficult to maintain that clitics are a unitary phenomenon, which can be defined with a uniform definition. However, we believe there is a tendency, in the majority of Romance languages, for clitic pronouns to behave like morphological elements. In particular, we conclude that their properties are very close to those of inflectional affixes; the clitics of Portuguese, and to some extent Romanian, pose problems for this hypothesis, notably in their positioning in relation to the verb. We believe that future research will be able to show more convincingly that the clitics of these two languages are in an intermediate stage of morphologization.

4

Complex Predicates in the Romance Languages

ANNE ABEILLE AND DANIELE GODARD

1 Introduction[1]

The term 'complex predicate' refers to the phenomenon whereby a series of verbs or, more generally, predicates, function like a single verb with respect to certain syntactic and semantic properties. Sentences with complex predicates thus have some monoclausal properties. Romance languages (RL) exhibit a simple syntactic criterion for monoclausality: 'clitic climbing'.[2] In

[1] For their judgments and comments, we wish to thank: Christine Aguilar-Adan, Alex Alsina, Adelaïde Amaral, Raúl Aranovich, Ana-Maria Barbu, Ignacio Bosque, Patricia Cabredo-Hofherr, Ileana Comorovski, Alexandra Cornilescu, Margarita Correia, Rodolfo Delmonte, Dana-Maria Dumitriu, Maria-Christina Echeverria-Skouras, Marai-Teresa Espinal, Josep Fontana, Ana Gavarró, Jean-Pierre Koenig, Emil Ionescu, Brenda Laca, Manuela Leahu, Alda Mari, Paola Merlo, Paola Monachesi, Fiammetta Namer, Sanda Reinheimer-Rîpeanu, Alain Rouveret, Carla Soares, Liliane Tasmowski, Lucia Tovena, Enric Vallduví.

[2] A clitic proform 'climbs' when it appears attached to a verb which does not subcategorize for it directly itself, but is the head of a phrase including the verb which does subcategorize for it. For convenience, we will retain this term which comes originally from transformational grammar. We treat all clitics as the realization of a (syntactic) argument, including those clitics which (as in idioms) do not have a corresponding non-clitic form as in *s'en aller* 'to go away' (Abeillé *et al.* 1998). We also include those clitics which appear to correspond to a modifier, like the locative or causative clitics (*J'en ai eu mal au dos* 'I had a bad back because of it'); to get this result, it is sufficient to adopt a rule which treats postverbal modifiers as syntactic arguments, see Abeillé and Godard 1997, Bouma, Malouf and Sag 2001.

Fundamental Issues in th Romance Languages
Danièle Godard (ed.).

(1b), the clitic occurs on the verb of which it is a complement (*mangiare, comer*), while it occurs on the matrix verb in (1c).

(1) a. I Giovanni può mangiare la torta.
S Juan puede comer la galleta.
John can eat the cake
b. I Giovanni può mangiarla.
S Juan puede comerla.
John can eat-CL
c. I Giovanni la può mangiare.
S Juan la puede comer.
Giovanni CL-can eat
John can eat it

We rely on this criterion in order to define the set of verbs which can be the head of a syntactically complex predicate. We limit ourselves to the most widely spoken European languages: French (F), Italian (I), Romanian (R), European Spanish (S), Catalan (C), and European Portuguese (P). Verbs which give rise to a complex predicate combine with a non-finite verb (or a non-verbal predicate). One does not find clitics 'climbing' out of a finite complement clause. Thus Romanian causatives, which are always constructed with a subjunctive complement clause, do not give rise to complex predicates, in spite of the fact that causative verbs give rise to complex predicates in the other RL. Similarly, modals or verbs of perception, which can take either infinitive or finite verbal complements, do not enter into a complex predicate in the second case: F *Paul y voit partir Jean* (Paul there sees go Jean, 'Paul sees Jean go there') contrasts with **Paul y voit que part Jean* (lit. Paul there sees that goes Jean).[3]

The verbs which give rise to complex predicates in the Romance languages are semantically heterogeneous: tense auxiliaries, modals, aspectuals, verbs of movement, predicative verbs (with predicative complements), causative verbs, and perception verbs. It is, however, tempting to look for a semantic correlation for the properties of monoclausality. These verbs seem to make a weak (or weakened) semantic contribution. In the Iberian Peninsula tradition, they refer to 'verbal periphrasis' (Yllera 1999, Gavarró and Laca 2002), when the semantics of the sequence of verbs is not obviously compositional. But semantic weakness is not a sufficient criterion for producing complex predicates in syntax: not all the periphrases studied in the cited texts for Spanish or Catalan are complex predicates in our sense. This is the same for certain future auxiliaries in French and Romanian (F *aller*

[3] In the Salentino dialect, certain finite verbs, which must be controlled, allow a clitic to raise in certain conditions (e.g. Monachesi 1999a).

+inf, R *o să* +subj, which do not allow clitic climbing: F *Paul va le lire* vs **Paul le va lire* 'Paul is going to read it').

It has also been claimed that complex predicates are associated with a single semantic domain, either in event terms, or propositional terms: the verbal complement would not denote an event or a proposition in itself (Napoli 1981 for Italian, Gonçalvès 1999 for Portuguese, Rochette 1990 for the Romance languages). However, modals are problematic for this proposal: their complement is generally taken to be a proposition, which does not prevent some of them from being part of a complex predicate. One cannot say either that a unique event is involved, since events denoted by the head and the complement verbs can have a different temporal localization:

(2) a. I Lo dovevi aver già finito.
S Lo debías haber terminado ya.
CL-you.should have already finished
You should have already finished it.
b. I Lo voglio fare domani.
S Lo quiero hacer mañana.
CL-I.want to.do tomorrow
I want to do it tomorrow.

It would be necessary therefore to appeal to more complex semantic notions. We leave the question open, concerning ourselves here with the syntax of the construction.

A survey of the Romance languages allows us to see general features of complex predicates in these languages, and to evaluate the differences between the languages or between different classes of verbs. The best-known properties demonstrate the monoclausality of complex predicate structures, and are interpreted in terms of the sharing of argument structure. Other properties, less well-studied, are distributed according to the language or the class of the predicate, and shed light on constituent structure. We show that not all complex predicates have the same structural properties. In other words, the formation of a complex predicate is compatible with different syntactic structures.

The chapter is organized in the following way: we illustrate first the set of verb classes which can head a complex predicate, then we examine in turn the monoclausality and the structural properties of complex predicates, according to the different predicates and the different Romance languages. Finally, we briefly discuss certain data which are unaccounted for by our analysis, and require attention to the specific properties of individual languages.

2 Defining complex predicates

Complex predicates in the Romance Languages are characterized by two related properties, clitic climbing and the non-finiteness of the complement predicate, which can be an infinitive, a gerund, a participle, a supine, or a non-verbal predicate.[4] We will review the different verb classes which manifest these criteria.[5]

2.1 Auxiliaries

The term 'auxiliary' does not receive a stable definition across grammatical frameworks, and it is used as either a syntactic or semantic term. We adopt here a syntactic definition, based on two properties: subject 'raising' (the subject of these verbs is identified with the one taken by the non-finite predicate), and the obligatoriness of clitic climbing (cliticized complements are obligatorily attached to the auxiliary).[6]

In French and Italian, the two past auxiliaries (*être* / *essere* and *avoir* / *avere*) alternate, and are selected by the participles. The two past auxiliaries in Romanian (*a avea* and *a fi*) do not alternate as a function of the participle: the first engenders a past tense interpretation and the second one a perfective tense.[7] In contemporary European Portuguese, only *ter* is used as a past auxiliary, *haver* now being used as a modal. Contemporary Spanish and Catalan only have one past tense auxiliary (*haber, haver*). Examples in (3) illustrate clitic climbing.[8,9]

---

[4] For clitics appearing on the second predicate see section 5.3. There is also at least one Italian dialect where clitics do not climb, but appear at the right-hand boundary of a verbal complex (Tortora 2000). As for non-finiteness, note that Portuguese inflected infinitives are treated as being finite, since they do not allow clitic climbing.

[5] We leave aside here light verb constructions (*avoir peur* 'to fear', *avoir raison* 'to be right' etc.), and more generally nominal complements (except with the copula).

[6] According to this syntactic criterion, the near-past (F *venir de (faire quelquechose)* 'to have just (done something)') or near-future (F *aller (faire qqch)* 'to be going to (do something)') forms in modern French, which do not allow the clitics to climb, are not auxiliaries; neither is Catalan *vaig*, with which climbing is optional (see section 2.2).

[7] The perfective auxiliary *fi* in Romanian is invariable, and appears where an infinitive or subjunctive is expected. It appears with *voi* and *aş* (R *voi fi cântat* 'I will have sung', *aş fi cântat* 'I would have sung'). See Avram (1999) for a discussion concerning the two Romanian auxiliaries.

[8] We make every effort to give parallel examples in the different languages. We generally give either a translation (in italics) or a gloss, and both where it seems necessary. Clitics are underlined, when their position is important.

[9] On clitics, see Miller and Monachesi (this volume), and for the more complex data in Portuguese, see especially Crysmann (1999, 2000a, 2002), Rouveret (1991, 1999), Monachesi 2005. The data of Romanian are complicated by the behavior of the singular feminine accusative clitic *o*, which can appear on the main verb or the auxiliary (obligatorily on the participle / infinitive with past and conditional auxiliaries *a, aş*, on the modal with *a avea de, a putea* and

(3) a. F Jean ne l'a pas vu / *n'a pas le-vu.
I Giovanni non lo ha visto / *non ha lo visto / *vistolo.
R Ion nu l-a văzut / *nu a-l văzut / *nu a văzutu-l.
P O João não o tem visto / *não tem-no visto / *não tem visto-o.
S Juan no lo ha visto / *no ha lo visto / *no ha vistolo.
C. En Joan no l'ha vist / *no ha el-vist / *no ha vist-el.
John has not seen him
b. R Nu cred să-l fi spus Ion / *să fi spusu-l Ion.
NEG believe SA-CL FI said Ion / SA FI says-CL Ion
I do not believe Ion said it

In addition to past auxiliaries, Romanian has *voi* (+inf) and *aş* (+inf) for the future and conditional, and the modal verbs *a avea de* (+supine, 'to have to'), and *a putea* (+inf, 'to be able to') are also auxiliaries in our sense. Portuguese has also aspectual or modal verbs which take a gerund complement (+ger) with obligatory clitic climbing (Mateus *et al*. 2004).

(4) R a. Ion o poate vedea / *poate vedea-o / *poate o vedea.
Ion can see her
P b. O João vai-os lendo / *vai lendo-os.
John is reading them

Italian and Portuguese, where clitics can attach to participles and gerunds when they are the head of an adjunct to the sentence (5), show that obligatory clitic climbing is a property of the construction in (3) rather than a morphological fact (example (5a) is from Monachesi 1999a):

(5) I a. Vistosi allo specchio, Vito decise di cominciare una nuova vita.
seen-CL in.the mirror, Vito decided to begin a new life
Having seen himself in the mirror, Vito decided to begin a new life.
P b. Telefonando-lhe amiúde, o João estava ao corrente.
By telephoning him often, Jean was in the picture

The set of Romance auxiliaries is given in Table 1 :

Tense auxiliaries	F *avoir, être*, I *avere, essere*, S *haber*, C *haver*, P *ter*, R *a avea, a fi, aş* (+inf), *voi* (+inf)
Modals and aspectuals	R *a avea de* (+sup), *a putea* (+inf), P *andar* (+ger), *ficar* (+ger), *estar* (+ger), *ir* (+ger), *vir* (+ger), *haver*.

Table 1: The auxiliaries (+participle, unless otherwise specified)

---

optionally or obligatorily, depending on speakers, on the infinitive with the future auxiliary *voi*).

2.2 Restructuring verbs

The term 'restructuring verb' historically goes back to a transformational treatment of monoclausality (Rizzi 1978, 1982). We will use it as a convenient label for a syntactic class. Restructuring verbs are all subject-raising or subject-control verbs; they are differentiated from auxiliaries by the optionality of clitic climbing,[10] and from causative verbs by the arguments they take.

In this sense, neither French nor Romanian have restructuring verbs.[11] By contrast, Italian, Spanish, Catalan and Portuguese have a certain number of them, which are often corresponding versions of the same lexeme. While there is a stable core of verbs which belong to the class, membership is subject to some variation.[12] It is therefore difficult to provide an exhaustive and stable list of restructuring verbs. Their complement is an infinitive or a gerund (noted with '+ger'). When these verbs are followed by a complement clause, they do not give rise to complex predicates, see the example in (6):

(6) I a. <u>Lo</u> voglio dare a Giovanni.
CL-I.want give to Giovanni
I want to give it to Giovanni.
b. *<u>Lo</u> voglio che dia a Giovanni.
CL-I.want that she.give to Giovanni
I want her to give it to Giovanni.

We contrast ordinary verbs (illustrated with TO APPEAR) which do not allow clitics to raise (7), with the two alternants with restructuring verbs (8):

(7) a. I Giovanni pare aver<u>le</u> mangiate.
S Juan parece haber<u>las</u> comido.
P O João parece tê-<u>las</u> comido.
C En Joan pareix haver-<u>les</u> menjades.
John appears to have eaten them

b. I *Giovanni <u>le</u> pare aver mangiate.
S *Juan <u>las</u> parece haber comido.

---

[10] Both possibilities being grammatical; we ignore here the stylistic, social, or regional preferences which can determine the choice (see for example for Italian Napoli 1981, Vanvolsem 1999).

[11] French occasionally allows complex predicate forms with the verbs *aller, devoir, pouvoir*, especially if the clitic is *en* or *y* (% *J'y devais rencontrer mes enfants* 'I needed to meet my children there'). They represent the remnants of an older variety of French where complex predicates were more widely available; this is not the colloquial French that we are focusing on here. For a recent discussion, see Cinque (2002) and references therein. The '%' sign indicates variable judgments among speakers.

[12] For a discussion of this problem in Italian, see Napoli (1981).

P *O João parece-as ter comido.
C *En Joan les sembla haver menjades.

(8)	I	Giovanni vuole mangiarle.	vs.	Giovanni le vuole mangiare.
	S	Juan quiere comerlas.		Juan las quiere comer.
	P	O João quer comê-las.		O João quere-as comer.
	C	En Joan vol menjar-les.		En Joan les vol menjar.
		John wants to eat them.		

Note that the future tense constructor *haver de* in Portuguese, and the past auxiliary one *vaig* in Catalan, are restructuring verbs in our sense, since clitic climbing is not obligatory. We give a list of restructuring verbs in table 2, grouping them by their common core meaning. They take an infinitive complement, unless otherwise indicated.

A property of clitics which is often mentioned is their non-separability; that is, if several complements of the same verb are cliticized, they must all attach to the same predicate, either by enclisis or proclisis (the 'bandwagon' effect):[13]

(9)	a.	I Te lo voglio dare.	S	Te lo quiero dar.
	b.	Voglio dartelo.		Quiero dártelo.
	c.	*Ti voglio darlo.		*Te quiero darlo.
	d.	*Lo voglio darti		*Lo quiero darte.
		I want to give it to you.		

Restructuring verbs differ regarding other syntactic properties.[14] In particular, they can be either subject-raising verbs, or subject-control verbs (Aissen and Perlmutter 1976, Rizzi 1978, 1982). Furthermore, while these verbs generally carry some tense, aspectual, or modal information, such semantic factors are generally insufficient to determine their complex predicate behavior. Many verbs (in the same language or in a different language) with similar meanings are not restructuring verbs. For example, in Italian *volere* contrasts with *desiderare* (which cannot be used in a complex predicate, for most speakers, Napoli 1981), while *querer* and *desear* are both

[13] The Italian impersonal clitic *si 'one'*, the subject of the head verb, can be separated from clitics subcategorized by the complement verb (*Si vorrebbe farlo* 'one would-want to do it'). Similarly for the pronoun *loro*, which does not have the same properties as clitics (*Lo voglio dare loro* Lit. It I-want to give them, 'I want to give it to them'); see section 5.3.1. For more on enclisis and proclicis, see Miller and Monachesi (this volume).

[14] For some authors (e.g. Quicoli 1976), restructuring verbs are defined by the following property: their infinitive complement alternates with a subjunctive clause. This proposal is reformulated in terms of obviation by Fontana (1996b): the infinitive *vs* subjunctive complement depends on the (non-) coreference of the two subjects. But Italian verbs like *detestare* or *desiderare* have this property, yet they are not restructuring verbs.

complex predicate heads in Spanish. Furthermore, whereas movement verbs lose their locative meaning in Portuguese complex predicates, they can retain it in Spanish and Italian.

Tense		P *haver de* (future, probability), C *vaig* (past)
Modals	TO HAVE TO	I *dovere, %avere da*, S *deber (de), haber de, tener que*, P *dever, haver de*, C *deure, haver de*
	TO BE ABLE TO	I *potere*, S-P-C *poder*
	TO KNOW HOW TO (do)	I *sapere*, C *saber*
	TO WANT	I *volere, intendere*, S *querer, desear*, P *querer, tencionar, %desejar*, C *voler*
	TO SEEM	I *%sembrare*
	Conatives	I *%cercare di, tentare di, %osare, %provare a*, S *intentar, tratar de, lograr*, P *buscar, conseguir, pretender, tentar*, C *pensar, gosar*
Aspectuals	TO BE IN THE PROCESS OF (doing)	I *stare* (+ger), *stare a/per*, S *andar* (+ger), *estar* (+ger), P *estar a, andar a, ficar a*, C *estar* (+ger), *anar* (+ger)
	TO BE GOING TO (do)	I *andare a, tornare a, venire, %stare per*, S *ir a*, C *anar a, estar a punt de* , P *ir*
	TO BEGIN TO (do)	I *cominciare a, %prendere a*, S *empezar a / comenzar a*, P *começar a*, C *començar a*
	TO CONTINUE TO (do)	I *continuare a, seguitare a*, S *seguir* (+ger), P *continuar a*, C *continuar* (+ger)
	TO BE ACCUSTOMED TO (do)	S-C *soler*, P *costumar*, C *acostumar a*, I *% solere, tendere a*
	TO FINALLY (do)	S *llegar a, acertar a*, P *chegar a*, C *arribar a*, I *%finire per*
	TO BE ABOUT TO (do)	S-C *acabar de*
	TO STOP (doing)	I *finire di, %smettere di*, S *terminar de, dejar de*, C *deixar de*
	Iteratives	S *volver a*, P-C *tornar a*
Movement verbs		I *venire a, andare a, correre, tornare*, S *pasar a, venir a*, C *venir a*

Table 2: Restructuring verbs (+infinitive, unless otherwise specified)

So while they are very widespread, the temporal, modal, and aspectual interpretations of a verb are neither sufficient nor necessary properties for restructuring verbs.

In section 3, we will show that clitic climbing is not, in fact, optional, but correlates with other properties. Restructuring verbs behave either like ordinary raising or control verbs (in which case clitics do not climb) or they are the head of a complex predicate (in which case clitics do climb).

2.3 Causative verbs

Another class which manifests the criteria of complex predicates, is made up of verbs which take a nominal complement (a 'causee'), in addition to an infinitive; the causee is co-indexed or identified with the (unexpressed) subject of the infinitive. Such verbs are sometimes called 'causatives' as a whole; they belong semantically to the class of verbs of influence and perception. Only Romanian, where infinitive complements are rare, lacks this class (Romanian causatives take a subjunctive complement clause). We can contrast the infinitive complement and the complement clause:

(10) F a. J'ai entendu dire de drôles de choses.
I heard (people) say funny things.
b. J'<u>en</u> ai entendu dire.
I-CL have heard say
I heard people say some things.
c. J'ai entendu qu'on disait de drôles de choses.
I heard that people say funny things.
d. *J'<u>en</u> ai entendu qu'on disait.
I-CL have heard that people say

Verbs of influence	F *faire, laisser,* I *fare, lasciare, %insegnare,* S *hacer, dejar, mandar, ordenar, permitir,* P *fazer, %mandar, deixar,* C *fer, deixar*
Verbs of perception	F *entendre, voir,* I *intendere, sentire, udire, vedere, guardare, osservare,* S *oir, ver,* P *ouvir, sentir, ver,* C *sentir, veure.*

Table 3: 'causative' verb heads of complex predicates

These verbs (except for TO MAKE) allow for the clitic subcategorized by the infinitive verb to appear on the causative verb or the infinitive. Again, this is not a question of optional climbing, but depends on whether there is a complex predicate. In the case of an ordinary complementation, the NP occurs between the causative and the infinitive verb (and can be cliticized like any other object); the complements of the infinitive can only be cliticized on the infinitive. There is no difference with the ordinary VP complementation illustrated in (11):

(11) F a. Nous avons forcé les enfants à aller à la gare.
We forced the children to go to the station.
b. Nous les avons forcés à aller à la gare
We forced them to go to the station.
c. Nous avons forcé les enfants à y aller.
We forced the children to go there.
d. Nous les avons forcés à y aller.
e. *Nous y avons forcé les enfants à aller.
f. *Nous les y avons forcés à aller.

We illustrate the impossibility of clitic climbing in the ordinary complementation with *y* / *ci* ('there') in French and Italian, and with an object clitic in Spanish and Portuguese (which lack equivalent clitics).[15]

(12) a. F Nous verrons / laisserons les enfants aller à la gare.
I Vedremo / Lasceremo i ragazzi andare alla stazione.
We will see / let the children go to the station.
b. F Nous les verrons / les laisserons aller à la gare.
I Li vedremo / Li lasceremo andare alla stazione.
CL-we.will.see / CL-we.will.let go to the station
We will see / let them go to the station.
c. F Nous verrons /laisserons les enfants y aller.
I Vedremo / Lasceremo i ragazzi andarci.
(we) will.see / will.let the children CL-go
We will see / let the children go to there.
d. F *Nous y verrons / laisserons les enfants aller.
I *Ci vedremo / lasceremo i ragazzi andare.
(we) CL-will.see / will.let the children go

(13) a. S Mandamos / Vimos a los niños cantar la canción.
P Mandámos / Vimos os meninos cantar o fado.
We made / saw the children sing the song.
b. S Mandamos / Vimos a los niños cantarla.

15 The *a* of *a los niños* in (13a) is the mark of the accusative. Note that the examples in (13) are less convincing than those in (12): the unacceptability of (13c) could be due to the fact that a verb cannot have an object and an accusative clitic at the same time. But using a dative clitic would not offer a tight argument either, because there are independent restrictions (still poorly understood) on the raising of a dative complement of an infinitive verb (F ?? *Je lui ferai parler Paul,* 'I will make Paul talk to him', see Kayne 1975, Tasmowski 1984). The restriction in Spanish is even wider (Moore 1990a,b, Franco and Landa 1995).

P Mandámos / Vimos os meninos cantá-lo.
we.made / we.saw A the children sing-CL
We made / saw the children sing it. (= the song)

c. S *(Se) la mandamos / vimos a los niños cantar.
P *Mandámo-lo / Vimo-lo os meninos cantar.
CL-we.made / saw / we.made / saw-CL A the children sing

When there is a complex predicate, both verbs are adjacent or separated only by an adverb: they cannot be separated by the causee which must follow the infinitive verb. It is an NP if the infinitive verb is intransitive, and a 'TO NP' or 'BY NP' form if the infinitive verb is transitive.[16] A complement which the infinitive verb subcategorizes for is cliticized onto the head verb. Thus, the examples in (14) with an NP causee contrast directly with those of (12) or (13). The examples in (15) show a BY causee.

(14) a. F Nous y verrons / laisserons aller les enfants.
I Ci vedremo / lasceremo andare i ragazzi.
(we) CL-will.see / will.let go the children
We will see / let the children go there.
b. S (Se) la mandamos / vimos cantar a los niños.
CL-CL-we.made / saw sing A the children
P Mandámo-lo / Vimo-lo cantar aos meninos.
We.made-CL / saw-CL sing A.THE children
We made / saw the children sing it (the song).

(15) a. F Il a entendu chanter La Traviata par La Callas.
I Ha sentito cantare La Traviata dalla Callas.
S Ha oído cantar la Traviata por la Callas.
P Ouviu cantar La Traviata pela Callas.
He has heard sing the Traviata BY La Callas
He heard La Callas sing La Traviata.
b. F Il l'a entendu chanter par La Callas.
I L'ha sentita cantare dalla Callas.
S La ha oído cantar por la Callas.
P Ouviu-a cantar La Traviata pela Callas.
(He) CL-has heard / heard-CL sing BY La Callas
c. F *Il a entendu la chanter par La Callas.
I *Ha sentito cantarla dalla Callas.

[16] We leave aside the discussion concerning the way the causee is expressed. The relevant questions are: is the alternation between NP and TO NP determined only by the syntax (according to the transitivity of the infinitive verb), or is it (in part) semantically conditioned? Is the infinitive verb with a BY argument passive or not? Does the alternation between TO and BY reveal a structural difference or is it only semantically conditioned?

S *Ha oído cantarla por la Callas.
P *Ouviu cantá-la pela Callas.
(He) has heard CL-sing / heard-CL BY La Callas

There is, therefore, a correlation between the properties of the causee and the possibility of clitic climbing. If the causee NP appears between the two verbs, there is no complex predicate, and the clitic complement of the infinitive cannot climb. If it appears after the infinitive, a complex predicate is formed, and the clitic climbs. This correlation shows that there is no optional clitic climbing, but rather an alternation between an ordinary complementation and a complex predicate.

With the verb TO MAKE this contrast is not always available. While both structures are indeed possible for the Portuguese *fazer* or *mandar*, Italian *fare* only has the complex predicate structure. Thus (16a,b) illustrate the object-control complementation while (16c,d) illustrate the complex predicate.

(16) a. P O João não mandou os meninos cantar La Traviata.
I *Giovanni non fece i ragazzi cantare La Traviata.
(THE) John not made the children sing La Traviata
b. P O João não mandou os meninos cantá-la.
I *Giovanni non fece i ragazzi cantarla.
(THE) John not made the children sing-CL
c. P O João não mandou cantar La Traviata pelos meninos.
I Giovanni non fece cantare La Traviata ai / ?dai ragazzi.
(THE) John not made sing La Traviata TO./BY.THE children
d. P O João não a mandou cantar pelos meninos.
I Giovanni non la fece cantare ai / ?dai ragazzi.
(THE) John not CL-made sing TO.THE/ BY.THE children
John did not make the children record La Traviata / it.

In French, Spanish and Catalan, the data are not so clear: one finds clitics on the infinitive while the V-NP-Vinf sequence is not acceptable. We briefly discuss this data in section 5.3.[17]

In summary, the verbs in Table 3 can (or must) give rise to a complex predicate, and the presence or the absence of clitic climbing is, generally, correlated with the existence of a complex predicate.

---

[17] The presence of a causee NP between *hacer* and the infinitive verb may be acceptable in certain varieties of Spanish, with an intransitive infinitive. Davies (1995) and Hernanz (1999) give as well-formed the following sentences (judged archaic or poetic by our informants):
(i) S La gran tormenta hacía los arboles salir de tierra.
The great storm uprooted the trees from the ground.
(ii) S Hizo las campanas sonar. *He made the bells ring.*

2.4 Predicative verbs

Clitic climbing is also seen with verbs which take predicative complements (a noun, adjective or passive participle), and which we refer to as 'predicative verbs'.[18] Note that passive auxiliaries are predicative verbs for us (Couquaux 1979, Milner 1986, Abeillé and Godard 2000b). We distinguish between two classes, according to whether the unexpressed subject of the predicative complement is identified with the subject of the verb (subject-raising verb) or with its NP object (object-raising verb).

A list of predicative verbs which can be the head of a complex predicate is given in table 4:

Subject raising verbs	BE	F *être*, C-S-P *ser*, *estar*, R *a fi*, I *essere*, *stare*
	SEEM	F *sembler*, *paraître*, C *?semblar*, I *%sembrare*
	BECOME	F *devenir*, I *divenire*, *diventare*, R *a deveni*, P *tornar-se*, S *volverse*
	STAY	F *rester*, *demeurer*, C *quedar*, *restar*, I *restare*, *rimanere*, R *a rămâne*, P *ficar*
Object raising verbs	BELIEVE	F *croire*, *?dire*, *?trouver*, *?voir*, I *credere*, P *achar*, *considerar*, C *creure*, *imaginar*, *trobar*, S *suponer*
	KNOW	F *savoir*, C *saber*,
	RENDER	F *rendre*, C *fer*, P *ficar*, I *fare*, *rendere*, R *a face*

Table 4 : The predicative verb heads of complex predicates

The subject raising predicative verbs are often heads of complex predicates, but there is some variation from one language to another, and according to different speakers.[19] The clitics here correspond to the complements of

[18] These same verbs may also take a prepositional predicative complement (PP) but in this case clitic climbing is not possible:

(i) F Paul est contre la révision de la constitution / *<u>en</u> est contre la revision.
Paul is against the revision of the constitution / of it.

[19] The predicative verbs giving rise to a complex predicate are not exactly the same in Spanish and Catalan. In particular, verbs with a BECOME meaning do not enter into complex predicates in Catalan (*C resultar, esdevenir, posar-se, tornar-se, fer-se*), nor do RENDER-type verbs in Spanish. With reflexive verbs, where one cannot test the formation of a complex predicate by clitic-climbing (the presence of SE on the infinitive prevents clitic climbing, because of the bandwagon effect), we use the possibility of extracting the adjective without its complements (see section 4.7, example (62)):

(i) S Por más fiel que se haya vuelto a sus amigos, ...
As faithful as he has become to his friends, ...

nouns, adjectives and passive participles: they are datives, Y (F *y*, I *ci*, C *hi*) or EN (F *en*, I *ne*, C *en*). We illustrate this property with the copula, whose behavior is remarkably homogeneous in the Romance languages (in S, C, P, *ser* and *estar* behave the same way, despite there being a semantic difference between them).

(17) F Jean lui était fidèle. P O João era-lhe fiel.
I Giovanni le era fedele. S Juan le era fiel.
R Ion îi era credincios. C En Joan li era fidel.
John was faithful to her.

The behavior of object raising predicative verbs is less stable and homogeneous. Overall, predicative causative verbs (of the RENDER type) allow clitic climbing more easily than predicative verbs denoting a propositional attitude (of the BELIEVE; KNOW types). The acceptability in case of clitic climbing is improved if the second predicate is not separated from the head verb by another complement, an ordering constraint which results possibly from discourse factors (see Cordin and Calabrese 1988, for Italian).[20]

(18) F a. On rendra Jean sensible à ces arguments.
a′. On y rendra sensible Jean / On l'y rendra sensible.
a″. %On y rendra Jean sensible.
One will render Jean / him sensitive to these arguments / to them.
R b. O face pe Maria ostilă lui Ion.
b′. I-o face pe Maria ostilă.
b″. I-o face ostilă pe Maria.
He makes Maria hostile to Ion / to him.
C c. En Pere fa en Joan capaç d'aquestes coses i de moltes més.
c′. ?En Pere en fa en Joan capaç.
c″ ?El en fa capaç en Pere.
Pere makes Joan / him capable of these things / of them and of many others.
I d. Crede Giovanni fedele a Maria.
d′. Le crede fedele Giovanni.
d″. %Le crede Giovanni fedele.
He believes Giovanni faithful to Maria / to her.

In Portuguese and Spanish, clitic climbing is only natural if the object is cliticized, or relativized, hence the contrasts in (19):

(19) a. P Eu considero o João hostil à Maria.
S Supongo a Juan hostil a María.

[20] The clitic *o* doubles the object in (18R).

I consider John hostile to Maria.

b. P *Eu considero-lhe o João hostil / hostil o João.
   S *Le supongo a Juan hostil / hostil a Juan.
   I consider John hostile to her.

c. P ?À Maria, eu considero-lho hostil.
   S ?A María, se lo supongo hostil.
   To Maria, I consider him hostile.

d. P O João, que eu lhe considero hostil, ...
   S Juan, que le supongo hostil, ...
   John, who I consider hostile to her, ...

3 Other properties of monoclausality

A certain number of other properties are correlated with clitic climbing, the phenomenon which we have been using as a criterion for the identification of a complex predicate. These correlations are especially clear with restructuring verbs, which allow us to compare two different complementations. Generally, the different Romance languages behave here in the same way. The properties in question are the formation of the two 'long' passive structures and the occurrence of complex predicates in bounded dependency structures.[21]

3.1 Middle-passive SE

Romance languages contain a SE construction, called the 'middle passive', where the subject corresponds to the object of the corresponding active construction, with an interpretation resembling that of the passive.[22]

(20) F a. On repasse facilement ces chemises.
   One irons these shirts easily.

b. Ces chemises se repassent facilement.
   These shirts SE-iron easily
   One can easily iron these shirts

Restructuring verbs have middle-passive forms, whose subject corresponds to the NP object of the complement verb.[23] This is impossible with ordinary

[21] One can find the main observations in Rizzi (1982), Burzio (1986), Skytte et al. (1991), Monachesi (1999a) for Italian, Aissen and Perlmutter (1976, 1983), Zagona (1988), Bordelois (1988), Moore (1990a, b), Gómez Torrego (1999) for Spanish, Quicoli (1976), Gonçalvès (1999) for Portuguese, Alsina (1996, 2002), Gavarró and Laca (2002) for Catalan, Kayne (1975), Rouveret and Vergnaud (1980), Legendre (1987), Abeillé *et al.* (1998) for French.

[22] This form is subject to interpretative constraints, which can differ according to the language. In general, one can distinguish between the property denotation, as illustrated in (21), (24), and the event denotation, as illustrated in (22), (23) (see Ruwet 1972, Zribi-Hertz 1982, Fellbaum and Zribi-Hertz 1989).

verbs. We illustrate this contrast with the restructuring verb TO BE ABLE TO and the ordinary verb TO APPEAR. The R auxiliary *a putea* behaves like restructuring verbs.

(21) a. I Queste camicie si possono stirare facilmente.
P Estas camisas podem-se passar facilmente.
S Estas camisas se pueden planchar fácilmente.
C Aquestes camises es poden planxar fàcilment.
R Cămăşile acestea se pot călca uşor.
These shirts SE-can / can-SE iron easily
These shirts can be ironed easily.

b. I *Queste camicie si paiono stirare facilmente.
P *Estas camisas parecem-se passar facilmente.
S *Estas camisas se parecen planchar fácilmente.
C *Aquestes camises es semblen planxar fàcilment.
These shirts SE-appear / appear-SE iron easily
These shirts appear to be ironed easily

A cliticized argument of the infinitive verb must be on the head of the complex predicate (which hosts SE), whether it is an ordinary (22a) (Rizzi 1982:16) or a doubling clitic (22b) (Aissen and Perlmutter 1976/1983).[24]

(22) I a. %Queste case <u>gli si</u> vogliono vendere a caro prezzo.
These houses CL.dat-SE-want sell at high price
a′. *Queste case <u>si</u> vogliono vender<u>gli</u> a caro prezzo.
These houses SE-want sell-CL.dat at high price
They want to sell these houses at a very high price.

S b. Estas casas <u>se le</u> quieren vender al general.
These houses SE-CL.dat -want sell TO.THE general
b′. *Estas casas <u>se</u> quieren vender<u>le</u> al general.
These houses SE-want sell-CL.dat TO.THE general
They want to sell theses houses to the general.

Causatives also have middle passive forms, whose subject corresponds to the object of the infinitive verb. We illustrate this with MAKE-TO constructions.

(23) S <u>Se le</u> han hecho construir nuevas casas a este arquitecto.
C <u>Se li</u> han fet construir noves cases a aquest arquitecte.

[23] This property does not make sense for tense auxiliaries. In Romanian, one finds the SE middle-passive with *a putea* ('can') but not with *a avea de* ('should').

[24] Italian speakers in general do not accept this construction as easily as has been claimed. Some only accept (22a) if the NP has some prosodic salience; we leave aside the question of whether this corresponds to a syntactic and / or a discursive property.

I Si sono fatte costruire nuove case a quest' architetto.
SE-(CL.dat)-have / are made build new houses TO this architect

P Mandaram-se construir novas casas a este arquitecto.
made-SE build new houses TO this architect
We made this architect build new houses.

French has a narrower usage of the middle passive with *faire*. In particular, it only seems possible with *faire* + intransitive verb, hence the contrast between *par* and *à* in (24a); [25] and, it is only regular with a generic subject and a modal interpretation (Koenig, 1994):

(24) F a. Une maison, ça se fait construire par / *à un bon architecte.
A house must be built by a good architect.
b. ?Un labrador, ça se fait courir tous les jours.
A Labrador has got to run every day.
c. *De nouvelles maisons se sont fait(es) construire par cet architecte.
New houses SE-were made build by this architect

3.2 The periphrastic passive

The periphrastic passive relies on the passive auxiliary. It is 'long' when an argument of the non-finite verb is the subject of the passive participle and passive auxiliary. It is possible with a causative verb under certain conditions, except for French:[26]

(25) F a. *Ce livre a été fait lire par Jean / à Jean.
This book has been made read BY / TO John
John was made to read the book.
b. *L'architecte a été fait intervenir.
The architect was made to intervene.
c. *L'enfant a été fait étudier longtemps.
The child was made to study for a long time.

As noted by Alsina (1996: 187), the infinitive verb with a passive *fer* in Catalan is either transitive or unaccusative, but cannot be unergative (26). The same seems to be true in Portuguese (27), though the construction is

---

[25] While FAIRE-À takes a transitive infinitive verb, FAIRE-PAR takes an intransitive (passive) infinitive verb (see Abeillé *et al.* 1997, 1998). There is also a reflexive form of *faire* with a passive meaning (*Jean s'est fait piquer par une abeille* 'John got himself stung by a wasp'), but it does not have the expected interpretation of the middle SE (≠ *On a fait piquer Jean par une abeille* 'One made John stung by a wasp'), see Tasmowski (1985), Tasmowski and van Oevelem (1987), Kupferman (1995).

[26] This passivization was possible in French, see Damourette and Pichon (1911-1933, tome III, section 1102), but is no longer well-formed today (*pace* Zubizarreta 1985:285, who gives it as good with an unergative verb).

less acceptable generally. This contrast does not exist in Italian if one accepts Burzio's examples (28).[27] Hernanz (1999) gives some examples of the passive as acceptable in Spanish:

(26) C a. El pont ha estat fet enderrocar per / a un specialist. (Alsina 1996)
The bridge has been made demolish BY / TO a specialist
A specialist was made to demolish the bridge.
b. Els conills van ser fets sortir del cau.
The rabbits were made to go out of their den.
c. *El nen ha estat fet treballar molt.
The child was made to work a lot.

(27) P a. ?Este livro foi-nos mandado ler pelo Mário.
This book was-CL.dat made read BY.THE Mário
Mario made us read this book.
b. ??O arquitecto foi mandado intervir.
The architect was made to intervene.
c. *A criança foi mandada estudar muito.
The child was made to work a lot.

(28) I a. Questo libro è stato fatto leggere a / da Mario. (Burzio 1986)
This book has been made to.read TO / BY Mario
b. L'architetto fu fatto intervenire.
The architect was made to intervene.
c. Il ragazzo è stato fatto lavorare molto.
The child was made to work a lot.

(29) S a. El testigo fue hecho comparecer ante el tribunal. (Hernanz 1999)
The witness was made to appear in front of the tribunal.
b. El palacio fue hecho reconstruir por el presidente.
The palace was made (to be) rebuilt by the president

Restructuring verbs generally cannot be passivized (30). However, one does find a few aspectual verbs in the passive in Spanish (*acabar de, terminar de,* Aissen and Perlmutter 1976/1983), and in Italian (*cominciare, continuare, finire,* Burzio 1986):

[27] Our Italian and Portuguese informants do not accept long periphrastic passives as easily as is generally claimed. The Spanish data are not completetely stable. This uncertainty may be linked to the fact that Spanish speakers prefer to use the middle-passive rather than the periphrastic passive.

(30) S *Esta madera es querida cortar.
I *Questo legno è voluto tagliare.
C *Aquesta fusta és volguda tallar.
P *Esta madeira é querida cortar.
This wood is wanted to carve

(31) S a. Estas paredes están siendo terminadas de pintar.
These walls are being finished being painted.
I b. %Il palazzo fu cominciato a costruire sotto Carlo V.
The palace began to be built under Charles V.

Interestingly, the same verbs also have passive participles in French (32a), with speakers' variation (see the '%' notation), although French does not have restructuring verbs in a general way. Note that clitics cannot appear on the infinitive, which shows that these are restructuring verb forms (see examples (32b,c) from Cinque 2005):

(32) F a. %Ces maisons ont été finies de construire l'an dernier.
These houses were finished to build last year
I b. I pezzi gli furono finiti di consegnare l'anno dopo.
c. *I pezzi furono finiti di consegnargli l'anno dopo.
The plays were finished to deliver to him the year after

These observations can be interpreted as follows. The passive participle of some restructuring aspectual verbs (in their complex predicate use) proves to be resilient: not only does it still exist in Spanish and Italian, while restructuring verbs in a general way cannot be passivized, but it remains in French when restructuring verbs have disappeared.

3.3 Occurrence in bounded dependencies

The preposition +VP*inf* complements of adjectives from the EASY class (F *facile* 'easy', *important* 'important', *impossible* 'impossible', etc.) and TO +VP*inf* modifiers of nouns, are bounded dependency structures in the Romance languages. We take our examples from the adjective complement. The highest V*inf* has a null complement, identified with the subject if the adjective is a predicative complement, or with the noun modified by the adjective:

(33) F Une carte difficile à faire
I Una carta difficile da fare
S Un mapa dificil de hacer
C Un mapa difícil de fer
A map difficult to make

Unlike ordinary infinitive constructions (34), complex predicates (35), can appear within this complement (see Aissen and Perlmutter 1976/1983, Rizzi 1978, Kayne 1975, Legendre 1987):[28]

(34) F *Ces cartes seront difficiles [à persévérer à faire].
I *Queste cartine gli saranno difficili [da insistere a fare].
S *Estos mapas les van a resultar dificiles [de perseverar a hacer].
C *Aquests maps resultaran difícils [de persistir a fer].
These maps will be difficult (for them) to persist on making.

(35) a. F Ces cartes seront difficiles à faire faire.
These maps will be difficult to get (people) to make.
b. I Queste cartine gli saranno difficili [da cominciare a fare].
S Estos mapas les van a resultar dificiles [de empezar a hacer].
C Aquests maps resultaran difícils [de començar a fer].
These maps will be difficult to begin to make.
c. I Queste cartine gli saranno difficili da cominciar<u>ci</u> a spiegare.
S ?Estos mapas les van a resultar dificiles [de empezar<u>nos</u> a explicar].
C ?Aquests maps resultaran difícils [de començar-<u>nos</u> a comentar].
These maps will be difficult to begin to explain to us.

(36) I *Queste cartine gli saranno difficili da cominciar a spiegar<u>ci</u>.
S *Estos mapas les van a resultar dificiles [de empezar a explicar<u>nos</u>].
C *Aquests maps els vénen a resultar difíciles [de començar a comentar-<u>nos</u>].

The contrast between a control verb which does not allow clitic climbing (34) and complex predicates which do (35) can be explained in the following way: the missing NP is indeed the object of the highest verb in a complex predicate, while it cannot be in ordinary control verb constructions. Note that, if the complement verb hosts a clitic, it cannot be part of a complex predicate, hence the contrast between (35c), with a raised clitic, and (36), with a downstairs clitic.[29]

---

[28] There is no equivalent structure in Romanian. We have not obtained clear judgments for Portuguese. In French, some speakers accept examples such as *%un livre difficile à pouvoir <u>te</u> résumer pour demain*, lit. a book difficult to be able to summarize to you for tomorrow (examples noted in Abeillé *et al.* 1998, and in Cinque 2002).

[29] Note, however, that certain clitics (resumptive clitics in particular) can appear on the second infinitive in Spanish and Catalan (Moore 1990b). For a brief discussion, see section 5.3.

3.4 Summary and analysis

The properties discussed in this section are summarized in Table 5.

	clitic climbing	middle-passive SE	periphrastic passive	occurrence in bounded dependencies
French	auxiliaries, causatives, predicatives	causatives (restrictions)	no	yes
Italian	auxiliaries, restructuring Vs, causatives, predicatives	causatives, restructuring Vs	causatives, some restructuring Vs (aspectuals)	yes
Catalan	auxiliaries, restructuring Vs, causatives, predicatives	causatives, restructuring Vs	causatives (restrictions)	yes
Spanish	auxiliaries, restructuring Vs, causatives, predicatives	causatives, restructuring Vs	causatives (restrictions) some restructuring Vs (aspectuals)	yes
Portuguese	auxiliaries, restructuring Vs, causatives, predicatives	causatives, restructuring Vs	causatives	–
Romanian	auxiliaries, predicatives	auxiliaries (except *a avea de*)	no	–

Table 5: Monoclausal properties of Romance complex predicates

Overall, the different languages behave in a remarkably homogeneous manner. The differences are mainly due to the absence of a structure or of a class of words in a given language, such as the absence of causatives in Romanian or restructuring verbs in French. There can also be certain restrictions that a language imposes on certain forms; such are the restrictions on the middle-passive SE-*faire* in French, and the passivization of *fer* in Catalan. Periphrastic passivization raises some questions: why is it that in general causatives but not restructuring verbs can be passivized, and why is

French distinct from the other Romance languages in this respect? For some discussion, see Zubizarreta (1985), S. Rosen (1989).

More generally, it seems that there is a general evolution towards the elimination not of complex predicates *per se*, but rather of the dual possibility associated with some verbs, with the possible exception of Portuguese. Thus, in French modals and aspectuals are ordinary raising or control verbs, while the specialization of *faire* as the head of a complex predicate is well under way. In Italian *fare* is always the head of a complex predicate, and it seems that restructuring verbs may undergo the same evolution. If passivization is perceived as a property of ordinary verbs, then the loss of this possibility would reinforce the classification of a verb as involving a complex predicate.

It is clear that complex predicates do not form a morphological unit, since one can insert elements between the two predicates (see section 4). They form a single syntactic unit in some respects: they behave like a simple verb with respect to all the properties already illustrated.[30] More precisely, such properties are explained if the defining property is the following: the head of a complex predicate inherits the complements subcategorized for by the predicate complement:

(i) Clitic climbing follows without any special rules, and obeys the general rule that arguments are cliticized on the verb which subcategorizes for them; clitic climbing is the manifestation of the general behavior of complements in complex predicates.

(ii) Passivization (middle or periphrastic) applies to the head verb of the complex predicate, characterized by this extended valence. Hence, the object subcategorized by the predicate complement is the subject of the passivized head of the complex predicate simply because it is the object of the complex predicate verb in the active construction.

(iii) The missing NP in the complements of adjectives of the EASY type is the object of the highest infinitive verb. In particular, it is the object of the head of a complex predicate.

Therefore, the data indicate that the complement predicate in a complex predicate construction transmits its arguments to the head. Depending on the grammatical framework, this phenomenon is called 'inheritance', ' argument composition', 'delegation', 'union' or 'valence fusion': complex predicates form an argumental (or functional) unit.

---

[30] As A. Rouveret has pointed out (p.c.), we might say that complex predicates form a single inflection domain, and that the clitic is realized on the head of this domain. But note that it is the syntax which determines if there is an inflection domain; there is no morphological clue in a general way: with restructuring verbs, the morphological properties are the same, whether the clitic is raised or not. The only morpho-syntactic correlation is offered by Portuguese, where inflected infinitives do not enter into complex predicates (Rouveret 1999).

This analysis allows us to explain how the verbs entering into complex predicates are a subset of 'raising' or 'control' verbs, in other words, how the non-finite verb is always unsaturated for its subject. If one assumes a hierarchy of accessibility of functions, we predict that in order to be able to inherit complements (of the non-finite verb), the verbs entering into complex predicates must firstly share the subject of the complement predicate, realized as the subject of the head verb in the case of auxiliaries or restructuring verbs, or as its object in the case of the causatives and verbs of perception.[31]

The properties mentioned thus far lead to a valence fusion or argument composition analysis, and say nothing about constituent structure. More generally, the analysis in terms of argument composition is compatible with several choices of syntactic structure. This is especially clear within frameworks like the phrase structure framework HPSG (see Pollard and Sag 1994, Sag et al. 2003), or Lexical Functional Grammar LFG (see Bresnan 1982, 2001), which represent structure and valence independently. It is this choice of structure that we turn to now.

4 Structural Properties

We turn to a different set of properties, which, unlike the previous ones, have not been systematically studied in the literature thus far, and show different patterns of behaviors. They will allow us to differentiate complex predicates in terms of their syntactic constituent structure.[32]

Three kinds of structures – which have all been proposed in the literature – are *a priori* possible for the complex predicate; see Figure 1.

In A, the verbal complex structure, the two predicates form a syntactic constituent; see Emonds (1978) for the French auxiliaries; Radford (1977) and Rizzi (1982) for Italian auxiliaries and restructuring verbs; Zagona (1988) for the tense auxiliary in Spanish, Monachesi (1999b, 2005) for the Romanian tense auxiliaries. In B, the flat structure, the head of the complex

[31] By the sharing of the subject, we mean that the subject of the non-finite V is (i) non-expressed locally and (ii) co-indexed or identified with an argument (subject or complement) of the verbal head of the complex predicate.

[32] The case of Catalan is put to one side, due to the high degree of variation in that language with respect to the problem at hand; see section 6.4.

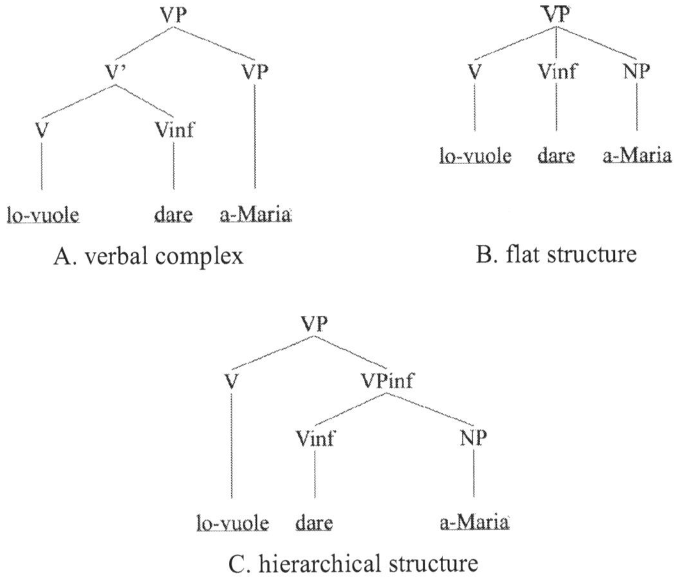

Figure 1: Three possible structures for complex predicates

predicate takes a lexical predicate and the complements this predicate subcategorizes for, as its own complements; see Legaré and Rollin (1976), Abeillé and Godard (1996, 2002) for French auxiliaries, Legendre (1987), Morin (1987), Miller (1992) for French causatives, Abeillé *et al.* (1998) for French auxiliaries and causatives; Aissen and Perlmutter (1976/1983) for Spanish restructuring verbs; Ionescu (1996) for the Romanian *a putea*, Monachesi (1999a,b, 2005) for those of Italian and the Romanian *a putea*; for the Romance languages in general, Davies and Rosen (1988). In C, the hierarchical structure, the head of the complex predicate takes a phrasal complement of which the second predicate is the head. Bear in mind that the difference between sentence/IP and VP is not relevant here, only the type of structure counts; for the last structure, see Kayne (1975), Rouveret and Vergnaud (1980), Tasmowski (1985) for French causatives; Burzio (1986), Bordelois (1988), Zagona (1988), Moore (1990a), Cinque (2005) for the Italian and or Spanish causatives and restructuring verbs; Salvi (1980), Pollock (1989), Miller (1992) for Italian and French auxiliaries; Dobrovie-Sorin (1994) for auxiliaries and modals in Romanian; Picallo (1990) and Alsina (1996) for the Catalan modals and causatives; Rochette (1990),

Lema and Rivero (1992), Andrews and Manning (1999) for Romance complex predicates generally.[33]

Our analysis is as follows. All three types of structure appear in the Romance languages: the C structure for the constructions with predicative verbs (in all the Romance languages), and structure A or B, according to the language, for the other types of complex predicate. We put the predicative verb constructions aside for the moment (see section 4.7).

4.1 Constituency test: Preposing

Preposing is generally judged to be a good test of constituency; by 'preposed constituent', we mean the initial constituent in Topicalization structures (with a corresponding missing constituent in the sentence) and in Left Dislocation structures (with a clitic or strong pronoun in the sentence). The sequences which follow the heads of complex predicates, composed of the second predicate and of the complements it subcategorizes for, cannot be preposed.[34] We illustrate this phenomenon here with the auxiliaries, which always enter into complex predicates:

---

[33] The flat structure is suggested rather than defended in studies in relational grammar, which stresses grammatical functions rather than structures (but see Aissen and Perlmutter 1976/1983). We leave aside the analysis of the causee, and we simplify certain analyses relying on movement rules (the structures resulting from movement in Zubizarreta 1985, and Guasti 1994 for instance are not completely clear).

[34] One sometimes finds other judgments concerning the Topicalization of the participle or of the infinitive verb with its complements. For Spanish and Romanian, (i) and (ii) are given as good in Davies (1995), and Lema and Rivero (1992), respectively:

(i) S Juana dijo que cocinaría temprano, y terminado de cocinar, ya había cuanda llegamos.
J. said that she would cook quickly, and finished cooking, she already had when we arrived.

(ii) R Citi cartea, Maria poate. *Read the book, Maria may*

Since these examples are consistently disallowed by all our informants, we consider these judgments to be mistaken. The situation is more complicated for Italian. A participle (with auxiliaries) with its complements, and even sometimes the infinitive verb (with a restructuring verb) with its complements, is given as good in Cinque (2005) (who talks about 'Focalization', cf. also Salvi 1980), and accepted by certain speakers:

(iii) I %Mangiato la torta non ho. *Eaten the pastry, I have not*
(context : a model says to herself 'Mangiato la torta non ho, quindi non posso essere ingrassata' *'Eaten the pastry, I have not, hence I cannot have gained weight'*)

(iv) I %Rubato la macchina gli hanno. *Stolen the car they have to-him*
(context : someone reports the actions of some wrongdoers 'Potevano limitarsi a spaventarlo, invece rubato la macchina gli hanno', They could (have) merely frighten him, instead they have stolen the car from him).

We leave aside the variation between Italian speakers, considering that (37) illustrates the main system. Note that, even for speakers who accept (iii) and (iv), cleft sentences never allow unsaturated verbs in focus. We leave the contrast between the two structures aside.

(37) F a. *Lu ce livre, vraiment, Jean n'a pas / ne l'a pas.
I b. *Letto questo libro, Giovanni non (lo) ha, veramente.
S c. *Leído este libro, Juan no ha, de verdad.
P d. *Lido este livro, o João não tem decerto.
R e. *Citit această carte, Ion nu a, în realitate.
Read this book, truly, John has not.

As shown by restructuring verbs, there is a correlation between clitic climbing and the impossibility of preposing the sequence 'non-finite verb + complements' (Rizzi 1982 for Italian, Aissen and Perlmutter 1976/1983 for Spanish).[35]

(38) Does Paul want to speak to Mary ?
P – Falar à Maria, quer com certeza (mas não quer falar à mãe dela).
I – Parlare a Maria, certamente lo vuole.
S – Hablarle a María, seguramente quiere (pero no a su madre).
Speak to Mary, he certainly wants to (but he does not want to speak to her mother).

(39) Does Paul want to speak to Mary ?
P – *Falar, quer-lhe / quer à Maria com certeza (mas não quer falar à mãe dela).
I – *Parlare, certamente glielo vuole / lo vuole a Maria.
S – *Hablar, le quiere / quiere a ella seguro (pero no mucho tiempo).

This contrast can receive two kinds of explanation: structural or semantic. In the first approach, it is due to an alternation between two structures: a complex predicate or an ordinary complement structure. In the latter case, the complement is a VP, and it can be preposed as in (38). If there is a complex predicate, the complement verb does not form a constituent with the complements it subcategorizes for and the sequence cannot be preposed (39). In the semantic approach, adopted in Lema and Rivero (1992) and Andrews and Manning (1999), the complement is always a saturated phrase (a VP), and the contrast must find another explanation, which they suggest is semantic or informational.

Lema and Rivero (1992) contrast 'weak auxiliaries', like the tense auxiliaries, which do not allow preposing, with 'strong auxiliaries', like modals, which do. In their analysis, the contrast is due to the presence or absence of theta role assignment on the complement: preposing requires association with a theta role, and only the strong auxiliaries are able to assign such a

[35] Rizzi (1982) observes the contrast based on cleft sentences and wh-movement structures in Italian (whose results are more homogeneous than those of Topicalization or Focalization, see note 34). Topicalization as in (40a) is judged to be a colloquial style in Portuguese.

theta-role. The formation of a complex predicate is correlatecd with a semantic property, the 'strength' of the head verb, responsible for theta role assignment. The problem here is that this semantic property is not independently justified. Since restructuring verbs can be, but do not have to be the head of a complex predicate, we expect them to be associated with two different strengths, in order to account for the contrast between (38) and (39). We would like evidence for this. In addition, the strength difference has to be correlated with the contrastive properties that have been discussed in the preceding section (clitic climbing, long passives, occurrence in bounded dependencies).

In Andrews and Manning (1999), who work in Lexical Functional Grammar, Romance complex predicates differ functionally rather than structurally from ordinary verbal complements. Structurally, the complements subcategorized by the second predicate are realized locally (within the VP complement, hence they adopt structure C), but their grammatical function is shared by the head verb. For instance, the object of the second predicate is also the object of the head verb. The contrast between (38) and (39) is attributed to the incompatibility between preposing and function sharing (due to some semantic or informational property). As explained in section 3, we agree that there is something like function sharing in complex predicates. Thus, the question is whether there is also a structural difference with ordinary verbs or not.

Andrews and Manning's analysis encounters a serious problem when we consider the behavior of the copula (for more, see section 4.7). In that case, not only can the sequence of the predicate and its complements be preposed (as in (38)), but the predicate without its complements can also be preposed (unlike in (39)) (Abeillé and Godard 1996 for French, Bosque 1999 for Spanish). It is worth noting that the data is identical in all the Romance languages (Abeillé and Godard 2000b):

(40) Is Paul faithful (to his friends)?

a. F – Fidèle à ses amis, Paul l'est plus qu'à ses convictions politiques.
Faithful to his friends, Paul is more than to his political convictions

I – ?Fedele ai suoi amici, Paolo (lo) è più che alle sue idee politiche

S – Fiel a sus amigos, Pablo lo es más que a sus convicciones políticas.

P Fiel aos amigos, o Paulo é-o mais (do) que às convicções políticas.

b. R Credincios prietenilor, mai mult decât ideilor sale politice, acesta este Paul!
Faithful to.his.friends, much more than to.the.ideas his politcal, that's Paul

(41) a. F Fidèle, Paul l'est plus à ses amis qu'à ses convictions politiques.
I Fedele, Paolo (lo) è più ai suoi amici che alle sue idee politiche.
S Fiel, Pablo lo es más a sus amigos que a sus convicciones políticas.
P Fiel, o Paulo é-o mais aos amigos (do) que às convicções políticas.
Faithful, (THE) Paul is more to his friends than to his political convictions

b. R Credincios, Paul le este mai mult prietenilor decât ideilor sale politice.
Faithful, Paul is much more to his friends than to his political ideas

In (40), the whole predicative complement is preposed, while only its head is in (41), leaving its complements behind. This data directly contradicts Andrews and Manning's assumption, since preposing is clearly compatible with unsaturation of the preposed constituent. Their proposal could be rescued if it were shown that the semantic or informational constraint responsible for this incompatibility in (39) was absent in (41). But it seems problematic to suggest a different semantics for preposing according to the type of verb whose complement is preposed.

We conclude that there is no satisfactory explanation of the constrast between (38) and (39) which is not based on a structural difference. Anticipating somewhat, we explain our analysis of the data. There are two constraints on preposed material: first, it must form a constituent; second, following the weight theory in Abeillé and Godard (2000a, 2004), it is non-light. Abeillé and Godard propose that linguistic expressions, words and phrases, are associated with a syntactic feature 'weight', whose values are light and non-light. Phrases, generally, are non-light, and only non-light expressions can be pronominalized or extracted, hence, preposed (see also sections 4.7, 5.2).

In complex predicates, the complements of the second predicate are inherited by the head verb, where inheritance implies both a structural and a functional difference with ordinary constructions. Tense auxiliaries enter into structure A or B; hence, the sequence of the participle and its subcategorized complements fails to form a constituent, violating the first constraint on preposing, hence the data in (37). With restructuring verbs either there is no complex predicate (in which case we have structure C), or there is a complex predicate (in which case we have structure A or B). The second verb and its complements form a (non-light) constituent in the first case, but not in the second, hence the contrast in (38)-(39).

The copula is interesting. On the one hand, the predicative complement can be saturated or not, as with restructuring verbs. On the other hand, the two cases are not distinguished in the same way as with restructuring verbs: the predicate complement is always phrasal (or non-light), whether it is saturated or not. Accordingly, it cannot enter into structure A or B, which both require it to be light.

4.2 Presence of a marker

An argument which is sometimes advanced in favor of the hierarchical structure C of Figure 1 is the fact that the non-finite verb in a complex predicate can be preceded by various markers (I *a*, *di*, *per*, S *a*, *de*, *que*, P *a*, R *de*) that have been analyzed as phrase markers (rather than the head of a PP).[36]

(42) a. I Gianni comincia a capirlo.
S Juan comienza a comprenderlo.
b. I Gianni lo comincia a capire.
S Juan lo comienza a comprender.
John begins to understand it.

In fact, this data does not show that the complement forms a phrase: these markers should be analyzed as marking a lexical verb rather than a VP. There are two arguments to this effect. First, no adverb can be inserted between the marker and the infinitive (only negation is possible); second, the marker fails to have wide scope over a coordination of sequences of 'non-finite V + complements' at least for part of the speakers (the marker must be repeated):[37]

---

[36] We use the expression 'marker' as a cover term, in order to avoid a discussion concerning their category (as preposition or not).

[37] An example cited by Andrews and Manning (1999) in favor of the hierarchical structure C (borrowed from Rizzi 1982) is (i):

(i) I ?Non ti saprei che dire.
Not to.you-I.would.know what to.say

(ii) I *Non ti saprei che cosa dire.
Not to.you-I.would.know what thing to.say
I would not know what to say to you

As long as this clitic climbing is limited to interrogatives introduced by *che* (which has the same clitic pronoun properties as the French interrogative *que*), and not allowed for interrogatives introduced by an interrogative phrase (*che cosa*), it is compatible with a flat structure, where '*che + V*' forms a verbal complement at the V° level, while '*che cosa + V*' does not.

(43) I a. Gianni lo comincia a scrivere per se stesso e a illustrare con molti particolari.
John is beginning to write it for himself and to illustrate it with many details.
a′. *Gianni lo comincia a scrivere per se stesso e illustrare con molti particolari.
S b. Dejó de leer el periódico y de escuchar la radio.
He stopped reading the newspaper and listening to the radio.
b′. %Dejó de leer el periódico y escuchar la radio.

4.3 Scope over a coordination

The coordination properties of the complements in complex predicate constructions are the following.[38] There is no syntactic constraint on the lexical coordination of non-finite verbs, as illustrated with auxiliaries in (44):[39]

(44) F a. Jean a acheté et lu ce livre.
I b. Giovanni ha comprato e letto questo libro.
S c. Juan ha comprado y leído este libro.
R d. Ion a cumpărat şi citit această carte.
John has bought and read this book.
P e. O João tem comprado e lido este jornal.
John has bought and read this newspaper (regularly).

There is more of a contrast when we consider the coordination of sequences of non-finite verbs and their complements without repetition of the main verb. With auxiliaries and restructuring verbs, this is possible in French, Italian, and Portuguese.[40] In Romanian, there is a difference between tense and aspect auxiliaries, which do not allow coordination, and the modals *a putea, a avea de*, which do allow it (Monachesi 1999b), hence the contrast between (45e) and (46a). In Spanish, there is speakers' variation: some speakers accept and some speakers do not accept such coordination.

(45) F a. Jean a battu les oeufs et fait la crème.
I b. Giovanni ha sbattuto gli albumi e fatto la crema.
John has beaten the whites and made the cream.
c. Giovanni lo vuole comprare subito e dare a Maria.

[38] See, e.g., for French, Abeillé and Godard (1996, 2002); for Romanian, Barbu (1999), Monachesi (1999b); for the Romance languages generally, Andrews and Manning (1999).

[39] The slightly different Portuguese example takes into account the (iterative) interpretation of the tense used.

[40] Some Italian speakers require the events denoted by the two participles to collectively form a 'complex event'. A comparable constraint exists in Romanian with modals, and also in Spanish for those speakers of the variety (S2) which accepts some such coordination. Hence, even for speakers of S2, not all examples are equally acceptable.

John CL.ACC-wants buy immediately and give to Maria.
P d. O João tem comprado este jornal e lido o caderno económico.
THE John has bought this journal and read the economics page
R e. ?Ion poate cumpăra această carte şi citi primul capitol.
John may buy this book and read the first chapter

(46) a. R *Ion a cumpărat această carte şi citit primul capitol.
John has bought this book and read the first chapter.
S %Juan ha comprado este libro y leído el primer capítulo.
b. R Ion a cumpărat această carte şi a citit primul capitol.
S Juan ha comprado este libro y ha leído el primer capítulo.

For Romanian speakers as well as those Spanish speakers who do not accept (46a), the tense auxiliary must be repeated. The structure is different from that in (45), where the coordination is good. Since the speakers' judgments seem to be consistent, we can speak of two varieties of Spanish. We will call Spanish-1 or S1 the variety which does not accept the coordination of sequences of 'non finite V + complements' in a general way, and Spanish-2 or S2 the other one. In S1, examples (47a,b), where the clitic is raised and shared (there is a complex predicate), contrast with (47c), where the clitic is repeated on each complement verb (there is no complex predicate):[41,42]

(47) S1 a. *Le quiso comentar el artículo y hacer algunas observaciones.
He wanted to comment the article for him and make him some observations.
b. *Le volvió a pedir un autógrafo y a hacer proposiciones.
He started again to ask him for an autograph and to make propositions to him.
S2 a′. Le quiso comentar el artículo y hacer algunas observaciones.
b′. Le volvió a pedir un autógrafo y a hacer proposiciones.

---

[41] The following coordination is also acceptable in Spanish, with the clitic repeated on the second verb complement:

(i) S Juan le quiere comprar este libro y leerle el primer capítulo.
John CL-wants to.buy this book and read-CL the first chapter
John wants to buy him this book and read him the first chapter

This is a coordination of two finite VPs, with deletion of the second *quiere* rather than that of two non-finite complements of a restructuring verb (A. Alsina, p.c.).

[42] Even for speakers of the S1 variety, it seems that the causative *hacer* can have scope over the coordination of intransitive infinitives.

(i) S Juan hace dormir a los más pequeños y jugar a los más grandes.
Juan makes the smaller ones sleep and the bigger ones play

This seems to be the remnant of an ordinary complementation, see also note 17 and section 5.3.

S c. Juan quiere comprar<u>lo</u> mañana y dárs<u>elo</u> a María.
Juan wants buy-CL.ACC tomorrow and give-CL.DAT-CL.ACC to Maria
Juan wants to buy it tomorrow and to give it to Maria.

The causatives (and verbs of perception) do not differ from auxiliaries and restructuring verbs. Thus, they scope over a coordination of infinitive verbs with their arguments in French, Italian and Portuguese:

(48) a. F Jean fait dormir les petits et jouer les grands.
John makes the little ones sleep and the big ones play.
I Giovanni fa dormire i più piccoli e giocare i più grandi.
P O João manda dormir os pequenos e brincar os grandes.
b. F Je ferai faire ses devoirs et prendre son bain à Marie.
I will make Marie do her homework and take a bath.
I Farò finire i compiti e fare il bagno a Maria.
P Mandarei fazer os deveres e tomar um banho à Maria.

Coordination therefore establishes an initial division of the Romance languages; in French, Italian, Portuguese and one variety of Spanish, all the verbal heads of complex predicates take scope over a coordination of non-finite verbs with their complements. In the other variety of Spanish, this scope-taking is not allowed in a general way. In Romanian, not all verbs behave in the same way: the verbs *a putea* and *a avea* allow wide scope, but the tense auxiliaries do not.

4.4 Adverbs occurring between the two predicates of a complex predicate

Let us now turn to the question of what elements can come between the head of a complex predicate and the non-finite verb. We know that in French and Italian, adverbs can generally appear between the two verbs:

(49) a. F Jean <u>lui</u> a généreusement donné des disques.
I Giovanni <u>gli</u> ha generosamente dato dei dischi.
John CL-has generously given some records
b. F Jean <u>lui</u> fera probablement travailler ce texte.
I Giovanni <u>gli</u> farà probabilmente studiare questo testo.
John CL-will.make probably work on this text
c. I Giovanni <u>gli</u> vuole generosamente dare dei dischi.
John CL-wants to give generously some records

In Romanian, however, adverbs generally cannot come between tense and aspect auxiliaries and the verbal complement (Dobrovie-Sorin 1994, Barbu

1999, Monachesi 1999b, 2005), while some (modal adverbs, for example) can come between *a putea* and the infinitive verb:[43]

(50) R a. *Maria îi va eventual asculta.
Maria CL will eventually listen.to
b. Maria îi poate eventual asculta.
Maria CL may eventually listen.to
Maria will eventually listen to them.

Spanish and Portuguese differ from French or Italian, as well as Romanian. With restructuring verbs, the acceptability of an intervening adverb depends on whether there is a complex predicate. As expected, adverbs are not good with the tense auxiliary (51c,f).

(51) P a. O João começará amanhã / calmamente a estudá-lo.
b. ?? O João começá-lo-á amanhã / calmamente a estudar.
John will begin tomorrow / calmly to study it.
c. *O João tem pontualmente partido para Paris.
John has punctually left for Paris.
S d. Juan quiere a menudo leerlo.
John wants often to read it
e. *Juan lo quiere a menudo leer.
f. %Los niños no habían todavía aprendido a hablar.
The children had still not learnt to speak.

These two languages behave similarly in one key respect: only a small set of adverbs are accepted between the two verbs of a complex predicate, with some variation according to different speakers. For Portuguese, Gonçalvès (1999) accepts: *só* 'only', *até* 'even', *também* 'also', *logo* 'immediately', *sempre* 'always', but not *ontem* 'yesterday' or *hoje* 'today'.[44] In Spanish, Zagona (1988) cites: *casi* 'nearly', *ya* 'already', *apenas* 'barely', *solo, meramente* 'only'; there is variation concerning some other adverbs (such as *todavía, justo*).

---

[43] In Romanian, there are five adverbs (*mai* 'more', *tot* 'still', *cam* 'a little', *prea* 'too much', *şi* 'also') which can appear between the tense auxiliary and the participle, or between the pronominal clitics and the finite V. However, they do not occur between *a putea* and the infinitive verb (Dobrovie-Sorin 1994):

(i) R Maria nu îi va mai asculta.
Maria not CL will longer listen.to (= *Maria is no longer going to listen to them*)
(ii) R *Maria nu-l poate mai vedea.
Maria not-CL can longer see (= *Maria can no longer see him*)

These forms can be analyzed as light adjuncts (see section 5.1), or affixes (Barbu 1999, Monachesi 1999b, 2005). We leave this discussion aside here.

[44] Some of our informants also accept intensifiers (*realmente, absolutamente, mesmo*):

(i) P Queres-me mesmo dar isso? (= *And you truly want to give me that?*)

(52) P a. Não a querem só ver, querem-lhe também falar.
They do not want to only see her, they also want to speak to her.
S b. Los niños habían casi aprendido a hablar.
The children had almost learnt to speak.
c. El tren había apenas llegado a la estación.
The train had barely arrived at the station.

4.5 Inverted subject between the two predicates

In the Romance languages, the subject NP can appear postverbally in certain constructions, in particular, in interrogative clauses in a general way. To the extent that the subject can immediately follow the verb, we must look to see whether it can appear between the head and the complement verb in complex predicate structures.[45, 46]

The occurrence of the subject between the two verbs of a complex predicate is possible in Portuguese (Ambar 1992, Rouveret 1991): the inverted subject can co-occur with clitic-climbing:

(53) P a. Começará a Maria a lê-los?
Begin.FUT THE Maria to read-CL
a′. Começá-los-á a Maria a ler?
Begin.FUT-CL THE Maria to read
Is Maria finally going to read them?
b. Pode a Maria explicá-los?
Can THE Maria explain-CL
b′. Pode-os a Maria explicar?
Can-CL THE Maria explain
Maria can explain them, no?

In Italian, the insertion of the subject between the two predicates in the question is also compatible with clitic-climbing (Salvi 1980), with speakers' variation and a special prosody (noted with capital letters):

(54) I %L'ha MARIA comprato, il vestito, oppure no?
Maria, she's bought it, the dress, yes or no?

---

[45] The insertion of a complement between the verbs of a complex predicate is not possible, except sometimes a bare quantifier (F *On lui a tout dit*, lit. We CL-have everything said); see e.g. Abeillé and Godard (1998), *infra* section 5.1.

[46] Insertion of the subject between the verbs of complex predicates is possible in interrogatives, not in a general manner (it is not possible in declarative clauses). For the pragmatic effects associated with a subject immediately following the verb, see Salvi (1980) for Italian, and Ambar (1992) for Portuguese.

In French, this order is not allowed, the subject always appearing after the verbs.

(55) F a. *Où sont tes parents partis en vacances ?
Where have your parents left.for on holiday?
b. ?Où sont partis en vacances tes parents?

In Spanish there is a contrast between the two varieties (section 4.3). All speakers accept a subject following all the predicates (56a), as well as a subject between the two verbs if there is no complex predicate (56b). However, only for speakers of S2 is a subject NP licensed between the two verbs of a complex predicate (56c,d,e). Finally, the pronominal subject is licensed in this position for all speakers (56f) (Suñer 1987).[47]

(56) S a. ¿ Había ido a Roma Juan?
Had left for Rome John
b. ¿ Comienza Juan a hablar inglés / a hablarlo?
Begins John to speak English / to speak-CL
c. %¿ Había Juan ido a Roma?
d. %¿ Lo comienza Juan a hablar?
e. %¿ Los hace Juan comprar para la biblioteca?
CL-makes John buy for the library
Does J. make (us) buy them for the library?
f. ¿ Había usted partido a Roma ?
Had you left for Rome?

Finally, Romanian offers a contrast between the tense auxiliaries, with which this order is not possible (57a,b), and the modals where it is (57c,d) (Dobrovie-Sorin 1994, Ionescu 1996, Monachesi 1999b, 2005):

(57) R a. *Ar Maria fi venit? / *Ar fi Maria venit?
COND Maria FI come / COND FI Maria come
b. Ar fi venit Maria ?
Would Maria have come?
c. O poate Ion fotografia?
CL-can John photograph
Can John photograph it?
d. Are Ion de citit o carte?
Has John DE read a book
Does John have a book he should read?

[47] In addition, even speakers of S1 may accept an inverted subject between *hacer* and the intransitive infinitive (see also note 42).

This property therefore contrasts the complex predicates of Portuguese, Italian, Spanish-2 and the modal auxiliaries of Romanian, on the one hand, with the complex predicates of Spanish-1, the tense auxiliaries of Romanian, and the complex predicates of French, on the other. However, in French, the order 'V + inverted NP + non-finite V' where the unexpressed subject of the non-finite V is co-indexed with the inverted subject is excluded independently (see section 5.2).

4.6 Interpretation of the data: a structural contrast

The results for the four structural properties are summarized in Table 6. The possibility of insertions between the two verbs is by and large well correlated with the possibility of coordinating the complement predicates saturated for their complements. The complex predicates in French, Italian, the Romanian modals *a putea* and *a avea de*, allow both, while the complex predicates of Spanish-1, like the tense auxiliaries of Romanian, allow neither. For Portuguese and Spanish-2, the correlation is not so good. The occurrence of the inverted subject NP between the verbs is only possible when coordination is also possible, but not always: French differs from the others on this point.

(with raised clitic)	Various adverbs between the two predicates	Subject NP between the two predicates	Coordination of the second predicate with complements	Preposing of the second predicate with its complements
French	yes	no	yes	no
Italian	yes	yes (%)	yes	no
Spanish-1	no	no	no	no
Spanish-2	no	yes	yes	no
Portuguese	no	yes	yes	no
Romanian tense auxiliaries	no	no	no	no
Romanian modals	yes	yes	yes	no

Table 6: Structural properties of Romance complex predicates (with auxiliaries and restructuring verbs)

Let us draw some conclusions from these observations. The inability to prepose the complement predicate with its complements argues against an analysis in terms of structure C, where the head of a complex predicate takes a phrasal complement. Take restructuring verbs, which allow us to contrast the complex predicate with an ordinary complementation: clitic climbing prevents preposing with verbs which allow it otherwise, see (38) *vs* (39). If one always has a phrasal VP complement, the two cases will differ according to its saturated or non-saturated status. One must therefore say that preposing is not possible for a non-saturated (or incomplete) constituent. But the behavior of the predicative verbs goes against this hypothesis, as explained in section 4.7.

The defenders of the phrasal complement structure often put forward the argument that sequences of complements can be coordinated: if the heads of complex predicates take phrasal complements, one expects these complements to be able to be coordinated. Let us note immediately the problems posed by the complex predicates of Spanish-1 and the tense auxiliaries of Romanian, which do not allow such coordination. In fact, one does not see how to prevent the coordination of an ordinary complement, since a lexical item does not specify whether its complement is simple or coordinated. Even in the other cases, the data from coordination does not supply a strong argument for a phrasal complement, if one takes into account coordinations with two conjunctions instead of one ('correlative coordination'). We illustrate these for French. The conjunction does indeed occur in front of the participles in (58), but that does not constitute an indication of structure. In the coordination of non-constituents in (59), the conjunction occurs in front of the sequences of complements. Yet, we do not see how these sequences could properly constitute phrases.

(58) F a. Paul aura (ou) trouvé une solution ou demandé de l'aide.
Paul will.have (either) found a solution or asked for help.
b. Paul n'a ni trouvé une solution ni demandé de l'aide.
Paul has neither found a solution nor asked for help.

(59) F a. Paul aura donné (ou) un livre à Jeanne ou un disque à Sophie.
Paul will.have given (either) a book to J. or a record to S.
b. Paul n'aura donné ni un livre à Jeanne, ni un disque à Sophie.
Paul will.have given (neither) a book to J. nor a record to S.
c. ??Paul aura ou donné un livre à Jeanne ou un disque à Sophie.
d. ??Paul n'aura ni donné un livre à Jeanne, ni un disque à Sophie.

The conjunction in correlative coordination is therefore placed before the first word of each parallel sequence of complements, rather than before the first word of each constituent. Similarly, the conjunction of a simple coordination ((58a) and (59a) without the first *ou*), is placed in front of the first word of the second (or last) sequence of complements. Consequently, coordination is not a strong argument in favor of one structure over another. So let us suppose that the verbal heads of complex predicates do not have phrasal complements. From this perspective, coordination of the second predicate (and its complements) is an instance of non-constituent coordination.

Having eliminated the phrasal complement structure, it remains for us to choose between the verbal complex structure (A) and the flat structure (B). In both, the head of the complex predicate takes for its complements a lexical predicate and the complements this lexical predicate subcategorizes for. There is a two-step combination in A while all the complements are on the same level in B.

The flat structure can accommodate the differences regarding the insertions, if the ordering rules are taken to be different in the different languages, but it cannot account for the differences with regard to coordination. Indeed, as long as all the Romance languages allow coordinations of sequences of complements at the same level, we do not see how to prevent coordinations of such sequences in some cases while allowing them in others if the structure is always the same. Thus, one cannot predict the contrast between (60a) and (60b).

(60) S1 a. *Juan ha [comprado] [este libro] y [leído] [el primer capítulo].
b. Juan (le) da [un libro] [a María] y [un disco] [a Pablo].

In contrast, the verbal complex structure is appropriate for blocking coordinations in Spanish-1 and Romanian, as long as a general constraint holds in the Romance languages, which prevents a coordination of sequences of constituents from different levels.[48] If, in sentences like (60a), the participle is not at the same level as the NP which follows it (see structure A), we can explain why the coordination is excluded. It is for the same reason as in (61a), where the degraded acceptability contrasts with that of (61b). Each time, one is trying to build a sequence of constituents one of which is embedded while the other is not:

(61) a. S ??Juan da [el libro de Proust] [a María] y [de Camus] [a Pablo].
F ??Jean donne le livre de Proust à Maria et de Camus à Paul.
J. gives the book by Proust to M. and by Camus to P.
b. S Juan da [el libro de Proust] [a Maria] y [el (libro) de Camus] [a Pablo.
F Jean donne le livre de Proust à Maria et le livre de Camus à P.
J. gives the book by Proust to M. and the book by Camus to P.
c. *[$_{NP}$ el libro [$_{PP}$ de Camus]] [$_{PP}$ a María] y [$_{PP}$ de Proust] [$_{PP}$ a Pablo]

[48] Romanian (at least spoken varieties) seems to be freer.

d. *[$_{V'}$ ha [$_{V}$ comprado]] [$_{NP}$ este libro] y [$_{V}$ leído] [$_{NP}$ el primer capítulo]

Since the participle and its complements are not sisters in the verbal complex structure, the constraint illustrated in (61) predicts the unacceptability of this sequence, while the flat structure does not.

The verbal complex structure is also well-suited to prevent the insertion of adverbs and of the inverted subject, as we will see in more detail later on. In the languages where it is proposed (German, Kathol 1998; Korean, Chung 1998), the verbal complex does not generally include an argument or an adverb. If the absence of insertion is natural with a verbal complex, then the complex predicates of Romance cannot all be verbal complex structures. Consequently, we suggest that not all complex predicates belong to a single structure.

For the complex predicates which allow coordination of sequences of complements, we propose a flat structure. In this analysis, the second predicate is the sister of the other complements, hence the acceptability of such coordinations. To account for the differences concerning the insertion of adverbs and subjects, we resort to different ordering rules (see below section 5.2).

Furthermore, for Romanian, one must note the difference between the facts observed with tense auxiliaries and those observed with modals. Yet, one expects the same word ordering rules and coordination rules to apply in both cases. Attributing to the first a verbal complex structure and to the second a flat structure, provides an interesting solution, already suggested by Monachesi (1999b), to accommodate the insertion data.[49]

The two structures are therefore distributed according to Table 7 (which does not include the predicative verbs):

	Verbal complex structure	Flat structure
French		auxiliaries, causatives
Italian, Portuguese, Spanish-2		auxiliaries, restructuring verbs, causatives
Spanish-1	auxiliaries, restructuring verbs, causatives	
Romanian	tense auxiliaries	modals

Table 7: Complementation associated with Romance complex predicates

[49] Dobrovie-Sorin (1994) highlights the contrast between tense auxiliaries and *a putea*, but gives a different analysis.

The complex predicate structures are illustrated in Figures 2 and 3 for tense auxiliaries, and in Figures 4 and 5 for restructuring verbs.

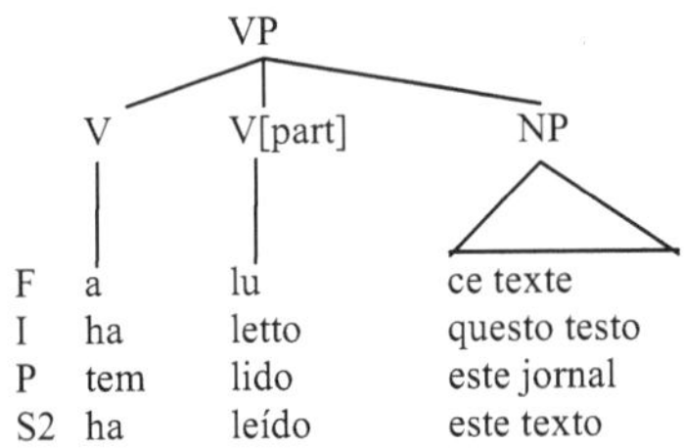

Figure 2: The flat structure with tense auxiliaries (F,I,P,S2)

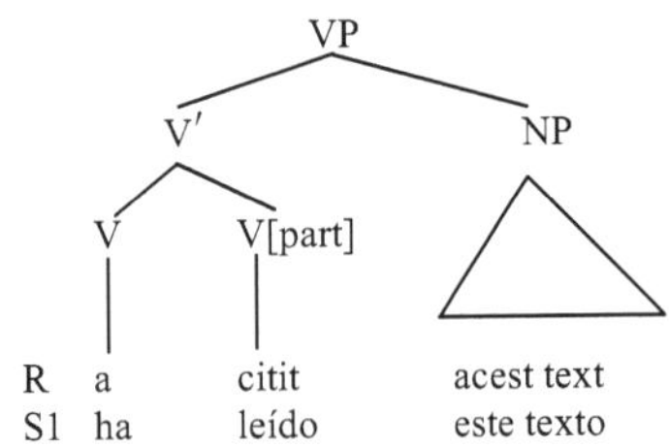

Figure 3: The verbal complex structure with tense auxiliaries (R, S1)

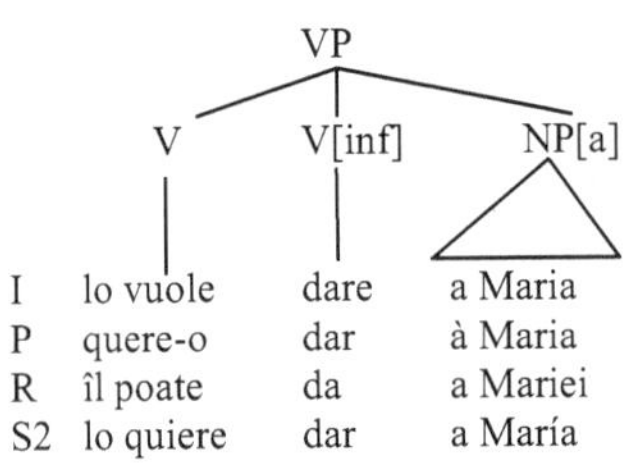

Figure 4: The flat structure with Restructuring verbs (I, P, R,S2)

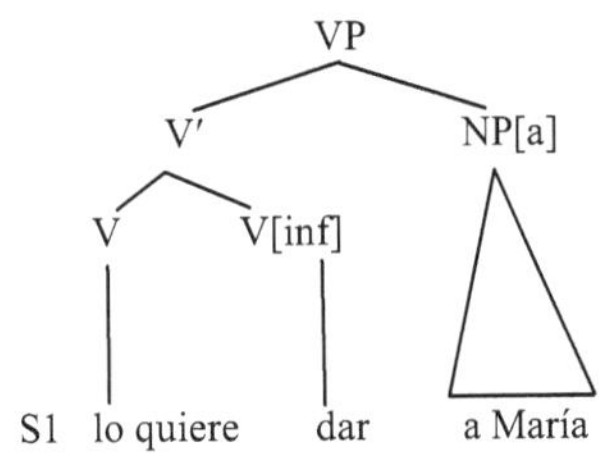

Figure 5: The verbal complex structure with Restructuring verbs (S1)

4.7 Predicative verbs

The predicative constructions, among which we count passive constructions, are doubly noteworthy. First, they are the only ones which have exactly the same properties in all the Romance languages; second, they are the only ones to motivate a phrasal complement structure, while rendering clitic-climbing obligatory.

We have illustrated above the fact that a predicative AP complement can be preposed with or without its complements (40)-(41). Similarly, it can be extracted with or without its complements in a concessive adjunct:

(62) F a. Aussi fidèle à ses amis qu'il soit, il ne perd pas de vue ses intérêts.
As faithful to his friends as he is, he does not lose sight of his interests.

b. Aussi fidèle qu'il soit à ses amis, il ne perd pas de vue ses intérêts.
As faithful as he is to his friends, he does not lose sight of his interests.

c. % Aussi fidèle qu'il leur soit, il ne perd pas de vue ses intérêts.
As faithful as he CL-is, he does not lose sight of his interests

In (62a), the extracted element is an AP, while it is an adjective without its complement in (62b,c), If one can only extract whole constituents, we must consider that the sequence *être fidèle à ses amis* 'to be faithful to one's friends' has a double structure: in the first, *être* has an AP complement (saturated for its complement), in the second, *être* has two complements (an unsaturated adjective and a PP) that can be extracted (and cliticized) independently of each other.[50] The copula contrasts with tense auxiliaries and restructuring verbs. Compare Left Dislocation in (63a,b) and in (63c,d).

(63) F a. *Parlé (avec Marie), Paul (l') a.
Spoken (with Mary), Paul has
b. *Parlé, Paul (l') a avec Marie
c. Amoureux de Marie, Paul l'est apparemment.
In love with Mary, Paul CL-is apparently
d. Amoureux, Paul l'est apparemment de Marie.
In love, Paul CL-is apparently with Marie

How do we account for this contrast? We appeal here to a different property that constituents must have in order to be extracted or preposed or cliticized: they must behave like phrases rather than lexical items. The complement of the copula behaves like a phrase, whether it is saturated or not, while the verbal complement of tense auxiliaries does not; in Abeillé and Godard's weight theory (2000a, 2004), the complement of the copula is non-light. This analysis is comforted by another observation. When the predicative complement expects two complements (64a), it can be extracted with only one of the two (64c) (Abeillé and Godard 2002), as illustrated with French and Italian:

(64) a. F Il est reconnaissant à Paul de son aide.
I È riconoscente a Paolo per il aiuto.
He is grateful to Paul for his help.
b. F Aussi reconnaissant qu'il soit à Paul de son aide, ...
I Per quanto riconoscente sia a Paolo per il aiuto, ...
As grateful as he is to Paul for his help, ...

---

[50] Some speakers do not accept (62c), where an adjective unsaturated for a complement clitic is extracted, but they accept (i), where an adjective whose complement is extracted is itself cliticized:

(i) F Je sais qu'il n'a pas été fidèle vis-à-vis de toi, mais des amis auxquels il l'a été, je peux t'en citer.
I know that he has not been faithful to you, but friends to whom he CL-has been, I can name some to you.

c. F Aussi reconnaissant de son aide qu'il soit à Paul, ...
%Per quanto riconoscente per il aiuto sia a Paolo, ...
As grateful be he to Paolo for his help, ...

Thus, on the one hand, the complement of the copula can be saturated, partally saturated or unsaturated, but, on the other hand, it always behaves like a phrase. In other words, the copula takes a phrasal predicative complement, from which it optionally inherits a complement or more. The difference between a word constituent that behaves like a lexical item and a word constituent that behaves like a phrase can be represented in the following way: only in the second case is the word dominated by a phrase (an XP).[51]

To sum up, we have three verb classes:

(i) tense auxiliaries obligatorily inherit the complements of their verb complement, which behaves like a lexical item;

(ii) the copula, and, more generally, predicative verbs, optionally inherit the complements of their predicative complement, which always behaves like a phrase;

(iii) restructuring verbs are associated with two different structures, one identical to that of tense auxiliaries, one identical to that of ordinary verbs, taking a non-finite VP complement (saturated for its complements).

Let us now look at the other structural properties of predicative verbs. If we look again at the insertion and coordination tests, we obtain the following results. All the Romance languages allow the insertion of an adverb between the verb and the predicative complement:

(65) F Roméo lui sera probablement fidèle.
I Romeo le sarà probabilmente fedele.
S Romeo le será probablemente fiel.
P O Romeu sera-lhe-á provavelmente fiel.
R Romeo îi va fi probabil credincios.
Romeo CL-will.be probably faithful

[51] In the terms of Abeillé and Godard (2000a, 2004), a word projecting a phrase is 'non-light', while a (light) word not projecting a (unary) phrase is 'light'. Only non-light constituents can be pronominalized or extracted:

(i) F C'est un bel hommage qu'on a rendu au président.
It is a beautiful homage that one has paid to the president

(ii) F *C'est hommage qu'on a rendu au président.
It is homage that one has paid to the president

In this perspective, the complement of the predicative verbs is analyzed as non-light, even when it is non-saturated, while the verbal complement of the restructuring verbs in complex predicates is always light. (see also section 5.1).

In Spanish, Portuguese, Romanian, the insertion of an inverted NP subject is also accepted (66a,b,c).[52] A different set of predicative verbs have two complements (see Table 4), an NP object and a predicate, predicated of the object. Here, there is some variation both across the languages, and within certain languages. The NP can separate the verb from the predicative complement in S, P, R while allowing clitic-climbing (66d); there is variation in Italian and French (66e,f):[53]

(66) S a. ¿ Está Pablo muy ofendido por sus palabras?
Is Pablo very offended by their speeches?
b. ¿ Está Pablo enamorado de María?
Is Pablo in love with Maria?
R c. A fost Maria lăudată pentru acest succes?
Has been Maria praised for this success
R d. I-o face pe Maria ostilă.
CL.DAT-CL.ACC-makes M. hostile
It makes Maria hostile to him.
I e. % Le crede Giovanni fedele.
CL.DAT-believes Giovanni faithful
He believes Giovanni faithful to her.
F f. % On y rendra Jean sensible.
One CL-will.render Jean sensitive
We will make Jean sensitive to it.

Predicative verbs allow the coordination of predicates with their complements, even if one of them is cliticized (and shared by the conjuncts):

(67) F a. Ce livre lui a été acheté par sa mère et envoyé par un ami.
I b. ?Questo libro gli è stato comprato da sua madre e inviato da un amico.
R c. Această carte i-a fost cumpărată de mama sa şi trimisă de un amic.
S d. Este libro le ha sido comprado por su madre y mandado por un amigo.
P e. Este livro foi-lhe comprado por sua mãe e mandado por um amigo.
This book was bought for him by his mother and sent to him by a friend.

[52] The contrast between passive participles and adjectives noted in Zagona (1988) (*¿Fueron estos libros *leídos / buenos?* 'Were these books read / good?') is not confirmed by our informants.

[53] Examples (66e,f) contrast with those of (18a',b'), where the object follows the non-saturated predicate.

We therefore have, for all the Romance languages, the following hierarchical structures for the predicative verbs, whose predicative complement can include its complements or not.

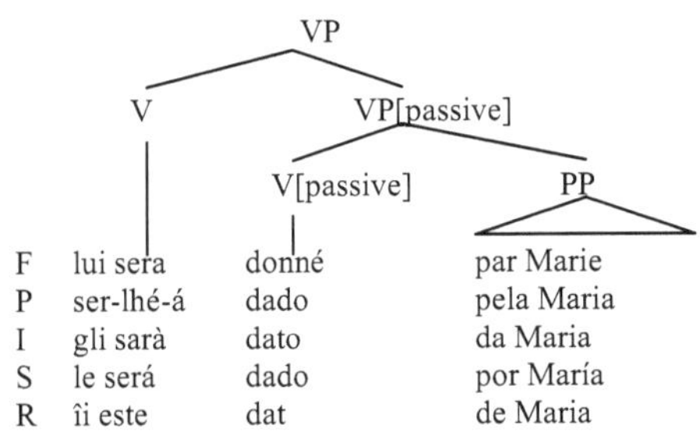

Figure 6: Predicative verbs with a saturated complement

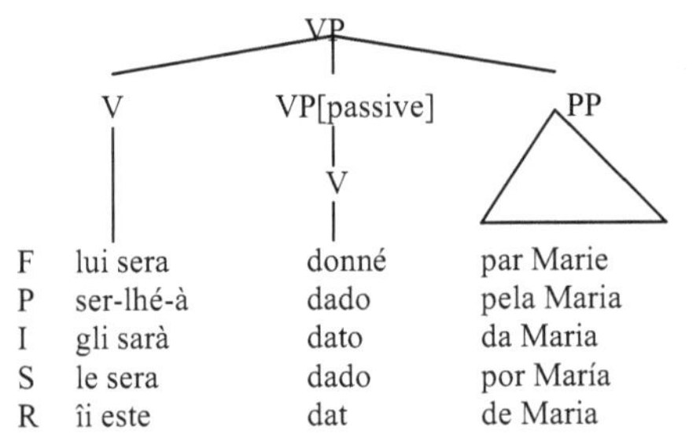

Figure 7: Predicative verbs with an unsaturated complement

5 Further Properties

We enter into more detailed analyses here, in order to account for data which remain accounted for in the analysis proposed thus far.

5.1 Constituents in verbal complex structures

We begin with the verbal complex structures (structure A in Figure 1). Although the insertion of constituents is generally excluded between the two predicates, one does find certain adverbs in this position, as well as Spanish pronominal subjects (e.g. *usted*). Furthermore, although the coordination of sequences of participles (or infinitives) with their complements is generally excluded, it is possible with a 'bare' nominal object (that is, one without a determiner or modifier) in Spanish (68a,b). This acceptability contrasts with the impossibility of conjoining sequences of 'complement V + NP' for speakers of the S1 variety.

(68) S a. Pablo ha comido galletas y bebido leche.
Pablo has eaten cakes and drunk milk.
b. Juan le quiere comprar libros y dar discos.
Juan CL.DAT-wants to buy books and give records
Juan wants to buy him books and give him records.
S1 c. *Pablo ha comido dos galletas y bebido toda la leche.
Pablo has eaten two cakes and drunk all the milk.
d. *Juan le quiere comprar un libro y dar un disco.
Juan CL.DAT-wants to buy one book and give one record

In order to deal with this data, we make use of the notion of the 'weight' of words and phrases, according to the analyses in Abeillé and Godard (2000a, 2001, 2004).

As already mentioned, the verbal complex, while being a phrase built in the syntax, nonetheless has properties which make it resemble a word. We express them using the weight feature. Lexemes and phrases have a weight property which belongs to their syntactic description: they are light or non-light. Light elements cluster with the lexical head of a phrase, while non-light ones are either an ordinary phrase or a heavy constituent. The intuition is that the light elements must precede non-light ones. In addition, light and non-light constituents have different properties regarding pronominalization, extraction and adjunction (see section 4.7). The distinction cuts across both words and phrases. The majority of phrases are non-light, but phrases which combine a head and an adjunct, or coordinations, can be light if they are composed of only light elements. Common nouns are light, proper nouns are non-light, the head V of a VP is light, and this distinction cuts across adverbs too. Thus, morphologically complex adverbs ending in *-ment(e)* in the Romance languages are non-light, while other adverbs can be light.

The light constituents (the N *raison, ragione*, the adverb *bien, bene in* (69)) appear in the VP before non-light constituents (with unmarked intonation contours, i.e. no emphatic or contrastive stress on *bien / bene,* no incidental prosody on the PP *sur ce point / su questo punte*).

(69) a. F Paul connaît bien ce texte.
I Paolo conosce bene questo testo.
Paul knows well this text (= *Paul knows this text well*)
b. F ??Paul connaît ce texte bien.
I ??Paolo conosce questo testo bene.
c. F Paul a raison sur ce point.
I Paolo ha ragione su questo punto.
Paul has reason on this head (= *Paul is right on this head*)

d. F ??Paul a sur ce point raison.
   I ??Paolo ha su questo punto ragione.

To account for the coordination data illustrated in (68) for speakers of S1, we propose the following hypothesis: the head of a verbal complex (auxiliary, restructuring, causative verb) and its complement verb are both light, and the verbal complex is also light. Hence, the verbal complex can contain other constituents, adverbs or arguments, as long as they are light. In particular, it can contain the pronominal subject *usted*, or a bare noun object, which is light, and coordinations, as long as the conjuncts are light. The conjuncts *comido galletas, bebido leche* are both light, and the coordination is also light. Hence, such a coordination is allowed as the complement of the tense auxiliary in the Spanish-1 verbal complex. On the other hand, an NP with a determiner is non-light. Hence, the coordination containing NPs in (68c,d) is not acceptable, given that the head of a complex predicate forms a light verbal complex with its verbal complement in the S1 variety of Spanish. The coordinations illustrated in (68a,b) are therefore coordinations within a verbal complex, as illustrated in Figure 8:[54]

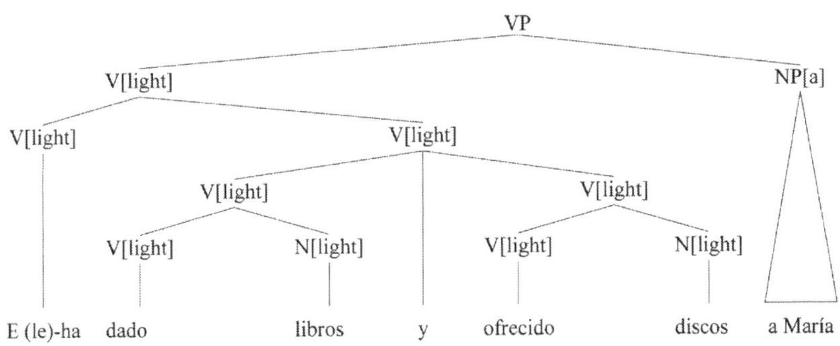

Figure 8: Coordination of verbal complexes with bare Ns in Spanish-1

Similarly, the verbal complex structure of complex predicates in S1 can include adverbs only if light, as shown in the following contrastive structures:

[54] We leave aside the question of whether these bare complements are adjuncts to the light verb (as Abeillé and Godard 1998 propose for bare quantifiers of French, as in *Il espère [[tout comprendre] de ton problème]* lit. He hopes to everything understand of your problem), or whether they are complements (like the second verb in the verbal complex, and certain nouns in German, such as *auto* in *autofahren*, see Kathol 1998).

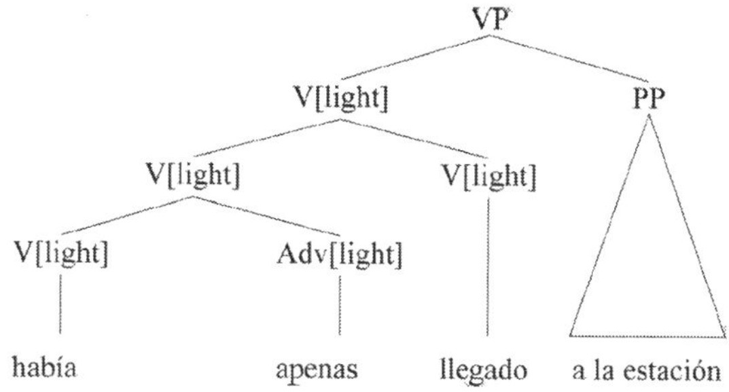

Figure 9: Light adverbs in the verbal complex in Spanish-1

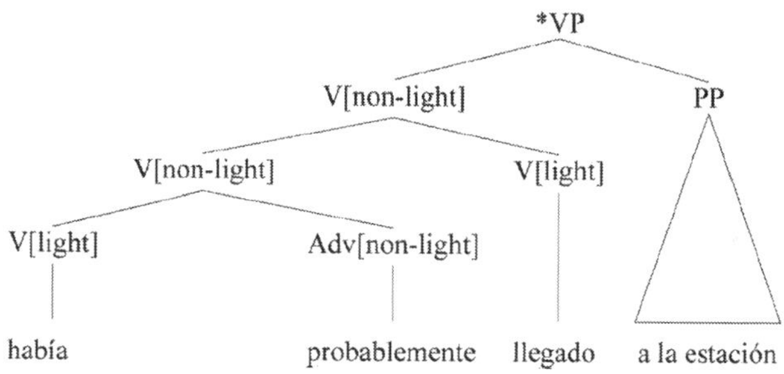

Figure 10: Non-light adverb in the verbal complex in Spanish-1

Let us briefly show that adverbs like *apenas, sólo* and bare nouns are indeed light. Independently of complex predicates, they are undoubtedly light if they obligatorily precede non-light constituents in the VP, which is what we find (with 'unmarked' intonation).[55] A light adverb must precede a non-light NP complement (70a,b), while a non-light adverb may precede or follow it (70c,d). A light N must precede a non-light adverb (70e,f), while a light adverb and a light N are unordered (70g,h).[56]

(70) S a. Cómete sólo las dos galletas.
Eat only the two cookies
b. *Cómete las dos galletas sólo.

---

[55] Like the light constituents of French and Italian, they can lose their lightness, if they have a contrastive stress, in which case they can appear after a phrasal complement. Romanian bare NPs behave differently: they can be separated from the verb by an ordinary adverb or non-light complement.

[56] The inverted subject cannot occur between the verb and a bare N for speakers of S1, but it can for speakers of S2. Leaving aside the analysis of inverted subjects, we restrict the orderng constraint to complements and adjuncts (see (71d)).

(i) S %¿ Se Come Pablo galletas? (*Does Pablo eat cookies?*)

c. Cómete deprisa las dos galletas.
   Eat quickly the two cookies
d. Cómete la dos galletas deprisa.
e. ??Comete deprisa galletas.
f. Cómete galletas deprisa.
g. Cómete sólo galletas.
h. Cómete galletas sólo.

5.2 Ordering constraints in flat structures

While the flat structure allows for the possibility of elements being inserted between the two verbs in a general way, the detail of the data is more complicated. In Romanian (with *a putea*), and in Italian, adverbs and the inverted subject (under certain conditions) are possible; in Portuguese, as well as the S2 variety of Spanish, the subject is possible, but not adverbs (except light ones), while in French, adverbs but not the subject, are possible. Ordering (or linearization) constraints are responsible for the differences between these languages. Lightness, which plays a crucial role in the verbal complex, also plays a role in flat structure, since the head verb is light, and the lexical (infinitive or participle) verb complement is also light.

Linearization constraints order the immediate constituents of the same phrase. They take into account the syntactic category (which includes the part of speech, and also the weight) and the grammatical function of the constituent. Orders which are not specified by a constraint are free. We specify here the constraints on the VP, containing the head verb, complements and adjuncts, all at the same level. The constraints are as follows:

(71) Ordering constraints in the VP
a. For all Romance languages: The head verb precedes the other constituents.
b. For all Romance languages: Verbs (and, more generally, predicates) precede their subcategorized complements.
c. French, Italian: Light complements and adjuncts precede the non-light complements.
d. Portuguese, Spanish-2: Light complements and adjuncts precede the non-light complements and adjuncts.
e. French: The inverted subject follows all the verbal predicates.

Rule (71a), which holds for all the Romance languages, orders the head verb before the other constituents (it comes first in the VP). The non-finite verb in complex predicates subcategorizes for the complements which are inherited by the head verb, and, according to (71b), it must appear before them even if they are light (F *a rendu hommage* 'has paid tribute' vs **a* *hommage rendu*).[57] In addition, rule (71c), which constrains French and Italian, orders the light nominal complements and the light adverbs before the non-light complements (*rendra hommage à Paul* 'will pay tribute to Paul' vs. **rendra à Paul hommage* lit. will pay to Paul tribute). This rule does not constrain the insertion of an adverb (taken to be an adjunct) before or after the complements: in French and Italian, any adverb (light or non-light) can be inserted between the head verb and the participle (or another light complement), see (49). For Portuguese and Spanish-2, non-light adverbs cannot precede the light verbal complement, while light adverbs may; non-light adverbs can precede non-light verbal complements (a VP saturated for its complements). In fact, the ordering is simpler in Portuguese and Spanish-2 than in French and Italian, as seen with rule (71d).

We illustrate the contrast between Portuguese and Italian with respect to the non-light adverb between the two verbs of a complex predicate in Figures 11 and 12.[58]

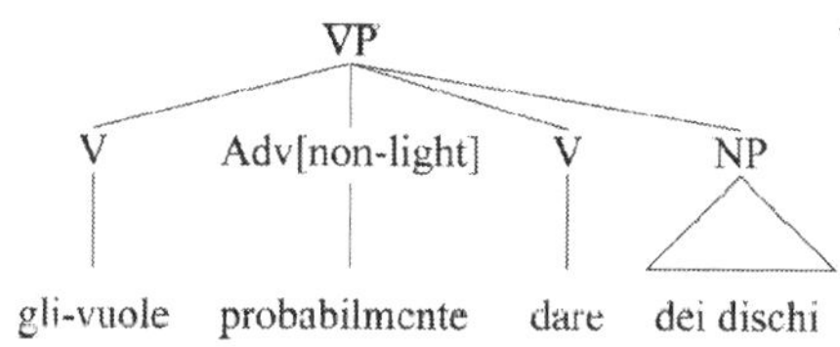

Figure 11: Insertion of a non-light adverb in the flat structure in Italian

---

[57] Some Romanian speakers accept the placing of the complements between the modal and the infinitive, although such complements are subcategorized by the infinitive:

(i) R Ion poate [citi] [această carte].
'Ion can read this book'

(ii) R %Ion poate [această carte] [citi].

It seems that the order in (ii) requires a special prosody on the inserted NP. We suspect that it is an incidental prosody, often associated with different linearization properties. For instance, in French, an incidental PP subcategorized by the participle can be linearized between the auxiliary and the participle (a position not possible for an integrated PP):

(iii) F Paul avait, à ses enfants, donné tout ce qu'il pouvait leur donner.
Paul had, to his children, given all that he could give them

We leave aside the linearization properties of incidental constituents (for the distinction between incidental and integrated French adverbs, see Bonami *et al.* 2004).

[58] Non-light adverbs in Portuguese cannot be adjoined to the lexical head, because the phrase would be non-light, while the head of a VP is always light.

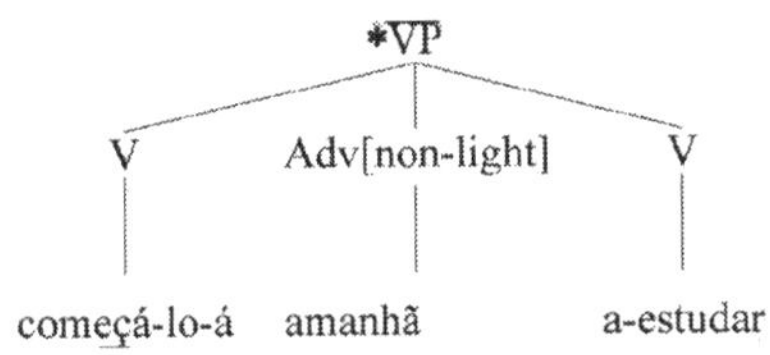

Figure 12: Insertion of a non-light adverb in the flat structure in Portuguese

Finally, French constrains the position of the inverted subject more than the other languages.[59] In fact, the impossibility of subject inversion between the verbs of a complex predicate is the result of a more general constraint, which requires the inverted subject of a verb to follow all complements which expect a subject co-indexed with it (be they control or raising predicates, lexical or phrasal). Thus, the inverted subject in (72b) follows not only the participle but the infinitival VP complement (*de partir*) (see Bonami and Godard 2001). Thus the inverted nominal subject must follow the participle (which it is a subject of).

(72) F a. *Quand est Jean parti?
When is John gone
(cf. Quand est parti Jean ?)
b. *le jour où avait décidé Jean de partir
The day when had decided John to leave
(cf. le jour où avait décidé de partir Jean)

5.3 Double complementation verbs

We have attributed to restructuring and causative verbs two complementation structures, according to whether a complex predicate is formed or not, following the tradition instigated by Rizzi (1982) and Aissen and Perlmutter (1976/1983). This approach has recently been challenged by Cinque (2005), who opts for a single structure, and optional clitic climbing. Here, we briefly justify our own choice, before looking in a little more detail at the case of MAKE in the different languages.

5.3.1 Justifying the double complementation structure

The double complementation hypothesis is based on the following correlation: clitics can appear either on the complement verb or on the head verb, but as soon as there is a clear indication of monoclausality (a long middle-passive, long periphrastic passive, or a bounded dependency), then the apparent optionality disappears and the clitic must appear on the head verb. Cinque (2001, 2005) challenges this correlation for French and Italian, rely-

59 However, recall that the acceptability of Italian (54) is variable.

ing on a different set of data. He observes the following for Italian: (i) the restructuring verb can 'change' auxiliary, adopting the *essere* auxiliary required by its verbal complement, even when the clitic is attached to this complement; (ii) the clitic can climb even when the infinitive is negated (by *non*); (iii) the pronoun *loro* can 'climb' while the clitic is downstairs; (iv) the pronoun *loro* can 'climb' in the absence of a change in auxiliary; (v) the pronoun *loro* can fail to climb despite a complex predicate being formed.

For these observations to challenge the double complementation structure, it would be necessary for the position of *loro*, the obligatory absence of negation, and the change of auxiliary to be clearly correlated with the existence of a complex predicate in Italian, which is not at all the case. We reject the changing of auxiliary as a criterial property of complex predicates in Italian (see section 6.3). Negation, if looked at more closely, is not a good criterion for Italian either (see section 6.1). The data concerning *loro* are in (73a-c) (Cinque 2001). Note that we do not analyze *loro* as a clitic, but as a light pronoun:[60]

(73) I a. %Ho loro cominciato a insegnarlo più di un anno fa.
I have them begun to teach-CL more than one year ago
I began to teach it to them more than one year ago.
b. %Avremmo loro potuto rimanere più vicini.
We would.have them been.able remain closer
We would have been able to remain closer to them.
c. Le ho dovute consegnar loro in ritardo.
CL.ACC-I.have had give them late
I have had to give them to them late.

The acceptability of the data where *loro* occurs before the restructuring verb (73a,b) is subject to variation. But even for the speakers who accept it, it does not show that a complex predicate is formed. In addition to complex predicates (which inherit complements indiscriminately), there are verbs which may inherit certain specific complements from their verbal complement. Consider the phenomenon referred to as 'Left *tous*' in Kayne (1975), to which Cinque also refers in the same article. As illustrated in (74), the quantifier can raise although the clitics stay downstairs.

(74) F Paul a tous voulu [les donner aux enfants].
Paul has all wanted CL.ACC-give to.the children
Paul has decided to give them all to the children.

---

[60] Cinque gives (73a,b) as acceptable while our informants do not accept them, hence the '%' mark.

French lacks restructuring verbs, as defined here. Nevertheless, there are some verbs, among which *vouloir* ('want'), which can inherit bare quantifier arguments from their VP complement, and only them (*tous, tout, rien*), see Abeillé and Godard (1998). Hence, the quantifier *tous* occurs upstairs while the clitic to which it is linked remains downstairs; since there is no complex predicate, we do not expect clitics to climb: the VP complement in (74) is saturated except for *tous*.[61] For the Italian speakers who accept (73a,b), the complement is an infinitive VP unsaturated for *loro*, just as the complement in (74) is a infinitive VP unsaturated for *tous*. Other speakers do not have this possibility of this selective inheritance for *loro*.[62]

The acceptability of (73c) does not pose a problem either. There is a complex predicate here, as shown by clitic climbing. For us there is a flat structure, with the auxiliary verb inheriting all arguments from *dovuto*, which itself inherits them from *consegnare*. In our analysis, *loro* is a light word, but not a clitic; therefore, it must appear before non-light complements (see constraint (71c)); this is the case in (73c).

5.3.2 MAKE verbs

The data concerning MAKE itself is less clear than for the other causative (or perception) verbs, at least in French and Spanish. In the analysis presented so far, the presence of a clitic on the infinitive verb complement should be sufficient to justify the existence of a second structure (with a complement saturated VP) as it is with restructuring verbs and the other causative verbs. But the situation is more complex.

In some cases, as expected, the presence of a clitic on the infinitive is correlated to clear indications that we are not dealing with a complex predicate (e.g. the causee is realized as an NP or a pro-NP rather than an A-NP although the infinitive is transitive). Such an ordinary complementation structure exists regularly for P *fazer*, *mandar* along with the complex predicate complementation. It does not exist at all for I *fare*, which is only compatible with a complex predicate. With French *faire*, and Spanish *hacer*, there is variation among speakers, and there are certain restrictions. In French, the causee must be a clitic (75a,b), and the structure is all the more acceptable when the co-occurrence of two raised clitics is impossible (75c),

---

61 The sets of French verbs which can inherit the bare quantifiers, and of Italian restructuring verbs overlap, but are not identical (see Abeillé and Godard 1998).

62 *loro* in (73a,b) and *tous* in (74), would be exceptions to constraint (71b) if they were in the same domain as the predicate which subcategorizes for them. This is not the case in our analysis (there is no complex predicate formation). It is the case with *tout* in F *Il a tout lu*, (lit. he has everything read), if both *tout* and *lu* are both complements of *a*; alternatively, *tout* may be adjoined to the past participle.

see Abeillé *et al.* (1997). In Spanish, the structure is sometimes acceptable in the same conditions.

(75) F a. %On les fera (ne pas) les laver.
One CL.ACC-will.make (not) CL.ACC-wash
We will make them (not) wash them.
b. *On fera les enfants (ne pas) les laver.
One will.make the children (not) CL.ACC-wash
We will make the children (not) wash them.
c. Elle nous fera vous gronder.
She CL.ACC-will.make CL.ACC-scold
She will make us scold you.
(cf. *Elle nous vous fera gronder.
She CL.ACC-CL.ACC-will.make scold)
S d. %Lo hicieron traer un paquete.
CL.ACC-they.made carry a package
They made him carry a package.
e. %Los hago (no) estudiarlo.
CL.ACC- I.make (not) study-CL.ACC
I make them (not) study it.

Elsewhere, one finds clitics on the infinitive verb along with signs of complex predicate structure (dative causee, acceptable bounded dependency). In French, the infinitive verbs host an idiomatic clitic or a reflexive, but this is not always the case in Spanish (Bordelois 1988, Moore 1990a,b, Hernanz 1999).[63] In any case, there is great variation in the judgments, as Hernanz (1999) especially points out.

(76) F a. %La pluie fait s'acheter des bottes aux familles.
The rain makes SE-buy boots A.the families
The rain makes families buy boots.
S b. %Yo le hice dárselo. (Bordelois)
I CL.DAT-made give-CL.DAT-CL.ACC
I made him give it to him.

[63] The variation concerning the realization of the clitic in Spanish (the accusative is not always morphologically distinguished from the dative) contributes to obscure the analysis. In addition, even with a VP complement, the causee could be a dative clitic, as happens in French in some cases (see note 64, Abeillé *et al.* 1997). Note that the examples proposed for Spanish also have a dative clitic rather than an A-NP (see, for example, Franco and Landa 1995). Thus, it is not clear whether we have a complex predicate with a downstairs clitic, or the remainder of a NP-VP control structure in (76b,c).

c. %Le hizo abrirlas. (cited in Hernanz)
CL.DAT-HE.made open-CL.ACC
He made him open them.

For French, one analyzes the verb bearing idiomatic clitics or reflexives as belonging to a different verb type than that which only carries ordinary clitics; the first can be a lexical verbal complement of *faire* in a complex predicate structure (Abeillé *et al.* 1998).[64] For Spanish, there are two possibilities. Either the ordinary structure (of the type V-NP-VP) with no complex predicate exists marginally for *hacer*, and the possibility of the dative causee must then be accounted for; or *hacer* allows the infinitive verb in the verbal complex to bear clitics. We leave this question open.

We summarize in Table 8 the distribution between single and double complement structures.[65] The single structure is not identical for all verbs. It is a phrasal complement (saturated for its complements or not) for predicative verbs in all Romance languages. It is a verbal complex for auxiliaries in Spanish-1 and Romanian, and a flat structure for the Italian, French, Portuguese, Spanish-2 auxiliaries and restructuring verbs, Italian *fare*, and the Romanian modals.

	Single structure	Two structures (complex predicate and ordinary complementation)
French	auxiliaries, predicative verbs	causatives (restrictions on *faire*)
Italian	auxiliaries, *fare*, predicative verbs	restructuring verbs, causatives (except *fare*)
Portuguese	auxiliaries, predicative verbs	restructuring verbs, causatives
Spanish	auxiliaries, predicative verbs	restructuring verbs, causatives (restrictions on *hacer*)
Romanian	(tense) auxiliaries and modals, predicative verbs	

Table 8: The distribution of double structures in Romance complex predicates

64 The fem. clitic *–o* which does not climb to the Romanian auxiliary could be analyzed in the same way as idiomatic clitics in French.

65 Abeillé and Godard (1996) for French, and Bosque (1999) for Spanish, propose two structures for the predicative verbs. We explain in section 4.7 why a single underspecified complementation is preferable (see Abeillé and Godard 2002).

6 Open questions

We mention here certain questions for which we do not have complete analyses: the absence of negation between the two predicates, and specific properties of certain complex predicates: the possibility of a null complement in Portuguese, and auxiliary 'change' in Italian. In addition, we briefly describe the problem posed by Catalan, where the properties of complex predicates are especially subject to variation.[66]

6.1 Negation of the complement verb in complex predicates

All complex predicates share a property in the Romance languages: the complement predicate cannot be syntactically modified by an adverb of sentential negation. In (77) and (78), negation prevents clitic climbing onto the main verb:

(77) a. F *Le mauvais temps le fera ne pas étudier par les enfants.
I *Il brutto tempo lo farà non studiare dai ragazzi.
C *El mal temps el farà no estudiar pels nens.
S *El mal tiempo lo hará no estudiar por los niños.
P *O mau tempo fá-lo-á não estudar pelas crianças.
The bad weather CL-FUT.make / make-CL-FUT NEG study by the children
The bad weather will make the children not study it.
b. R *Vremea rea poate nu îndepărta copiii.
The bad weather may not drive away the children.

(78) a. I Giovanni intende non comprarlo.
S Juan quiere no comprarlo.
C En Joan vol no comprarlo.
P O João quer não comprá-lo.
b. I *Giovanni lo intende non comprare.
S *Juan lo quiere no comprar.
C *En Joan lo vol no comprar. (Gavarró and Laca 2002)
P *O João quere-o não comprar.
John wants (to) not buy it.

As expected, complex predicates contrast with ordinary infinitives (or gerunds) which can be negated (79a,b,c,d):

---

[66] We analyze the coordinations of predicates with their complements in flat structures as instances of non-constituent coordination (see section 4.6). However, we do not claim to know which structure to adopt for non-constituent coordination, a separate problem in its own right (for a recent analysis for French, see Mouret 2006).

(79) a. F Jean regrette de ne pas l'étudier.
I Giovanni rimpiange di non studiarlo più.
C En Joan lamenta no estudiar-lo.
S Juan siente no estudiarlo.
P O João lamenta não estudá-lo.
John regrets not studying it.
b. R Pentru a nu pierde trenul,
In order to not miss the train, ...

The interpretation of this phenomenon is not straightforward, and the analysis is not necessarily the same for all the languages we consider.

To the extent that the verbal head of a complex predicate does not take a phrasal VP complement, in contrast to ordinary control or raising verbs, one could say that negation is excluded because it requires a VP. Thus, in a surface-based framework, negation would be analyzed as an adverb which (left) adjoins to an infinitive VP (rather than to the infinitive lexical verb); therefore, in complex predicates in a general way, negation does not find the right constituent to adjoin to.[67]

This analysis is plausible for French, Portuguese and Spanish, where negation can have wide scope over a coordination of infinitive VPs, see Abeillé and Godard (1997) for French:[68]

(80) F a. Paul affirme ne pas [lire le journal ou même regarder les nouvelles à la télévision].
P b. ?O Paulo afirma não [ler o jornal ou mesmo ver as notícias na televisão].
S c. ?Pablo afirma no [leer el periódico o ver las noticias en la televisión].
Paul claims to not read newspapers or even watch the news on television.

[67] Alternatively, in a grammar with functional heads (see e.g. Pollock 1989, Zanuttini 1997), one would say that negation is a functional head that takes for its complement a category (e.g. IP) other than the one found in complex predicates (e.g. VP). This kind of representation would not better explain the absence of wide scope in Italian or Romanian.

[68] The judgments are a little uncertain, depending on the conjunction. As expected, in Italian and Romanian, wide scope is equally impossible with the finite VP, or the gerund. In R, with the VPinf, the pre-VP particle *a* must also be repeated.

(i) I *Paolo non legge giornali o ascolta la radio.
R *Paul nu citeşte ziare sau ascultă radioul.
P. not reads the newspaper or listens the radio
Paolo does not read the newspaper or listen to the radio.

(ii) I *Non comprando giornali o noleggiando nessuna cassetta, Paolo vive fuori dal mondo.
Not buying newspapers nor hiring any cassette, Paolo lives outside the world.

I d. Paolo sembra [non leggere giornali] [e guardare le notizie in televisione].
Paul seems to not read newspapers and to watch the news on television.

R e. Pentru [a nu citi ziarul] [sau / şi *(a nu) se uita la ştiri], ...
In order [not to read the newspaper] [or / and not to look at the news on television], ...

This analysis is less likely for Italian and Romanian, where negation cannot take wide scope: in (80d,e), the negation has scope over the first member of the coordination only. This is unexpected if it adjoins to VP. On the other hand, if negation requires a lexical verb (rather than a VP) in Italian and Romanian, we expect it to not have wide scope over a coordination of VPs. But, in this analysis, it becomes necessary to explain why it is excluded from complex predicates, where the complement is a lexical verb.

There are several possible lines of analyses for the negative adverb in Romanian and Italian. Possibly negation is a lexical affix (ie. it forms a single word with the verb) rather than an adjoined word; this would explain why it must be repeated in a coordination (Miller 1992). This seems to be a plausible solution for Romanian (Barbu 1999). Alternatively, the negative adverb is an independent word, adjoined to the lexical verb. This is the most likely solution for Italian, where certain authors have noted the possibility of negation in certain examples of complex predicates, with prosodic conditions (Napoli 1981, Cinque 2005). Note that the negation can appear between the infinitive and the marker, for certain speakers, as in *%Lo continua a non capire* 'He continues to not understand it'. We have analyzed the marker as marking the lexical verb rather than the VP (see section 4.2); in this perspective, it is expected that the adverb *non* adjoins to the lexical verb. Under such analyses, the negative adverb would not be excluded on syntactic grounds, but there would be a pragmatico-semantic effect associated with the construction. We leave the question of the absence of negation in complex predicates open for further inquiry in these two languages.

6.2 The null complement in Portuguese

A well-known property of Portuguese is the possibility of a null complement for verbs which can be the head of a complex predicate (84a,b).[69]

(84) P a. O João tem visto a Maria, mas o Pedro não (tem).
THE João has seen THE Maria, but THE Pedro not / (has not)

---

[69] The problem is similar with the Romanian modal *a putea*, which, unlike the R auxiliaries, can be found without a complement:

(i) R Vei veni? – *Voi. (= *Are you going to come? – I'm going to*)

(ii) R Poţi veni ? – Pot. (= *Can you come ? – I can*)

b. O João quer falar à Maria, mas o Pedro não (quer).
THE João wants to speak to THE Maria, but THE Pedro not (wants)

This property seems to indicate that the auxiliary or restructuring verb has a phrasal complement, which can be left unrealized.[70] Therefore, we must take another look at the Portuguese data, to see whether this property challenges the flat structure analysis proposed above.

An alternative to the flat structure in Portuguese would be a phrasal complement (a VP), either saturated or not saturated for its complements, as we propose for the copula. But this analysis encounters two major difficulties. First, it is difficult to understand why the possibility of preposing the verbal complement is correlated with the absence of clitic climbing on the head (38)-(39). As we explained above, one cannot simply say that a non-saturated complement cannot be extracted, since it can be with the copula (41). On the other hand, the preposing data follows from a well-accepted constraint on preposing: a sequence can be preposed only when it is a constituent.

The properties of adverbs also run counter to the phrasal complement hypothesis. Remember that, with restructuring verbs, non-light adverbs appear before an infinitive verb if it is (complement) saturated, but not if the clitics climb (51). In our analysis, non-light adverbs appear before a VP complement, but not before a lexical verb complement in the flat structure. In our analysis, this follows from an ordering constraint (74d) and the fact that the VP is non-light while the lexical verb is light. Since light elements in Portuguese appear before non-light ones, non-light adverbs cannot occur before a light verb complement, while they can before a non-light complement. On the other hand, if the complement is in every case phrasal, it is always non-light, and one can no longer call upon this difference. It would be necessary to say that non-light adverbs are possible before a category saturated for clitic complements, but not before a category which is not

---

[70] Clitic climbing is incompatible with a null complement.

(i) P O João tem visto a Maria, mas o Pedro não (*a tem).
THE João has seen THE Maria but THE Pedro not / (CL-has)

(ii) P O João quer falar à Maria, mas o Pedro não (*lhe quer).
THE João wants to speak to. THE Maria, but THE Pedro not (CL- wants)

However, this is the case in a general way, as shown by the unacceptability of (iv) with the copula.

(iii) P O Paulo foi grato à Maria, mas a Marta não (foi).
Paulo was grateful to Maria, but Marta was not

(iv) P *O Paulo foi grato à Maria, mas a Marta não lhe foi.
Paul was grateful to Maria but Marta was not to him

saturated for clitics. Again, the data from predicative verbs challenges such a constraint, since non-light adverbs are possible between the copula and the passive participle, even if the clitics climb (65).

The existence of a null complement does therefore not suffice to challenge our analysis of the Portuguese complex predicate. The case of restructuring verbs is straightforward: they have two possible complementations, a VP and a flat structure; the null complement corresponds to a null VP. But more must be said of tense auxiliaries, which always enter into complex predicates, and yet may have a null complement. To account for (84a), we extend the double complementation to auxiliaries, with the constraint that their VP complement must be null. In this perspective, even the auxiliaries have the signs of double complementation.

6.3 Auxiliary change in Italian

We have not discussed the well-known data about auxiliary change with Italian restructuring verbs (see, among others, Rizzi 1982, Burzio 1986). Verbs like *volere*, which take *avere* when they are not part of a complex predicate (85a), take *essere* in complex predicates if the complement verb itself takes *essere* (85e). Thus *volere* takes *avere* where its complement takes *avere* (85c), but it can take *essere* in (85e), where its complement verb takes *essere* (see (85b)). Verbs like *andare*, which take *essere*, do not change auxiliary (85d,i). The choice of auxiliary in (85e) depends on whether there is a complex predicate or not, as shown by (85f,g), where clitic climbing indicates a complex predicate, and (85h), where absence of clitic climbing indicates absence of a complex predicate.

(85) I a. Rocco ha / *è preso il libro.
Rocco has taken the book.
b. Rocco è / *ha andato a Roma.
Rocco has left for Rome.
c. Rocco ha / *è voluto prendere il libro.
Rocco wanted to take the book.
d. Rocco è / *ha andato a prendere il libro.
Rocco has gone to take the book.
e. Rocco ha / è voluto andare a Roma.
Rocco wanted to leave for Rome.
f. Rocco <u>lo</u> ha / *è voluto prendere.
R. CL-has / is wanted to take
Rocco wanted to take it.
g. Rocco <u>ci</u> è / *ha voluto andare.
R. CL-is / has wanted to go
Rocco wanted to go there.

h. Rocco ha voluto andarci.

i. Rocco lo è / *ha andato a prendere.
   R. CL-is / has gone to take

j. %Rocco è voluto andarci
   R. has wanted to go-CL
   Rocco wanted to go there.

To the extent that the change of auxiliary is obligatory for verbs like *volere* if there is a complex predicate, one can say that it characterizes the complex predicate. But certain speakers also accept the change of auxiliary outside the complex predicate, as seen in (85j). Indeed, if it were the change of auxiliary rather than clitic climbing which was the criterion for a complex predicate in Italian, as proposed in Cinque (2005), it would be necessary to explain why (i) the acceptability of (85j) is variable, in contrast with examples like (85f,g), where the clitic climbs; (ii) one finds the correlations between properties that have been shown above (such as the obligatoriness of clitic climbing if the sequence occurs in a bounded dependency (36)).

In our perspective, the formation of a complex predicate implies the change of auxiliary, but the reverse correlation does not hold. We must therefore consider two possibilities. One is that the selection of *essere* has the same source in all cases. The formation of a complex predicate is then not crucial for the change of auxiliary, and it would be necessary to introduce semantic factors. The other possibility is that it is necessary to dissociate the case of the complex predicate from (85j), and to introduce nonsyntactic factors in the second case only. We leave the problem open (on the selection of the auxiliary in Italian, see, among others, Levin and Rappaport 1995, Sorace 2000, Legendre and Sorace, this volume).

6.4 The structure of complex predicates in Catalan

As we have seen, Catalan is not different from the other Romance languages with respect to the monoclausal properties of its complex predicates. However, speaker judgments show strong disagreement regarding all the structural properties of the Catalan auxiliaries, restructuring verbs or causatives. The points of agreement are:

(i) Preposing is not possible of the non-finite verb with the complements it subcategorizes. Thus, the data in (86) is parallel to that of the other Romance languages: (86a) corresponds to (37), and the contrast between (86b) and (86c) corresponds to the examples in (38)-(39) (see also Gavarró and Laca 2002).

(86) C a. *Llegit aquest llibre, realment, en Joan no (ho) ha.
   Read this book, really, THE Joan not (CL.ACC) has

b. En Pau vol parlar a la Maria?

Does Paul want to talk to Maria?
– Parlar-li a la Maria, ho vol sens dubte.
Talk-CL.DAT to M., CL.ACC wants undoubtedly
(però no vol parlar-li a la seva mare).
(but not wants talk-CL.DAT to her mother)

c. En Pau vol parlar a la Maria?
– *Parlar, (ho) vol a la Maria / li vol sens dubte.
Talk, (CL.ACC)wants to M. / (CL.DAT)wants undoubtedly
(però no a la seva mare)
Talk to Maria, certainly he wants to (but not to her mother).

(ii) The subject cannot intervene between the two verbs in a question (87a). But this has to do with a general ordering constraint, rather than a property of complex predicates. In yes-no questions, the subject appears either to the left of the verb (87c,d), or after the complements if it is focused (87e,f) (Wheeler *et al.* 1999):

(87) C a. *Ha en Pau comprat un llibre?
Has THE Paul bought a book

b. ??Comprarà en Pau un llibre?
buy.FUT THE Paul a book

c. En Pau ha comprat un llibre ?
THE Paul has bought a book

d. En Pau comprarà un llibre?
THE Paul buy.FUT a book

e. Ha comprat un llibre en Pau ?
Has bought a book THE Paul
Was it Paul who bought a book?

f. Comprarà un llibre en Pau ?
buy.FUT a book THE Paul
Is it Paul who will buy a book?

(iii) There are restrictions on the adverbs which can appear between the two verbs of a complex predicate (Gavarró and Laca 2002 give *aviat* 'soon', *sempre* 'always', *ben* 'well', *pas* 'not').[71] But the interpretation of this fact is not straightforward. To start with, there is some variation in speakers' judgments: some, but not all, accept modal adverbs (88b); there are also some speakers who do not allow an adverb to come between a verb and its complements, even when it is not a complex predicate construction (88c).

[71] The adverbs are possible as long as they are accompanied by a particular prosody (Alex Alsina, p.c.). We believe this prosody means that the adverbs are incidental rather than being prosodically integrated in the sentence, a prosodic property which is correlated with scoping as well as linearization properties (for French, see Bonami *et al.* 2004, and here note 57).

(88) C a. Els començarà aviat a fregar.
CL-SHE.begin.FUT soon to clean
She will soon begin to clean them.
b. %En Pau ho voldria potser acabar pel matí.
c. %En Pau voldria potser acabar-ho pel matí.
THE Pau like.COND perhaps finish.CL in the morning
Paul would perhaps like to finish it in the morning.

The judgments diverge with respect to the scope of coordination. As we expect, two non-finite verbs are freely coordinated (see the participles in (89a) and the infinitives in (89b)). But the head (auxiliary, restructuring, or causative verb) can have scope over a coordination of infinitives with their complements for certain speakers while others reject it outright, and a third group are uncertain, or treat the auxiliaries differently to the restructuring verbs. Sentences (89c,d) are therefore subject to variation.

(89) C a. En Joan ha comprat i llegit aquest llibre.
THE Joan has bought and read this book
b. En Joan el vol comprar i llegir.
THE Joan CL.ACC wants buy and read
c. %En Joan ha comprat aquest llibre i llegit el primer capítol.
THE Joan has bought this book and read the first chapter
d. %En Joan el vol comprar per ell i llegir immediatament.
THE Joan CL.ACC wants buy for her and read immediately

Notice, however, that even for speakers who do not accept wide scope in the coordination cases in (89), there is no problem if the object is a bare NP.

(90) C a. %En Pau ha menjat totes les galetes i begut tota la llet.
THE Pau has eaten all the cakes and drunk all the milk
b. En Pau ha menjat galetes i begut llet.
THE Pau has eaten cakes and drunk milk
c. %En Pau li vol comprar un llibre i donar un disc.
THE Pau CL.DAT wants buy a book and give a record
d. En Pau li vol comprar llibres i donar discos.
THE Pau CL.DAT wants buy books and give records

We suggest the following analysis. Like Spanish, Catalan has two systems competing for the complex predicate structure: the verbal complex and the flat structure. But speakers do not always seem to choose one or the other consistently, so that we cannot easily distinguish between two varieties. In addition, the properties of adverbs have to be investigated. A socio-linguistic study of this variation remains to be carried out.

7 Conclusion

We have taken up the idea, from early work on restructuring verbs, that clitic climbing is explained by the fact that a combination of verbs projects a single syntactic or monoclausal domain (with one head verb). Properly speaking, the clitics here do not climb, but are always analyzed as complements of the verb to which they attach. Their position on the upper or lower verb is not free, but depends upon whether or not a complex predicate has been formed. Clitic climbing, along with SE middle passives, long periphrastic passives, and the occurrence of complex predicates in bounded dependencies, are indicators of the general process of inheritance of the arguments of a verb (or, more generally, a predicate) by a higher verb (a process which is also referred to a 'valence fusion' or 'argument composition' or 'clause union'). This is relevant for argument structure.

We have also distinguished the properties of monoclausality, which are shared among the different types of complex predicate and the different Romance languages, from the properties indicative of syntactic constituency, and responsible for the distinctions among the different Romance complex predicates. In our analysis, the sequence of the second predicate and its subcategorized complements does not always form a syntactic constituent in the Romance languages. Rather, leaving aside predicative verbs, complex predicates have two kinds of constituent structure: a verbal complex structure, where the two verbs form a sub-constituent, to the exclusion of the other complements, or a flat structure, where the second (lexical) verb, is on the same level as the head verb and the other complements. With tense auxiliaries, causative, aspectual, modal, or movement verbs, the Romance languages or speakers tend to choose one structure or the other. Romanian has both, the verbal complex for its tense auxiliaries and the flat structure for its modals, while Spanish speakers choose one or the other. In both structures, the second verb is a lexical or, in terms of a weight property, a light complement. Languages have a choice between a purely linear treatment of weight differences (a flat structure with ordering constraints) and a more structural treatment (first combining light or lexical complements with the head, before non-light or phrasal complements). In this perspective, we are led to an unexpected grouping of French, Italian, one Spanish variety and Portuguese (which choose the flat structure) on the one hand, and the other Spanish variety and Romanian (which have the verbal complex structure) on the other.

On the other hand, the predicative verbs (the copula in particular), have the same syntactic structure in all Romance languages. They contrast with the preceding cases in always taking a phrasal or non-light complement, which can itself be saturated, partially saturated or unsaturated for its complements. If it is indeed the lightness property which is at the heart of

plements. If it is indeed the lightness property which is at the heart of the special syntactic (structural or linear) properties of the other complex predicates, we understand why the Romance predicative verbs are treated differently: nothing distinguishes this structure from an ordinary one, besides the possible non-saturation of the complement predicate (which creates a structure analogous with, but not identical to, the flat structure).

These structural differences among Romance complex predicates, which are compatible with identical monoclausality properties, favor grammatical frameworks like Lexical Functional Grammar (Bresnan 1982, 2001) or the phrase structure grammar HPSG (Pollard and Sag 1994, Sag *et al.* 2003), which have the means to distinguish between the representation of valence (or argument structure) and the representation of phrase structure. Relational Grammar or Government and Binding / Principles and Parameters theory (e.g. Chomsky 1981), which tend to only use one type of representation, would fail to easily represent these differences. Finally, if one looks at the differences between Romance languages in more detail, we find that different ordering constraints are needed for the same syntactic structures. This clearly calls for a model which is able to separate the question of constituency from that of ordering.

5

Auxiliaries and Intransitivity in French and in Romance

GÉRALDINE LEGENDRE AND ANTONELLA SORACE

1 Introduction[1]

The Unaccusative Hypothesis (Burzio 1986, Perlmutter 1978, Rosen 1984)[2] states that intransitive verbs divide into two subsets — unaccusatives and unergatives — with distinct syntactic properties. The single argument of unaccusative verbs is an underlying or deep direct object, and thus displays many syntactic properties of direct objects of transitive verbs. In contrast, the single argument of unergative verbs is a subject at all levels of representation, and thus displays the same syntactic behavior as the subject of transitive verbs. This syntactic difference is typically represented configurationally as in (1).

(1) Intransitive structures
    Unergative: NP [$_{VP}$ V]
    Unaccusative: ___ [$_{VP}$ V NP]

The simplicity and elegance of Perlmutter's Unaccusative Hypothesis stands in sharp contrast with the many, largely unsuccessful, attempts at

1 We are grateful to Paul Smolensky for his comments on various aspects of the present chapter and to Danièle Godard for her editorial suggestions.

2 Several early versions of the Unaccusative Hypothesis actually predate Perlmutter (1978), including Postal (1963) and Hall-Partee (1965). See Pullum (1988) on its history.

Fundamental Issues in the Romance Languages.
Danièle Godard (ed.).

formulating a solid and systematic semantic basis for such a syntactic distinction and establishing its cross-linguistic validity.

The earliest formulations of the Unaccusative Hypothesis noted that the distinction is systematically related to certain semantic characteristics of the predicate: 'Agentivity' tends to correlate with unergativity and 'patienthood' correlates with unaccusativity (Dowty 1991, Perlmutter 1978). Much subsequent research has shown, however, that the alignment between syntactic and semantic properties is not 100%, nor is it as consistent as originally predicted (Rosen 1984). Some verbs with similar semantics have different syntactic behavior across languages: For example, 'blush' is unaccusative in Italian but unergative in French (and Dutch), on the basis of their auxiliary selection and appearance in participial constructions. Some verbs are classified as both unaccusative and unergative by the same diagnostic. For example, It. *continuare* 'continue' and Fr. *paraître* 'appear' can take both auxiliaries *essere/être* 'be' and *avere/avoir* 'have'. Within a given language, syntactic tests do not overlap completely, either. This is especially true of French, where auxiliary selection identifies only a small subset of unaccusative verbs, compared with participial constructions:

(2) F a. La neige a / *est fondu(e) pendant la nuit.
The snow melted during the night.
b. La neige fondue, toutes les stations de ski ont fermé.
With the snow melted, all the ski resorts have closed.

Context, too, may play a role. It is well known that *correre* 'run' selects *essere* or *avere* in Italian, depending on the presence of a stated goal. Yet the role of context is not systematic across languages. French *courir* 'run' selects *avoir*, regardless of whether a goal is specified or not.

(3) I a. Il bambino è corso a scuola.
F b. L'enfant a couru à l'école.
The child ran to school.

(4) I a. Il bambino ha corso nel giardino.
F b. L'enfant a couru dans le jardin.
The child ran in the garden.

Nevertheless, a substantial body of research has shown that these 'unaccusative mismatches' are problematic only to the extent that one expects unaccusative and unergative verbs to represent syntactically and semantically homogeneous classes. Most of the syntactic diagnostics of unaccusativity/unergativity (e.g. auxiliary selection in Italian, impersonal passives in Dutch, resultative constructions in English) do tend to identify semantically coherent subsets of verbs (Levin and Rappaport Hovav 1995, 2005).

The challenge has long been the identification of the syntactically relevant components of meaning in different languages and the search for a theory that could account for their reciprocal interaction. The principle underlying this endeavor is that neither a verb's ability to be found in the unaccusative or unergative syntactic configuration, nor the verb's particular semantic characteristics are, by themselves, sufficient conditions to satisfy particular diagnostics: Split intransitivity is both syntactically encoded and semantically determined (Legendre *et al.* 1991, Levin and Rappaport Hovav 1995). Despite views to the contrary (e.g. Bentley 2006; Bentley and Eythórsson 2004), many theories maintain that a syntactic characterization of unaccusativity is necessary to account for phenomena not easily reducible to purely semantic explanations, such as the similarity between unaccusatives and passives, the resultative construction in English, the cliticization of the partitive clitic pronoun *ne* in Italian, etc. The identification of syntactic constraints, however, is not sufficient. It is also crucial to explain how lexical semantic or aspectual representations underlying individual verbs are mapped onto the binary syntactic representations defining the Unaccusative Hypothesis.[3,4]

A decade and a half of discussion of split intransitivity has revealed that French is a serious challenge to all traditional accounts of the phenomenon (e.g. Cummins 1996, Labelle 1992, Legendre 1989, Ruwet 1988, Zribi-Hertz 1987). It has remained basically unexplained so far. Nor has cross-linguistic variation in auxiliary selection in French and Italian been successfully accounted for. The approach developed in this chapter attempts to remedy both situations.

It should come as no surprise that French and Italian dominate the empirical discussion in the present chapter. Among the main Romance languages, French and Italian are the only languages that still make use of two auxiliaries in forming compound tenses.[5] Most other languages have

---

[3] Various theories of argument structure (focused on the syntactically relevant properties of verb arguments) and event structure (focused on the temporal and aspectual organization of the event described by a verb) developed in recent years have set out to pursue this goal (Grimshaw 1990, van Hout 1996, Pesetsky 1995, Pustejovsky and Busa 1995, Rappaport Hovav and Levin 1998, among others).

[4] For example, the resultative construction in English is subject to a 'Direct Object Restriction' (see Levin and Rappaport Hovav 1995) — that is, it can be predicated only of a direct object NP governed by the verb, as shown in (i) :

(i)	E	a. John licked his finger clean.	(transitive)
		b. The bottle broke open.	(unaccusative)
		c. *John shouted hoarse.	(unergative)

[5] Among the less studied Romance languages, Occitan, Piedmontese, Sardinian, and Catalan (spoken outside of Barcelona) maintain two auxiliaries.

dropped their counterparts of *être* altogether, replacing it with a counterpart of *avoir* or some other auxiliary at some point in their history (e.g. Spanish *haber*, Catalan (Barcelona) *haver*, Portuguese *tener*). Romanian does make use of two auxiliaries but they do not alternate as markers of one and the same tense. A derived form of its *avoir* counterpart is used in the compound past tense (*a avea*) while the invariable form *fi* is used in the perfect (Avram 1999; Abeillé and Godard, this volume).

Specifically, we argue that we can make genuine headway in understanding the complex facts of French in the context of Romance variation if we adopt the optimality-theoretic premise that well-formedness constraints on the mapping between the lexicon and syntax are universal, but soft and highly conflicting. For example, verbs denoting existence of state select different perfect auxiliaries in the two languages: *essere* in Italian vs. *avoir* in French. In our terms, such variation results from re-ranking a single constraint with respect to all others in the universal constraint hierarchy defining (part of) Universal Grammar (UG). Among other things, our analysis is shown to account for auxiliary selection developments in the history of Spanish.

The chapter is structured as follows. Section 2 introduces the problem of accounting for gradience in the lexicon/syntax mapping and compares existing classes of solutions to the problem. It is argued that only a hierarchical approach to the lexicon/syntax mapping may capture what is common to and what is different in auxiliary selection in Italian and French. The resulting Auxiliary Selection Hierarchy (Sorace 2000) can in turn be shown to derive from an optimization-based approach to constraint interaction.

Section 3 focuses on French and the controversies surrounding the nature of syntactic evidence for an unaccusative/unergative distinction among its intransitive verbs. Several syntactic tests are probed, including impersonal constructions, partitive clitic *en*, unaccusative inversion, auxiliary selection, and participial constructions. Of the tests reviewed, only auxiliary selection and participial constructions are shown to provide reliable evidence for a split among intransitive verbs.

Section 4 returns to the issue of cross-Romance variation in auxiliary selection and offers an optimality-theoretic solution to that long-standing problem. Section 5 summarizes the main contributions of the paper.

2 Solutions to the mapping problem

In very general terms, 25 years of research on the semantic basis of the unergative/unaccusative distinction have revealed the primacy of lexico-semantic and aspectual features and emphasized the central role played by telicity in capturing regular patterns both across lexico-semantic verb classes and across languages. What remains are controversies about the significance of other features or feature bundles, the theoretical status of verb classes, as well as the formal apparatus necessary to provide an explicit typology of possible lexicon/syntax mappings. Several classes of approaches to the mapping problem have emerged in the last decade or so (see the collection in Aranovich 2006 for an overview), and we examine them in turn. Because Sorace's Auxiliary Selection Hierarchy was designed to solve the Romance problem it is discussed in much greater details than its competitors.

2.1 The projectionist approach

Levin and Rappaport Hovav are the leaders of what has become known as the 'projectionist' approach (see Sorace 2004, Levin and Rappaport Hovav 2005 for discussion). They maintain that the lexical semantics of a verb deterministically specifies the hierarchical classification of its arguments, and that this in turn produces the syntactic behavior associated with unaccusativity or unergativity (Hale and Keyser 1986, 1993; Levin and Rappaport Hovav 1992, 1994, 1995, 2005, among others).

The most comprehensive account of this type is Levin and Rappaport Hovav's (1995) model based on English, in which a small number of linking rules map lexical semantic components of verb meaning (such as 'immediate cause', 'directed change' and 'existence') onto positions at argument structure. Within this approach, verbs with variable behavior have different meanings, and therefore different lexical semantic representations, each with its own regular argument structure realization.

Confronted with the complexities of Romance auxiliary selection, the projectionist approach faces the challenge of accounting for variation without resorting to systematic duplication in the lexicon.

2.2 The constructional approach

Alternatives to the projectionist view have gained ground in recent years. Collectively they can be identified as 'constructional' approaches (Arad 1998a; Borer 1994, 1998, 2005; Cummins 1996; van Hout 1996, 2000; McClure 1995; etc.). These models regard unaccusativity and unergativity not as lexical properties of verbs, but rather as clusters of properties derived from the syntactic configurations in which verbs appear, which in turn determine their aspectual interpretation. Since the lexical entries of verbs do not contain any specification of whether an argument is internal or external, any verb is free to enter into more than one syntactic configuration and consequently to receive multiple aspectual interpretations.

Unlike the projectionist model, the constructional approach predicts flexibility in the syntactic realization of arguments, but at the price of overgeneration. Constraints on overgeneration therefore have to be present at other levels (e.g. Cummins 1996, van Hout 1996). The constructional model is also a direct challenge to the Universal Alignment Hypothesis (UAH, Perlmutter 1978) and the Uniformity of Theta Assignment Hypothesis (UTAH, Baker 1988) according to which the mapping between thematic relations (agent, patient, etc.) and underlying syntactic configuration is invariable and universal.

2.3 The Auxiliary Selection Hierarchy

The starting point of Sorace's 2000 Auxiliary Selection Hierarchy (ASH) is a set of facts which characterize split intransitivity in a number of Western European languages:[6]

(a) Across languages, some verbs tend to show consistent unaccusative/unergative behavior, whereas others do not;

(b) Within languages, some verbs are invariably unaccusative/unergative regardless of context, whereas others exhibit variation. Sorace *et al.*'s studies provide supporting evidence for these generalizations, mostly based on experiments testing native speakers' intuitions about auxiliary selection (perhaps the best known diagnostic of unaccusativity) in various languages that have a choice of perfective auxiliaries (such as Dutch, German, Italian, and Paduan). In all these languages — and to some extent in French — unaccusative verbs tend to select the counterpart of *essere* and unergative verbs tend to select the counterpart of *avere*. However, native intuitions on auxiliaries are categorical and consistent for certain types of verb, but much less stable for other types. For example, native speakers have a very strong preference for counterparts of *essere* with change of location verbs, but express a weaker preference for the same auxiliary (or have no preference at all) with stative verbs.

Sorace's (2000) account of these systematic differences within the syntactic classes of unaccusative and unergative verbs is that there exists a hierarchy which distinguishes 'core' unaccusative and unergative monadic verbs from progressively more 'peripheral' verbs. This hierarchy, which is based on (potentially universal) aspectual parameters, places the notion of 'telic dynamic change' at the core of unaccusativity and that of 'agentive non-motional activity' at the core of unergativity. The extremes of the hierarchy thus consist of maximally distinct core verbs — verbs of change of

---

[6] Sorace *et al.* concentrate on all languages making use of two alternating auxiliaries, including Dutch and German. We by and large omit evidence from Germanic languages in the present discussion.

location (e.g. *arrivare/arriver* 'arrive') and verbs of agentive non-motional activity (e.g. *lavorare/travailler* 'work') — which consistently display the greatest degree of consistency in auxiliary selection. In contrast, peripheral verb types between the extremes are susceptible to variation. The overall hierarchy is represented in (5).

(5) The Auxiliary Selection Hierarchy

CHANGE OF LOCATION *essere / être* (least variation)
CHANGE OF STATE
CONTINUATION OF A PRE-EXISTING STATE
EXISTENCE OF STATE
UNCONTROLLED PROCESS
CONTROLLED PROCESSES (MOTIONAL)
CONTROLLED PROCESSES
(NON MOTIONAL) *avere / avoir* (least variation)

The verbs at the extremes of the hierarchy ('core' verbs) are change of location verbs at the *essere/être* end and non-motional process verbs at the *avere/avoir* end. They are characterized by the following properties:

- categorical/consistent syntactic behavior across languages
- consistent behavior within individual languages; insensitivity to compositional properties of the predicate
- determinacy of native speakers' intuitions
- primacy in acquisition
- diachronic stability

Let us examine some evidence in support of these generalizations, focusing in particular on the first three (for a full discussion see Sorace 2000, 2004).

2.3.1 Core verbs

Core verbs tend to be categorical and consistent in auxiliary selection across languages/language varieties. This is exemplified in (6)–(7), which show that the auxiliary selected by change of location verbs in the present perfect is *essere/être*, and that selected by non-motional process verbs is *avere/avoir*, in all the languages that have a choice of auxiliaries.[7]

(6) I a. Paolo è venuto / *ha venuto in ritardo.
Paolo came late.
F b. Ma soeur est arrivée / *a arrivé hier.
My sister arrived yesterday.

[7] The abbreviation *Sd* stands for Sardinian.

Sd c. Maria est / *at arrivata a domo.
Maria arrived at home.

(7) I a. I delegati hanno parlato / *sono parlati tutto il giorno.
The delegated spoke all day.
F b. Les délégués ont parlé / *sont parlés toute la nuit.
The delegates spoke all night.
Sd c. Los profesores ont faeddadu / *son faeddados totu su die.
The professors spoke all day.

Core verbs display consistent behavior within individual languages; in particular, they tend to select the same auxiliary regardless of the contribution of other aspectual or thematic elements in the sentence in which they appear. So in (8), *arrivare* 'arrive' selects *essere* even though the predicate is atelic; the verb *cadere* 'fall' in (9a) selects *essere* despite the fact that the event described by the verb clearly denotes intentionality, just as it does when the event is clearly unintentional (9b). Similarly, the verb *lavorare* 'work' selects *avere* regardless of the telicity of the predicate, as in (10). Similar remarks apply to their French counterparts.

(8) *atelic predicates*
a. I Sono arrivate lamentele in continuazione.
F Des plaintes sont arrivées continuellement.
Complaints arrived continually.
b. I Sono apparse imitazioni per anni.
F Des imitations sont apparues depuis des années.
Imitations have appeared for years.

(9) a. *agentive*
I Maria è caduta apposta per non andare a lavorare.
F Maria est tombée volontairement pour ne pas aller travailler.
Maria fell on purpose in order not to go to work.
b. *non-agentive*
I Il vaso è caduto dal tavolo.
F Le vase est tombé de la table.
The vase fell off the table.

(10) *telic predicate*
I I poliziotti hanno lavorato fino all'alba.
F Les policiers ont travaillé jusqu'à l'aube.
The police worked until dawn.

The data from studies on other languages (e.g. Paduan, see Sorace and Cennamo 2006) confirm that, in general, inherent lexical aspect determines auxiliary choice with core verbs, whereas compositional aspect (i.e. the event structure of the whole predicate) affects auxiliary selection with peripheral verbs. These findings support the conclusion that auxiliary selection with core verb types is a *lexical* phenomenon and is relatively insensitive to compositional factors. The degree of sensitivity to these factors increases for non-core verb types as they get more distant from the core.[8]

Native speakers of languages with auxiliary selection have clear and determinate intuitions on core verbs; they categorically accept sentences in which these verbs appear with the 'correct' auxiliary and reject those in which they appear with the 'wrong' auxiliary. Evidence of differential judgments is particularly strong for Italian (Sorace 1993a, 1993b, 1995a,b; Bard, Robertson and Sorace 1996 for experimental evidence). Furthermore, descriptive studies of Italian (e.g. Berruto 1987, Rohlfs 1969) indicate that there is more variation in auxiliary usage for peripheral verbs than for core verbs, which is consistent with the predictions of the hierarchy.

The ASH is further supported by developmental data. Auxiliary selection with core verbs is acquired early both in first and second language acquisition. Data from the acquisition of Italian as a non-native language show that the syntactic properties of auxiliary selection are acquired first with core verbs and then are gradually extended to more peripheral verb types (Sorace 1993a, 1995a). Moreover, Italian learners of French find it more difficult to acquire *avoir* as the auxiliary for verbs closer to the core than for peripheral verbs (Sorace 1993b, 1995b), and do not completely overcome this difficulty even at the advanced level. These developmental regularities can be explained by assuming that the acquisition of the syntax of unaccusatives crucially depends on the internalization of two elements: the hierarchical ordering of meaning components, and the lexicon-syntax mapping system instantiated by the target language.

A cursory look at the early acquisition of French verbs by young Grégoire (Champaud Corpus, available from the CHILDES Database, McWhinney and Snow 1985) confirms the general findings. In his earliest four files (age 1;9–1;10), the only intransitive verbs Grégoire uses are unaccusative; he produces 'passé composé' forms with the correct auxiliary (E) with verbs of location first (specifically *tomber* 'fall', *monter* 'go up', *partir* 'leave', in this order). The first unergative verbs to show up in the' passé composé'

[8] A reviewer comments that 'this text illustrates a hypothesized set of diverse properties through lists of verbs provided out of context. However we all know that a given verb can take on different semantic properties in particular contexts. I believe that only full, contextualized examples should be included'. The point is that not all verbs change syntactic behavior according to context: core verbs select the same auxiliary regardless of context, whereas non-core verbs are sensitive to factors contributed by the sentence in which the verb appears.

(A) are controlled motional processes *bouger* 'move' (2;0; file #5) and *rouler* 'move (for a car)' (2;3; file #7).

Finally, core verbs tend to be diachronically stable. There is evidence from studies on the historical development of auxiliaries in Romance (e.g. Benzing 1931, Tuttle 1986) showing that core verb types tend to be the last to be affected by the replacement of auxiliaries derived from Latin *esse* with those derived from *habere* whereas peripheral verb types are the most vulnerable to change (see further discussion in section 4). A recent study by Cennamo (1999) suggests that the development of reflexives *se / sibi* in Late Latin as markers of split intransitivity followed a path largely consistent with the unaccusative/unergative hierarchies.

2.3.2 Intermediate (non-core) verbs

While core verbs tend to be categorical in their auxiliary selection behavior, non-core verbs show increasing variation. The greater flexibility of these verbs is illustrated here with Italian examples (for cross-linguistic evidence see Sorace 2000).

A class that exhibits regular alternations is that of verbs denoting 'indefinite change' in a particular direction (e.g. Fr *monter* 'go up'), change of condition (e.g. Fr *faner* 'wither'), appearance (e.g. Fr *apparaître* 'appear'). *Essere* is strongly preferred by these verbs in Italian, but *avere* is not completely rejected (as in (11b,c).[9] The strength of preferences is a function of the inherent telicity of the verb: As the Italian sentences in (11)-(12) show, many of these verbs allow two readings, one telic and one atelic, which may be disambiguated by the context.

(11) a. I La popolarità del governo è scesa / ha sceso notevolmente.
F La popularité du governement a (visiblement) monté.
The government's popularity has increased notably.
b. I Mia figlia è cresciuta / ?*ha cresciuto molto quest'anno.
F Ma fille a (beaucoup) grandi (cette année).
My daughter has grown a lot this year.

[9] The diacritics in the examples, here and throughout, refer to the degrees of unacceptability of a sentence in terms of strength of preference that native speakers have for one auxiliary over the other. The do not refer to the normative acceptability of sentences in terms of prescriptive grammars. So a sentence marked as "?*" may be ungrammatical according to a prescriptive grammar of Italian, but is judged by native speakers as more acceptable than a sentence marked with "*".

For a discussion on the quantification of relative judgments of linguistic acceptability, and experimental results, see Bard, Robertson and Sorace (1996).

c. I Lo spettro è apparso / ?*ha apparso nel castello.
F Le fantôme est apparu (dans le château).
The ghost appeared in the castle.

(12) a. I La pianta è fiorita / ha fiorito due volte quest'anno.
F La plante a fleuri deux fois cette année.
The plant has flowered twice this year.
b. I I pomodori sono marciti / hanno marcito al sole.
F Les tomates ont pourri au soleil.
The tomatoes rotted in this sun.
c. I Il girasole è / ha finalmente germogliato.
F Le tournesol a enfin fleuri.
The sunflower finally bloomed.

The French versions select *avoir* in the same contexts, with two exceptions: *Monter* 'go up' (and *descendre* 'go down') select *être* or *avoir* for most speakers depending on the agentivity of its subject. For some speakers either auxiliary is possible in these contexts with a subtle change in meaning. *Être* emphasizes the fact that the goal is reached, while *avoir* conveys more of the difficulty during the ascension and somewhat unexpected success of reaching the summit.

Apparaître 'appear' typically selects *être* but it is not uncommon to see it with *avoir* (14a). In fact, the class of verbs of appearance is the class that displays the most variation in French. Yet, the change in auxiliary does not seem to correlate with a change in meaning for this class.

(13) F a. Pierre est / a monté jusqu'au sommet.
Pierre climbed to the summit.
b. La température a / est monté(e) pendant la journée.
The temperature rose during the day.
(14) F a. C'est ici que le petit prince a apparu sur terre. (Saint-Exupéry)
It is here that the little prince appeared on Earth.
b. Ambrose Pierce a / est disparu en 1913. (cited by Cummins 1996:39)
Ambrose Pierce passed away in 1913.
c. Le dernier livre de Chomsky a / est paru en 1995.
Chomsky's last book appeared in 1995.
d. Eve a / est passé(e) de la chambre à coucher à la salle de bain. (Ruwet 1988)
Eve went from the bedroom to the bathroom.

Verbs denoting continuation of a pre-existing condition (e.g. 'stay') are less determinate in Italian: *Essere* is preferred but *avere* is not ruled out categorically, and is in fact accepted with many of these verbs. The agentivity of the subject correlates with the degree of acceptance of *avere* — see the contrast in (15b–c) and (15e–f) — suggesting that these verbs, unlike core verbs, are sensitive to the feature contributed at the predicate level.

(15) a. I Ancora una volta sono / ?ho rimasto solo.
F Je suis resté seul une fois de plus.
I stayed alone once again.
b. *non-agentive*
I La discussione è durata / ?ha durato a lungo.
F La discussion a duré pendant longtemps.
The discussion lasted a long time.
c. *agentive*
I Il preside è / ha durato in carica tre mesi.
The dean has been (lit. lasted) in office three months.
d. I I miei genitori sono sopravvissuti / ?hanno sopravvissuto alla guerra.
F Mes parents ont survécu à la guerre.
My parents survived the war.
e. I Questo atteggiamento è / ?ha persistito per troppo tempo.
F Cette attitude a persisté pendant trop longtemps.
This attitude has persisted for too long.
f. I Gianni *è / ha persistito nella sua ostinazione.
F Jean a persisté dans son obstination.
Jean persisted in his stubbornness.

The French examples in (15) select *avoir* with one exception: *rester*. In fact, all remaining verb classes discussed below invariably select *avoir*, in sharp contrast to the variation displayed in Italian.

Stative verbs (including both verbs of physical and abstract existence and psychological verbs) are the most indeterminate in Italian, consistent with the findings from other studies. Auxiliary alternations (some restricted to regional or non-standard varieties) are shown in (16)–(17).

(16) I a. I primi mammiferi sono esistiti / ??hanno esistito molti milioni di anni fa.
The first mammals existed many millions of years ago.
b. Lo zucchero non è bastato / ??ha bastato per fare la torta.
There was not enough sugar to make the cake.
c. Il film è sembrato / ?*ha sembrato troppo violento a tutti gli spettatori.
The film seemed too violent to all the audience members.

(17) I a. Questo palazzo ha appartenuto / è appartenuto alla mia famiglia.
This palace once belonged to my family.
b. I viveri sono scarseggiati / hanno scarseggiato tra i terremotati.
Basic necessities have become very scarce among the earth quake victims.
c. Il partito è / ?ha sussistito senza i contributi dei politici.
The party continued to exist without contributions from politi cians.
d. La sua dichiarazione non è servita / ?ha servito a nulla.
His declaration didn't serve any purpose.

The use of *avere* induces an agentive reading, whereas *essere* does not. So in (18), the verb *mancare* is understood as intentional in (b) and non-intentional in (a).

(18) I a. Il soldato è mancato all'appello.
The soldier was missing at roll-call. (non-agentive)
b. Il presidente ha mancato all'appuntamento.
The president missed the meeting. (agentive)

Peripheral verbs closer to the 'unergative' core include verbs denoting motional processes (e.g. 'swim'). Native intuitions are less absolute: *Avere* is preferred but *essere* is not completely rejected, as shown in (19) and (20).[10]

(19) I I bambini hanno saltato / ?*sono saltati in giardino tutto il pomeriggio.
The children jumped in the garden all afternoon.

(20) I a. Michela ha corso / ? è corsa più velocemente di tutti.
Michela ran the fastest of all.
b. Paola ha nuotato / ?*è nuotata fino all'altra sponda.
Paola swam all they way to the other bank.

The effects of agentivity on auxiliary selection are shown in (21), where *avere* is the preferred auxiliary with a human subject, *essere* is the preferred one with an inanimate subject.

---

[10] A reviewer argues that 'I imagine that 'jump' will be classified along with 'swim' as denoting a controlled process. Yet, in 'This noise made me jump (in the air)', 'jump' does not denote a controlled process'. The examples above show that verbs like *saltare* 'jump' in Italian display a different syntactic behavior according to whether the subject is agentive or not. *Sauter en l'air* 'jumsp in the air' in this context means *sursauter* 'jump (in surprise)'; it belongs to the subclass of involuntary actions along with *trembler* 'shiver', etc.

(21) I a. Il pilota ha / ?è atterrato sulla pista di emergenza.
The pilot landed on the emergency runway.
b. L'elicottero è / ?ha atterrato sul tetto del grattacielo.
The helicopter landed on the roof of the skyscraper.

Next, the hierarchy includes various types of uncontrolled processes such as bodily functions (e.g. 'sweat'), involuntary reaction (e.g. 'tremble') and emission (e.g. 'clink') (for definitions of controlled vs. uncontrolled processes, see Levin and Rappaport Hovav 1995). These verbs are internally caused but tend to be non-volitional.

(22) I a. Il convincimento politico ha tentennato / ?è tentennato anche nei più anziani.
Political convictions vacillated even among the oldest.
b. Paolo ha tentennato / *è tentennato a lungo prima di prendere una decisione.
Paul hesitated for a long time before making a decision.
c. La terra ha tremato / ?è tremata.
The earth shook.
d. Mario ha tremato / *?è tremato dallo spavento.
Mario shook with fear.
e. Il mendicante ha rabbrividito / è rabbrividito dal freddo.
The beggar shivered from the cold.

(23) I a. L'innesto non è attecchito / ha attecchito.
The transplant didn't take.
b. L'acqua ha scarseggiato / ?è scarseggiata.
Water has become scarce.
c. La bicicletta ha sbandato / ?è sbandata senza preavviso.
The bicycle suddenly skidded.

(24) I a. La sveglia ha squillato / ?è squillata.
The alarm clock rang.
b. L'eco ha / è risuonato.
The echo resounded.
c. Il tuono ha / è rimbombato.
The thunder rumbled.

To sum up, auxiliary selection in Italian displays a gradient sensitivity to the aspectual and lexical-semantic properties of individual verbs, which is uniquely captured by the ASH. Telicity is the main factor that separates verbs that select *essere* from verbs that select *avere*. Agentivity is a secondary factor that further differentiates among verbs selecting *avere*. Core verbs at the extremes of the hierarchy tend to select the same auxiliary categorically both within and across languages. Verbs between the extremes are less specified with respect to telicity and agentivity, and it is among these verbs that most cases of 'unaccusative mismatches' are found.

French, too, displays some gradient sensitivity to the aspectual and lexical-semantic properties of individual verbs, with one significant difference. The core unaccusative verbs are a subset of their Italian counterparts and the resulting cut-off point between intransitive verbs selecting *être* and those selecting *avoir* is much higher in the hierarchy, as shown in Table 1 ("*" indicates variation as discussed above). The high cut-off point in French entails that variation and instability occurs closer to the top, i.e. among change of state verbs. As many verb classes from the bottom up have already switched to *avoir*, there is less variation and gradience than in Italian. Viewed from the perspective of the history of Romance languages, French appears to be relatively close to eliminating *être* as an alternating auxiliary.

auxiliary		Verb classes
French	Italian	
E	E	Change of location: *arrivare / arriver* 'arrive', *venire / venire* 'come', etc.
		Change of state
E	E	a. Change of condition: *morire / mourir* 'die', etc.
E*	E	b. Appearance: *apparire / apparaître* 'appear', etc.
		c. Indefinite change in a particular direction:
E*	E	*salire / monter* 'go up', *scendere / descendre*'go down'
A	E*	*appassire / faner* 'wither', *peggiorare / empirer* 'worsen', etc.
A	E*	Continuation of pre-existing state: *durare / durer* 'last', etc.
		Existence of state:
A	E	a. *essere / être* 'be'
A	E*	b. *esistere / exister* 'exist', *bastare / suffire à* 'suffice'
		Uncontrolled processes
A	A*	a. Emission: *risuonare / résonner* 'resound', etc.
A	A	b. Bodily functions: *sudare / suer* 'sweat', etc.
A	A*	c. Involuntary actions: *tremare / trembler* 'shiver', etc.
A	A*	Motional controlled processes: *nuotare / nager* 'swim', etc.
A	A	Non-motional controlled processes: *lavorare / travailler* 'work', etc.

Table 1: Auxiliary selection in French and Italian

The ASH challenges existing theories of the syntax-lexicon interface. It cannot be accommodated within a projectionist account because it would entail too much duplication in the lexicon, and it does not fit a constructional account either because the amount of variation is related to specific verb types. At the same time, it has features of both accounts. Like the projectionist approach, it assumes a systematic relation between the syntax of auxiliary selection and the semantics of individual verbs. Like the constructional approach, it allows for verbs (though not all of them) to have multiple syntactic projections.

2.4. An Optimality-Theoretic approach

Establishing that cross-linguistic variation in auxiliary selection is best understood in terms of a hierarchy of lexico-semantic verb classes still leaves important theoretical questions unanswered. The ASH is a generalization that reveals different cut-off points for the unergative unaccusative distinction in French and Italian. It does not automatically translate into a set of mapping rules referring to the verb classes in Table 1, for two main reasons. A single verb class may not map onto a single auxiliary — as in the case of change of state verbs in French. More important still is the fact that these classes do not by themselves reveal what is common to two verb classes selecting one and the same auxiliary.

We propose that the ASH arises from an optimization-based view of grammar whereby the verb classes listed in Table 1 and the hierarchy itself *emerge* from a competition among soft constraints on mapping a given lexico-semantic or aspectual feature (e.g. telicity, control, etc.) onto a syntactic configuration.

We borrow the features themselves from the existing literature on split intransitivity and propose that a set of five binary features is sufficient to exhaustively describe classes and subclasses in Table 1: ± telic, ± motion, ± directed change, ± protagonist control (or agentivity), ± state (see Table 2 in section 4). The mapping rules or constraints that employ these features, however, are novel.

We know that there is a universal tendency for the argument of a verb bearing features like +telic, +motion, +directed change not to map onto an unergative configuration. We can therefore specify a set of constraints against pairing each feature of the verb with its argument in subject position (*subject/telic, *subject/directed change, etc.) and evaluate both auxiliaries against it. Since selecting *avoir* correlates with an unergative configuration, the argument of a +telic, +motion, +directed change verb like *arriver* 'arrive' would violate all these constraints. Note that selecting *être,* which correlates with an unaccusative configuration, would satisfy them all. The fact that not all verbs select *être* means that the above constraints against pairing any feature with an unergative configuration are in conflict with at least one constraint penalizing an unaccusative configuration. The choice of auxiliary depends on the relative priority of that constraint – whether it is more or less important than the constraints *subject/telic, *subject/directed change, etc. See section 4 for an analysis that implements these ideas.

The key idea is that auxiliary selection is the outcome of a competition between unergative (subject) and unaccusative (object) configurations. The most well-formed configuration wins, as determined by soft or violable mapping constraints. It is not fatal to violate one or more constraints as long as this allows a higher priority constraint to be satisfied.

In Optimality Theory, cross-linguistic variation results from re-ranking constraints. As we shall see in section 4, only one constraint needs to be re-ranked to account for both French and Italian patterns of auxiliary selection. The analysis also makes a number of predictions. In fact, a complete typology of auxiliary selection systems is formally predicted, and empirically confirmed (Legendre 2006, Legendre, Sorace and Smolensky 2006).

3 Syntactic tests for unaccusativity in French

We first return to the issue of the limited evidence that auxiliary selection provides for an unergative/unaccusative distinction in French. Because this distinction has far reaching consequences for the study of French syntax in general, it is imperative to re-evaluate the main syntactic tests proposed in the literature. Obviously the issue is also of paramount importance for other Romance languages (e.g. Spanish, Catalan, Portuguese, Romanian) that do not avail themselves of alternating auxiliaries.

We proceed with examining the status of widely accepted syntactic tests in French, namely impersonal constructions, the distribution of partitive *en*, and so-called unaccusative inversion. In section 3.2 we probe the lexico-semantic basis of auxiliary selection in French and the status of reflexive verbs (which we have ignored so far). In section 3.3 we argue that the only reliable independent evidence for unaccusativity in French is provided by the participial constructions exemplified in (25). Where appropriate we present parallel evidence gathered from the existing literature on other Romance languages.

(25) F a. La personne morte hier soir sera enterrée demain matin.
The person who died last night will be buried tomorrow morning.
b. On croyait son père mort d'une crise cardiaque.
We thought his father had died of a heart attack.

c. Le père mort, les enfants vendirent la propriété familiale.
With the father dead, the children sold the family property.

d. Mort d'une crise cardiaque à 20 ans, son frère n'avait pu reprendre la direction de la ferme familiale.
Dead of a heart attack at 20, his brother was unable to take over the family farm.

3.1 Unreliable syntactic tests

Among the most frequently invoked syntactic tests in the context of unaccusativity in French are (active) impersonal constructions and the distribution of partitive *en*. For example, the syntactic literature is replete with claims that impersonal constructions group together passive and unaccusative verbs while they exclude unergative and transitive verbs, based on examples like (26) (Cinque 1990, Labelle 1992, Marandin 2001, Pollock 1986, Ruwet 1989, etc.). Similar claims have been made for *en*.

(26) F a. Il a été arrêté plusieurs terroristes à la frontière.
Several terrorists were arrested at the border.

b. Il est arrivé trois personnes.
Three people arrived.

c. *Il a travaillé trois personnes.
There worked three people.

d. *Il a mangé de la glace trois enfants.
There ate ice cream three children.

3.1.1 Impersonal constructions (ICs)

Despite numerous claims to the contrary ICs do not syntactically distinguish two subclasses of intransitives in French. To begin with, a significant number of well-formed examples of ICs (with and without partitive *en)* have been reported which involve verbs classified as unergative on the basis of their ungrammaticality in participial constructions, their selection of *avoir* in the perfect tense, and their low rank on the ASH (Bouchard 1995, Cummins 1996, and Legendre 1989).

(27) F a. Il travaille des milliers d'ouvriers dans cette usine.
Thousands of workers work in this factory.

b. Pendant des siècles il a régné des tyrans sur cette petite île de l'Atlantique.
For centuries tyrants have reigned over this small Atlantic island.

c. Il a sauté beaucoup d'otages par la fenêtre.
Many hostages jumped through the window.

d. Il a éternué beaucoup d'enfants pendant le concert.
Many children sneezed during the concert.

The claim that there are by and large no lexical restrictions on intransitive verbs appearing in ICs is echoed in two large studies of ICs. One is the corpus analysis of Hériau (1980), which forms the basis of the discussion in Cummins (1996). This corpus includes well-formed ICs of 273 monadic verbs, all drawn from Modern French literature of the 19th and mostly 20th centuries. Hériau points out that the verbs listed below can hardly be subsumed under the existence and appearance classes, traditionally held to be the verb classes that ICs are restricted to. Yet, they are attested in his corpus: *saigner* 'bleed', *rêvasser* 'daydream', *répondre* 'answer', *bâiller* 'yawn', *pleurer* 'cry', *pâlir* 'grow pale', *crisser* 'squeak' *grisonner* 'go gray', *frissonner* 'shiver', *frémir* 'shudder', *baver* 'drool', *poudroyer* 'produce clouds of dust', *palpiter* 'flutter'. These are all unergative in French.[11] Additional support is provided in Rivière's 1981 analysis of an extensive corpus of elicitations from a large sample of native speakers. A number of examples in this section are drawn from these two corpora.

In the generative literature, the occasional recognition that unergative verbs are not excluded in ICs is typically accompanied by two comments: (a) Only a few unergative verbs display this exceptional behavior (i.e., the pattern is non-productive), (b) These unergative verbs display properties in ICs that are not found in unaccusative verbs. Compared with unaccusatives, unergatives are said to have an existential reading, to be stylistically marked, and less acceptable (e.g. Labelle 1992:381). At first glance, the first restriction appears to be confirmed by the fact that verbs of existence and continuation of state — which fail all unaccusativity tests — are extremely common in ICs.

(28) F a. Il est des pays où les gens sont heureux.
There are countries where people are happy.
b. Il persiste de nombreuses rumeurs sur le nouveau président.
There persist numerous rumors about the new president.
c. Il ne demeure aucun doute sur sa culpabilité.
There remains no doubt about his guilt.

Yet, according to Lambrecht (1994), the function of ICs is not primarily that of asserting the existence of the referent of the postverbal NP. Rather, ICs give a presentational value to a previously unidentifiable entity, as shown by the indefinite restriction on the postverbal NP and the fact that all examples can be paraphrased as presentational clefts [*il y a ... qui*] as in *Il*

---

[11] And so are verbs of existence of state. See evidence in sections 3.2 and 3.3.

y a du lait qui aigrit dans le frigo 'There is some milk going sour in the fridge'. One may further tease apart presentational ICs proper (often called existential) which serve to introduce a new, not yet pragmatically available entity in the world of discourse to make it available for reference in subsequent discourse from event-reporting ICs, which introduce a new referent as an element in some unexpected or surprising piece of information.[12] Thus, examples in (30) — in contrast with (29) — merely introduce a new event. They are all natural answers to *Que se passe-t-il?* 'What is happening?' Moreover, (29) — in contrast with (30) — have a generic or habitual reading, which explains their affinity with the present and past imperfective tense.

(29) Presentational:

F a. Il meurt beaucoup d'enfants dans le Tiers-Monde.
Many children die in the third World.

b. Il aigrissait deux litres de lait dans le frigo.
Two liters of milk were going sour in the fridge.

c. Il gisait un homme sur le trottoir.
A man was lying on the sidewalk.

d. Il bourdonnait des milliers d'insectes autour de nous.
Thousands of insects were buzzing around us.

(30) Event-reporting:

F a. Il sort des enfants de partout.
Children are appearing out of everywhere.

b. Il brille mille étoiles dans le ciel ce soir.
A thousand stars are shining in the sky tonight.

c. Il dort un chat au coin du feu.
A cat is sleeping by the fire.

d. Il a échappé une bourde au président.
A blunder slipped from the president's lips.

e. D'ici peu il voyagera de nombreux millionaires dans l'espace.
Soon many millionaires will travel to space.

f. Il est resté beaucoup de vin qu'il faudra maintenant finir.
There is a lot of wine left, that will now have to be finished.

We find examples of semantically varied verbs in both types of ICs, including directed motion (30a), change of state (29a–b), spatial configuration (29c), emission (29d, 30b), etc. Clearly, these verbs do not correlate with a particular class on the ASH, nor with a particular aspectual property. Some

---

[12] Lambrecht (1988:150) notes that it is not always possible to define an utterance as belonging to one rather than the other type.

are telic, others are atelic. (29a, 30a) involve unaccusative verbs, (29c–d, 30b–f) unergative verbs (on the basis of auxiliary selection and their behavior in participial constructions). In sum, there is no subclass of ICs that strictly correlates with unaccusative verbs.

Many linguists have pointed out that unergative ICs often sound better with a locative or temporal adjunct. In some cases an adjunct is even required. As it turns out, this constraint does not distinguish unergative from unaccusative ICs, either. (31a–e) demonstrate that both syntactic classes can exhibit a strong preference (or requirement) for an adjunct. The reader may verify that this constraint (whatever its exact nature may be) cross-cuts the presentational vs. event-reporting dimension.

(31) F a. Il paraît des nouvelles contradictoires tous les jours.
vs. *Il paraît des nouvelles.
Contradictory news reports appear every day. vs. *News reports appear every day.*

b. En 1970 il roulait encore quelques trams dans Paris.
vs. ?*Il roulait quelques trams.
In 1970 a few trams still ran in Paris. vs. *A few trams still ran.*

c. Il rôtit deux oies dans le four. vs. ?*Il rôtit deux oies.
Two geese are roasting in the oven. vs. *Two geese are roasting.*

d. Hier à Bobino il chantait un artiste espagnol inconnu en France.
vs. ?*Il chantait un artiste espagnol.
Yesterday a Spanish artist unknown in France was singing at Bobino. vs. *A Spanish artist was singing.*

e. Chaque jour il change des milliers de personnes à la station Châtelet. vs. *Il change des milliers de personnes.
Every day thousands of people change at Châtelet station. vs. *Thousands of people change.*

We suspect that there are a number of factors behind the obligatoriness of or strong preference for adjuncts in (31). With alternating (transitive/intransitive) verbs like *changer* 'change', adjuncts may well be necessary to disambiguate the structure (31e). According to Lambrecht (1994) a main function of ICs is to 'demote' the agentivity of the referent and 'promote' the presentational function of the structure. Further specification of an event in terms of the location or temporality of the universe of discourse (e.g. *chanter à Bobino* 'sing at Bobino' (a famous Paris theater)) can be understood as serving that main function. It spreads the focus over properties of the event that are typically backgrounded in canonical sentences rather than having to concentrate it on the referent of the postverbal NP in the absence of an adjunct.

That an existential interpretation is also enhanced by a specification of the location or temporality of the universe of discourse is not surprising either. The locative or temporal PP anchors the state of affairs in the universe of discourse, adding a dimension beyond its mere existence. However this explanation does not straightforwardly account for the fact that the locative clitic pronoun *y* is highly favored in ICs. The question is: Why are the ICs in (32) more felicitous with *y* than with their non-pronominal counterparts (which themselves are much more felicitous than their bare counterparts), if both serve to anchor the state of affairs in the universe of discourse?

(32) F a. Il y circule des voitures. (y = dans les rues pavées de la ville)
Cars move around there (in the cobbled streets of the city).
b. Il y pousse des fraisiers. (y = le long du sentier)
Strawberries grow there (along the path).
c. L'autre jour je suis allé à la rivière, il y pêchait des dizaines de personnes.
The other day I went to the river, dozens of people were fishing there.
d. ?*L'autre jour il pêchait des dizaines de personnes dans la rivière.
The other day dozens of people were fishing in the river.

Following Lambrecht (1994) we tie the preference for *y* to the informational status of ICs. ICs introduce new information. This is particularly clear from the fact that contrastive focus *ne ... que* 'only' or *surtout* 'above all' always yields an 'improved' IC:

(33) F a. Dans les rues il ne rôdait que des créatures de rêve.
Only fantastical creatures were prowling in the streets.
b. Il y pousse surtout des fraisiers.
Strawberries grow there, above all.

Lambrecht relates the *y* preference to a cognitive constraint limiting the number of inactive referents that can be introduced at a time to one. It is well known that clitic pronouns encode old information. Expressing a locative adjunct as *y* allows satisfaction of the cognitive constraint without losing the anchoring function of the locative. As a consequence, *y* does not detract from the focus on the existence of a particular state of affairs.

Summing up our discussion, we have provided empirical evidence that there is no unaccusative restriction on French ICs in general. Nor is there such a restriction on subclasses of French ICs as defined by their discourse function. All the well-known properties pertaining to the postverbal elements in the structure are tied to their presentational function.

3.1.2 Partitive *en* and unaccusative inversion

Marandin (2001) argues that inversion in non-*wh* contexts is restricted to unaccusative verbs, based on the possibility of *en* (in appropriate contexts of referring to old information) and the failure of some intransitive verbs to appear in the construction.

(34) F a. Je voudrais que vienne Marie.
I would like for Marie to come.
b. Alors sont entrés deux hommes.
Then two men entered.
c. Quelques minutes plus tard en arrivèrent deux autres.
A few minutes later two more arrived.
d. Paul craignait que n'en viennent plus d'autres.
Paul feared that no others would come.

From our previous discussion we know that *en* is ubiquitous in impersonal constructions. Not surprisingly, the partitive clitic pronoun *en* enhances an IC just like *y* does. In fact, most spontaneous elicitations of ICs start as *Il en* V ..., and many examples in Hériau (1980) involve *en* rather than a full postverbal NP when it is the quantifier that has the status of new information. Given that ICs impose no restrictions on their intransitive verbs, the presence of *en* cannot be tied to a particular type of verb, unaccusative or otherwise.

Based on an observation by Abeillé (1997) that object NPs are the only constituents that trigger *en* and take the form *de N* in negative contexts (see 35b), Marandin argues that *en* reveals the function (object) rather than the position (postverbal) of its referential source. If Marandin is right, then all verbs that appear in ICs are unaccusative because *en* is possible with all of them. Yet, this conclusion cannot be correct, because some verbs in (35) — in particular *bourdonner* 'buzz', *voyager* 'travel' — are among the lowest on the ASH and they do not pattern syntactically like verbs at the top of the hierarchy, both with respect to auxiliary selection and appearance in PCs.

(35) F a. Il en meurt beaucoup dans le Tiers-Monde.
A lot of them die in the Third World.
b. Il n'en rôtit que deux dans le four.
Only two of them were roasting in the oven.
c. Il en gisait un sur le trottoir.
One of them was lying on the sidewalk.
d. Il en bourdonnait des milliers autour de nous.
Thousands of them were buzzing around us.

e. D'ici peu il en voyagera de nombreux dans l'espace.
Soon several of them will travel in space.

The distribution of Italian *ne* is significantly more restricted that that of French *en*. In the standard language, the well-known pattern associated with unaccusativity obtains: *Ne* occurs with transitive, passive, and unaccusative verbs; unergative verbs do not allow *ne*, as shown in (36).

(36) a. I Gianni ne ha mangiate tre (di mele).
F Gianni en a mangé trois (pommes).
Gianni ate three of them (apples).
b. I Ne sono stati venduti molti (di appartementi).
F Beaucoup en ont été vendus (d'appartements).
Many of them were sold (apartments).
c. I Ne sono arrivati trenta (di studenti).
F Trente en sont arrivés (étudiants).
Thirty of them arrived (students).
d. I *Ne hanno lavorato molti (di impiegati).
F *Beaucoup en ont travaillé (d'employés).
Many of them worked (employees).

But the comparison is not as simple as (35)–(36) might first suggest because (36d) is equally ungrammatical in Italian and French. The correct generalization about partitive *en* is this: *En* does not distinguish unaccusative from unergative verbs. Rather, *en* provides evidence for the structure of ICs themselves, independently of the lexical verb they may contain. To the best of our knowledge, Cummins (1996) is the first one to have zeroed in on the necessity of distinguishing the unaccusative structure of ICs (the post-verbal NP occupies a position within V′) and the distribution of the verbs that occur in ICs.

Marandin further claims that, among intransitive verbs, only verbs denoting a 'non-Actor' relation may appear in unaccusative inversion. He defines 'Actor' in terms of immediate cause of an eventuality (Levin and Rappaport Hovav 1995:135), which covers both internally and externally caused events. The following ungrammatical examples of agentive verbs are offered in support of his claim.

(37) F a. *Alors passa à l'action le commando.
Then the commando went into action.
b. *Alors commencèrent à travailler les candidates.
Then the candidates started working.

We reject this claim on the basis of two observations. First, the verbal structures in (37) are complex. *Passer à l'action* 'go into action' is an idiomatic expression while *commencer à travailler* 'start working' is an aspectual construction. The length/heaviness of the verbal string relative to that of the subject affects the overall acceptability of the sentence. Compare (37) with examples in which the subject NP is lengthened (38a) or the unergative verb shortened (38b–c).

(38) F a. ?Alors se mirent à rire trois joyeux lurons.
Then three happy fellows started laughing.
b. Ainsi parlait Zarathoustra.
Thus spake Zarathustra.
c. Alors sonna le glas.
Then the death-knell tolled.

Levin and Rappaport Hovav (1995) cite Italian *sorridere* 'smile', *scherzare* 'joke', *chiaccherare* 'chat', etc., English *cough*, *shiver*, *sleep*, *snore*, etc., verbs of emission as well as verbs of spatial configuration as examples of the immediate cause of eventuality subclass of unergative verbs. Note that (38) fall squarely into Levin and Rappaport Hovav's subclass.

Second, the type of inversion exemplified in (38) is a highly stylized construction that is found almost exclusively in literary French. A quick look at Le Bidois's study of inversion in 20th century prose yields many examples of such inversion after a temporal adverbial. Many involve unaccusative verbs denoting motion or appearance but a surprising number of examples involve unergative verbs (39) and even some transitive verbs (40). For additional examples in both main and non-*wh* complement clauses, see Le Bidois (1950:132–37).

(39) F a. Parfois retentissait la sirène comme un appel déchirant de Walkyrie. (Proust)
Sometimes the sirene resounded like the tearing call of a Wal karie.
b. Déjà régnait en ce matin de juillet une chaleur sulfureuse. (Mauriac)
A sulfur-like heat already reigned on that July morning.
c. Déjà depuis longtemps sommeillait ma tête lassée. (Gide)
My tired head had already been asleep for a while.
d. De nouveau soufflait le grand vent du premier soir. (Fournier)
The strong wind of first evenings was blowing again.
e. Enfin glissa lentement, entre les rideaux, la face.... d'un long pierrot. (Fournier)
At last the face of a long pierrot slided slowly between the curtains.

(40) F a. Alors m'envahit plus complètement la tristesse. (Gide)
Then sadness invaded me more completely.
b. Alors avait dû éxercer sur elle un grand prestige la femme pour laquelle Rachel avait été quittée. (Proust)
Then the woman for whom Rachel had been abandoned had to have had great prestige exercised on her.

The evidence is overwhelming. Among unergative verbs we find a variety of semantic classes, including verbs of existence, verbs of sound and substance emission, manner of motion, spatial configuration, and activity verbs. If we add these to the lexico-semantic classes that map onto an unaccusative configuration, we have examples of so-called unaccusative inversion with all intransitive verbs (including reflexive ones).

It is tempting to suggest that the label 'unaccusative' inversion may in fact pertain to its structure rather than the distribution of relevant verbs — on a par with the conclusion reached for ICs above. The main argument Cummins (1996) invokes for the unaccusativity of IC structures is the complete ban against having transitive verbs in ICs.

(41) F a. *Il y guette Pierre des renards. (vs. Des renards guettent Pierre.)
Foxes are lying in wait for Pierre.
b. *Il les y guette des renards. (vs. Des renards les guettent.)
Foxes are lying in wait for them there.

To the extent that transitive verbs may occur at all in unaccusative inversion (see (40)), extending the IC analysis to unaccusative inversion is surely premature.

3.2. Auxiliary selection

In a nutshell, there are two auxiliary selection patterns in French, an easy one and a challenging one. The easy pattern is that all verbs occurring with reflexive morphology — regardless of the function/meaning of the reflexive clitic, and without any exceptions — select *être*. Among non-reflexive verbs however, there is a split in auxiliary selection, which — as we shall see — is best analyzed in terms of a hierarchical approach. We start with the complex pattern of split intransitivity that follows the ASH.

3.2.1 Auxiliary selection with non-reflexive verbs

In French only about 20 non-reflexive verbs obligatorily select *être* (Cumming 1996), compared with large numbers (a hundred or so) in Italian. They include *advenir* 'occur', *aller* 'go', *arriver* 'arrive', *apparaître* 'appear', *décéder* 'die', *devenir* 'become', *entrer* 'enter', *intervenir* 'happen, intervene', *mourir* 'die', *naître* 'be born', *partir* 'leave', *parvenir* 'reach', *prove-*

provenir 'arise', *rester* 'remain', *retourner* 'return', *sortir* 'go out', *survenir* 'happen', *tomber* 'fall', *venir* 'come' (see also Grevisse 1975).

In terms of the ASH most of these verbs are at the very top of the hierarchy (as predicted). They include verbs of change of location (*arriver (à)* 'arrive', *partir* 'leave', *venir (à)* 'come (to)', *parvenir à* 'reach', *accourir* 'come running', *sortir* 'go out', *tomber* 'fall') and change of state (*mourir* 'die', *naître* 'be born', etc.), which are inherently telic and express a directed change rather than a change of location. Telicity is an aspectual property widely associated with unaccusativity (see Zaenen 1993 on Dutch, Zribi-Hertz 1987 on French). Yet, telicity alone (either inherent or contextual) is not sufficient to predict *être* in French. As Melis (1985) notes, agentive *aller* 'go' denotes a non-directed motion process with an atelic reading (*aller vers la gare* 'go toward the train station') or with an endpoint and a telic reading (*aller à la gare* 'go to the train station'). Regardless of context, it selects *être*. Nordhal (1977) reports that *aller* could appear with both auxiliaries in Old French. This typically resulted in an activity reading (with *avoir*) or an achievement reading (with *être*). In Modern French *aller* has to be further specified with *à pied* 'on foot', *en voiture* 'by car', *à skis* 'on skis', etc., to express manner and denote an activity rather than motion. Because activity is conveyed by the adverbial phrase, the basic lexico-semantic properties of *aller* are retained and *être* is still the auxiliary of choice. This shows that contextual meaning does not necessarily entail auxiliary change.

In general, a combination of telicity and directed motional change is required for selection of *être*, but some aspectual properties are common to verbs that select *être* and those that select *avoir* (see also Cummins 1996). This in turn necessitates a more elaborate and fine-grained analysis than traditional analyses based on telicity alone are able to provide.

A few telic change of state verbs focusing on the end state select *être*: *mourir* 'die', *décéder* 'pass away', *naître* 'be born'. Many telic verbs of the same narrowly defined class, however, select *avoir* for no obvious semantic reason: *expirer* 'expire', *succomber à* 'succumb', *périr* 'perish', *trépasser* 'pass away'. An anonymous reviewer remarks that *expirer* behaves like *inspirer* 'inspire' /*respirer* 'breathe', which occupy a lower position on the ASH. *Périr* 'perish' (from Latin *per-ire*) and *trépasser* 'pass away' appear to behave like *traverser* 'cross'. Finally, *succomber* 'succumb' may be etymologically related to *suc-cumbere* (*tomber sous* 'fall under') but this does not explain its choice of *avoir*. The same reviewer suggests a structural analogy: *Succomber à NP* 'succumb to' selects *avoir* in analogy with *résister à NP* 'resist'. In sum, a number of exceptions defy any lexico-semantic account, possibly due to mere analogical processes.

The ASH predicts that as we move down the hierarchy we find more variability. This is indeed the case. Among verbs of appearance denoting a transition to a state and emphasizing the beginning of the event, we find a few verbs which select *être*: *apparaître* 'appear' and verbs derived from *venire* 'come' (*parvenir* 'reach', *survenir* 'occur', *intervenir* 'intervene').[13] Others (*transparaître* 'transpire', *surgir* 'appear suddenly', *émerger* 'emerge', etc.) select *avoir*. Yet others select either auxiliary, sometimes without any detectable change in meaning (Cummins 1996; Grevisse 1975; Ruwet 1989): *paraître* 'appear', *disparaître* 'disappear', *passer* 'pass by'. See the examples given earlier in (14).

Overall, verbs of appearance are [+inherent telicity], [–motional displacement][14], i.e. less specified than core verbs selecting *être*, which in turn means that they are more variable.

Most verbs of indefinite change in a particular direction, regardless of their telicity status in context, select *avoir* (unless they are reflexive).[15] This large class of verbs denotes degree achievements (Dowty 1979) and display variable aspectual behavior (Hay *et al.* 1999). Depending on whether their affected argument undergoes a change to a closed-range or open-range state, their interpretation is telic or atelic. *Rancir* 'turn rancid', *verdir* 'turn green', *rougir* 'redden', etc., are in fact ambiguous between a telic reading (*rougir* = 'become red') and an atelic one (= 'be more red'). Verbs with a typical telic reading include deadjectival verbs like *sécher* 'dry', *noircir* 'blacken', *refroidir* 'cool', *durcir* 'harden', which denote processes leading to a non-gradable final state. The verbs themselves are modifiable by the temporal adverbial *en x heures* 'in *x* hours' and the resulting state by *complètement* 'completely': *sec* 'dry', *froid* 'cold', *noir* 'black', *dur* 'hard', etc.

Verbs which have the same aspectual properties but are not derived from adjectives include *bouillir* 'boil', *fonder* 'melt', *faner* 'wither', *flétrir* 'wilter', *moisir* 'grow moldy', *pourir* 'rot', *tarir* 'dry up', etc.[16] The verbs denoting processes leading to a open-ended state are typically atelic; they include deadjectival *grandir* 'grow taller', *grossir* 'grow fatter', *rétrecir* 'shrink', *rapetisser* 'grow smaller', *embellir* 'grow more beautiful', and non-deadjectival verbs like *empirer* 'worsen', *baisser* 'decrease', *fermenter*

---

[13] *Convenir* 'suit' can select *avoir* in Modern French (*être* in Old French). Note that it denotes a state rather than a transition of state. All existence of state verbs select *avoir* in French.

[14] The meaning of *apparaître* 'appear' does not include motional displacement on the part of the person who is said to appear. It only requires that the person becomes visible to the speaker.

[15] One exception is *monter* 'go up' (and *descendre* 'go down'), as discussed in section 2.3.

[16] In the present tense, some change of state verbs including *bouillir* 'boil', *sécher* 'dry', *durcir* 'harden', etc., are in fact ambiguous between 'being in the state of boiling' (atelic) and 'coming to a boil' (telic).

'ferment', *augmenter* 'increase', *diminuer* 'diminish', *décliner* 'decline', etc. All can be modified by the temporal adverbial *pendant des heures* 'for hours' and *se mettre à* 'to start V-ing', *petit à petit* 'little by little' (Zribi-Hertz 1987).

Verbs of spatial configuration include atelic maintenance of position verbs (*reposer* 'rest', *gésir* 'lie', etc.) as well as assuming position verbs that denote a directed change of state: *reculer* 'back up', *rebondir* 'bounce'. They are stative in their basic meaning and they select *avoir* which is the auxiliary of choice for existence of state in general: *survivre (à)* 'survive', *persister* 'persist', *stagner* 'stagnate', *languir* 'vegetate', *durer* 'last', *exister* 'exist', *appartenir à* 'belong', etc.

Surprisisingly, a few atelic verbs denoting absence of change select *être*: *rester* and *demeurer*. One might impute their selecting *être* to the fact that *rester* and *demeurer* express continued presence therefore existence. But *être* itself expresses continued presence and existence, yet it selects *avoir* (*essere* in Italian).[17]

(42) F a. Il reste / est resté à l'université.
He is staying / stayed in college.
b. Il est / a été à l'université.
He is / was in college.
c. Il est / a été des nôtres.
He is / was one of us.

The fact that most verbs of existence of state select *avoir* was a puzzle in traditional accounts typically requiring some extra rule to explain their choice of auxiliary (e.g. Legendre 1989). On the present account, they occupy the midpoint in the ASH and are amongst the most peripheral of both unaccusative and unergative verb classes. We predict significant variation cross-linguistically as well as variation within a given a language. This is very much what we observe both in French and Italian. See section 2.3. for examples.

Going still further down the ASH, the remaining classes select *avoir*. They include uncontrolled bodily processes (*trembler* 'tremble', *éternuer* 'sneeze', *suer* 'sweat', *rougir* 'blush', *suffoquer* 'suffocate', *dormir* 'sleep', etc.) and verbs of emission (*briller* 'shine', *luire* 'glow', *résonner* 'echo', *jaillir* 'spurt', *couler* 'flow', *rugir* 'roar', *éclabousser* 'spatter', etc.) as well as manner of motion verbs typically used with an agentive argument (*courir*

[17] The real reason behind *être* selection may have been lost in the history of French. In his dictionary of Old French, Greimas (1989) gives *rester* 'stay' (Lat. *restare*) as originally meaning *s'arrêter* 'come to a stop', *se lever* 'get up', and *résister* 'stand up against'. Note that all three are directed motion verbs.

(à) 'run', *marcher* 'walk', *sauter* 'jump', *nager* 'swim', *rouler* 'roll', etc.), and activity verbs (*travailler* 'work', *jouer* 'play', *parler* 'talk'). Most are atelic but some are telic: *triompher* 'triumph', *réussir à* 'succeed', *capituler* 'capitulate', etc. As Sorace (2000) shows, non-core 'unergative achievement verbs' (McClure 1995) such as *triompher, réussir à, capituler* are strongly agentive (i.e., they imply intentionality) but they also imply a permanent change of state for the subject argument (unlike core unergatives such as *travailler* 'work', which do not have this implication). However, this change of state is not the endpoint of the action, but rather the logical consequence of the event.

It is clear that more traditional proposals have failed for French because none have explicitly focused on the interaction of eventive factors. For example, event-structure based analyses relating selection of *être* singlehandedly to a state component in the logical structure of a verb (Van Valin 1990), or to an affected argument of a stative predicate in logical structure, as proposed for Italian in Centineo (1996) cannot account for French. Verbs of existence and achievement verbs meet this definition, and yet, they select *avoir*.

3.2.2. Auxiliary selection with reflexive verbs

The one verb class for which auxiliary selection in French can be predicted without any regard for their event structure is a morpho-syntactically defined class: reflexive verbs. (See Abeillé and Godard 2002, this volume for a similar claim). As we shall see, every single class of verbs considered in our survey includes reflexive members whose morphology overrides any of their event structure properties. These include change of state verbs, which alternate between transitive and reflexive including *(s')améliorer* 'improve', *(s')assombrir* 'darken', *(s')obscurcir* 'darken', etc. At first glance one might be tempted to ascribe their selecting *être* to the fact that they are telic verbs. The following list of verb classes organized around their lexico-semantic properties shows, however, that telicity is irrelevant when the morphology is reflexive.

(43) Aspectual classes of reflexive intransitive verbs (all selecting *être*):
  Telic verbs of directed motion with the focus on the end point: *se rendre à* 'go to', *se transporter à* 'move to', or the departure point: *s'en aller* 'leave'; atelic *se promener* 'go leisurely' and telic *se déplacer (à)*'move (to).
  Telic change of state verbs focusing on the end state: *s'éteindre* 'die (of a fire or person)', *s'anéantir* 'become useless'.
  Telic verbs of change of state like *s'évaporer* 'evaporate' as well as (atelic) verbs denoting processes leading to a open-ended state like

deadjectival *s'élargir* 'grow larger', *s'enrichir* 'become richer', *s'assombrir* 'darken', *s'obscurcir* 'become very dark' and non-deadjectival verbs like *s'étouffer* 'choke', *se détériorer* 'deteriorate', etc.

Verbs of (dis)appearance denoting a transition to a state: *se dissiper* 'dissipate', *se volatiliser* 'disappear by flying', *s'envoler* 'fly away', *se manifester* 'appear', *se produire* 'take place', *se montrer* 'show up', *se révéler* 'appear'.

Inherently reflexive verbs including telic verbs like *s'emparer de* 'take possession of', *s'envoler* 'fly away', *se repentir* 'repent', etc. and atelic ones which typically denote a psychological state (*se moquer de* 'laugh at', *se pâmer* 'faint', *se douter de* 'suspect', *se souvenir de* 'remember', *se méfier de* 'fear'). In other syntactic contexts (e.g. the participial constructions discussed in section 3.3) many behave like non-reflexive unergative verbs.

Atelic verbs describing a continuation of state such as *s'éterniser* 'stay around forever', *s'attarder* 'stay on', *se maintenir* 'hold'.

Verbs of spatial configuration including imperfective maintenance of position verbs (*se tenir* 'stand', *se trouver* 'be located at') as well as assuming position, which are typically perfective: *se blottir* 'huddle up', *se recroqueviller* 'curl up' , *s'avancer* 'move forward', *se cabrer* 'rear up', *se lever* 'stand up', *s'asseoir* 'sit down', *se tasser* 'settle', *s'affaler / s'effondrer / s'écrouler* 'collapse', *s'affaisser* 'sag'.

Verbs of uncontrolled bodily processes (*s'évanouir* 'faint'), verbs of emission (*s'illuminer* 'light up', *s'embraser* 'be set ablaze'), agentive manner of motion (*se retourner* 'turn around', *se pavaner* 'strut about'), and activity verbs. Most are atelic: *se garder de* 'refrain from', *s'apercevoir de* 'realize', *s'adonner à* 'devote oneself to', *s'efforcer de* 'try', *se crever à* 'exhaust oneself in' , *s'employer à* 'apply oneself to', etc.; others are telic: *s'écrier* 'shout', etc.

All morphologically reflexive verbs without any exception select *être*, whether *se* is a marker of semantic reflexivity/reciprocity, inalienable possession, middle/passive, or has no semantic content ('inherent *se*').[18] Note that novel intransitive verbs entering the language are likely to be reflexive: e.g. *s'afghaniser* 'become Afghanized', *s'iraniser* 'become Iranized', by

---

[18] On factual grounds we reject the view put forward by Zribi-Hertz (1987) that *se* is a marker of perfectivity. Nor should *se* be analyzed as a marker of low elaboration of an event (Cummins 1996). We side with Grimshaw (1982) and many others in claiming that *se* is fundamentally a valency reducing morpheme.

analogy to fairly recent *s'américaniser* 'become Americanized' with a transitive causative counterpart but no intransitive inchoative like **américaniser, *afghaniser, *iraniser*.

In fact, both the absolute character of *être* selection by reflexives and its productivity — the class of reflexive verbs is huge and expanding — point to a morphosyntactic explanation. Early on, Perlmutter (1989) and Rosen ([1981] 1988) identified these properties as providing one of the two main arguments in favor of a syntactic representation of (underlying) unaccusativity.

Their other argument for a syntactic encoding of the unergative/unaccusative distinction is grounded in the well-known parallelism between (personal) passive and unaccusative verbs. Passive operates on transitive verbs whereby an internal argument (direct object) surfaces as the subject of the verb endowed with passive morphology. Under Perlmutter's (1978) Relational Grammar analysis or Burzio's (1986) Government and Binding version, both passive and unaccusative receive essentially the same syntactic analysis. In Burzio's terms, these verbs fail to assign a theta-role to their subject position and Case to their internal argument (thereby accounting for their intransitivity). The internal argument moves to subject position to receive Case.

In addition, passive verbs share several eventive properties of reflexive verbs. First, their surface subject is semantically unrestricted. Passive applies to activities (*arrêter* 'stop'), change of state (*casser* 'break', *briser* 'break'), and psychological states (*aimer* 'love', *connaître* 'know') alike, as long as they involve two core arguments. Second, reflexives and passive are morphologically marked. Zribi-Hertz (1987) argues that it is the non-reflexive member of an alternating pair that is idiosyncratic, and this receives confirmation from novel verbs entering the language, as discussed earlier. That is, inchoativity is typically expressed by *se* just as passive is expressed by special morphology. Third, the event structure corresponding to a passive verb is similar to that of an unaccusative verb like *se casser*: The entity undergoing change is a passive participant of a process brought about by external factors; the focus is on the end of the process. In sum, we see no reason to abandon the parallelism between passive, reflexive, and unaccusative constructions on which the syntactic analysis of unaccusative verbs rests.

Summing up, our discussion of auxiliary selection has revealed the extent to which two main factors underlie the choice of *être* in French. One is reflexive morphology, which overrides any other consideration. All French reflexive verbs, regardless of argument structure or lexico-semantic properties, select *être*. Similarly, all Italian reflexive verbs select *essere*.

The other factor is a verb's placement on the ASH, on the basis of which French and Italian establish two different syntactic subclasses, so-called unaccusative and unergative classes. The French cut-off point is high, with the consequence that few unaccusative verbs select *être* today, compared with their Italian counterparts.

Crucially, the ASH reveals that the split into two subclasses is not random across the two languages. The French unaccusative class is merely a subset of the Italian unaccusative class. In fact, the systematicity of the mapping argues against analyses that assimilate auxiliary selection in French to an idiosyncratic property of individual verbs requiring a stipulation in the lexicon (Cummins 1996). On the contrary, auxiliary selection is a reliable test for unaccusativity in Romance — notwithstanding the small size of the resulting unaccusative class in French.

Our conclusion runs against other claims made in the literature. Labelle (1992) states that selecting *être* is a test for unaccusativity and selecting *avoir* a test for unergativity based on the fact that verbs of change of state like *casser* alternate between selecting *avoir* (as opposed to *essere* in Italian) when used in the intransitive inchoative construction and *être* in the reflexive construction.

(44) F a. Le vase a cassé.
b. Le vase s'est cassé.
The vase broke.

We reject the claim that verbs selecting *avoir* are unergative once and for all in French, for three main reasons. First, the subclass of verbs that select *être* is only a subset of the unaccusative class (see discussion in section 3.3.). Second, part of Labelle's evidence relies on assuming that ICs are a reliable test for unaccusativity in French, which they are not (see discussion above and below in section 4.2). Third, Labelle's claim entails that Spanish and Romanian with their single perfect auxiliary *avoir* do not have *any* unaccusative verbs. However, occurrence in participial absolute constructions, adnominal participial adjectives (45), and bare NP subject constructions (46) positively identifies unaccusative verbs in Spanish (Aranovich 2003a, Mendikoetxea 1999, and Torrego 1989). Romanian unaccusative (but not unergative) verbs also productively occur in participial absolute constructions (Dobrovie-Sorin 1994:182).

(45) S a. Los chicos salidos de la casa a las nueve no han llamado.
The kids who left the house at 9 have not called.
b. *Los chicos gritados a las nueve no han llamado.
The kids who shouted at 9 have not called.

(46) S a. Llegaron invitados a la fiesta.
Invited (people) came to the party.
b. *Hablan representativos mañana.
Representatives are speaking tomorrow.

3.3 A reliable diagnostic test for unaccusativity: participial constructions

The strongest and most productive evidence in favor of a syntactic distinction among French intransitive verbs comes from participial constructions (PCs for short). These include adnominal participial adjectives (APAs), *croire* 'believe' unions (CRs), participial absolute (PA), and participial equi (PE) constructions — all discussed at length in Legendre (1989). APAs function like a reduced relative modifying a noun (33a). *Croire* unions are representative of biclausal structures in which the complement clause consists of an argument modified by a participial adjective.[19] They are 'unions' (a term borrowed from Relational Grammar) because they trigger clitic climbing, as shown in (47b). PAs are different from CR in two respects. They are adjunct clauses (i.e., they are not governed by a class of main verbs), and they must precede the main clause (47c). PEs are the control counterpart of PAs (47d): Their non-overt argument is in a control relation to (i.e. coreferential with) the subject of the main clause. Targeting the object of a transitive verb in PCs (47) as opposed to its subject (48) always yields an absolute contrast in grammaticality.

(47) F a. L'athlète éliminé en quart de finale a décidé de prendre sa retraite.
The athlete eliminated in the quarterfinals decided to retire.
b. On le croyait éliminé en quart de finale.
We thought he had been eliminated in the quarterfinals.
c. Son compatriote éliminé en quart de finale, l'athlète américain reprit espoir.
With his compatriot eliminated in the quarterfinals, the American athlete felt hopeful again.
d. Eliminé en quart de finale, l'athlète américain reprit espoir.
Eliminated in the quarterfinals, the American athlete felt hopeful again.

---

19 Other main union verbs governing participial clauses include *juger* 'judge', *supposer* 'suppose', and *considérer* 'consider' (Legendre 1989).

(48) F a. *L'athlète américain éliminé son compatriote en quart de finale a perdu en demi-finale.
The American athtete, having eliminated his compatriot in the quarterfinals, lost in the semis.
b. *On le croyait éliminé son compatriote en quart de finale.
We thought he had eliminated his compatriot in the quarter-finals.
c. *L'athlète américain éliminé son compatriote en quart de finale, le champion de la coupe du monde reprit espoir.
The American athlete having eliminated his compatriot in the quarterfinals, the World Cup champion felt hopeful again.
d. *Eliminé son compatriote en quart de finale, l'athlète américain reprit espoir.
Having eliminated his compatriot in the quarterfinals, the American athlete felt hopeful again.

(Non-reflexive) intransitives display a split highly reminiscent of the one found in auxiliary selection. The verbs that may appear in PCs are high on the ASH (i.e. telic change of location verbs), while the ones that invariably fail are lowest (e.g. non-motional activity verbs). (49)–(50) illustrate the split. [(49) = (25)]

(49) F a. La personne morte hier soir sera enterrée demain matin.
The person who died last night will be buried tomorrow morning.
b. On croyait son père mort d'une crise cardiaque.
We thought his father had died of a heart attack.
c. Le père mort, les enfants vendirent la propriété familiale.
With the father dead, the children sold the family property.
d. Mort d'une crise cardiaque à 20 ans, son frère n'avait pu reprendre la direction de la ferme familiale.
Dead of a heart attack at 20, his brother was unable to take over the family farm.

(50) F a. *Le candidat hésité trop longtemps a été rejeté.
The candidate who had hesitated too long was rejected.
b. *On considérait le candidat hésité trop longtemps.
We considered the candidate to have hesitated too long.
c. *Le premier candidat hésité trop longtemps, ...
With the first candidate having hesitated too long, ...
d. *Hésité trop longtemps, ...
Having hesitated too long, ...

As we move down the ASH from change of location verbs we encounter the predicted pattern as well as a different cut-off point, compared with auxiliary selection.[20] First, we encounter some variation within the larger class of change of state verbs: *expirer* 'expire/die', *fonder* 'melt', *refroidir* 'cool', *moisir* 'grow moldy', *durcir* 'harden', *tarir* 'dry up', etc., yield well-formed PCs, but *succomber à* 'succumb to', *trépasser* 'pass away', *empirer* 'worsen', *rétrécir* 'shrink', etc., do not. Among verbs of (dis)appearance, some non-reflexive ones appear in PCs (*apparaître* 'appear', *disparaître* 'disappear', *paraître* 'appear', etc.) and some do not (*transparaître* 'transpire').

Most of these change of state verbs select *avoir* in the perfect tense. Hence the class of verbs that may appear in PCs is a superset of those that select *être*. In other words, as a classificatory test, PCs identify more French verbs as unaccusative than auxiliary selection does. In particular, these include the large class of verbs of indefinite change in a particular direction, an example of which is given in (51). Note that this class, too, displays some variation. For example, *empirer* 'worsen', *rougir* 'redden', *pâlir* 'become pale', etc., are by and large not acceptable in PCs (see (55) below).

(51) F a. La neige fondue pendant la journée avait tourné en glace.
The snow that had melted during the day had turned into ice.
b. On croyait la neige fondue dans toutes les stations de ski.
We thought the snow had melted at all the ski resorts.
c. La neige (une fois) fondue, toutes les stations ont fermé.
With the snow melted, all the resorts have closed.
d. Fondue, la neige tournait en boue.
Having melted, the snow turned into mud.

The remaining non-reflexive verbs selecting *avoir* — including verbs of spatial configuration *reposer* 'lie', of assuming position *reculer* 'back up', *rebondir* 'rebound', of existence *être* 'be', *sembler* 'seem', *exister* 'exist', *survivre* 'survive', *persister* 'persist' — are ungrammatical in PCs (as are lower classes on the ASH).

There appears to be no aspectual restriction on either APAs and CR unions. Both telic and atelic participles are grammatical.

(52) F a. Un poulet mariné en moins de deux heures est bien meilleur.
A chicken marinated for less than two hours is much better.

[20] The pattern starts with *aller*, which selects *être* but is ungrammatical in PCs, either in a telic or atelic context: **allé à / vers la gare* 'gone to/toward the strain station'. Note that *aller* denotes motion along a path rather than a directed change of location. This is possibly why *aller* (unlike *arriver* 'arrive' but like manner of motion verbs *nager* 'swim', *errer* 'wander') is ungrammatical in participial contexts.

b. Les documents disparus pendant des semaines ont été retrouvés.
The documents, missing for weeks, were found.

c. On le croyait évadé de prison en moins d'une journée.
We thought he had escaped from prison in less than a day.

d. On imaginait Marie restée seule à la maison pendant des heures.
We imagined that Marie had stayed at home alone for hours.

This is not the case for participial adjunct clauses where the secondary event denoted by the adjunct clause stands in a cause-effect relation with the main event. In particular, the secondary event must be completed prior to or overlap with the main event. In fact, in PAs the secondary event must be completed prior to the main event. This temporal relation is often rendered explicit or improved by the addition of *une fois* 'once' to the participial clause, an indication of the relevance of telicity: *Une fois le lait bouilli, la neige fondue*, ... 'once the milk (had) boiled, the snow (had) melted...'. This is also true of Italian (Perlmutter 1989, Rosen 1984). The form of the participle — identical to that found in compound tenses like the passé composé and passives — provides additional evidence for a telicity restriction on PAs. Contra Labelle (1992), these aspectual restrictions do not invalidate PAs as a test for unaccusativity, let alone invalidate the remaining PCs. It simply means that appearing in a PA is a sufficient condition but not a necessary one (Legendre 1989).

The second restriction is one of event dynamicity. The state denoted by the adjunct clause must be the result of a change, as revealed by a comparison between copular constructions and PAs. While adjectives and nominals are standard in copular constructions, they are ungrammatical in PAs. In contrast, their dynamic counterparts are fine. The fact that *rester* 'stay' and *demeurer* 'remain' are not acceptable confirms the existence of a dynamicity restriction on PAs.

(53) F a. *Son mari innocent, Marie refusa de divorcer.
With her husband innocent, Marie refused to get divorced.

b. Son mari innocenté, Marie refusa de divorcer.
Her husband having been found innocent, Marie refused to get divorced.

c. *Son père (un) héros de la résistance, Pierre était respecté de tous.
With his father a resistance hero, Pierre was respected by all.

d. Son père devenu un héros de la résistance, Pierre était respecté de tous.
His father having become a resistance hero, Pierre was respected by all.

e. *?Sa fille restée / demeurée (seule) à la maison, Marie écourta sa visite.
With her daughter having stayed alone at home, Marie cut her visit short.

In PEs, these aspectual restrictions are clearly relaxed. The secondary event need only overlap with the main event. It need not even be a state resulting from a change. It is not surprising then that *rester* and *demeurer* are perfectly acceptable in PEs.

(54) F a. Assis au premier rang, les enfants ne quittaient pas la scène des yeux.
Seated in the first row, the children didn't take their eyes off the stage.

b. Jaillie d'on ne sait où, l'eau coulait claire et limpide.
Having gushed out from who knows where, the water flowed crystal clear.

c. Innocent / innocenté, Pierre refusa de reprendre son travail.
Innocent/having been found innocent, Pierre refused to resume his work.

d. Héros de la résistance, il était respecté de tous.
A resistance hero, he was respected by all.

e. Restée / demeurée seule à la maison, Marie se mit à pleurer.
Having stayed alone at home, Marie started crying.

Telicity and dynamicity together appear to impose a necessary condition for appearance in PAs. However, the combination of telicity and dynamicity is not a sufficient condition for appearing in PAs: It cannot rescue a verb otherwise doomed in PAs. In particular, selecting unergative participles denoting more dynamic processes (e.g. uncontrolled bodily processes and some activities) and adding the aspectual adverbial *une fois* to force a completed reading does not render them acceptable in PAs (or any PC):

(55) F a. *Une fois pâli / rougi / bâillé / sué, Pierre se dissimula derrière un pare-à-vent.
Once gone pale / blushed / yawned / sweated, Pierre hid himself behind a screen.

b. *Une fois réagi / triomphé / résisté, Pierre embrassa sa femme et ses enfants.
Once reacted / triumphed / resisted, Pierre kissed his wife and children.

This shows that the primary condition on PAs is not aspectual in nature. Rather, the primary condition is one that splits the classes of verbs into two main subclasses, those that are grammatical in PAs as long as they are also [+telic], [+dynamic], and those that are ungrammatical, regardless of their aspectual properties. Hence the class of verbs that appear in PAs is a subset of the class that appear in other PCs. By characterizing both classes as syntactically unaccusative we can formulate a generalization that cuts across aspectual restrictions. Nevertheless, the subset-superset relation among unaccusativity tests is confirmed: auxiliary selection (selects the fewest number of unaccusatives at the small class at the top of the ASH) < PAs (selects a larger class anchored at the top of the ASH) < other PCs (select the largest class also anchored at the top of the ASH).

All intransitive verbs that appear in PCs turn out to have an important common property. They are intransitive verbs whose participle alternatively appears in a predicative structure with the copula *être*. The predicative form is homophonous with the passé composé form of only the small class of non-reflexive verbs selecting *être*: *est parti* 'is gone', *est monté* 'is gone up', *est mort* 'is dead', *est apparu* 'is appeared', *est resté* 'is stayed', etc. For all other verbs, the copular construction is clearly distinct from the passé composé (because of a different auxiliary or absence of reflexive morphology): *est fondu* 'is molten', *expiré* 'is expired', *moisi* 'is moldy', *refroidi* 'is cooled off', *blotti* 'is hudlled up', *évanoui* 'is fainted', etc. In all cases, the copular construction denotes a state resulting from change or motion.

Stative, uncontrolled processes, manner of motion, and activity verbs typically fail in the copular construction: **est existé* 'is existed', *relui* 'is gleamed', *résonné* 'is resonated', *pâmé* 'is fainted', *rougi* 'is reddened'[21], *pâli* 'is paled', *grandi* 'is grown', *nagé* 'is swum', *couru* 'is run', *hésité* 'is hesitated', *travaillé* 'is worked', etc. They also fail in all PCs. Note that *survivre* 'survive' conveys a result, yet it is ungrammatical. In sum, appearance in a copular construction is in fact as much a separate test as any of the

[21] A reviewer mentions that some accept *est rougi* 'is reddened' and *est pâmé* 'is fainted' as in *ses mains rougies* 'his/her reddened hands', *une femme pâmée* 'a fainted woman'. We suggest that *rougi* is a passive participle in this context: *ses mains rougies par le froid* 'his/her hands reddened by the cold'.

PCs discussed above. Like them, it follows the prediction made by our analysis.

(56) F a. *Ils sont survécus.
They are survived.
b. *Les personnes survécues ...
The people who have survived ...
c. *On les croyait tous survécus.
We thought they had all survived.
d. *Ses parents survécus, ...
With his parents having survived, ...
e. *Survécus, ses parents ...
Having survived, his parents ...

Abeillé and Godard (2002) have demonstrated that copula/passive *être* is not syntactically identical to perfect tense *être*. Hence, to say that only the verbs appearing in the copula construction may also appear in PCs — and thereby be identified as unaccusative (as one reviewer suggests) — is distinct from claiming that a subset of unaccusative verbs select *être* as an auxiliary.

Our earlier comparative discussion of partitive *en* and *ne* in section 3.1.2 highlighted the fact that the existence of similar structures with similar meanings in both languages does not translate into similar distributional properties. A similar point is made by Loporcaro (2003) concerning participial constructions. Loporcaro notes that one subtype of PCs, namely PEs (unlike PAs) are not restricted to unaccusative and passive verbs in Italian. He provides the following examples including unergative and transitive verbs (57a-d), which are all absolutely ungrammatical in French.

(57) a. I Vendemmiato, i contadini lasciarono il paese.
F *Vendangés, les fermiers quittèrent le village.
Having harvested the grapes, the farmers left the village.
b. I Bussato alla porta, Gianni entrò.
F *Frappé à la porte, Gianni entra.
Having knocked at the door, Gianni entered.
c. I Maltrattato Gianni, Carla partì.
F *Maltraité Gianni, Carla partit.
Having mistreated Gianni, Carla left.
d. I Arrestatili, la polizia poté sedare il tumulto.
F *Les arrêtés, la police a pu mettre fin à l'émeute.
Having arrested them, the police were able to calm the riot.

e. I Svegliatasi Maria, la festa poté cominciare.
F *Se réveillée Maria, la fête pouvait commencer.
With Maria having woken up, the party could begin.

Returning to French, one significant difference between auxiliary selection and PCs is that reflexive morphology is irrelevant to the latter.[22] Yet, not all reflexive verbs appear in PCs despite the fact that they select *être* and (at least some of them) can have a telic interpretation. Many are ungrammatical in PCs, including verbs of (dis)appearance: *se volatiliser* 'escape by flying', *se manifester* 'occur', *se produire* 'happen', *se montrer* 'show up', *se révéler* 'appear'; stative *s'éterniser* 'stay forever', change of state *(s')empirer* 'worsen', inherently reflexive *s'emparer de* 'grab', *se souvenir de* 'remember', *se moquer de* 'laugh at', *se pâmer* 'faint', and spatial configuration verbs like *se tenir* 'stand', *se trouver* 'be located at', etc. Because reflexive morphology is relevant to auxiliary selection but not to PCs, the conclusion seems inevitable that intransitive verbs which appear in PCs constitute neither a subset not a superset of verbs that select *être*.

An important consequence of motivating PCs as productive unaccusativity tests is that it leads to an unergative classification of some reflexive verbs. Recall that auxiliary selection does not tell us anything about the unaccusativity status of reflexive verbs because the reflexive morphology constraint overrides any constraint pertaining to aspectual features mapping onto an object position in the syntax. Reflexive verbs may or may not appear in PCs without any obvious aspectual restriction to explain the difference in grammaticality. Ungrammatical reflexive verbs in unrestricted and restricted PCs include atelic maintenance of position verbs: *se tenir droit* 'stand straight', *se trouver sans ressources* 'find oneself without any resources'; stative *s'éterniser à réviser,* 'keep revising forever', *se révéler contraire* 'prove to be opposed to', uncontrolled processes *s'embraser* 'be set ablaze', *s'évaporer* 'evaporate', *s'étouffer* 'choke', as well as psychological states *s'apercevoir de qch* 'realize something', *se souvenir de qch* 'remember something', *se douter de qch* 'suspect something', and activities *s'adonner à la politique* 'devote oneself to politics'; *s'engager dans la bataille* 'enter the fray', etc.

To sum up, we have argued that PCs (with or without aspectual restrictions) provide substantial evidence for identifying a subclass of intransitive

---

22 The reflexive clitic *se*, like any other clitic in French, never appears attached to a participle form, hence reflexive verbs that appear in PCs appear without the reflexive clitic. In Standard Italian and Franco-Provençal, pronominal clitics do encliticize to some participials (Loporcaro 2002). See examples (57d–e) in Standard Italian.

verbs as unaccusative in French.[23] The fact that PCs identify a superset of the non-reflexive unaccusative verbs classified as such on the basis of selecting *être* in the perfect tense following the ASH provides an important confirmation of our hierarchy-based approach.

More generally speaking, our discussion so far leads to several far-reaching claims:

- The empirical difficulties of reducing auxiliary selection in French and Italian to a simple verb-class based distribution argues against traditional analyses, in favor of a hierarchical feature-based approach.
- Though this is hardly a new discovery, it bears repeating that selection of *être* cannot be taken to define the entire class of unaccusative verbs in French. It only characterizes core unaccusative verbs (the ones figuring at the top of the ASH). To the best of our knowledge, only participial constructions taken as a whole define the class of non-reflexive unaccusative verbs.
- Our detailed discussion reveals that auxiliary selection and participial constructions stand in a subset-superset relation with respect to non-reflexive unaccusative verbs in French. This accords well with our basic hierarchical analysis and its outcome — the ASH. Participial constructions further define the scope of the unaccusative subclass in other languages, in particular languages that do not have alternating auxiliaries.
- Across Romance languages participial constructions overall constitute the most reliable and common syntactic test for unaccusativity.
- We hope that our reexamination of other tests cited in the literature on French unaccusativity, in particular impersonal constructions, partitive *en* cliticization, and unaccusative inversion will serve to dispel the belief that these structures positively contribute to identifying the subclass of unaccusative verbs.

4 Optimizing auxiliary selection

In the remainder of this chapter we informally sketch an analysis that rests on the concept of optimization, as defined in Optimality Theory (Prince and Smolensky 1993/2004) and adapted to syntax (e.g. Grimshaw 1997; Legendre *et al.* 1998; 2001). The main idea of this alternative to Principles-and-Parameters Theory (Chomsky 1981) is that constraints are universal, but

[23] Note that all the unaccusativity tests discussed so far identify weather verbs as unergative in French, *contra* Ruwet (1988).

they are soft or surface-violable.[24] In other words, a grammatical structure generated by a language-particular grammar is likely to violate some universal constraint(s). This is acceptable, as long as all alternative structural representations of the same input to the grammar (a specification of argument structure, lexical items, and lexico-semantic features in the case at hand) fare worse, i.e. violate at least one constraint that outranks the constraint(s) violated by the grammatical structure.

Such a general approach has two important advantages. One is that universal constraints can be stated in simple and general terms, thereby avoiding disjunctions and other formal complications needed to insure their universal inviolability. The other is that OT is in fact a theory of typology that constrains the typological space to language-particular re-rankings of the same set of constraints. Thus, the difference between say French, Italian, and Spanish auxiliary selection is fundamentally one of re-ranking a single set of mapping constraints.

The first step is to provide the material for the constraints themselves based on a featural decomposition of all relevant subclasses. Table 2 combines Table 1[25] (from section 2.3) with an exhaustive decomposition of each subclass into binary features borrowed from the existing literature: ± inherent telicity (TE), ± motional displacement(MO), ± directed change (DIR), ± protagonist control (CON), and ± state (ST, i.e. no change).

Suppose UG includes not only the well known relational scale from the typological-functional literature: Subject > (Direct) Object (Bresnan 1994, Croft 1990, Jakobson [1965] 1995, Keenan and Comrie 1977, Perlmutter 1983, Silverstein 1976) but also scales that pertain to each feature/property listed in Table 2: atelic > telic (Dowty 1979, Grimshaw 1990, Vendler 1967, etc.), non-directed change > directed change, no motion > motion, etc. By aligning two scales at a time we arrive at a set of relations that express how marked the mapping of a certain feature — say [+telic] — is with a certain grammatical relation — say Object:

---

24 Analyses of unaccusativity mismatches and gradience in the ASH in terms of soft constraints go back to Legendre *et al.* (1991). Some technical differences (which we need not go into) exist between the model of Harmonic Grammar proposed in 1991 and the Optimality Theory analysis sketched here.

25 Indications of variation in auxiliary selection are absent in Table 2 because an analysis of such variation within a language goes beyond the simpler analysis of cross-linguistic variation discussed below. Such an analysis requires, among other things, partial constraint rankings (as opposed to total constraint rankings illustrated below) of the type found in young children's developing grammars (Legendre *et al.* 2002). They are needed to account for free variation of auxiliaries. Variation tied to register or regional varieties involves re-rankings of the type discussed below.

Aux		Semantic/aspectual features →	TE	MO	DIR	CON	ST
Fr	It	emergent verb classes ↓					
		Change of location:					
E	E	*arriver/arrivare* 'arrive'	+	+	+	±	–
E	E	*aller/andare* 'go'	+	+	+	±	–
E	E	*venir/venire* 'come'	+	+	+	±	–
		Change of state					
		a) change of condition					
E	E	*mourir/morire* 'die'	+	–	+	–	–
E	E	b) appearance:					
		apparaître / apparire 'appear'	+	–	+	–	–
E	E	c) indefinite change in a particular					
A	E	direction:					
		monter / salire 'go up' , *descen-*	–	±	+	±	–
		dre / scendere 'go down'					
		faner /appassire 'wither', *em-*	–	–	+	–	–
		pirer / peggiorare 'worsen'					
		Continuation of a pre-existing state:					
A	E	*durer / durare* 'last'	–	–	–	–	+
		Existence of state:					
A	E	*être / essere* 'be'	–	–	–	–	+
A	E	*exister / esistere* 'exist', *suffire /*	–	–	–	–	+
		bastare 'suffice'					
		Uncontrolled processes:					
A	A	a) bodily functions: *suer / sudare*	–	–	–	–	–
A	A	'sweat'	–	–	–	–	–
A	A	b) involuntary actions: *trembler /*	–	–	–	–	–
		tremare 'shiver'					
		c) emission: *résonner / risuonare*					
		'resound'					
A	A	Controlled processes (motional):	–	+	–	+	–
		nager / nuotare 'swim'					
A	A	Controlled processes (non-motional):	–	–	–	+	–
		travailler / lavorare 'work'					

Table 2: Featural composition of monadic intransitive verbs in French and Italian

(58) O/[+telic] > S/[+telic]
In words: 'The mapping of [+telic] onto an Object configuration is less marked than (>) the mapping of [+telic] onto a Subject configuration'

These mappings turn into a hierarchy of constraints or filters once their polarity is reversed (note the change in symbol). See Aissen (2001) for analyses of cross-linguistic voice patterns relying on formally similar constraints.[26]

(59) *S/[+telic] >> * O/[+telic]
In words: The constraint 'Do not map [+telic] onto a Subject configuration' outranks has priority over (>>) 'Do not map [+telic] onto an Object configuration'

Putting all mapping constraints pertaining to a Subject configuration together, we obtain a hierarchy or *ranking* of constraints which is hypothesized to be universally fixed (see Smolensky 2006, Legendre et al. 1998 for a formal demonstration). (60) reads as follows, starting from the bottom constraint. It is bad to map the feature [+motional displacement, +MO] onto a Subject configuration, but it is worse to map the feature [–protagonist control, –CON] onto a Subject configuration.[27] It is even worse to map the feature [+state, +ST] onto a Subject configuration, etc. In other words, the leftmost constraint has priority over the constraint immediately following the next double arrow (>>), which in turn has priority over the next constraint following the next double arrow to the right, etc.

(60) Universal hierarchy:
*S/[+TE] >> *S/[+DIR] >> *S/[+ST] >> *S/[-CON] >> *S/[+MO]

Obviously, if no constraint against mapping onto an Object configuration ever entered the picture, Object configurations would always be optimal and we would never encounter any cross-linguistic mismatches. That is, all languages would reflect the ranking in (60) and exhibit no split intransitivity effects. Since mapping onto a Subject configuration ranks from bad to worse, all verb classes would be syntactically unaccusative. The fact that at least some languages do show split intransitivity effects is evidence that a *O constraint is at work, universally speaking.

---

[26] As is customary in Optimality Theory, the constraints in (59) and (60) are stated as negative constraints. Restating them as positive constraints is possible and unlikely to yield different results.

[27] In order to maintain constraint uniformity (in the sense of penalizing the mapping of all feature values onto a Subject configuration), it is necessary to use the value "–" for [protagonist control]. This captures the well-known generalization that unergative verbs tend to be agentive.

(61) *O ('Do not map onto an Object configuration')

We propose that this *O constraint universally slides along the hierarchy of the mapping constraints in (60), resulting in a cut-off point which is movable cross-linguistically. The difference between French and Italian, we claim, results from a distinct constraint interaction due to the fact that the same constraint *O is interposed in different locations on the same hierarchy, as shown in (62). The cut-off point determines unergative unaccusative subclasses.

(62) a. French:
*S/[+TE] >> ***O** >> *S/[+DIR] >> *S/[+ST] >> *S/[–CONT] >> *S/[+MO]
b. Italian:
*S/[+TE] >> *S/[+DIR] >> *S/[+ST] >> ***O** >> *S/[–CON] >> *S/[+MO]

The need to interpose *O in different locations on a single hierarchy of individual *S/X constraints in turn provides theoretical evidence that a solution to unaccusativity mismatches relying on mapping rules cannot be stated in terms of verb classes themselves (*contra* Levin and Rappaport Hovav 1995).

How particular verbs are evaluated against this hierarchy is discussed next. Consider verbs at the top of the ASH like *arriver / arrivare* 'arrive' first. Their featural description is as follows (from Table 2): [+TE, +DIR, –ST, ±CON (depending on the context), +MO]. Hence the constraints relevant to this particular optimization are: *O, *S/[+TE], *S/[+DIR], (*S/[–CONT] if the argument is non-agentive), and *S/[+MO]. *S/[+ST] is irrelevant — technically vacuously satisfied — because *arriver / arrivare* has the value "–" for the feature [ST].

A direct mapping from Object and Subject configuration to auxiliary choice *être* and *avoir* respectively is assumed. This means that selecting *être* always results in violating *O, while selecting *avoir* results in violations of *S/X, where X stands for the relevant features (of a given verb) and polarity, as stated in the universal constraint hierarchy (60). In both French and Italian, selecting *être / essere* with *arriver / arrivare* violates the *O constraint. However, selecting *avoir / avere* violates three constraints: *S/[+TE], *S/[+DIR], *S/[+MO]. As shown in (62), two of these constraints (*S/[+TE], *S/[+DIR]) outrank the *O constraint in Italian, and one (*S/[+TE]) outranks *O in French. Since only *O is violated if *être / essere* is selected, selecting *avoir / avere* is worse than selecting *être / essere* for a verb like *arriver / arrivare*. *Être / essere* is the grammatical choice in both languages.

Note that the different position of the *O constraint on the constraint hierarchy in the two languages yields different results for verbs that are neither telic nor express directed motion. For existence of state verbs like *être* and *exister* [–TE, –DIR, +ST, –CON, –MO], three constraints are active: *O, *S/[+ST], and *S/[–CON]. Selecting *être* entails a worse violation (of *O) than selecting *avoir,* which entails violations of lower-ranked constraints (*S/[+ST], *S/[–CON]) only. For *être* 'be' and *exister* 'exist', selecting *avoir* is thus the optimal choice. The reverse is true for Italian *essere* 'be' and *esistere* 'exist'. Because of the relative ranking of *S/[+ST] and *O in Italian (S/[+ST] outranks *O; see (62)) it is more costly — therefore non-optimal — to select *avoir* rather than *être*.

Significantly, the proposed general OT analysis does *not* predict total, unconstrained variation in auxiliary selection. Rather, it predicts a very specific typology of languages, including languages in which all verb classes are syntactically unaccusative, languages in which all verb classes are unergative, and languages that display a split.

First of all, languages in which all verb classes select *être* and languages in which all verb classes select *avoir* are predicted to exist. The latter formally result from *O outranking all *S/X constraints and the former from all *S/X constraints outranking *O. Both are found within Romance languages: Spanish (to name only one) uses only *haber* and the central Italian dialect Terracinese has only one auxiliary derived from Latin *esse*, as discussed in Tuttle (1986).

Another correct prediction made by the present analysis is that other languages have different cut-offs along the universal hierarchy. Besides Standard Italian and its low cut-off point, Standard French with its high cut-off point, we find Dutch and German with a cut-off point somewhere in between those of Italian and French. In both these Germanic languages, change of location and change of state verb classes select the auxiliary corresponding to *être* while the remaining verb classes — expressing continuation of a pre-existing state, existence of state, uncontrolled processes, as well as controlled processes — select *avoir*.

A remarkable example is provided by Spanish through the course of its history, as described in Aranovich (2003a). In Old Spanish, verbs like *trabajar* 'work' and *pecar* 'sin' never occurred with *ser* (= *être* / *essere*). The change from *ser* to *haber* (= *avoir* / *avere*) started with the peripheral classes as predicted by our analysis. The first to go were verbs of manner of motion like *errar* 'wander' and verbs of existence of state *rastar* 'stay' (14th century). Next to change were dynamic verbs of existence and appearance (*aparecer* 'appear', *desaparecer* 'disappear', etc.) in the 15th century. *Morir* 'die' and *ir* 'go' were the last ones to give up *ser* (17th century).

Our OT analysis also predicts some languages to be impossible. For example, there could not be a language where existence of state verbs select *être* but change of state verbs select *avoir*. As far as we know this is a correct prediction.

Summing up, we have proposed that the ASH derives from alignment of simple scales referring to lexico-semantic and aspectual features and syntactic configuration. In other words, verb classes like 'change of state', etc. (see vertical axis in Table 2) have no theoretical status in our OT analysis. They are emergent classes. Yet, they serve the important function of making explicit how, given a set of constraints stated on relatively fine-grained lexico-semantic and aspectual features, and given a (typically binary) choice between two auxiliaries, *être* or *avoir* are alternatively selected, albeit differently in the two languages.

Another property of the OT analysis worth emphasizing is that the constraints are the same in different languages. What varies is the position of a single constraint (*O) relative to all others in the hierarchy of *S/X constraints. Thus, variation results from different interactions of the same set of mapping constraints. This stands in contrast with an analysis like Bentley and Eyrthórsson (2004), which is grounded in the ASH but posits different mapping rules in different languages.

4.2. Beyond the ASH

Our analysis can be straightforwardly extended to formalize overriding effects, as the following sketch demonstrates. Formally, if reflexive morphology overrides all other constraints, it is because there is a constraint *S/REFL[28] outranking all *S/[X] constraints in French.

(63) *S/REFL >> *S/[+TE] >> ***O** >> *S/[+DIR] >> *S/[+ST] >>
*S/[–CON] >> *S/[+MO]

Compare *arriver* with *se rendre à*, both verbs of directed location. In both cases, selecting *avoir* entails worse violations (of all relevant *S/[X] constraints) than selecting *être* (which incurs only a violation of *O). Hence *être* is the auxiliary of choice. Note that *S/REFL is vacuously satisfied when the morphology is non-reflexive. Hence the constraints violated by *arriver* are a subset of the constraints violated by *se rendre à* and the fatal constraint violation is a different one in the two optimizations.

The more interesting case is when a different auxiliary is selected based on difference in morphology. Take for example two agentive manner of

---

[28] Obviously, the label Refl will need to be refined, possibly in terms of Case. *S/Refl is not part of the *S/[X] hierarchy because Refl is not a lexico-semantic feature.

motion verbs [–TE, –DIR, –ST, +CON, +MO]: *errer* 'wander' vs. *se pavaner* 'strut about'. *S/REFL is relevant only to *se pavaner*. Selecting *avoir* means violating this high-ranked constraint. It is therefore preferable to select *être*. The same high-ranked constraint is irrelevant to (i.e. vacuously satisfied by) non-reflexive *errer*. A violation of *O, in turn, eliminates *être* because selecting *avoir* in this case is less costly: only a violation of lower-ranked *S/+MO is incurred.

A main advantage of the OT analysis lies in its typological predictions. In another language *S/REFL might be overridden by *O. As a result, all reflexive verbs would select *avoir*. This is the case in Spanish. In a third language, *S/REFL might outrank *O which in turn outranks all *S/[X] constraints. The result is that all reflexive verbs would select *être*, and all non-reflexive verbs would select *avoir*.

Our OT analysis also predicts the following scenario of diachronic change. Suppose a constraint ranking starts with *S/REFL at the bottom of the ranking. Then all reflexive verbs select *être*. As *S/REFL rises up the universally fixed constraint hierarchy step by step over time, *être* disappears, being replaced by *avoir*, starting with lower classes on the ASH and ending with the top classes. Remarkably, this is precisely what happened in Spanish, as documented by Aranovich (2003a). Volitional achievement verbs like *vengarse* 'take vengeance' and verbs of existence and appearance (*demostrarse* 'show oneself', *quedarse* 'stay', etc.) were the first to drop *être*, followed by assume-position verbs (*levantarse* 'get up'), and finally directed motion (*salirse* 'leave', *irse* 'leave') and change of state (*afogarse* 'drown', *desencasarse* 'separate/divorce') roughly at the same time.

Note that the analysis does not entail that all reflexives are unaccusative in French (*contra* Grimshaw 1990 who claims that *se* is a marker of absorption of the external argument). Some reflexive verbs might be unergative and still select *être* because of the high ranking of *S/REFL. In particular, reflexive verbs belonging to the lower classes on the ASH select are predicted to select *être* despite denoting controlled and uncontrolled processes. This is indeed a correct prediction for activity verbs (e.g. *s'écrier* 'shout', *s'efforcer de* 'try', etc.) and manner of motion verbs (e.g. *se retourner* 'turn around (+/- control)', *se pavaner* 'strut about'). Evidence for classifying these reflexive verbs as unergative was presented in section 3.2.2.

5 Concluding remarks

In our terms, to say that a verb is unaccusative or unergative is to make the following claims:

- Intransitive verbs split into exactly two subclasses that differ with respect to their distributional properties.
- Important generalizations across passives, reflexives, and only a subset of intransitive verbs can be stated in a precise and simple way.
- What is common to French and Italian in the absence of a complete distributional overlap can be stated in a simple and elegant way. Although the ASH reveals that the existing overlap is not of a random kind, event semantics are by themselves not sufficient to account for the distributional properties of the phenomena associated with split intransitivity. For example, the subclass of verbs which select *être*/*essere* in French and Italian do not constitute a single class of verbs defined in lexico-semantic terms but only an overlapping one.
- For a given verb in both French and Italian the particular choice of auxiliary is the result of resolving a conflict among lexicon/syntax mapping constraints favoring one or the other auxiliary, based on the verb's semantic decomposition. Thus, the semantics of events does play a crucial role in our analysis because it provides half the content of the constraints governing the lexicon/syntax interface.

6

Bare nouns in the Romance languages

CARMEN DOBROVIE-SORIN AND BRENDA LACA

1 Introduction

Most theorists agree that in the absence of a determiner, nouns, as well as their projections (the constituent N+Adj, for example) are predicates which denote properties of individuals (for singular nouns), pluralities (for plural nouns) or quantities of matter (for mass nouns): *student, students,* and *sugar* denote respectively the properties of being a student / students / sugar. For languages with determiners, one can formulate the following generalization:

(1) Bare nouns denote properties.

Property-type denotation explains why bare nouns can occur in predicate positions.[1] All the Romance languages allow the use of bare nouns in predicate positions:[2]

(2) S a. Juan y Maria son profesores.
I b. Gianni e Maria sono professori.
R c. Ion şi Maria sunt profesori.
P d. O João e a Maria são professores.
F e. Jean et Marie sont (des) professeurs.
John and Mary are teachers.

[1] The term 'bare nouns' also covers nouns without determiners which are modified by adjectives or prepositional phrases. Where the difference between nouns with or without modifiers is relevant, we will refer to nouns with modifiers as 'modified bare nouns'.

[2] In the examples, the different languages are identified as follows: E(nglish), S(panish), F(rench), I(talian), P(ortuguese), R(omanian).

Fundamental Issues in the Romance Languages.
Danièle Godard (ed.).

However, bare nouns can also be used in argument positions. In these positions, Spanish, Italian, and Romanian (SIR hereafter)[3] allow bare plurals and mass nouns.[4] Unlike the Germanic languages, where bare nouns can have an existential or a generic interpretation, only the existential interpretation illustrated in (3a, b) is possible in SIR. In addition, the distribution of bare nouns is highly restricted in these languages: they are difficult, for example, in the preverbal subject position (3c):

(3) a. S Juan comía bizcochos y bebía leche.
I Gianni mangiava biscotti e beveva latte.
R Ion mînca prăjituri şi bea lapte.
John used to eat cakes and used to drink milk.
b. S En la calle jugaban niños.
I Giocavano bambini per strada.
R Pe stradă se jucau copii.
In the street, children were playing.
c. S * Niños jugaban en la calle.
I ?Bambini giocavano per strada.
R ??Copii se jucau pe stradă.
Children were playing in the street.

French displays a particular type of nominal expression, phrases with a DE article (so-called 'partitive article', *des, du, de la*), whose distribution and interpretation are comparable to those of bare nouns in SIR. DE-phrases in French are (with a few rare exceptions) plurals or mass nouns, just like bare nouns in SIR:

(4) a. Dans la rue jouaient *(des) enfants.
In the street, children were playing.
b. Jean était en train de manger *(des) gâteaux et de boire *(du) lait.
John was eating cakes and drinking milk.

Although in French bare nouns can occur in predicate positions, the use of DE-phrases is still possible, and is often obligatory in this position.

The use of bare nouns is less restricted in Portuguese. On a par with the Germanic languages and unlike SIR, Portuguese allows the generic reading and the preverbal subject position for bare nouns:

---

[3] For reasons of space, we do not present any data from Catalan. This language behaves, in all relevant respects, like Spanish and Romanian. It differs from Italian in that it excludes generic readings of modified bare nouns (see section 5), and from Portuguese, in not allowing bare nouns in preverbal subject positions, or generic readings (see section 7).

[4] We leave aside here the much more restricted use of bare singular count nouns. For some general comments, see section 7.2 below.

(5) P Clientes atrasam-se numa média de doze minutos.
Clients are on average twelve minutes late.

The data that we have just summarized raises two sorts of questions:

(6) (i) What is the denotation of bare nouns in argument positions?
(ii) How can we account for the linguistic variation among the Romance languages as well as between them and the Germanic languages, particularly English?

The analysis that we present in this article relies on the hypothesis that bare nouns with an existential interpretation denote properties, and correlatively function as co-predicates rather than as semantic arguments of the verbal predicate (McNally 1995, 1998a,b, van Geenhoven 1996, Dobrovie-Sorin 1995, 1997a,b, Dobrovie-Sorin and Laca 1996, 1998, Laca 1996). This hypothesis goes against a principle traditionally considered fundamental in linguistics, according to which the syntactic distinction between the predicate and argument positions correlates with a semantic distinction between types of denotation: predicates denote properties (of type $\langle e, t\rangle$) or relations, while their arguments denote individuals (type e) or generalized quantifiers (type $\langle\langle e, t\rangle, t\rangle$).

In section 2, we show that those analyses which have attempted to satisfy this demand for homomorphism do not satisfactorily account for the properties of bare nouns in SIR. Those analyses which assimilate bare nouns with indefinites are unable to explain the important contrasts which distinguish them from (singular or plural) indefinites introduced by indefinite determiners.[5] Furthermore, Carlson's (1977) analysis, supported by data from English, cannot be extended to the SIR languages. According to Carlson, bare nouns are to be analyzed as constants denoting a particular type of individual, kinds; in SIR, bare nouns are excluded from contexts which characteristically require kind-denoting nominals. In section 3, we show that the hypothesis that bare nouns denote properties is adequate not only for the predicate position but also for arguments. This analysis accounts for the sensitivity of bare nouns to the type of predicates they are the argument of, as well as for the aspectual and anaphoric properties of these predicates. In section 4, this analysis is extended to nouns preceded by the 'partitive' article in French. Section 5 examines generic readings; following

[5] We label 'indefinite' those determiners which are characterized by the properties of intersectivity and symmetry, such as cardinal numbers or *several, some, a few* etc. (see Corblin 1996). A determiner is intersective when the truth value of the clause which contains it only depends on the intersection between the set of the N and the set denoted by the predicate. A determiner is symmetric when the inversion of the set denoted by N with that denoted by the predicate produces a truth-conditionally equivalent sentence, such as in *Two students are polyglots* and *Two polyglots are students*.

Longobardi (2002) and Delfitto (2002), we show that a Carlsonian analysis, which is adequate for English, cannot be extended to Italian data (contra Chierchia 1998b): while in English, generic bare nouns can be assimilated with generic definite expressions, in Italian they behave like generic indefinites. In section 6, we suggest that certain syntactic constraints which apply to bare nouns in SIR, in particular the ban on their being in a preverbal subject position, are due to their semantic type (property-type denotation). In section 7, we examine Brazilian Portuguese, which displays not only bare mass nouns and bare plurals, but also bare singular count nouns, which are neutral with respect to the semantic singular/plural distinction. We show that these facts, while appearing to diverge quite surprisingly from the other Romance languages, in fact support the correlations established in the preceding sections.

2 What bare nouns are not

In this section we will briefly review Carlson's (1977) arguments, which show that bare nouns cannot be assimilated with indefinites, adapting them to the Romance languages. We then present Carlson's hypothesis, according to which bare nouns in English are analyzed as constants denoting kinds. This analysis cannot be extended to the SIR languages.

2.1 Bare nouns are not indefinites

2.1.1 Scope

Carlson (1977) highlighted several important contrasts between the existential reading of bare plurals in English and that of singular indefinites, in particular with respect to their scope: whereas singular indefinites are scopally ambiguous, bare plurals only allow a narrow scope reading.

Thus, for example, propositional attitude contexts create an ambiguity in the interpretation of singular indefinites, whereas the bare plural is unambiguous:

(7) a. S María piensa que Pedro robó un libro.
Mary thinks that Peter stole a book.
I Pietro crede che Maria conosca un politico importante.
Peter believes that Mary knows an important politician.
R Maria presupune că Petre a vorbit cu un logician.
Mary assumes that Peter spoke with a logician.
b. S María piensa que Pedro robó libros.
Mary thinks that Peter stole books.
I Pietro crede che Maria conosca politici importanti.
Peter believes that Mary knows important politicians.

R Maria presupune că Petre a vorbit cu logicieni.
Mary assumes that Peter spoke with logicians.

All these examples are compatible with an opaque or non-specific reading, in which the implication of existence associated with the italicized expressions remains confined to the epistemic universe of the subject of the propositional attitude (narrow scope); but the transparent, specific or wide scope reading is only possible for the examples in (7a), built with singular indefinites. In other words, the examples in (7b), with bare plurals, do not have the interpretation 'there are some books which, according to Mary, have been stolen by Peter', or respectively 'there are some important politicians which Peter believes Mary knows', 'there are some logicians which Mary assumes Peter has spoken with'.

The same type of effect can be observed for all bare nouns embedded in modal contexts. The fact that bare nouns in these contexts demand a subjunctive in a relative clause modifying them,[6] is another sign of their narrow scope, since the subjunctive signals the dependence of an expression with respect to a modal context (Farkas 1985):

(8) a. S María quiere leer un libro que describe$_{IND}$ / describa$_{SUBJ}$ la conquista de México.
Mary wants to read a book which describes the conquest of Mexico.
I Conosci per caso un linguista che si occupa$_{IND}$ / occupi$_{SUBJ}$ di lingue agglutinanti?
Do you happen to know a linguist who works on agglutinating languages?
b. S María quiere leer libros que *describen$_{IND}$ / describan$_{SUBJ}$ la conquista de México.
Mary wants to read books which describe the conquest of Mexico.
I Conosci per caso linguisti che si *occupano$_{IND}$ / occupino$_{SUBJ}$ di lingue agglutinanti?
Do you happen to know linguists who work on agglutinating languages?
(examples taken from Laca and Tasmowski 1994)

The impossibility of a wide scope reading can also be observed in relation to a quantified expression in the same sentence:

(9) a. S Todos los profesores nos recomendaron un libro.
Every teacher recommended a book to us.

[6] Some Italian speakers accept an indicative in the context of (8b).

I Ogni giorno telefona uno studente.
Each day a student telephones.

b. S Todos los profesores nos recomendaron libros.
Every teacher recommended books to us.

I Ogni giorno telefonano studenti.
Each day students telephone.

Only the narrow scope reading, in which the books co-vary with the teachers (each teacher recommends one/some different book(s) or different students telephone each day), is acceptable for bare plurals, while the examples in (9a), with singular indefinites, additionally allow a wide scope reading (a specific book or student).

In an analogous manner, bare plurals always take narrow scope with respect to negation, whereas singular indefinites can normally outscope negation. This is why the sentences in (10b), in contrast to those in (10a), are contradictory:

(10) a. S Llegó una carta y no llegó una carta.
A letter has arrived and a letter has not arrived.

I Ho trovato un libro e non ho trovato un libro.
I found a book and I didn't find a(nother) book.

b. S Llegaron cartas y no llegaron cartas.
Letters have arrived and letters have not arrived.

I Ho trovato libri e non ho trovato libri.
I found books and I did not find books.

The absence of scope ambiguities which characterizes bare plurals makes them look like referential expressions (definite descriptions, especially proper nouns), and could be understood as an indication of their status as proper names of kinds (Carlson 1977, Chierchia 1998b). However, the resemblance only relates to the absence of scope variability, not to the type of scope: the scope of bare nouns is always the narrowest possible, whereas that of proper nouns is always the widest scope possible. In other words, bare plurals are referentially dependent expressions, and as such contrast with proper nouns and definite descriptions, which are referentially independent.

The scope contrasts which we have just examined distinguish bare plurals not only from singular indefinites, but also from plurals introduced by indefinite determiners. Indeed, NPs introduced notably by cardinals or by 'indefinite articles' (such as S *unos*, I *dei*, R *nişte*) behave like the singular indefinite in terms of their scope. Thus, for example, (11)S can have a transparent reading, (11)I can mean that it is the same students that telephone each day, and (11)R has a non-contradictory interpretation:

(11) S María piensa que Pedro robó unos libros.
Mary believes that Peter stole some / certain books.
I Ogni sera telefonano tre studenti.
Every evening, three students telephone.
R Trei profesori au fost prezenţi şi trei nu.
Three teachers are present and three are not.

These plurals thus behave as the true plural counterparts of singular indefinite expressions. Just as singular indefinites can be translated as individual variables (Kamp 1981, Heim 1982), plurals introduced by an indefinite determiner can be analyzed as 'group variables', which range over a set of groups (or plural individuals), of a precise or vague cardinality.

Extending this analysis to bare plurals (Kratzer 1988, 1995, Diesing 1992) does not explain their behavior in relation to scope.

2.1.2 Aspectual and anaphoric properties

Dowty (1979) and Carlson (1977) highlighted other interesting properties of bare nouns, which concern their aspectual and anaphoric behavior. The facts all seem to point in the same direction: in contrast to indefinites with a determiner, bare plurals do not introduce delimited and stable entities into the discourse. On the assumption that individuals are delimited and stable entities, these effects show that bare plurals cannot function as denotations of individuals (type *e* expressions).

With respect to their aspectual properties, bare plurals are not able to supply the boundary-marking required by telicity. Both predicates which denote achievements and those that denote accomplishments when their object has an indefinite determiner, acquire the characteristics of activities when their object is a bare plural.[7] Thus, examples (12a,b) show that the alternation between interval adverbials denoting delimited duration (that is, expressions of the kind *in X amount of time*) and non-culminating measure adverbials (ie. expressions of the kind *for X amount of time*) correlates with the alternation between a plural indefinite and a bare plural in object position.

(12) a. S Escribió dos artículos en tres meses / *durante tres meses.
He wrote two articles in three months / for three months.
I Ha stirato molte camicie in due ore / *per due ore di seguito.
He ironed many shirts in two hours / for two hours.

[7] It is however necessary to stress that indefinite plurals with *dei* in Italian behave in an exceptional manner which brings them close to bare plurals, to the extent that they can bring about de-telicization effects.

b. S Escribió artículos *en tres meses / durante tres meses.
He wrote articles in three months / for three months.
I Ha stirato camicie *in due ore / per due ore di seguito.
He ironed shirts in two hours / for two hours.

Similarly, the use of bare plurals leads to a durative interpretation of predicates which are normally non-durative such as *kill* or *discover*. Hence, the possibility of embedding such predicates under the aspectual verb *continue*:

(13) a. S *El zorro siguió matando varias gallinas.
The fox continued to kill several chickens.
I *Continua a scoprire tre errori di calcolo.
He continued to discover three calculation mistakes.
b. S El zorro siguió matando gallinas.
The fox continued to kill chickens.
I Continua a scoprire errori di calcolo.
He continued to discover calculation mistakes.

The same facts can be observed for post-verbal subjects, in particular with intransitives which denote a change of state of the subject:

(14) S Seguían llegando invitados / *unos invitados.
Guests / Some guests continued to arrive.
I Sono scoppiate bombe / *quattro bombe per tre giorni di seguito.
Bombs / Four bombs exploded for three days in a row.

The fact that bare plurals are not able to supply the delimitation necessary for bounded processes excludes them from any telic context, notably from the object position of aspectual verbs such as *begin* or *finish* (this observation is due to Godard and Jayez 1993, who are concerned with *des* in French) and from constructions with ethical dative reflexives which act as telicity markers:

(15) S Comenzó varias novelas / ??Comenzó novelas.
He began several novels. / He began novels.
I Ha finito tre ritratti / ??Ha finito ritratti.
He finished three portraits / He finished portraits.

(16) S Me leí muchas novelas / ??Me leí novelas.
REFL read many novels / REFL read novels
I read (up) several novels. / I read (up) novels.
I Mi sono mangiata tanti di quei gelati / *Mi sono mangiata gelati.
REFL AUX eaten many ice creams / REFL AUX eaten ice creams
I ate up a lot of ice cream. / I ate up ice cream.

Bare plurals also have particular properties when they provide antecedents for pronominal expressions. Thus, for example, they cannot serve as antecedents of anaphoric elements of the type *other ones / the other ones* (see (17a) vs. (17b)) and they allow anaphors that are not strictly co-referential (see (17c), Laca 1996):

(17) a. S Juan recomendó unos / tres libros y María recomendó otros / los otros.
John recommended some / three books and Mary recommended other ones / the other ones.
I Oggi sono arrivati tre / molti ospiti stranieri. Domani arriveranno altri / gli altri.
Three / Several foreign guests arrived today. Others / The others will arrive tomorrow.
b. S * Juan recomendó libros y María recomendó otros.
John recommended books and Mary recommended other ones.
I * Oggi sono arrivati ospiti stranieri. Domani arriveranno altri / gli altri.
Today foreign guests arrived. Tomorrow others / the others will arrive.
c. S Porque Usted quema libros, y Sánchez los escribe.
Because you burn books and Sánchez writes them.
I Prendeva libri in prestito in biblioteca o li rubava nelle librerie del centro.
He borrowed books from the library or he stole them from bookshops in the town centre.

These facts distinguish bare nouns from singular indefinites as well as from plural indefinites introduced by a determiner. The scope restrictions can be explained by the hypothesis of a strictly local licensing of bare plurals, which is dependent on the predicate of the sentence. The aspectual effects seem to show that these expressions do not denote individuals, and the anaphoric properties suggest that bare plurals do not introduce discourse referents. We may thus conclude that bare nouns cannot be assimilated to indefinites.

2.2 Bare nouns do not denote kinds

Drawing on the fact that in English, bare plurals (as well as bare mass nouns) have not only the existential reading illustrated in (18), but also the generic reading illustrated in (19), Carlson (1977) proposed a unified analysis which takes the generic reading as primitive:

(18) E a. Students are dancing in the streets.
b. John is eating apples.

(19) E a. Gorillas are on the verge of extinction.
b. Cats are intelligent.
c. John loves cats.

According to Carlson, bare nouns can be seen as constants denoting kinds, which directly accounts for the generic reading. The existential reading is then based on spatio-temporal stages of kinds, resulting from the use of expressions denoting kinds in the context of particular events. Carlson's analysis can be summarized in the following way:

(20) a. Bare plurals are analyzed as proper names of kinds.
b. The two readings, generic and existential, are contextually determined:
i. The existential reading is due to the presence of a stage-level predicate.
ii. The generic reading is correlated with an individual-level predicate.

Carlson's analysis cannot be extended to the Romance languages. Thus, in SIR bare nouns are not compatible with kind-predicates, and they do not give rise to generic interpretations when they combine with individual-level predicates:[8]

(21) S En la India se están extinguiendo los tigres / *tigres. (cf. 19a)
In India, the tigers / tigers are going extinct.
I In questa regione, sono riusciti a sterminare i conigli / *conigli.
In this region, they have succeeded in exterminating the rabbits / rabbits.
R O lege din 1950 protejează urşii / *urşi.
A law of 1950 protects the bears / bears.

(22) a. S A Juan le gustan los gatos / *gatos. (cf. 19b)
John likes the cats / cats.
I A Gianni gli piacciono i gatti / *gatti.
John likes the cats / cats.
R Lui Ion îi plac prăjiturile / *prăjituri.
John likes the cakes / cakes.

[8] The ungrammaticality of the bare nouns in (21) and (22) contrasts with the grammaticality of the bare nouns in the English examples in (19). We use examples with post-verbal subjects or with objects in order to neutralize the independent constraint by which bare nouns in SIR can't appear in the preverbal position (see section 6).

b. S Juan detesta los gatos / *gatos. (cf. 19c)
John hates the cats / cats.
I Gianni odia i gatti / *gatti.
John hatesthe cats / cats.
R Ion respectă profesorii / *profesori /.
John respects the teachers / teachers.

Although there is a certain amount of variation among Romance languages regarding the possibility of generic readings, in particular for modified bare nouns (see section 5), this possibility is so constrained that the hypothesis that bare nouns in SIR denote kinds (Chierchia 1998b) cannot be maintained.

Carlson's analysis thus does not allow us to explain the existence of languages such as SIR, which allow the existential reading of bare nouns while excluding or strongly restricting their generic reading. Furthermore, it is noteworthy that the opposite situation does not seem to be instantiated in well-described languages: to our knowledge, there are no languages in which bare nouns allow generic readings but not existential readings.

3 Bare nouns denote properties

In the preceding section we showed that bare nouns in SIR cannot be analyzed as either indefinites or kinds. In what follows, we will adopt another hypothesis, recently proposed independently by McNally (1995, 1998a, b), van Geenhoven (1996), Dobrovie-Sorin (1997a, b), that bare nouns denote properties, even when they occupy argument positions.[9]

This hypothesis allows us to simultaneously account for the existential interpretations of bare nouns, their scope properties, and their distribution. Our analysis takes up the fundamental intuition of Carlson (1977), according to which the use of bare nouns in argument positions relies crucially on an existential quantifier introduced by the verbal predicate. However, we diverge from Carlson regarding the denotation of existential bare nouns (which we assume to be properties, not kinds) and regarding the characterization of predicates which supply an existential quantifier.

---

[9] Analyses of this kind have in fact been suggested in older work, see in particular de Hoop (1992), who refers to 'detransitivization' for verbs with direct objects unmarked for accusative case (in the terms of de Hoop, these objects have a 'weak' case). Speaking of detransitivization is undoubtedly inaccurate from a strictly syntactic point of view, but correct from a semantic point of view: certain syntactic arguments do not function as true semantic arguments, but rather as co-predicates. For a recent discussion of the relation between syntax and semantics with respect to the predicate/argument distinction, see Landman (2000).

3.1 Nouns without determiners in predicate position

Defined in functional terms, a property is a function of type (*e, t*), which applies to an individual (type *e*), and returns a truth value (type *t*). In set-theoretic terms, a property is equivalent to the set of individuals for which the function returns the value 'true'.[10] Sets of individuals corresponding to properties (type (*e, t*)) are crucially distinct from plural individuals (groups) which are first order entities (type *e*) with a particular structure.

Property-denotation is commonly accepted for nouns as lexical units, as well as nouns which appear inside a Determiner Phrase (*all the / three students*).[11] Property-denotation also explains why bare nouns can appear in predicate positions: one-place predicates denote functions of type (*e, t*).

The predicate position allows a wider use of bare nouns in all the Romance languages. In particular, we find bare singular count nouns:

(23) S Juan es professor.
I Gianni è professore.
R Ion este professor.
John is [a] teacher.

However, predicates formed with a bare singular are only possible with a restricted sub-class of nouns, which denote professions, roles, social functions or relations. If the predicate does not express a role or a social function, but class membership, the indefinite article is obligatory for the singular in Spanish and Italian, and optional in Romanian:

(24) S Bobby es *(un) gatto.
I Bobby è *(un) gato.
R Bobby e (o) pisică.
Bobby is a cat.

In classifying predications, one therefore finds in Spanish and Italian exactly the same nominal forms as in argument positions: an indefinite article for the singular and a bare noun for the plural. The corresponding French examples require *de*:

---

[10] Properties must be treated intensionally, since they can be associated with different sets according to worlds and times. We will ignore this complication here, which can be accounted for in the standard manner notated by introducing indices of worlds and times.

[11] In the framework of the theory of generalized quantifiers, determiners are expressions of type ((*e,t*),((*e,t*), *t*), which combine with the denotations of properties to yield generalized quantifiers. This analysis matches the syntactic analysis according to which determiners are functional heads which take nouns or their lexical projections as arguments (the DP (Determiner Phrase) hypothesis). We assume, however, that certain indefinite determiners function, in certain contexts, like adjectives, more precisely as predicates of cardinality. See in particular Higginbotham (1985, 1987) and Landman (2000).

(25) S Estas flores son rosas.
I Questi fiori sono rose.
R Aceste flori sunt trandafiri.
F Ces fleurs sont des roses.
These flowers are roses.

(26) S Las ballenas son mamíferos.
I Le balene sono mammiferi.
R Balenele sunt mamifere.
F Les baleines sont des mammifères.
Whales are mammals.

The use of plurals with an indefinite determiner (S *unos*, I *dei*, R *nişte*) in a predicate position results in special meaning effects. These determiners are used when the predicate is formed with a 'qualifying noun' (Milner 1978) or when it is a metaphorical predication (Laca and Tasmowski 1994):

(27) S Eran unos pobretones.
They were poor people.
I Sono dei mascalzoni.
They are rascals.
R Sunt nişte dobitoci.
They are imbeciles.

(28) S Esas mujeres son unas víboras.
These women are vipers.
I Siamo tutti dei cani.
We are all dogs.
R Femeile astea sunt nişte vipere.
These women are vipers.

The indefinite determiners are equally obligatory when the noun is accompanied by evaluative modifiers, whether it is in a predicate position or in an argument position:

(29) a. S Son rosas blancas / ??(unas) rosas magníficas.
I Sono rose bianche / ??(delle) rose magnifiche.
They are white roses / magnificent roses.
b. S Me regaló rosas blancas / ??(unas) rosas magníficas.
I Mi ha regalato rose bianche / ??(delle) rose magnifiche.
He gave me white roses / magnificent roses.

This type of context is undoubtedly comparable to examples (27) and (28) with qualifying nouns and metaphorical predications: the common property of the three contexts is that of expressing the attitude of the speaker towards particular referents. The Romance languages other than French thus signal, with the help of the alternation between bare plurals and plurals preceded by a determiner, a difference between 'classifying' predications and 'qualifying' predications which, in French, are not distinguished.

Summing up, we stress again the fact that the predicate position is not a great deal more permissive than argument positions for bare nouns. In particular, bare singulars are only possible in well-circumscribed contexts (titles, professions, etc.). In all other predications, only plurals and mass nouns can be used without determiners (and a DE article is required in French). Furthermore, these forms themselves need an article if the predication is qualifying. The notable parallelism between the predicate position and the argument positions regarding the use of bare nouns strongly suggests that property-denotation, generally accepted for the predicate position, equally underlies the use of bare nouns as arguments.

3.2 The reference domain of plural and mass nouns

We are now in a position to ask why the SIR languages allow the absence of a determiner for plurals and mass nouns, but need the indefinite article for singular countable nouns (however see section 7.2 below). It is well-known that plural and mass nouns share crucial denotational properties: in particular, their reference is cumulative (if a quantity of a substance A is coffee and a quantity of a substance B is coffee, then A and B are coffee, and, similarly, if a group of animals A are cats and a group of animals B are cats, then A and B are cats). Cumulativity is a consequence of the particular structure of their denotation domains: the set of plural individuals (groups) and the set of quantities of matter, respectively (see Link 1983, Landman 1989, 1996, Chierchia 1998a). Plural individuals and quantities of matter are entities of a particular ontological sort: they are composed of parts of the same kind. Plurals and mass terms denote ordered sets, with 'is a part of' as the ordering relation. In contrast, the denotation domain of singular countable nouns is a set of atomic individuals, and therefore necessarily disjoint and unordered.

We thus arrive at establishing a correlation between the absence of a determiner and the structure of the denotation domain: singular expressions, which take their denotation in the unordered domain of atomic individuals, cannot occur without determiners (however see section 7 for a presentation of Brazilian Portuguese); plurals and mass nouns, which denote sets of non-atomic entities with an internal structure based on an ordering relation, can occur without a determiner.

Bearing in mind these common denotational properties of plurals and mass nouns, we expect structural parallelisms in their distribution and interpretation. Bare mass nouns always take narrow scope (30), they can cancel telicity (31) and they are excluded from the argument positions of certain predicates (32):[12]

(30) S Maria cree que Juan robó leña.
Mary believes that John stole wood.
I Pietro vuol comprare caffè.
Peter wants to buy coffee.
R Trei studenţi au adus vin.
Three students brought wine.

(31) S *Maria se comió fruta.
Mary REFL ate fruit
I Pietro ha bevuto caffè (*in un ora).
*Peter drank coffee (*in an hour).*
R Ion a terminat *vin / OK vinul.
John finished wine / the wine.

(32) a. S Está caliente *agua / el agua.
I È calda *acqua / l'acqua.
R E caldă *apă / apa.
Water / The water is hot
b. S Juan adora *café / el café.
I Gianni adora *caffè / il caffè.
R Ion adoră *cafea / OK cafeaua.
John loves coffee / the coffee.

However, there is a salient difference between the behavior of plurals and that of mass nouns. Mass nouns take the narrowest possible scope even when they are preceded by quantifying expressions. The scope ambiguities exhibited by the sentences in (33) thus contrast with the non-ambiguity of the sentences in (34):

(33) S Maria cree que Juan robó algunos libros.
Mary believes that John stole some books.
I Pietro vuole comprare molti libri.
Peter wants to buy a lot of books.
R Petre n-a primit multe scrisori.
Peter has not received many letters.

(34) S Maria cree que Juan robó mucha leña.
Mary believes that John stole a lot of wood.

---

[12] The data give rise to some variation in Italian. The judgments reflect the acceptabilities of speakers from Rome.

I Pietro vuol comprare un po di caffè.
Peter wants to buy a little coffee.
R Petre n-a primit mult tutun.
Peter has not received a lot of tobacco.

This goes hand in hand with the fact that mass nouns, even when they are preceded by quantifying expressions, cannot appear in the argument positions of predicates such as *like, detest, hate,* which do not allow bare nouns in their object positions:

(35) S *María detesta mucha agua.
I *Maria odia molta acqua.
R *Maria detestă multă apă.
Mary hates a lot of water.

Mass nouns, with or without quantifying expressions, seem therefore to behave like bare plurals, and contrast with plurals that take indefinite determiners. This particular behavior is due to the fact that mass nouns are incompatible with individuation: in contrast to plurals, their denotation domain is not associated with a domain of disjoint atomic individuals that generates it. This explains why, even in combination with quantifying expressions, mass nouns are not able to supply discourse referents which can escape the scope of other elements or saturate the argument positions of predicates such as *like* (see section 3.4). Plurals introduced by indefinite determiners have the double possibility of introducing discourse referents (they can have wide scope and they can saturate predicates such as *like*), or denoting complex cardinalized properties, (which explains how they can appear in the predicate position, as in *Peter and John are two hardworking students* as well as in the argument position of existential constructions, as in *There are two students in the courtyard).*[13]

Although quantified mass nouns are equivalent to bare (plural or mass) nouns from the point of view of their denotation (they do not introduce individuals), they behave differently with regard to telicity effects. Indeed, quantified mass nouns can provide the boundedness required for telicity:

(36) S Maria se comió dos kilos de fruta.
Mary REFL ate two kilos of fruit
Mary ate up two kilos of fruit.
I Pietro ha bevuto mezzo litro di caffè (in un ora).
Peter drank half a liter of coffee (in an hour).

---

[13] McNally (1998a) convincingly shows that existential constructions select denotations of properties.

R Ion a terminat două sticle de vin.
John finished two bottles of wine.

This behavior is expected; while the delimitation of a quantity of matter is not sufficient to individuate it, it does guarantee boundedness.

Summing up, the absence of determiners is allowed for plurals and mass nouns, which denote in a domain structured by the relation 'is a part of'. Countable singulars, whose domain is a set of atomic individuals, need an indefinite article. However, the presence of the determiner should not be analyzed as indicating that singular indefinites cannot denote properties. In fact, this kind of denotation must be assumed at least for certain contexts which are open to countable singulars, particularly in the predicate position. Generally, singulars preceded by the indefinite article are systematically ambiguous: they can denote an individual, a generalized quantifier or the property of being a student, a bear, etc.

3.3 Property-denoting NPs in argument positions

By adopting the hypothesis that bare noun arguments denote properties, we abandon the notion of a trivial homomorphism between syntactic argumenthood and semantic type. It is however possible to put forward semantic composition rules which allow a verbal predicate to be composed with a property-denoting NP occupying a syntactic argument position. These rules rely on predicates of a particular type. We assume that besides their standard denotation, which can be represented as a lambda abstraction over individual-variables (see (37a)), a large sub-class of predicates – which we shall call 'existentials' – can have lexical representations which include an existential quantifier binding certain argument variables (see (37b)). Predicates which are not existential (which do not introduce an existential quantifier) will be called 'entity-predicates' (see examples (40a,b), below):

(37) a. λx sleep (x)
b. $\lambda \mathrm{P}\, \exists x\, (\mathrm{sleep}(x)\ \&\ \mathrm{P}(x))$

Represented as in (37b), predicates like *sleep, wash* or *available* have argument positions saturated in the lexicon by existential closure, yet they remain partially unsaturated: they still require properties to specify the domain of the argument variable. In (37b), this is formalized by a property-variable P which restricts the argument variable.[14] We can now propose representations as in (38') for sentences containing property-denoting expressions as arguments:

[14] The domain of variables bound by the existential quantifier can, in certain cases, be unrestricted. This is what we find for implicit arguments, present in the thematic grid of the predicate but not projected lexically, as in *John ate, Mary reads a lot.*

(38) S Duermen niños.
are sleeping children
There are children sleeping.

(38') $(\lambda P\ \exists x\ (\text{sleep}(x)\ \&\ P(x)))(\text{children})$

(38'') $\exists x\ \text{sleep}(x)\ \&\ \text{children}(x)$

By reduction (λ conversion), we obtain the representation in (38''). In this analysis, bare nouns in argument positions do not function like real arguments, but rather like co-predicates.

Generally then, existential predicates can be represented in two different ways, the choice between the two possibilities being determined by contextual factors. Thus, (37b) will be chosen for arguments expressed by bare nouns. The same representation is also necessary for proper names, when they appear in thetic sentences.[15] In (39''), *John(x)* reads as 'x has the property of being John'.

(39) When I entered the room, John was sleeping peacefully.

(39') $(\lambda P\ \exists x\ (\text{sleep}(x)\ \&\ P(x)))(\text{John}) \Rightarrow$ (lambda conversion)

(39'') $\exists x\ (\text{sleep}(x)\ \&\ \text{John}(x))$

Some predicates, however, cannot combine with bare nouns:

(40) S a. *Eran grandes / inteligentes niños.
Children were big / intelligent.
b. ??Estaban tristes / inquietos / enfermos médicos.
Doctors were sad / worried / sick.

In the framework proposed here, the ungrammaticality of such examples can be seen as a consequence of a semantic type-mismatch: bare nouns denote properties, but the predicates which appear in (40a,b) require entity-denoting NPs, whence the term 'entity-predicates', taken from Dobrovie-Sorin (1997a, b). These predicates do not allow an existential quantifier in their lexical representation, and therefore only allow representations of the type (37a):

(40') a. $\lambda x\ x$ is intelligent / big / beautiful / tasty
b. $\lambda x\ x$ is sick / sad / fresh / soft

15 The only nominal expressions that cannot be analyzed as denoting properties are quantificational NPs. In order to be composed with quantificational NPs, the predicate of the sentence must be analyzed as a lambda abstraction over individuals (see (37a)), a representation which is possible for any lexical type of predicate.

It is useful to clarify our analysis of bare nouns in relation to the treatment of indefinites in the different variants of DRT (Discourse Representation Theory, Heim 1982, Kamp 1981, Kamp and Reyle 1993). The central idea of DRT is that indefinites introduce individual-variables, the existential quantifier being introduced by rules of existential closure. According to Heim (1982), the existential quantifier can be inserted either in the scope of another quantifier, or at the level of the text (*text-level existential closure*), as in (41a) and (41b), respectively:

(41) a. Each pupil will write a poem.
b. A pupil told me some bad news.

(41') a. $\forall x\, \exists y$ (x is a pupil) (y is a poem) [x will write y]
b. $\exists x\, \exists y$ (x is a pupil) (y is some bad news) [x told me y]

This analysis seems very close, if not identical, to the one we have proposed here for bare nouns: the existential quantifier is provided by the context, and the nominal predicate contained in the indefinite denotes a property which restricts the range of the variable.

However, the two analyses differ in one central respect. According to DRT, indefinites have the canonical type of arguments: they are individual-variables (type e), whereas according to the analysis proposed here, a certain type of indefinite – bare nouns – has a semantic type which requires sentential predicates of a particular type (37b). In the absence of such a predicate, bare nouns in argument positions are excluded because of a semantic type mismatch. No such mismatch is predicted by DRT analyses of indefinites.

3.4 Classes of predicates

Thus far we have suggested that only existential predicates, which can be represented as in (37b), with an existential operator, license bare nouns denoting properties. But what are the empirical criteria which allow us to distinguish between existential predicates and entity-predicates, which are represented as in (37a)? In what follows we will first show that this distinction does not correspond to the distinction between *stage-level* predicates and *individual-level* predicates (Carlson 1977, Kratzer 1988). We then propose a different criterion, which relies on spatial localization.

In Carlson's (1977) approach, bare nouns in English are analyzed as proper names of kinds, and the predicates which trigger their existential interpretation play a double role: on the one hand, they introduce an existential quantifier, and on the other they make it possible to change from an individual or kind denotation, to a 'stage of individual' and 'stage of a kind' denotation. With this analysis in mind, the relevant predicates must be at once existential and episodic, hence the hypothesis that the existential quantifier is linked to the episodic character of the predicate. This hypothesis, which is necessary for Carlson's analysis, is not necessary for ours: the existential interpretation of bare nouns depends on the property denotation and not on stages of an individual/kind. The only relevant property of the predicate is that of introducing an existential quantifier, which is crucial for a representation like (37b).

The correlation between episodic predication and existential quantification not being necessary, it is not expected to appear in all contexts. Several authors have indeed noticed for English that there are episodic predicates which do not allow an existential reading for bare nouns in argument positions, and that certain stable, individual-level predicates do allow them. The same situation arises with bare nouns in SIR: bare nouns, which in these languages only allow in principle the existential reading, fail to be always the arguments of episodic predicates, or excluded as arguments of individual-level predicates. Thus, adjectives composed with the copula *estar* in Spanish give rise to episodic predications, but the majority of these predicates cannot combine with bare nouns (40b).

Only a restricted sub-class of adjectives which take *estar*, those which do not express the state of the subject, but which localize it in some way, allow bare nouns as arguments (42a). Conversely, even though the predicates of examples (42b,c) express permanent situations, they are compatible with bare nouns in an argument position:

(42) S a. Estaban presentes / disponibles médicos.
Doctors were present / available.
b. Bordeaban cipreses el camino.
Cypresses lined the path.
c. Este manuscrito contiene errores.
This manuscript contains errors.

Since there is no perfect correlation between the class of episodic predicates and the class of existential predicates, it is necessary to find another empirical way of identifying the class of existential predicates. Following Dobrovie-Sorin (1997a,b), it is the possibility of localizing their arguments in space which defines existential predicates. Indeed, the following correlation holds: predicates which combine with adverbials of spatial localization also allow argumental bare nouns with an existential interpretation, and those that do not readily combine with such adverbials, exclude existential bare nouns:[16]

---

[16] Spatial localization has been used in a quite different way, as a criterion for delimiting the class of predicates which allow 'existential' or 'weak readings', by McNally (1995, 1998a,b)

(43) S a. ?? ¿ Dónde estaba triste / inquieto / enfermo Juan?
Where was John sad / worried / sick?
b. ¿ Dónde estaba presente Juan?
Where was John present?

In contrast to the stage-level vs. individual-level distinction, which affects the entire predication, and consequently all the arguments of a predicate, the criterion of spatial localization allows us – according to the proposal in Dobrovie-Sorin (1997a,b) – to accommodate cases in which only one of the arguments of a given predicate finds itself in the scope of the predicate's existential quantifier. Certain permanent predicates show this dissociation of their arguments with respect to localization. So, for example (42b) and (42c), which localize the subject in relation to the object and the object in relation to the subject, respectively. Only the localized argument (the subject in (42b), the object in (42c)) can be a bare noun with an existential interpretation.

Spatial localization also plays a role in the contrast between (40b) and (42a), but in a way that remains to be explored in detail. Only those predications with *estar* which express localized existence allow bare nouns in an argument position.

Dobrovie-Sorin (1997a,b) showed that this analysis also makes it possible to explain the well-known – but until then little understood – ungrammaticality of examples like (44) (Laca 1990), which show that bare nouns in SIR (just like DE indefinites in French, examined in section 4) cannot appear in the object position of verbs such as *like, hate,* etc. We can see that these predicates do not allow place adverbials, and are consequently entity-predicates:

(44) a. S *María adora café.
R *Maria adoră cafea.
Mary loves coffee.
b. S *Juan detesta manzanas.
R *Ion detestă mere.
John hates apples.
c. S *María adora el café en la cafetería.
R *Maria adoră cafeaua în cofetărie.
Mary loves the coffee in the cafeteria.

---

and Glasbey (1998), and more recently by Kleiber (2001). Kleiber distinguishes predicates which localize their arguments, from those predications on which the spatial localization of arguments has no influence. It is precisely this second type of predicate which excludes bare nouns in argument positions.

d. S *Juan detesta las manzanas en la cocina.
R *Ion detestă merele în bucătărie.
John hates the apples in the kitchen

Examples (43a, b) are therefore ungrammatical because (i) *like, hate,* etc. are entity-predicates, in other words predicates which must be applied to individuals, and (ii) bare nouns in SIR denote properties.

In summary, spatial localization seems to provide a better empirical criterion for distinguishing existential predicates from entity-predicates, which cannot supply an existential quantifier and therefore are necessarily represented as λ-abstractions over individuals. These predicates cannot combine with bare nouns due to a type mismatch between their denotation (which demands arguments of type entity or individual) and the denotation of a property which characterizes bare nouns.

We must note, however, that there is no necessary relation between spatial localization and the introduction of an existential quantifier. It is simply an empirical observation which may be invalidated by new data (see in particular the counter-examples adduced by Cohen and Erteschik-Shir, 2002). All the same, the problems linked to the empirical criterion do not have a direct effect on the analysis proposed here: the analysis (that predicates which can combine with bare nouns are represented as in (37b)) may well be correct, even if the criterion of spatial localization needs to be refined.

4 Partitive articles in French

For syntactic reasons which are peculiar to French, this language does not allow the use of bare nouns in argument positions. In fact NPs introduced by the 'partitive' article (*des, de la, du*) constitute in French an almost perfect counterpart to the existential bare nouns in SIR. These indefinite NPs must be distinguished from forms with *de* which are not followed by the definite article and which are required in negative contexts or after certain adverbs such as *beaucoup* or *peu* (*je n'ai pas vu de fille(s)* 'I didn't see a/any girl(s)', *j'ai vu beaucoup / peu de filles* 'I saw a lot of / few girls'). We leave aside here this other type of expression and refer to DE-phrases for phrases introduced by partitive articles.

The contrasts between plurals introduced by *des*, on the one hand, and singular indefinites and plurals introduced by other determiners, on the other, have been noticed by Attal (1976). Attal put forward a hypothesis which can be seen as a direct precedent of the analysis which we propose in this article. According to Attal, plurals introduced by *des* function as modifiers of the sentence-predicate. He assumes that their semantic role in relation to the process is analogous to that of the adjective's in relation to the noun (1976:139). His hypothesis is based on the type of behavior we have discussed for bare plurals: *des*-NP can neither have wider scope than negation, nor do they have specific readings in intensional contexts, and they do not occupy the argument position of certain verbs. Although he notes the different uses of *des*, Attal (1976:142) leaves open the question of whether there is one or two *des*. Subsequent research (for an overview, see Bosveld-de Smet 1997:5-54) shows that there is indeed reason to characterize a marked use of *des*, in which the NP can escape negation as well as appear as an argument of an entity-predicate and provide the antecedent of the anaphoric *d'autres*, as can be seen in (45a-c):

(45) F a. Des élèves ne m'ont pas rendu leurs devoirs.
Some pupils haven't given in their homework to me.
b. Des élèves étaient malades.
Some pupils were sick.
c. Des enfants tambourinaient sur leurs tables, tandis que d'autres criaient à tue-tête.
Some children were drumming their fingers on their tables, while others were shouting at the top of their voices.
d. Pendant mon cours, des étudiants étaient ivres / malades / affamés / endormis.
During my lesson, some students were drunk / sick / starving / asleep.
e. Des verres sont vides.
(Some) glasses are empty.
f. Des fauteuils sont bancals.
(Some) armchairs are rickety.
(examples d-f from Galmiche 1986)

In examples (45a-c), the meaning of *des N* is clearly partitive, referring to a subset of a contextually determined set. This meaning is close to that of *some N*, which is analyzed as a quantificational NP.

Examples (45d-f) illustrate a third use of *des*, noted by Dobrovie-Sorin (1997b). The predicates of (45d-f) are entity-predicates, which as such are not able to apply to properties. However, the interpretation of these examples is not necessarily partitive or contrastive. Dobrovie-Sorin (1997b) proposes analyzing the indefinite with *des* in examples of this type, as introducing a group variable (see the analysis suggested by Villalta 1995 for *unos* in Spanish).

As for mass nouns, the parallelism with bare nouns in SIR is perfect. NPs introduced by *du* / *de la* never give rise to uses comparable to those illustrated in (45).

NPs with a partitive article can also be found in the predicate position. The absence of the article is only possible for particular types of predicate, those which refer to professions, functions, titles or relations.

(46) F a. Ces animaux sont *(des) girafes.
Those animals are giraffes.
b. Cette substance est *(de l') or.
This substance is gold.
c. Jean et Marie sont professeurs.
John and Mary are teachers.
d. Jean est professeur.
John is a teacher.

It is highly significant that the use of bare plurals in French should parallel the use of bare singular count nouns in SIR (see section 3.1). Indeed, in the same contexts singular count nouns can be used without an indefinite article, in every Romance language, including French (46d). If we leave aside this particular context, the absence of a determiner in SIR on the one hand, and DE-NPs in French on the other, concern the same types of nouns: mass nouns and plurals, which are comparable in that they denote in the non-atomic domain (quantities of matter and plural individuals/groups, respectively) ordered by the relation 'is a part of'. The absence of a determiner in SIR and the presence of a partitive article in French therefore constitute two different procedures by which a nominal expression is marked as denoting a non-atomic entity. The parallelism between the two types of expression is all the more noteworthy as (i) it concerns both the predicate position and argument positions and (ii) generic interpretation is excluded in both cases. We thus conclude that two distinct syntactic forms, NPs with DE in French, and bare nouns in SIR, must be analyzed as having the same type of denotation (a property). In the following section, we will illustrate the opposite situation: bare nouns in English, while sharing the same syntactic form as bare nouns in SIR, are ambiguous, denoting not only properties (type (e, t)), but also maximal groups (type e) which have the corresponding property.

5 Genericity, (in)definiteness and bare nouns

In common with most theories about genericity, we assume that there are two different kinds of generic reading. Nominal genericity relies on NPs functioning as proper names of kinds, while sentential genericity crucially involves an overt adverb of quantification or an implicit generic operator notated as GEN which is introduced by default, and is equivalent to an adverb of quantification. It is also accepted that the generic reading of indefinites does not build on denotations of kinds, but rather depends on a generic quantificational structure resulting from the adverbs of quantification, particularly GEN. However, the existing approaches differ in their analyses of different scenarios, and in particular in their analysis of bare plurals in English. In contrast to Spanish, Italian, and Romanian (SIR), English bare plurals give rise to a generic reading in a totally productive way. We assume that bare nouns in English are analyzed as proper names of kinds (Carlson 1977), or more precisely as kind-denoting definite expressions (Dobrovie-Sorin and Laca 1998; see section 5.1 below).

A generic reading for modified bare nouns is possible in Italian, for a limited number of examples. This lead Chierchia (1998a) to propose that Italian bare nouns – and by extension those of all the Romance languages other than French – denote kinds.[17] But as Longobardi (2002) and Delfitto (2002) show, modified bare nouns in Italian cannot appear in the characteristic contexts of kind nouns. A Carlsonian analysis therefore cannot be extended to the data of Italian. Like Longobardi and Delfitto, we think that the generic reading of bare plurals in Italian is comparable to that of generic indefinites, in so far as it is based on a quantificational structure. But bare plurals cannot be assimilated to indefinites, because bare plurals denote properties.

5.1 From property to kind denotation

In the Germanic languages, particularly English, bare nouns can not only be interpreted as denoting properties, but also as definite descriptions denoting kinds (Carlson 1977, Dobrovie-Sorin and Laca 1998). This generalization is particularly clear for examples such as (47a), containing predicates which can only be applied to kinds. The possibility of bare nouns in English being interpreted as definite expressions denoting kinds also explains the grammaticality of examples (47b-c):

(47) E a. Cats are on the verge of extinction.
b. Cats are intelligent.
c. John hates cats.

Predicates like *intelligent, big,* or *like, hate,* etc., are entity-predicates, which must be combined with NPs which denote individuals. Examples

[17] The impossibility of a generic reading for bare nouns without modification could be attributed to a syntactic constraint which applies to bare nouns in general: in Italian (and also in Spanish and Romanian), bare nouns can only occupy a preverbal position if they are modified or coordinated (see section 6 below). The issue is more complex however, in so far as one can find examples of generic bare nouns in post-verbal positions. And in this case too, modification is necessary for the generic reading (but not for the existential reading). We will set aside this problem here (see Longobardi 2002).

(47b-c) are grammatical because bare nouns in English can denote entities of a specific type, kinds.

The counterparts to the examples in (47) are ungrammatical in SIR, due to a semantic type mismatch: bare plurals in SIR denote properties, while the predicates in (48) demand either individuals of the sort kind, or ordinary individuals.

(48) a. S *Gatos se están extinguendo.
I *Gatti sono in via d'estinzione.
R *Pisici sunt pe cale de dispariţie.
b. S *Gatos son inteligentes.
I *Gatti sono intelligenti.
R *Pisici sunt inteligente.
c. S *Juan odia gatos.
I *Gianni odia gatti.
R *Ion urăşte pisici.

Kind-denotation, which characterizes the generic use of bare nouns in English (Carlson 1977) has been analyzed by Chierchia (1998a,b) as resulting from a type-shifting function comparable to the one denoted by the definite article: from a property such as *cats* one obtains the unique individual which satisfies (in a given context) the property *cat*. Where *cats* is plural, it refers to a property of plural individuals (groups). The unique individual that satisfies this property corresponds to the maximal collective entity constituted of individuals who satisfy the property 'cat'. Kinds are maximal collective entities which have the peculiarity of being totally independent from contextual domain restriction. To sum up, generic bare nouns in English can be assimilated to definite expressions which refer to kinds.

Dobrovie-Sorin (1997a) and Dobrovie-Sorin and Laca (1996, 1998) have extended the analysis of bare nouns as denotations of maximal collective entities to the quasi-universal reading (see the 'functional' reading of Condoravdi 1994):[18]

(49) E a. We're reaching the end of term. Students are exhausted.
b. It hadn't rained for three months. Farmers were worried and speculators were happy at the prospect of rising food prices.

In these examples, the bare nouns denote maximal plural entities restricted by the discourse context: the students of a particular university, the farmers of a particular region or village.

[18] For a detailed description of the properties of the quasi-universal reading, see Condoravdi (1994). However, we will not follow the analysis of Condoravdi, who considers the quasi-universal reading of bare nouns to be entirely distinct from the generic reading, and analyzes bare nouns with a quasi-universal interpretation as *indefinite* expressions.

There is a striking parallelism between the generic and quasi-universal readings of bare nouns: both are possible in English, but impossible in SIR. Thus, in parallel with the contrasts illustrated in (47) and (48), the English examples like (49a) contrast with their counterparts in SIR:

(50) S Se acerca el fin del semestre. *Estudiantes están agotados.
I Si avvicina la fine del semestre. *Studenti sono esauriti.
R Se apropie sfîrşitul trimestrului. *Studenţi sunt epuizaţi.

This parallelism between the generic and quasi-universal readings suggests that the two types of readings are based on an identical type of denotation, which is possible for bare nouns in English but impossible in SIR. We are thus led to follow the suggestion of Dobrovie-Sorin (1997a) and Dobrovie-Sorin and Laca (1996, 1998), whereby the maximal collective individual corresponding to the property denoted by the bare noun is not necessarily a kind. Contextual domain restriction leads to a quasi-universal interpretation, whereas its absence forces the kind-interpretation.

The fact that bare nouns in English, in contrast to those in SIR, are able to denote maximal collective entities can be related to a syntactic parameter: one could for example assume a null definite determiner, without phonetic realization, which would exist in English but not in SIR. Or else, one could adopt the analysis of Longobardi (1994), according to which bare nouns in English, but not in SIR, can occupy (following a syntactic rule of 'raising') the position provided for the determiner. We believe that there are at present no decisive empirical arguments in favor of the existence of a null definite determiner or a rule of Noun Raising. Adopting a null definite determiner is a way of saying that the type-shifting which characterizes bare nouns in English is a particular property of this language (as opposed to other languages), not a semantic type-shifting brought about by the context, which should apply in any language. In the Romance languages, the same type-shifting must be marked by a lexically realized definite article. This use of the definite article must be distinguished from its anaphoric use, for which an overtly realized definite article is required not only in the Romance languages, but also in English.

5.2 Generic bare nouns in Italian don't denote kinds

Modified bare nouns in Italian allow generic interpretations (Renzi 1988, Chierchia 1998b, Longobardi 2002, Delfitto, 2002):[19]

[19] All the authors cited point out that the acceptability judgements concerning these generic readings vary considerably. We only report the most widely accepted examples here.

(51) I a. Cani di grosse dimensioni creano seri guai.
Large dogs cause great misfortunes.
b. Assenze che non siano segnalate per tempo, non verrano giustificate.
Absences that are not signaled in advance will not be justified.

This type of example is less acceptable in Spanish and Romanian.[20] This difference between Italian and the other Romance languages with bare nouns indicates the existence of additional constraints in Spanish and Romanian, which are probably linked to the differences in word order, and accentuation and focalization devices, but we will leave this question open. In concentrating on Italian, we will try to show the *necessary* conditions for the generic reading of modified bare nouns in the SIR languages. These conditions are also sufficient for Italian, but not for Spanish or Romanian.

According to Chierchia (1998b), generic bare nouns in Italian denote kinds. To support this hypothesis, Chierchia draws on examples such as those given in (52), constructed with predicates such as 'rare' or 'abound', that he analyzes as being kind-predicates:

(52) I a. Qui, ragazze in minigonna sono rare.
Here, girls in miniskirts are rare.
b. In questa zona, belle farfalle abbondano.
In this region, beautiful butterflies abound.

However, Krifka *et al.* (1995) have clearly established that these predicates, which express quantified existence, must not be assimilated to kind-predicates. Thus, modified bare nouns in Italian are not compatible with *bona fide* kind-predicates (Longobardi, 2002):

(53) I *Uomini intelligenti sono in via d'estinzione.
Intelligent men are on the verge of extinction.

---

[20] In these languages, only bare nouns modified by expressions of the type S *de esta especie*, I *di questa fatta*, allow generic interpretations in a completely productive manner (they are equally possible in I):

(i) S a. Delfines de esta especie son más inteligentes que sus entrenadores. (Zubizarreta 1996)
Dolphins of this species are more intelligent than their trainers.
b. Individuos como ése no suelen tener paciencia.
Individuals like this usually lack patience.

(ii) I a. Mascalzoni di questa fatta non sono rari, purtroppo. (Renzi 1988)
Louts of this kinds are not rare, unfortunately.
b. Incidenti così hanno spesso delle conseguenze imprevedibili.
Incidents of this type often have unpredictable consequences.

By virtue of their content, these modifiers can be assimilated to expressions such as *this type / this sort of* N, which are kind-denoting (Wilkinson 1995, Longobardi 1999).

Examples such as (52) do not therefore constitute a solid argument in favor of Chierchia's proposal. This proposal does not allow us to account for the contrasts between English and SIR that we summarized in section 5.1. If modified bare nouns in Italian were able to denote kinds, it would be difficult to understand why they are excluded in the majority of contexts which allow the generic interpretation of bare nouns in English.

5.3 The genericity of indefinites and bare nouns

Longobardi (2002) has given evidence of striking parallelisms between contexts which allow generic readings of modified bare nouns in Italian and those which allow generic readings of (singular or plural) expressions preceded by an indefinite determiner.

(54) I a. Stati di grandi dimensioni sono pericolosi.
Large states are dangerous.
b. Uno stato di grandi dimensioni è pericoloso.
A large state is dangerous.
c. Cani da guardia di grosse dimensioni sono più efficienti.
Large guard dogs are more efficient.
d. Un cane da guardia di grosse dimensioni è più efficiente.
A large guard dog is more efficient.

(55) I a. ??Stati di grandi dimensioni sono prosperi.
Large states are prosperous.
b. ??Uno stato di grandi dimensioni è prospero.
A large state is prosperous.
c. ??Cani da guardia di grosse dimensioni sono più pelosi.
Large guard dogs are hairier.
d. ??Un cane da guardia di grosse dimensioni è più peloso.
A large guard dog is hairier.

In order to explain the contrast between (54) and (55), Longobardi proposes a sub-classification of individual-level predicates which results from their being more or less eventive. In reality, one can in fact analyze the predicates classified as 'permanent eventives' by Longobardi as ambiguous between individual-level and stage-level. By the logic of Longobardi's analysis, one would therefore say that only stage-level predicates allow a generic reading of indefinites (54), due to the fact that only these predicates allow the introduction of GEN.

Contrary to Longobardi, however, we do not think that individual-level predicates, such as those in (55), block the introduction of GEN. Indeed, they clearly authorize the generic reading of singular indefinites (*A cat is intelligent*). One also finds, in French, examples of generic plural indefinites in the context of individual-level predicates:[21]

(56) F a. Des droites parallèles se coupent à l'infini.
Parallel lines intersect at infinity.
b. Des droites convergentes ont un point en commun.
Converging straight lines have a common point.
c. Des pays limitrophes ont souvent des rapports difficiles.
Bordering nations often have difficult relations.

These examples express generalizations about pairs of parallel lines, converging lines, or bordering countries, to which are attributed permanent defining properties: 'if any pair is a pair of parallel lines, then (the elements belonging to) this pair intersect at infinity'. Given the grammaticality of this type of example in French, it follows that individual-level predicates, in particular those of (55), allow, in principle, the default introduction of GEN, hence Logical Forms (LF) like (56′), where GEN quantifies over pairs of individuals:[22]

(56′) GENx (x is (a pair of) parallel straight lines) [x intersect at infinity]

However, the Italian examples corresponding to (56) are ungrammatical:[23, 24]

(56) I a. * Rette parallele s'incrociano all'infinito.
b. * Rette convergenti hanno un punto in comune.
c. * Paesi limitrofi hanno spesso rapporti difficili.

---

[21] Corblin (1987) gives comparable examples with cardinals instead of indefinites with *des*:

(i) Deux droites convergentes ont un point en commun.
Two convergent straight lines have a point in common.

(ii) Deux pays limitrophes ont souvent des rapports difficiles / finissent par se fédérer.
Two bordering countries often have difficult relations / end up forming a federation.

(iii) Deux amis intimes se critiquent toujours.
Two close friends always criticize each other.

[22] This LF is perfectly parallel to the one generally accepted for singular indefinites:

(i) A cat is intelligent

(ii) GENx (x is a cat) [x is intelligent]

The only difference between (56′) and (ii) concerns the domain of the variable: the domain of atomic individuals for (ii), and the domain of plural individuals / groups for (56′).

[23] Neither Longobardi (2002) nor Delfitto (2002) discuss examples of this type. We thank Pino Longobardi, Cecilia Poletto and Roberto Zamparelli for the grammaticality judgements.

[24] Examples like (56) must be distinguished from those like (i), which do not attribute stable properties, but merely give definitions of terms:

(i) I Strofe di tre versi sono terzine.
Verses of three lines are tercets.

In the framework proposed by Longobardi, which assimilates bare nouns with indefinites, the contrast between Italian and French remains mysterious. In the framework of our analysis of bare nouns, one can attribute this ungrammaticality to the fact that LFs of the same type as that given in (56′) cannot be assigned to the examples (56)I: bare plurals denote properties, but the predicates 'intersect at infinity', 'have a point in common' or 'have difficult relations' are entity-predicates, which as such cannot be applied to properties. The French examples given under (56)F are acceptable due to the fact, noted in section 4, that indefinite plurals with *des* are not necessarily analyzed as denoting properties, but can, in certain contexts, introduce group variables.

This analysis also explains the ungrammaticality of the Italian examples given in (55). However, we still cannot understand why the corresponding French examples, given in (55)F, as well as those like (48)F, repeated here, are also ungrammatical, contrasting with the examples of (56)F:

(55) F a. ??Des états de grande taille sont prospères.
Large states are prosperous.
b. ?Des chiens de garde de grande taille sont plus poilus.
Large guard dogs are hairier.

(48) F * Des chats sont intelligents.
Cats are intelligent.

It is not a type mismatch which explains the ungrammaticality of these examples, since we have seen that indefinites with *des* can be analyzed as introducing group variables (see(56)).[25] A different explanation must therefore be proposed. According to Dobrovie-Sorin and Laca (1998) and Dobrovie-Sorin (2002), the ungrammaticality of examples like (48)F and (55)F is due to a selectional restriction: while the plural indefinite introduces groups (group variables), predicates like 'prosper', 'hairy', 'intelligent', etc., must be applied to atomic individuals. In contrast, the examples in (56) are grammatical, because they are constructed with individual-level predicates which select groups ('intersect at infinity', 'have a point in common' or 'have difficult relations').

---

[25] Note that all these examples are grammatical in the singular, which is contrary to the perfect parallelism between generic indefinite singulars and plurals, put forward by Longobardi:

(i) S Un gato es inteligente.
I Un gatto è intelligente.
R O pisică e intelligentă.
F Un chat est intelligent.
A cat is intelligent.

It remains for us now to understand the contrast, internal to Italian, between (54)I and (55)I. Dobrovie-Sorin (2002) suggests that adverbs of quantification can quantify, according to the context, either over individuals or over situations (or events).[26] Due to the type mismatch invoked above for example (55), quantification over individuals (atomic or plural) is excluded for bare plurals in Italian, which can therefore only obtain a generic interpretation due to generic quantification over situations or events. As a consequence of the type of predicate (individual-level vs. stage-level), this possibility is excluded in (55), but allowed in (54). Thus we obtain LFs like (54′), in which GEN quantifies not over individuals, but over situations:

(54′) GEN *s*,*x* (*x* is in *s* & *x* is (a group of) states of large size) [*s* is dangerous]

This representation is compatible with our central hypothesis, according to which bare nouns denote properties: in (54′), the bare noun 'states of large size' does not function as the semantic argument of the predicate 'dangerous' (if that were the case, the LF would be ill-formed, due to a type mismatch, like (55) and (56)), but like a predicate which constrains the domain of an individual-variable postulated as existing in the situation. The intuitive interpretation associated with this LF is of the type: 'If a situation contains a group of states of large size, then this situation is dangerous'; 'If there are / the world has a group of states of a large size, then there is danger / the world is in danger'.

In conclusion, our analysis of the generic readings of modified bare nouns in Italian resembles those of Longobardi (2002) and Delfitto (2002) to the extent that we assume that they involve generic quantification (and not kind-denotation). However, we diverge from these authors on several points: (i) We do not assimilate bare nouns to indefinites. Due to the fact that bare plurals denote properties, generic quantification over plural individuals (groups) is impossible for bare nouns, but possible for indefinite plurals. That allows us to understand the contrast between bare plurals in Italian and plurals with *des* in French (see (55)I-(56)I vs. (56)F). (ii) We assume, following Dobrovie-Sorin (2002) that adverbs of quantification – and GEN in particular – can quantify either over individuals or over situations or events. This allows us to explain the contrast between (54) and (55): the generic reading of bare nouns in Italian is possible in examples like (54), analyzed in terms of quantification over events, but it is excluded

[26] Dobrovie-Sorin and Laca (1996, 1998) assume that the generic reading of plural indefinites relies on generic quantification over individuals, while Longobardi accepts recent semantic analyses, according to which adverbs of quantification necessarily quantify over situations or events (see the introduction, as well as the majority of the articles in Krifka *et al.* 1995).

in examples like (55), which can only be analyzed in terms of quantification over individuals. (iii) We assume, following Dobrovie-Sorin and Laca (1998), that in examples which can be represented by generic quantification over individuals (as opposed to situations or events), indefinite plurals give rise to generalizations over groups, and as such cannot be combined with predicates which select atomic individuals. This explains the ungrammaticality of (55)F in French.

6 Syntactic constraints

The distribution of bare nouns in SIR is subject to important restrictions with respect to the syntactic positions which they can occupy. Beyond the common restrictions on bare nouns in SIR and *des* / *du* phrases in French, that we explain by semantic type mismatches between the denotation of these expressions and the denotation required by the argument positions of entity-predicates, there are other constraints which are peculiar to bare nouns in SIR. They affect preverbal subjects and they can be overridden by contextual factors, which is not the case for the constraints due to the type of the predicate.

The most robust constraint, which affects the preverbal subject position, has been formulated for Spanish by Suñer (1982:209) under the label of *Naked Noun Constraint*:

(57) An unmodified common noun in the preverbal position cannot be the surface subject of a sentence under conditions of normal stress and intonation.

This generalization accounts for the examples in (58) from Spanish; the data of Romanian and Italian are parallel (Longobardi 1994). Bare nouns are excluded from the preverbal subject position in (58a, b), but they are possible in the post-verbal position (58c). Sequences with preverbal bare nouns become acceptable in the presence of an adnominal modification (58d) or when they exhibit a marked intonation contour. The intonation contour indicated by the capital letters in (58e) marks the preverbal subject as the (narrow) Focus of the sentence;[27] the contour suggested by the context in (58f) indicates that the subject is a dislocated Topic.

[27] Dislocated bare nouns in Spanish are not generally associated with a clitic, and only the intonation allows us to discern this type of construction. In Italian, in contrast, the presence of the clitic *ne* in the examples which illustrate this structure is at once a sign of dislocation and of the postverbal origin of the subject. Indeed, *ne* is strictly correlated in Italian with a direct object or the postverbal subject of an unaccusative verb. In this language, in addition, the dislocation can be explicitly marked by *di*:

(58) S a. *Olas batían contra las rocas.
Waves were beating the rocks.
b. *Ratones salieron del armario.
Mice came out of the cupboard.
c. Salieron ratones del armario.
Mice came out of the cupboard.
d. Olas gigantescas batían contra las rocas.
Huge waves were beating the rocks.
e. RATONES salieron del armario.
Mice came out of the cupboard.
f. Ratones salieron, pero arañas no.
Mice did come out of it, but no spiders.

In the framework of the Government and Binding theory, the most widely accepted explanation appeals to the notions of empty category and lexical government (Contreras 1986, 1996, Longobardi 1994). Phrases with bare nouns contain a functional head (a null determiner or quantifier, not realized phonetically) which, like all empty categories, must be licensed by a lexical head which governs it.[28] The Subject-Verb configuration not being a configuration for lexical government, bare nouns are excluded from this position.

However, modification, as well as the structures with narrow Focus or a dislocated Topic, make bare plurals acceptable in the preverbal position. The explanation required by this fact is not easy to provide in the framework of the hypothesis involving lexical government (for an attempt to ex-

(i) (Di) Elicotteri, non se ne sono visti.
Helicopters, they haven't been seen.

[28] Besides the preverbal subject position, bare nouns are also seldom acceptable in the dative position and, in Spanish, they are for the most part incompatible with differential object marking ('prepositional accusative'):

(i) S *Le habló de la cuestión a colegas.
He spoke about the question to colleagues.
(ii) S Juan quiere conocer (*a) profesores.
John wants to know teachers.

In these cases too, modification or focus with the help of a particular contrastive contour or a focus particle improve the sentences (Brugè and Brugger 1994, Laca 1996, Bosque 1996). To account for the unacceptability of bare nouns in the dative position or prepositional direct object position in Spanish in the same framework, Brugè and Brugger (1994) hypothesize that prepositions do not constitute proper governors. Although they try to support their hypothesis with the help of examples in which other complements or prepositional adjuncts with bare nouns are unacceptable, they notice variability in acceptability judgments in relation to their own examples, and it seems perfectly possible to find acceptable examples (Lois 1996). The facts concerning the distribution of bare nouns with prepositions are too complex to be used to evaluate the null determiner hypothesis. They contrast with the quite clear unacceptability judgments that one obtains for datives and prepositional accusatives.

plain the role of modification in syntactic terms, see Delfitto and Schroten 1991 as well as Delfitto, 2002).

The purely syntactic explanation poses problems even for unmodified bare nouns if we take into account the data from other languages: English, indeed, allows bare nouns in the preverbal subject position. It is not clear why the preverbal subject position would be lexically governed in English but not in SIR. Longobardi's (1994) answer is that in English the bare noun moves to the determiner position, so that no null determiner would appear there, and correlatively lexical government is not demanded. We cannot accept this explanation here, because it implies that the existential interpretation of bare nouns in English is based on the same syntactic structure as the one which is responsible for their generic interpretation (see above section 5.1).[29]

We are far from having a satisfactory explanation of the observed regularities, and can only propose a direction for future research here. We would like to derive the restriction of bare nouns in the preverbal subject position from the following constraint (Dobrovie-Sorin 2000):[30]

(59) Topic NPs cannot denote properties.

If we accept this constraint, the unacceptability of bare nouns in the preverbal subject position in SIR can be explained by the fact that in these languages the preverbal subject position is necessarily, in the unmarked case, a Topic. The contrast between SIR and English is not due – as Longobardi (1994) suggests – to a syntactic parameter concerning DP, but rather to a parameter concerning the structure of the sentence, and more specifically the status of the preverbal position of the subject: in English and in French, preverbal subjects are not necessarily Topics. The differing status of the preverbal subject position follows from whether the language in question generally allows post-verbal subjects or not:

(60) a. In a language with free inversion of the subject, a non-dislocated preverbal subject is either a Topic or contrastive Focus.
b. In a language without free inversion of the subject, the preverbal subject is susceptible to two analyses: it can be a Topic, or it can belong to the Comment.

---

[29] Longobardi's solution (1994) has the effect of making the existential interpretation of English bare nouns a marked phenomenon. Everything seems to indicate, on the contrary, that it is the generic interpretation which constitutes the marked phenomenon.

[30] This constraint follows from the very notion of a Topic, if one agrees with Strawson (1950) and Reinhart (1995) that a Topic-Comment configuration presupposes the existence of the individual to which the predicate expressed by the Comment is attributed. Property-denoting expressions do not presuppose existence.

The SIR languages are of the type described in (60a): an unmarked preverbal subject is a Topic, which is incompatible with the denotation of a property; a preverbal subject marked by contrastive accent – or composed with modifiers – can be interpreted as a Focus, and consequently is compatible with a denotation of a property. English is a language like those described in (60b), the preverbal subject can belong to the Comment, and consequently it can denote a property, whence the acceptability of bare nouns with an existential interpretation. Preverbal subjects in French have the same syntactic and information status as those in English, which renders them compatible with NPs denoting properties. Hence the possibility of using NPs with *de(s)* in the preverbal subject position.

7 Brazilian Portuguese

In this section we draw on Munn and Schmitt (1999), who have clearly established that the facts of Portuguese, particularly Brazilian Portuguese, diverge quite significantly from those that we have described for SIR. We will first look at plurals and mass nouns (section 7.1) and then singular count nouns (section 7.2). We will show that, while diverging from the facts described for SIR, Brazilian Portuguese confirms certain correlations established in the previous sections.

7.1 Plurals and mass nouns

The distribution of bare nouns is much wider in Portuguese (European and Brazilian), where they are allowed in the preverbal subject position, unconstrained by the particular conditions required by SIR (see section 6 above):

(61) P a. Elói olha volta com indiferença. Cabeças espreitam-no umas por cima das outras.
Elói looks around him with indifference. Heads surround him, some above others.
b. Crianças brincavam na rua.
Children were playing in the street.

Furthermore, in Brazilian Portuguese, bare nouns allow not only an existential interpretation, but also a generic reading:

(62) BP a. Epífitas nascem sobre outras plantas, sem contudo tirar delas a nutrição.
Epiphytes are born on other plants, without necessarily feeding off them.
b. Pela sua experiência, clients atrasam-se numa media de doze minutos.

From his experience, clients are on average twelve minutes late.

c. Roupa suja lava-se em casa.
Dirty linen is washed at home.

d. Ela adora orquídeas.
She loves orchids.

e. Naquela época, vinho era grande novidade nos países nórdicos.
At that time, wine was a great novelty in the northern countries.

Note that generic bare nouns appear not only in contexts expressing characterizing generalizations (62a-c), but also as an argument of entity-predicates (62d-e). It therefore appears that bare nouns in (Brazilian) Portuguese are comparable to those of English, in that they can denote not only properties but also the maximal collective entities corresponding to the properties in question. This analysis is confirmed by the data of (63), which show that bare plurals in Brazilian Portuguese can give rise, in the context of an episodic predication, to quasi-universal readings, as we also noticed for English (in this case they denote a contextually determined maximal plural entity, see ex. (49) above):

(63) BP Continua a lua cheia. Relógios pararam e o som de um carrilhão rouco escorre pelo muro.
There is still a full moon. Clocks have stopped and the sound of harsh chimes spreads along the wall.

This data confirms the parallel between generic readings and quasi-universal readings for bare nouns, established for English in section 5.1.

Unlike English, which does not allow the definite article to be used for generic interpretations, this is optional in Brazilian Portuguese (64a, b). It is also clearly preferred, or even obligatory, for kind-predicates and for readings involving a representative part of a kind (64c-d):[31]

(64) BP a. Os animais não riem.
(the) *Animals do not laugh.*

b. As flores são muito delicadas.
(the) *Flowers are very fragile.*

c. *(As) baleias são uma espécie em vias de extinção.
(the) *Whales are a species on the verge of extinction.*

[31] We thank Rita Godet for this information. European Portuguese seems to reject generic readings as much as quasi-universal ones, and prefers the definite article in these cases (Carla Soares, p.c.). There is, however, a certain amount of variability in the judgments, and bare NPs are more acceptable as objects of entity predicates and in certain characterizing generalizations.

d. *(Os) cavalos foram introduzidos no Novo Mundo pelos europeus.
(the) *Horses were introduced into the New World by the Euro peans.*

These facts are reminiscent of those which have been noticed for German, where bare nouns as well as nouns preceded by the definite article allow generic interpretations (Krifka *et al.* 1995): the transition from the denotation of a property to the denotation of a kind can happen, as in SIR, with the help of an overt operator or, as in English, without overt marking.

7.2 Singular count nouns

The distribution and denotational properties of singular count nouns distinguish Brazilian Portuguese not only from the SIR Romance languages, but also from English and German.

In SIR, bare singular nouns are only allowed in argument positions under very specific conditions, and their use presents idiosyncrasies which might be a symptom of their idiomatic status.[32] Putting aside the case of expressions equivalent to complex predicates, existing also in French (F *faire preuve de,* S *echar mano a*, I *prendere nota di*, R *a ţine cont de*), bare singulars appear in negative contexts, though with important restrictions which still have not been thoroughly explored (the preferred option under negation being the plural or singular preceded by a negative polarity indefinite):[33]

(65) S a. Nunca he visto estudiante más revoltoso.
I have never seen [a] more rebellious student.
I b. Non si trovava taxi in tutta la città.
One couldn't find [a] taxi in the whole town.
R c. N-am văzut student mai turbulent.
I have never seen [a] more rebellious student.

In Spanish and Romanian, bare singulars can occasionally appear in object position, but these combinations are subject to quite specific lexical constraints:

(66) S a. Este edificio tiene ascensor.
'This building has [a] lift.

[32] Bare singulars have a wider distribution when they are introduced by a preposition, according to constraints which vary from one language to another. Bare singulars are particularly common in Italian in locative expressions. In other languages, certain prepositions and certain nouns favor bare singulars (F *en clinique*, E *to church* etc.) We do not develop this matter here.

[33] See footnote 12 for (65)-I.

b. Pedro compró coche / casa / apartamento.
Peter bought [a] car / [a] house / [an] apartment.
c. A veces se pone corbata / sombrero.
Occasionally he puts on [a] tie / [a] hat.
R d. Din cînd în cînd Ion îşi pune cravată / pălărie.
From time to time John puts on [a] tie / [a] hat.

In Brazilian Portuguese, in contrast, bare singulars have a comparable distribution to that of bare plurals and bare mass nouns. They can give rise to existential interpretations (67a, b) or generic interpretations (68a, b):

(67) BP a. Aqui passa trem (sg).
[A] train passes / Trains pass here.
b. Chegou criança (sg).
[A] child / Children arrived.

(68) BP a. Flor dos trigais só dá no meio do trigo.
[The] wheat flower only grows in the middle of the wheat.
b. Tigre ferido é perigoso.
[A / The] wounded tiger is dangerous.
Wounded tigers are dangerous.

It is particularly interesting to notice that these bare singulars do not imply atomicity. Firstly, they combine with predicates which only apply to plural entities, like reciprocal predicates:

(69) BP a. Criança briga uma com a outra. (Schmitt and Munn 1999)
Children argue with each other.
b. Homem se beija na França. (Schmitt and Munn 1999)
In France, men kiss each other.

Secondly, they cancel telicity, like bare plurals or mass nouns:

(70) BP a. Eu escrevi carta por duas horas / *em duas horas. (Schmitt and Munn 1999)
I wrote letter[s] for two hours / in two hours.
b. Eu escrevi uma carta *por duas horas / em duas horas.
I wrote a letter for two hours / in two hours.

There is a particularly clear contrast here with bare singulars in Spanish which do not give rise to detelicization effects, but behave as if they were introducing bounded entities:

(71) S a. Juan compró casa en quince días.
John bought [a] house in fifteen days.
b. Juan consiguió taxi en cinco minutos.
John found [a] taxi in five minutes.

And finally, even with the existential reading, bare singulars in Portuguese can supply the antecedent for plural pronouns or take up a plural referent:

(72) BP a. Tem criança na sala. E ela está / elas estão ouvindo. (Schmitt and Munn 1999)
There is [a] child / children in the room. And he is / they are listening

b. Davam tapas em nossas bocas, indignadas por criança se meter onde não devia.
They were giving us taps on the mouth, indignant at the fact that children were meddling in what didn't concern them.

As suggested by Schmitt and Munn (1999), these facts indicate that bare singulars in Brazilian Portuguese are not semantically specified for singular number. Recall that we have assumed that the singulars of uncountable nouns take their denotation in the unstructured domain of atomic individuals, while the plurals and mass nouns take their denotation in a domain structured by the relation 'is a part of'. The special feature of bare singulars in Brazilian Portuguese is that they can take their denotation in both domains in question. The effects we've just seen indicate that they can denote in the domain of quantities of matter and plurals. But they can also denote in the domain of atomic entities:

(73) BP Criança pesa 20 quilos nesta idade.
[A] child weighs / Children weigh 20 kilos at this age.

This type of example, as well as the possibility of referring to an existential bare singular by a singular pronoun illustrated in (72a) above, shows that bare singulars in Brazilian Portuguese are not comparable to mass uses of countable nouns that one notices in examples like F *Il y a du flic dans les parages* 'There are policemen around'. Bare singulars in Portuguese do not rely on a metonymic transfer which would produce particular meaning effects, but are actually neutral with respect to the semantic distinction singular/plural.[34]

This property of bare singulars can be compared with what we also know about the treatment of morphological number marking in the non-

---

[34] It is important to underline that this property is not verified for singulars preceded by a determiner:

(i) P O homem se beija na França.
The man SE-kisses in France
Men kiss themselves in France. (reflexive / *reciprocal)

(ii) P (* A) criança briga uma com a outra
The child fights the one with the other
Children fight with each other.

standard and contact varieties of Portuguese, whose influence makes itself felt much more clearly in Brazilian Portuguese than in European Portuguese (Da Silva Neto 1977). Indeed, in these varieties one notices the tendency to only use the plural morpheme in the two following cases: (a) with specific noun phrases, referring to individuated groups, and (b) if there are no other indications of plurality in the noun phrase ('only one plural marking per NP', Gregor 1988). The morphological plural proves to be a marked category (morphologically and semantically), while the morphological singular is semantically neutral.

In section 3, we noticed that the absence of an article is only possible in SIR for an expression which denotes in the domain of non-atomic entities. In contrast, expressions which denote exclusively in the domain of atomic entities demand a determiner. This generalization remains valid for Brazilian Portuguese. The difference between the two types of languages comes down to the different status of the morphological singular. It is semantically specified in SIR: a singular count noun denotes exclusively in the domain of atomic entities and demands, consequently, a determiner. In Brazilian Portuguese, in contrast, the morphological singular is semantically neutral: a singular count noun can indifferently denote in the domain of atomic or non-atomic entities, and because of this allows articles to be absent.

A Note on bare count singulars (by C. Dobrovie-Sorin)

The analysis of bare nouns proposed above concerns bare plurals and bare mass nouns but count bare singulars only marginally, with a brief examination limited to Brazilian Portuguese. Bare singulars have recently come to the foreground of the investigation and their distribution has been carefully examined in languages which possess articles, e.g., in Albanian, Norwegian, Hungarian, Spanish and Romanian (see Kallulli 1999, Borthen 2003, Farkas and de Swart 2003, Dobrovie-Sorin, Bleam and Espinal 2005, 2006). There is a general agreement that the distribution of bare singulars is more restricted than that of bare plurals, a situation which yields a tripartite distinction between indefinites, bare plurals and bare singulars. This distinction can be represented syntactically (full DPs vs. NumPs vs. NPs), and correlated to different modes of semantic composition: in addition to the canonical rule of predicate-saturation, we would need two distinct rules: 'semantic incorporation' (proposed by van Geenhoven 1996 and adopted in the text above) and 'predicate-modification' (which covers Dayal's 'Pseudo-Incorporation' 2003, Farkas and de Swart's 'Theta-unification' 2003, and Chung and Ladusaw's 'Retrict' 2003). The tripartite distinction in syntactic category calls for a tripartite distinction in semantic type, and since bare singulars are unanimously assumed to denote properties, the semantic analysis of bare plurals needs to be revised. Dobrovie-Sorin's proposal (2007) is that bare plurals (and bare mass nouns) are to be represented as variables bound by existential closure over the VP-domain. As regards indefinites, they can be represented as referential terms formalized as Skolem terms, as proposed by Steedman (2006), who builds on Farkas (1997a,b, 2001).

Analyzing bare plurals as referring to a particular type of entity rather than as denoting properties would allow us to distinguish them from bare singulars, while at the same time keeping them distinct from indefinites, represented as Skolem terms. The empirical generalizations that were captured within the property-analysis can be maintained, because the variables supplied by bare plurals must be bound by existential closure, which is restricted to apply to the VP-domain (as in Diesing 1992), and is subject to lexical restrictions imposed by the main predicate (as in Carlson 1977).

7

Negation in the Simple Clause in the Romance Languages

FRANCIS CORBLIN AND LUCIA M. TOVENA

1 Introduction[1]

In this chapter we aim to provide an overview of the system of negation in the Romance languages. We will concentrate on the phenomenon of negative concord in French, Italian, Romanian, Spanish, and Portuguese.

The term *negative concord* was introduced by Labov (1972) to describe a phenomenon in certain non-standard dialects of American English.[2] In contrast to standard English, for example, where the abstract negative element is attracted by the first indefinite in a sentence (realized for instance as *nobody* in the sentence *Nobody did anything*), Labov characterizes these non-standard dialects as follows: 'We might say for these dialects that the negative is attracted to indefinites generally' (1972:784). The sentence thus expresses a single negation, whose expression is copied onto each indefinite to produce, for example, *Nobody did nothing* (with a single negation in the semantics). We can extend the term *negative concord* to other languages in which a sentence can contain several negative words and yet fail to give rise to a multiple negation interpretation. For example, the Italian sentence in (1)

[1] We would like to thank in particular R. Calciu, I. Comorovski, M. Huber, B. Laca, J. Peres, R. Pop, L. Santos, and the many colleagues who helped us with the data. Danièle Godard aided us enormously with her careful reading of the manuscripts and her suggestions for form and content. Our thanks also to an anonymous reviewer for detailed comments.

[2] As far as we know, Mathesius (1937) is a precursor to Labov on this point and provides the first occurrence of this concept in the literature. His exact expression is 'negation concord'.

Fundamental Issues in the Romance Languages
Danièle Godard (ed.).

does not have an interpretation corresponding to 'Everyone said something'; it can only mean 'Everyone stayed silent'.

(1) I Nessuno ha detto niente. lit. 'no one has said nothing'

The term *N-word*, attributed to Laka Mugarza (1990), has been used to identify (without necessarily making any strong analytical claims) expressions that have certain properties typical of truly negative elements—see for example their behavior in (2a)—and other properties typical of negative polarity items, as illustrated in (2b). In (2a), *nessuno* is the only explicit negative element, and the sentence has only a negative interpretation. In (2b) the same word appears after a negative marker, but the sentence does not allow a double negation reading.

(2) I a. Nessuno mangia. *No one eats.*
b. Qui non mangia nessuno. lit. 'here not eats no one'

In general, then, we use the term 'N-word' for languages with negative concord. In addition to words like Italian *nessuno* that contain a negative morpheme, the term N-word applies, by extension, to expressions used as arguments of a predicate that are interpreted (at least in some of their uses) as negative quantifiers—that is, they introduce the equivalent of a classical logical negation, and depending on the analysis, a universal or existential quantifier. This is true for *personne* in French, for example, and for *cap* in Catalan.

The languages in which negative concord is standard are called negative concord languages. They are contrasted with languages in which the co-occurrence of several N-words associated with the same verb is either ungrammatical or necessarily yields a multiple negation reading. One must distinguish the case of generalized negative concord, where the co-occurrence of the negative marker and N-words is grammatical and produces a single logical negation (which is the case for African American English, for example, but also for many of the Romance languages), and negative concord restricted to N-words (which is the case for standard French).

Negative concord is a phenomenon common to the Romance languages, but the details differ from one language to another. This is why we find the phenomenon so interesting. While all researchers would agree that (1) is an instance of negative concord, there is no universally accepted account of the mechanisms that give rise to the interpretation with a single negation. The different analyses proposed in the literature, discussed in detail in section 4, are concerned essentially with this technical problem, without really attempting to explain why so many natural languages should have adopted such a 'problematic' method of expressing meaning. In section 5, we present our view of negative concord, which shifts the perspective and derives the concord from the interaction of general (not formal) constraints or principles on the way languages work. The first principle expresses the fact that languages have to mark negative variables lexically, and the effect of the second is to disallow self-embedding of negation in the predicate-argument space. This proposal is a synthesis of previous work (Corblin 1996, Tovena 1998), which is also outlined in Corblin and Tovena (2001).

In this chapter, we focus on the semantic problems that negative concord poses, and we only indirectly address syntactic issues.[3] Our proposal amounts to a typology of simple sentences involving negative concord in the Romance languages. Three main cases are identified. First of all, Romanian illustrates the case of a language that marks every negative sentence with its preverbal negative marker, while N-words can occupy argument positions, or more precisely they can be used to represent participants in the event described in the sentence or spatio-temporal parameters. The second case covers Italian, Portuguese, and Spanish. In these languages, the negative marker occupies a preverbal position, but its presence is not required if there is a participant expressed by an N-word in preverbal position. Southern Italian dialects also belong to this group. Catalan seems to be moving out of the first group and into the second, but the classification is complicated by the possible interference of sociolinguistic factors. French exemplifies a third case, where the negative marker (which we identify as *pas*) occupies a postverbal position. Northern Italian dialects and Western Romansh also belong to this group, with the additional peculiarity that the postverbal negative marker migrated from an earlier preverbal position.[4]

[3] For the syntax of sentential negation, the reader is invited to consult (for French) Gaatone (1971), Emonds (1978), Pollock (1989), Abeillé and Godard (1997), Godard (2004), Kim and Sag (2002), (for Italian) Zanuttini (1991), (for Spanish) Rivero (1970), Bosque (1980), and (for Romanian) Barbu (1999), among many others. See also the discussion in section 4, and Abeillé and Godard, this volume, section 6.1.

[4] The transition from a preverbal to a postverbal negation is often described in terms of the Jespersen cycle, which identifies a general tendency in the diachronic development of negation. The classic formulation can be found at the beginning of Jespersen (1917):

> The history of negative expressions in various languages makes us witness the following curious fluctuation: the original negative adverb is first weakened, then found insufficient and therefore strengthened, generally through some additional word, and this in its turn may be felt as the negative proper and may then in course of time be subject to the same development as the original word.

The cycle is subdivided into three phases. In the beginning, a certain element is positive and totally independent of the sentential negation marker. It then becomes a 'reinforcer' of this marker, with which it combines. Finally it becomes an independent expression of negation. A classic example is French *pas*. In Old French (i) negation is expressed by *ne*, a phonetically

This classification ignores the question of embracing negation, obviously relevant for French, where the status of the preverbal element *ne* is a matter of debate, but also for Eastern Romansh (Schwegler 1983), and for Portuguese, where double negation as in (3) is emphatic in European Portuguese but not in Brazilian (Schwegler 1983).

(3) P Ele não fala português não. *He doesn't speak Portuguese.*

Nevertheless, it should be noted that the postverbal negative element *pas*, which functions as a negative marker in French, was originally a minimizer,[5] whereas in Portuguese it is the negative marker *não* that is repeated. Since we do not treat French *ne* as part of the negation (section 2.2.1, but see Muller 1991), and since we are concentrating on 'standard' languages and European Portuguese, we will leave this question aside.

The chapter is organized as follows. Section 2 presents a series of examples involving the lexical negative elements in the Romance languages considered. Section 3 discusses the various possible syntactic combinations of these elements and their interpretation. In section 4 we give a (non-exhaustive) presentation of analyses proposed in the literature for negative concord in the Romance languages. Finally, in section 5, we propose our own analysis of negative concord.

2 The Lexicon of Negation

In this section, we examine the words associated with negative interpretation in the Romance languages.

2.1 Criteria for Negative Sentences

A sentence is negative if its semantic representation contains a negation. In general, 'negation' refers to the symbol in the semantic representation language that corresponds to negation in predicate logic. This correspondence is understood denotationally (inversion of the truth value of a proposition),

---

weakened form of Latin *non*. Then, *ne* is reinforced by a form indicating a minimal quantity (ii) and subsequently disappears in modern casual French (iii).

(i) Jeo ne di.

(ii) Je ne dis pas.

(iii) Je dis pas.
I do not say.

Italian *affatto* 'at all' provides another example of an originally affirmative element that has become an expression of negation.

[5] This term refers to expressions like *une goutte*, *un brin*, etc., which denote a minimal quantity in positive contexts. In negative contexts, in interaction with negation, they denote the absence of a minimal quantity (Bolinger 1972).

and dynamically: negation is a logical operator capable of taking scope over variables and being situated in a scope hierarchy with other logical operators. For example, the representation of *Je ne lis pas un journal* or *Non leggo giornali* contains a negation.

Je n'accepte pas is a negative sentence, but *Je refuse* is not, even if the two sentences are practically equivalent. They are distinct with respect to variable binding relationships and scope hierarchy. Consider examples (4) and (5).

(4) F Je n'ai pas accepté un compromis. *I did not accept a compromise.*

(5) F J'ai refusé un compromis. *I refused a compromise.*

The representation of (5) does not include a negation that could take scope over the variable introduced by *un compromis*. In contrast, sentence (4) does contain such a negation.

Negative sentences can often be identified with a series of semantic, syntactic, or discourse properties. For example, in French, a negative sentence can be identified by applying the following criteria (see Godard 2004):

A. Possibility of scope ambiguity with an indefinite:

(6) F a. Je n'ai pas accepté une récompense.
I did not accept a reward. (ambiguous)
b. Personne n'a accepté une recompense.
Nobody accepted a reward. (ambiguous)
c. J'ai refusé une récompense.
I refused a reward. (unambiguous)

B. Special form of coordination:

(7) F a. Je n'ai pas accepté, ni refusé d'ailleurs.
I did not accept, nor did I refuse, for that matter.
b. Personne n'a accepté, ni refusé d'ailleurs.
No one accepted, nor did they refuse, for that matter.
c. *J'ai refusé, ni accepté d'ailleurs.
I have refused, nor accepted for-that-matter

(8) I a. Non ho accettato, né d'altronde rifiutato.
I did not accept, nor for that matter did I refuse.
b. Nessuno ha accettato, né rifiutato.
No one accepted, nor did they refuse.
c. *Ho rifiutato, né d'altronde accettato.
(I) have refused, nor for-that-matter accepted

C. Discourse continuation:

(9) F a. A: Je n'ai pas accepté. B: Moi non plus.
A: I didn't accept. B: Me neither.
b. A: Personne n'a accepté. B: Moi non plus.
A: No one accepted. B: I didn't either.
c. J'ai refusé. *Toi non plus.
A: I refused. B: You neither.

(10) I a. A: Non ho accettato. B: Neanch'io.
A: I didn't accept. B: Me neither.
b. A: Nessuno ha accettato. B: Neanch'io.
A: No one accepted. B: I didn't either.
c. Ho rifiutato. *Neanche tu.
A: I refused. B: You neither.

D. Complement of the form *de* + N:

(11) F a. Je n'ai pas accepté de récompense.
I didn't accept any reward.
b. Personne n'a accepté de récompense.
No one accepted any reward.
c. *J'ai refusé de récompense.
I have refused DE reward

E. Temporal complement of the form *de* + NP[duration]

(12) F a. Je n'ai pas accepté de toute la journée.
I have not accepted all day long.
b. Personne n'a accepté de toute la journée.
No one has accepted all day long.
c. *J'ai refusé de toute la journée.
I have refused all day long.

In the following discussion, we enumerate the lexical elements that appear in negative sentences, before presenting their various possible combinations from a syntactic and semantic perspective.

2.2 The Lexical Elements

The main negative forms in the Romance languages considered here are given in Table 1.

negative marker		F *pas, point,* R *nu,* I *non,* P *não,* S *no*
negative response		F *non,* I *no,* R *nu,* P *não,* S *no*
co-negator		F *ne*
N-word	entity NP	F *personne, aucun, rien,* I *nessuno, niente, nulla,* R *nimeni, nicicare, nici unul, nimic,* P *nenhum, nada, ninguem,* S *nadie, nada, ninguno*
	entity Det	F *aucun, nul,* I *nessuno,* R *niciun,* P *nenhum, ninguem,* S *ninguno*
	time	F *jamais,* I *mai,* R *niciodată, nicicînd,* P *nunca, jamais,* S *nunca, jamás*
	place	F *nulle part,* R *nicăieri,* P *nenhures* (obs.)
	manner	R *nicicum*
emphasizer		F *aucunement, nullement,* R *nicidecum,* I *affatto*
privative		F *sans,* S *sin,* P *sem,* I *senza,* R *fără*
conjunction	SV	F *ne... ni ne,* I *non... né,* S *no... ni,* P *não... nem,* R *nu... nici nu*
	SN, SP	F *ni... ni,* I *né... né,* S *ni... ni,* P *nem... nem,* R *nici... nici*

Table 1 – The main negative forms

2.2.1 Negative marker and co-negative

We use the term 'negative marker' or more concisely 'negator' to refer to the expression that (i) can appear in any simple sentence with a finite verb, whatever the argument structure or the complementation pattern of the verb, (ii) imposes a negative semantic representation, and (iii) is not an argument of the verb. The term 'co-negator' refers to an expression, such as *ne* in French, that is licensed by the presence of a negator or an N-word in a negative sentence. A negator can become a co-negator in the evolution of a language, as happened in French.

Let us first examine the position of the negator in the sentence. The negator in contemporary French is the adverb *pas* placed after the finite verb or auxiliary; in written French it is associated with the preverbal co-negator *ne*, which is optional in spoken French. There remain, however, a few rare verbal forms or constructions in contemporary French where *ne* alone expresses negation, and therefore has the status of negator (see Muller 1991 for a list of these cases); see (13c).

(13) a. Pierre est pas venu. *Pierre did not come.* (spoken French)
b. Pierre n'est pas venu. (written French)
c. Je ne puis. *I cannot.* (negator *ne*)

In all of the other languages considered here, the negator precedes the finite verb (14a) or the auxilary (14b), even when there is no subject (14c). The negator cannot be separated from the verb, except by pronominal clitics (14d).

(14) S a. No vino Pedro . *Pedro did not come.*
R b. Petre nu a venit. *Petre did not come.*
I c. Non piove. *It is not raining.*
P d. Maria não lhe deu o livro. *Maria did not give him a book.*

The negative markers in Portuguese, Italian, and Spanish also appear with infinitives and event nouns, see (15) and (16), but with certain constraints.[6] In Romanian and French, this is only possible with the infinitive, see respectively (15d) and (15e).[7] To negate an event noun in Romanian, the form *ne* is used, and in French, the form *non*, also used for negative short answers (as noted in Milner 1982).

(15) S a. No asistir sería descortés.
I b. Sarebbe scortese non andarci.
P c. Seria impolido não ir.
R d. A nu merge ar fi nepoliticos.
F e. Il serait impoli de ne pas y assister.
Not to attend would be impolite.

(16) S a. la no existencia de trazas
the non-existence of traces
I b. Il non pagamento della tassa causa l'espulsione.
The non-payment of the tax leads to expulsion.
P c. O não pagamento da taxa ...

In the case of French and Italian, the negative marker cannot be used as a sentential pro-form to give a negative response (17). A distinct element is used for this function (18). In contrast, Romanian, Spanish, and Portuguese allow this double function for the negator (Bernini and Ramat 1992).

(17) F a. A: Fini ? B: *Pas.
I b. A: Finito? B: *Non.
A: Finished? B: No.

---

[6] For example, in Italian, in the case of an event noun, the form *mancato* 'failed / missed', which is not negative according to the definition above, is preferred. Consider for instance (i), used in preference to (16b), which sounds somewhat affected.

(i) I Il mancato pagamento della tassa causa l'espulsione.
The failure to pay the tax leads to expulsion.

[7] In this case the marker must precede the verb.

(18) F a. A: Fini ? B: Non.
I b. A: Finito? B: No.

French and Italian differ, however, with respect to the behavior of the negator in verbal ellipsis, as we can see in (19) and (20).

(19) F a. Daniel mange de la viande, mais moi pas / non.
I b. Daniele mangia la carne, ma io *non / no.
Daniel eats meat, but I don't.

(20) F a. ?Mais Marie pas.
b. Mais Marie non.
I c. *Ma Maria non.
d. Ma Maria no.
But not Mary.

In the literature, for example Milner (1979, 1982), the French negator *pas* is grouped together with elements like *nullement*, *aucunement*, and *point*, because none of them can occur in a sentence that contains another negative adverb or N-word, see (21), and because none of them can occur in non-negative contexts, unlike N-words, as we will see below.

(21) F a. *Daniel ne mange pas point / aucunement / nullement.
lit. Daniel does not eat not-at-all / in no way
*Daniel n'est nullement content de personne.
lit. Daniele is in no way happy with nobody

It should nevertheless be noted that the resulting class of words is hardly homogeneous. First, *nullement* and *aucunement* can be used as negative sentential pro-forms (22), while *point* and *pas* can only serve this function in combination with *du tout*. Furthermore, *nullement* is the only member of this class that is morphologically negative.

(22) F A: Content ? B: Nullement / Aucunement / ??Point / *Pas.
A: Happy? B: In no way / In no way / Not at all / Not.

Second, unlike *pas*, they can appear with *sans* (with the exception of *point*):

(23) F a. Il frémit, mais sans aucunement s'affoler. (Gaatone 1971)
He is agitated, but without panicking in any way.
b. Il frémit, mais sans nullement s'affoler.
c. *Il frémit, mais sans point s'affoler.
d. *Il frémit, mais sans pas s'affoler.

Third, *pas* is the only element commonly used as a negative marker without *ne* in the spoken language. And finally, it does not allow the emphatic use typical of *nullement* and *aucunement*.

To return to our classification of markers, contemporary French is the only language that has a co-negator. The placement of *ne* has been taken to be an indication of the scope of negation (Milner 1979, 1982, Kayne 1984):

(24) F a. Pierre a l'intention de ne voir personne. (Il veut rester seul.)
Pierre intends not to see anyone. (He wants to be alone.)
b. Pierre n'a l'intention de voir personne. (Il n'a pas de programmes de visite.)
Pierre does not intend to see anyone. (He has no visits planned.)

The omission of preverbal *ne* is not a recent phenomenon, but exactly when it began is a matter of controversy. According to Price (1993), it was long after the appearance of minimizers with negative force. This author dismisses the idea that *ne* omission could have started before the 15th century and argues that the minimizers found in questions prior to this period are in fact emphasizers, without polar force. The negative force associated with minimizers stabilized around the 16th century (see also Yvon 1948).

Another open question is whether the current situation is stable, or if it is still evolving. Ashby (1981) notes an increase in the frequency of *ne* omission, thus suggesting an ongoing evolution, but also shows that there are several factors that discourage its omission, not only stylistic and sociolinguistic, but also phonological and syntactic (see also Coveney 1998). In Ashby (1991), the author reconsiders the issue, in response to criticism, and concludes that while variation in the use of *ne* may not necessarily imply an ongoing typological change, the fact that younger speakers omit *ne* much more often than older speakers, independently of social status and speech context, must still be explained. The significance of age seems to be constant across all French-speaking communities. In Ashby (2001) the comparison of two corpora from the same region, collected 20 years apart, allows the author to demonstrate that *ne*-drop is not (only) a generational phenomenon (i.e., a change in a speaker's linguistic behavior during the course of his or her life). The fact that the frequency of omission of *ne* increased during the interval studied is better explained by the hypothesis of an ongoing change.

2.2.2 N-words

The Romance languages exhibit a wide range of possible morphological origins for N-words. French, which hardly has any originally negative N-words, is situated at one extreme, while Romanian is at the other extreme, having only N-words with a negative origin. The other languages lie between these two, with Italian closest to Romanian, since *mai* is the only one of its N-words that is not etymologically related to a negative item.[8]

As we can see in Table 1, all of the languages have N-words for entities and time, but this is not the case for place and manner N-words.

The presence of an N-word in a simple sentence is enough to make the sentence negative. These elements can realize a thematic role of the verb. When used alone as short answers to a question, they are obligatorily interpreted as negative responses:

(25) F a. A: Qui a répondu ? B: Personne.
A: Who responded? B: No one.
b. A: Qu'as-tu vu ? B: Rien.
A: What did you see? B: Nothing.
c. A: Quand viendra-t-il ? B: Jamais.
A: When will he come? B: Never.

The syntactic category of N-words is not uniform: some of them are determiners (for example F *nul*[9] and R *niciun* in construction with a noun), others have a double categorization NP determiner (for example F *aucun*, I *nessuno*[10]), and others are perhaps adverbs (for example F *jamais*, R *nicicum*) or in any case expressions that cannot combine with a noun.

These forms sometimes have idiosyncratic properties. We will highlight some of them. The determiners *aucun* and *nessuno*, for example, have a distribution wider than their characterization as singular determiners would suggest, but more constrained than that of unrestricted determiners; see (26). More specifically, they can combine with singular count nouns, as expected, and also with certain mass nouns, but not with concrete mass nouns[11] (see the discussion in Tovena 2001, 2003).

(26) F a. Il n'a pris aucun livre. *He took no book.*
b. *Il n'a utilisé aucun sable. *He used no sand.*
c. Il n'a montré aucun courage. *He showed no courage.*

---

[8] Spoken Italian also has the form *mica* 'crumb', which looks like a minimizer but behaves like a presupposition modifier (Cinque 1977, Tovena 2000).

[9] It tends to be used in generic or non-referential contexts, as illustrated by the contrast between (i) and (ii).

(i) Je n'en ai nulle envie. *I have no desire for that.*

(ii) ?Je n'ai participé à nulle élection. *I took part in no election.*

[10] In general, *niente* and *nulla* are only used as semantic quantifiers and cannot be combined with a noun. Nevertheless, in some sentences without a verb, *niente* has some of the properties of a negative determiner (Tovena 2002, 2004). In these cases its interpretation is something like that of French *pas de*.

[11] The taxonomic reading is not relevant, for example the interpretation 'type of sand' in (26b).

Turning now to NPs, all of the languages (except for Italian) have two forms for discrete entities, for example S *nadie* and *ninguno*, F *personne* and *aucun*, or P *nenhum* and *ninguém*. These forms are not simply interchangeable: one of the two is particular in that it is always context-dependent, and presupposes the existence of the entities in the domain of quantification. This form is therefore the one used in partitive constructions (cf. *aucun de tes étudiants vs *personne de tes étudiants*). This particularity also manifests itself in existential sentences (27), which show that *ninguno* is context-dependent (the sentence is acceptable if *ninguno* is anaphoric), while *nadie* is not (Gutiérrez-Rexach 1999).

(27) a. S *No hay ninguno en el jardín.
F *Il n'y a aucun dans le jardin.
P *Não há nenhum no jardim.

b. S No hay nadie en el jardín.
F Il n'y a personne dans le jardin.
P Não há ninguém no jardim.
There is no one in the garden.

Moreover, the determiner *ningún* is not context-dependent, whereas *ninguno de los N* is. This dependence also seems to be related to the possibility of clitic doubling (Gutiérrez-Rexach 1999) in Spanish and Romanian.[12] Note that the form *niciunul* in Romanian contains a definite article.

(28) S a. *No lo he visto a ningún político.
I did not see any politician;
b. No lo he visto a ninguno de los políticos.
I did not see any of the politicians.

(29) R a. Am 3 studenţi, dar ieri nu, (l)-am văzut pe niciunul.
I have 3 students, but yesterday I saw no one.
b. Am 3 studenţi, dar ieri nu (*l)-am văzut pe nimeni.
I have 3 students, but yesterday I saw no one.
c. Am 3 studenţi, dar ieri n-am văzut pe niciun student.
I have 3 students, but yesterday I saw none of the students.

Finally, the Spanish N-word determiner *alguno / a* can appear after the nominal head, as in (30a). This construction also exists in Italian (30b), but the element involved is a negative polarity item (NPI)[13] as shown by the ungrammaticality of (30c).

---

[12] On clitic doubling, see Miller and Monachesi (this volume).

[13] The label 'negative polarity item', which first appears in the literature in Baker (1970), is used traditionally to identify an expression that must be licensed by a trigger within a limited

(30) S a. En caso alguno debes dejar tu puesto.
In no case should you abandon your post.
I b. Ha sollevato la cassa senza sforzo alcuno.
She lifted the crate without any effort.
I c. *In caso alcuno devi abbandonare il tuo posto.
In no case should you abandon your post.

2.2.3 N-words and negative polarity contexts

In presenting the list of N-words in the different languages, we gave some indication of their morphological origin. The differences seem to be reflected, at least in part, in the distribution of the N-words in non-negative contexts. In Romanian, N-words can never be used as NPIs,[14] whereas a certain number of non-negative contexts allow this use in French, in ver-

---

syntactic domain. Broadly speaking, the distribution of these expressions has been modeled by explicitly taking into consideration information about the polarity of the context in which they occur. The question of their characterization is complicated by the fact the notion of *negative context* here goes beyond those cases where there is a manifestation of negation. The most frequently cited example of an NPI is English *any*:

(i) E *Anybody attended that meeting.
(ii) E I don't think that anybody attended that meeting.
(iii) E Nobody said anything.

The negative marker and N-words are the typical licensers for NPIs; the most well-known (but not universally accepted) theory is that NPI licensers are monotone decreasing expressions (Fauconnier 1975 and Ladusaw 1979). Many studies have shown that individual NPIs are often subject to idiosyncratic constraints. Other studies have shown that the distribution and interpretation of NPIs follow from constraints related to properties of their semantic domain.

For most of the languages that have been studied, the class of NPIs is much larger than that of N-words. Since the 1980s, there have been proposals in the literature for treating the phenomenon of negative concord in terms of negative polarity.

[14] Besides negative polarity items, certain analyses of sensitivity to polarity also introduce the notion of *positive polarity items* (PPI), to characterize cases like (i).

(i) I ??Non ho visto qualcuno. *I didn't see someone.*

The particularity of (i) is that the interpretation where the indefinite *qualcuno* 'someone' is in the scope of negation is not available. The sentence, insofar as it is acceptable, only has the reading in which the existence of someone whom I have not seen is presupposed. The most frequently cited example of a PPI is *some* in English. It must be noted that, in spite of their name, PPIs are not in complementary distribution with NPIs. First of all, as we noted for (i), PPIs induce an *outscoping* effect, instead of yielding total ungrammaticality (Baker 1970). Second, the distribution of PPIs is described by an anti-licensing condition, not by identifying licensing contexts. Third, the negative marker is taken to be the sole anti-licenser, in contrast to the wide range of licensers for NPIs. And finally, the set of PPIs is significantly smaller than that of NPIs and includes almost no idiomatic expressions (which constitute a large proportion of NPIs). In short, if PPIs exist, they are not the mirror image of NPIs.

formal or archaic registers.[15] What distinguishes these NPI uses from negative uses is the fact that the co-negator *ne* does not appear:

(31) F a. Croyez-vous que personne ait jamais dit cela ?
Do you think that anyone has ever said that?
b. Savez-vous si personne a jamais essayé de le savoir ?
Do you know if anyone has ever tried to find out?

Italian, Spanish, and Portuguese allow a very limited range of NPI uses, not all of which moreover are possible for all speakers.

We can observe the following generalizations. First, for N-words referring to entities, as we have just seen, NPI use is highly restricted. It is characteristic of careful, sometimes old-fashioned language, and it tends to be used in fixed expressions and in sentences that invite a rhetorical interpretation. It is interesting to note that, when it is possible, we find this use in analogous contexts in the different languages. These contexts include: interrogative sentences, the antecedent of a conditional, the nominal or sentential complement of a comparative, the complement of an adversative verb (for example *nier*), and a few other monotone decreasing contexts, such as *avant que* (but not the restriction of the universal quantifier).

Broadly speaking, all of these contexts allow N-words used as NPIs in French. Another particularity is that this use is facilitated by the presence of a context with a negative interpretation (whether or not the context actually includes a negation). Compare for instance (32a), which is only marginally acceptable, and (32b,c), which are much better, though still not accepted by all speakers. Examples with *aucun* seem to be the most acceptable; see (33).

(32) F a. ??Croyez-vous que Marie ait vu personne ?
Do you believe that Marie saw anyone?
b. Pierre ne croit pas que Marie ait vu personne.
Pierre does not believe that Marie saw anyone.
c. Le juge refuse que le condamné voie personne.
The judge does not allow the condemned man to see anyone.

(33) F a. Croyez-vous que Marie ait vu aucun suspect ?
Do you believe that Marie saw any suspect?
b. Pierre ne croit pas que Marie ait vu aucun client.
Pierre does not believe that Marie saw any client.

[15] This characterization finds support in the fact (observed by an anonymous reviewer) that if the question is formulated without inversion, as is often the case in spoken French, the sentences in (31) are no longer acceptable:

(i) F *Vous savez si personne a jamais dit ça ?

For Italian, Portuguese, and Spanish, the data can be organized by context, starting with questions. In Italian, NPI use is uniformly recognized as possible only in yes-no direct questions where the N-word is postverbal (34a). Indirect questions are much more controversial (34b).

(34) I a. Viene nessuno in negozio?
Does anyone come into the store?
b. ??Mi chiedo se venga nessuno in negozio.
I wonder if anyone comes into the store.
c. Mi chiedo se nessuno venga in negozio.
I wonder if nobody is coming into the store. (negative interpretation only)

The use of these N-words as polarity items seems to be facilitated by the presence of a context with negative interpretation. Compare (35a), quite marginal, with (35b), which is better, although a more natural realization is the one without Neg-raising in (35c). Note that (35b) can reduce to a simple instance of the phenomenon of negative concord, depending on the analysis of Neg-raising.

(35) I a. ??Pensate che Maria abbia visto nessuno quella sera?
Do you think that Maria saw anyone that evening?
b. Pietro non pensa che Maria abbia visto nessuno quella sera.
Pietro thinks that Maria saw no one that evening.
c. Pietro pensa che Maria non abbia visto nessuno quella sera.
Pietro thinks that Maria saw no one that evening.

In Spanish, too, NPI use in questions is limited to N-words in postverbal position. It should be said, however, that these questions are strictly interpreted as rhetorical (that is, with a presupposed negative response) and that the presence of *cuándo*, interpretable as 'never', or *acaso* 'maybe', is obligatory.

(36) S a. ¿Cuándo me has regalado nada?
When have you ever offered me anything?
b. ¿Acaso dije nunca nada?
Did I ever say anything?

In Portuguese, NPI uses are also very rare, and they are becoming rarer. They sound old-fashioned in questions, even rhetorical ones.

(37) P Há lá nada tão bonito como isto?
Is there anything as beautiful as that?

NPI uses of N-words in conditional sentences, are rejected by speakers of Italian in most cases, as in (38), and they are not possible in Portuguese and Spanish.

(38) I ??Se vedi nessuno, ricordagli la riunione di stasera.
If you see anyone, remind them about the meeting tonight.

In Italian, there is a great deal of variation with respect to N-words in comparatives, and some speakers reject this configuration entirely, even though this is a context that is unanimously recognized as allowing expletive negation (39c). In general, (39a) requires the addition of the word *altro* 'other' in order to be interpreted, as in (39b), although *più veloci di chiunque* is the most natural wording.

(39) I a. *??Sono più veloci di nessuno.
They are faster than anyone.
b. ??Sono più veloci di nessun'altro.
They are faster than anyone else.
c. Sono più veloci di quanto non sia Daniele.
They are faster than Daniel (is).

In contrast, Portuguese seems to allow NPI uses in comparatives, but they have fallen out of use in superlatives.

(40) P a. Ele fala melhor (do) que ninguém.
He speaks better than anyone.
b. Ele sabe isso melhor (do) que ninguém.
He knows that better than anyone.
c. ?A Ana revelou-se mais competente do que ninguém tinha imaginado.
Ana turned out to be more competent than anyone could have imagined.

(41) P ?Ele tem o gabinete mais confortável que nenhum professor alguma vez teve.
He has the most comfortable office that any professor ever had.

Finally, we turn to NPI uses with 'before', possible only in French and (marginally) in Portuguese, see (42), and in the propositional complement of verbs like *dubitare* 'doubt' in Italian (43), where NPI use seems to be accepted, but quite controversially.

(42) P Antes de dizeres ??(mais) nada, pensa duas vezes.
F Avant de rien dire ??(de plus), réfléchis deux fois.
Before saying anything (more), think twice.

(43) I ??Dubito che venga nessuno. *I doubt that anyone is coming.*

Table 2 summarizes the data and highlights the instability of the use of N-words as NPIs, a usage reserved for formal styles and subject to variation according to the context, the language, the individual lexical item chosen, and the speaker.

language → ↓ context	F	I	S	P	R
question (rhetorical)	*jamais, aucun, personne*, (*rien* licensed by *jamais*)	yes, in postverbal position (yes-no questions)	marginal, licensed by *cuándo* and *acaso*	obsolete	no N-words in these contexts
comparative	yes	marginal	no	yes	
superlative	*jamais, aucun*	no	no	obsolete	
conditional antecedent	*jamais*	*mai*	no	no	
negative predicate	marginal	marginal	no	no	
'before'	*jamais, aucun, personne*, (*rien* licensed by *jamais*)	no	no	marginal	

Table 2 – N-words in negative polarity contexts

The second generalization that emerges concerns temporal N-words in NPI uses. The presence of *jamais* in French and its equivalents in the other languages always improves the acceptability of the sentence, and in some cases it is indispensable. This use is widespread and is not limited to formal or archaic registers, in contrast to what was said above for the other N-words.

(44) F a. ??Croyez-vous que personne ait dit cela ?
Do you think that anyone said that?
b. ??Savez-vous si personne a essayé de la voir ?
Do you know if anyone tried to see her?

(45) F a. Croyez-vous que personne ait jamais dit cela ?
Do you think that anyone has ever said that?

b. Savez-vous si personne a jamais essayé de la voir ?
Do you know if anyone has ever tried to see her?

It is very difficult to use N-words as polarity items in French without *jamais* if none of the N-words occurs preverbally. None of these constraints applies to other NPIs such as *le moindre*, or *qui que ce soit*.

(46) F a. Croyez-vous que Marie ait fait le moindre geste ?
Do you believe that Marie made the slightest move?
b. Savez-vous si Marie a fait le moindre effort pour le savoir ?
Do you know if Marie made the slightest effort to find out?

It should be noted that (N)EVER is the only 'abstract element' to be realized as a morphologically non-negative N-word in all of the languages allowing NPI uses. Furthermore, Italian *mai* is the only element accepted by all speakers when used as an NPI in interrogative and conditional sentences; see (47) and (48) and footnote 7. The French form *jamais* is the only productive NPI in the contemporary language.

(47) I Mi chiedo se venga mai nessuno in negozio.
I wonder if anyone is ever coming to the store.

(48) I Se mai ti servisse, fammelo sapere.
If you ever need it, let me know.

2.2.4 Some remarkable cases of negation

In this section we briefly examine some examples of negative conjunctions, prepositions and adverbs that are relevant to the discussion at hand, since they give rise to negative concord.

The first case is *sans* 'without' in French and its counterparts S *sin*, P *sem*, I *senza* and R *fără*. *Sans* functions as a negative preposition introducing an NP, an infinitival clause or a finite *que*-clause, see (49). The main observation is that it does not negate the main proposition of the sentence ('he works' in (49a)) but reduces the number of situations that can be correctly described by this sentence, by removing all situations involving working with a net.

(49) F a. Il travaille sans filet. *He works without a safety net.*
b. Il est parti sans saluer. *He left without saying goodbye.*
c. Il est parti sans qu'elle le remarque.
He left without her noticing.

In French, *sans* licenses an object of the form *de N*, identified above as a property of negative sentences.

(50) F Il a survécu sans boire d'eau pendant toute sa cavale.
He survived without drinking (any) water during his flight.

In general, *sans* and its counterparts in the Romance languages trigger negative concord in the constituent they govern (51), but the negation that they express cannot take scope outside of this constituent (52). These cases thus constitute exceptions to the characterization of negative concord as a clause-level phenomenon, based on the idea that negation is a semantic property of propositions.

(51) I Ha risposto senza nessuna esitazione.
F Il / elle a répondu sans aucune hesitation.
He/she answered without any hesitation.

(52) I *Senza aiuto ha fatto nessun compito.
F *Sans aide il / elle a fait aucun devoir.
Without help he/she did no assignment.

The second case to be mentioned here is the negative conjunction. This type of conjunction introduces the second element in a coordination, while indicating that it should be interpreted in the scope of the negation in the first conjunct. For example, (53a) contains the conjunction *e* (and) and only allows the reading where the second conjunct is positive,[16] while (53b), containing the negative conjunction *né*, requires the second conjunct to be negated, too. The second conjunct introduced by *né* can host N-words, as in (53c).

(53) I a. Non va in bicicletta e corre nel parco solo col walkman.
He does not ride a bicycle and (he) runs in the park only with his walkman.
b. Non va in bicicletta né corre nel parco solo col walkman.
He does not ride a bicycle nor does he run in the park only with his walkman.
c. Non sorride né dice niente a nessuno.
She does not smile or say anything to anybody.

In addition, a negative conjunction can mark each of the conjuncts in the scope of negation:

(54) I Non va né in bicicletta né in moto.
He rides neither a bicycle nor a motorcycle.

Finally, the third case that we will mention is that of negative additive adverbs/particles. The development of additive adverbs from coordinating conjunctions has been observed in the positive case (König 1991). For instance, Latin *et* 'and' can also mean 'also' and 'even'. We note that there is

[16] The use of *e* when the first conjunct is negated is also constrained. In general, in this case, the conjunction is replaced by *ma* 'but'; see Barwise and Cooper (1981).

a negative counterpart to this observation: Negative conjunctions also give rise to additive and scalar particles. Moreover, negation sometimes has an impact on the range of readings available. We will briefly describe this effect in Italian.

Italian, like several other languages (König 1991), is characterized by the clustering of additive (as in *also, too, neither*) and scalar readings (as in *even*) in single lexical forms. For instance, while in French we find two different forms, the positive additive particle *aussi* and scalar *même*, in Italian we find forms like *neanche* and *neppure*, which both have the two readings and are specialized for negative contexts. Interestingly enough, they derive from positive forms which are additive with no stable scalar use (respectively *anche* and *pure*). For instance, *anche* corresponds to *also* in (55a), but *neanche* with a negative component can be additive (55b) as well as scalar (55c).

(55) I a. Maria ha comprato dei cioccolatini e anche dei fiori.
Maria bought chocolates and also some flowers.
b. Maria non ha comprato dei cioccolatini. E neanche dei fiori.
Maria didn't buy chocolates. She didn't buy flowers either.
c. Maria non ha neanche comprato dei fiori.
Maria didn't even buy flowers.

As discussed in Tovena (2005, 2006) the use of *neanche* and *neppure* triggers the presupposition of an alternative negative proposition, similar to the 'existential presupposition' in the positive counterparts. The alternative(s), for instance in (55b) 'not buying flowers' and 'not buying chocolates', form an unordered set in the additive case and they are ordered in the scalar case, with the element put into focus by the particle at the top of the order, e.g. 'not buying flowers' in (55c).

These particles behave like N-words, in that they can make a sentence negative without a negator when they occur in preverbal position (see section 3), and free-standing occurrences have only negative interpretations (56).

(56) I a. Neppure lo champagne lo ha soddisfatto.
Not even champagne made him happy.
b. A: Ha almeno risposto? B: Neppure.
A: Did he answer you, at least? B: Not even that.

French has a dedicated additive negative particle, *non plus* (57) derived from a comparative construction (Corblin 2005), but no negative scalar form. Spanish has a negative additive form of comparative origin, *tampoco*, but it also has a negative scalar form *ni siquiera*, which contains the negative conjunction *ni*. As shown by (58), *tampoco* behaves like an N-word.

(57) F a. Marie n'a pas acheté des chocolats. Elle n'a pas acheté des fleurs non plus.
Maria didn't buy chocolates. She didn't buy flowers either.
b. Marie n'a même pas acheté des fleurs.
Maria didn't even buy flowers.

(58) S a. No vino y tampoco llamó.
He didn't come and didn't call either.
b. Tampoco el lunes vino.
Neither did he come on Monday.

As for Portuguese and Romanian, their negative conjunctions (respectively *nem* and *nici*) can also serve as negative additive and scalar particles. Portuguese also uses the adverbial *nem sequer* to get more emphatic scalar readings.

A full discussion of these elements would take us too far from the main topic of this chapter. We simply offer these observations to call attention to the crucial role of negation in the production of additive expressions.

3 Syntactic Combinations and their Interpretation

In this section we will present a simplified comparison of the main properties of simple negative sentences in several Romance languages.

3.1 Co-occurrence of Negative Forms

There is a degree of diversity in the manifestations of negative concord across the Romance languages. We contrast cases of negative concord and cases that are exempt from concord.

3.1.1 The syntax of negative concord

In Romanian, an N-word systematically requires the presence of the negator *nu* in the same sentence:

(59) R a. Nimeni nu a venit. *Nobody came.*
b. *Nimeni a venit.
c. Nu a venit nimeni. *There came no one.*
d. *A venit nimeni.

For Portuguese, Spanish, and Italian, the following generalization holds: Exactly one N-word must appear preverbally, cf. (60) and (61). If there is a negator, then the N-word must instead appear postverbally, cf. (62) and (63). Example (63) is marginal with normal intonation, but see the discussion in section 3.2 below about interpretations with double logical negation. If there are several N-words and a negator, the N-words must all appear postverbally. Finally, if there are only N-words (and no negator), one of the N-words must appear in preverbal position, and the others must be in postverbal position (64).

(60) I a. Nessuno è venuto. *Nobody came.*
b. A nessuno piace il caldo. *Nobody likes the heat.*

(61) I a. *È venuto nessuno.
b. *Il caldo piace a nessuno.

(62) I a. Non è venuto nessuno. *There came no one.*
b. Il caldo non piace a nessuno. *The heat pleases no one.*

(63) I a. ??Nessuno non è venuto. *Nobody didn't come.*
b. ??A nessuno non piace il caldo. *Nobody doesn't like the heat.*

(64) I a. Nessuno vede niente. *No one sees anything.*
b. ??Nessuno non vede niente. *Nobody sees nothing.*

Italian *mai* constitutes a counterexample to this generalization, as we can see in (65). While it can appear alone in preverbal position (as expected), as in (65a), which has a slight emphatic effect, or in postverbal position with a preverbal negator (65e), it can also join another N-word in preverbal position (65b,c), and it cannot appear by itself preverbally if there are other postverbal N-words (65d).[17]

(65) I a. MAI accetterò questa decisione.
Never will I accept this decision.
b. Nessuno mai accetterà questa decisione.
No one will ever accept this decision.
c. Mai nessuno accetterà questa decisione.
Never will anyone accept this decision.
d. *Mai accetterà nessuna decisione di Pietro.
e. Non accetterà mai nessuna decisione di Pietro.
He will never accept any decision of Pietro's.

In Portuguese, too, we can find *nunca* and another N-word in preverbal position, as in (66a), but in contrast to (65d), *nunca* has negative force in this position, as confirmed by (66b).[18]

[17] For other details about the behavior of this word, see section 5.6.

[18] This is also true of the form *jamás* 'never', but it is stylistically marked as 'stiff' and formal.

(66) P a. Ninguém nunca disse nada. *No one ever said anything.*
b. Nunca a Maria viu nada. *Maria never saw anything.*

In French, the co-negator *ne*, optional in the spoken language, is licensed whenever a negator or an N-word is present in the sentence. On the other hand, N-words and negators cannot appear together to give rise to a negative interpretation (i.e. the negative concord reading) in European (standard) French (21b).[19] In principle, their co-occurrence always yields a double negation. Finally, a simple sentence can contain arbitrarily many N-words. The resulting combinations are perfectly grammatical.

(67) F a. Personne ne dit rien à Marie.
No one says anything to Marie.
b. Personne ne présente Jean à personne.
No one introduces Jean to anyone.
c. Jean ne donne rien à personne.
Jean gives nothing to anyone.
d. Personne ne dit jamais rien à personne.
No one ever says anything to anyone.

3.1.2 Absence of negative concord

There are a number of cases where the co-occurrence of several N-words, or of a negative marker and N-words, does not give rise to a negative concord reading. The interpretation of these examples is discussed in the next subsection; here we focus on their syntactic characteristics.

For French, the combination of a negator and an N-word produces a structure that can only be acceptable in a very specific context of denegation in an echo statement,[20] and this condition is generally satisfied in the presence of an intensifier, contrastive focus or topic, etc.

(68) F a. Ça n'est pas rien. *It's not nothing.*
b. Je ne commence pas avec rien. *I am not starting with nothing.*
c. (?)Personne ne vient pas. *No one is not coming.*

Apart from (68a), which is an example of litotes and corresponds to *C'est quelque chose* 'It's something', these combinations are judged to be ungrammatical out of context, especially if the N-word is the subject, as in (68c). These judgments are independent of stylistic register, and are also observed in varieties of French without *ne*.

---

[19] This combination is attested in Quebec French.

[20] Prosody also plays an important role in making explicit that the sentence is a denegation. For example, the sentences in (68) acquire a double negation reading if *pas* and *rien* do not belong to the same prosodic constituent, and *pas* bears an emphatic accent.

For Portuguese, Spanish, and Italian, we need to look at combinations of negator and N-word in preverbal position, which are generally only possible in denial echo contexts.

(69) I a. ?NESSUNO non viene. *NOBODY isn't coming.*
b. NIENTE non giova mai.
NOTHING is never useful.

Out of context, these combinations are judged to be ungrammatical. This effect can be mitigated by the informativity of the sentence, that is to say if the sentence allows the construction of a clear denial context:

(70) I Nessun bambino non va a scuola in questa società.
No child does not go to school in this society.

Next, there is the case of constituent negation, which constitutes an exception to negative concord because it gives rise to postverbal N-words without a preverbal negative marker or N-word. Sometimes labelled as idiosyncratic or idiomatic, these examples are restricted to N-words in NPs that express a peripheral participant in the event described by the sentence, such as purpose (Tovena 1998).

(71) I a. Hai telefonato per niente.
F b. Tu as téléphoné pour rien.
You phoned for nothing (i.e. in vain).

But not all adjunct positions can give rise to this exceptional structure; see (72). Also, this configuration seems to be restricted to N-words for inanimate entities, such as *niente*.

(72) I *Ha prenotato per nessuna meta. *He reserved for no destination.*

Note also that these cases cannot be explained in terms of N-word nominalization or the use of N-words as minimizers, as in (73), for example.

(73) S a. Se enfada por nada. *He gets angry about nothing.*
b. Lo compré por nada. *I bought it for nothing.*

While constituent negation is possible in the Romance languages in this type of example, it is impossible in Romanian, which seems to require systematic negative concord. Example (71) cannot be translated using an N-word.

(74) R Ai telefonat degeaba. *You phoned in vain.*

Finally, one nuance needs to be mentioned. As observed in Tovena (1998), negative concord is easier with N-words functioning as NPs (i.e. as quantifiers, semantically) than with N-word determiners. Consider the following contrast:

(75) I a. Nessuno legge niente. *No one reads anything.*
b. ?*Nessun bambino coi capelli rossi ha letto nessun libro sulla lista. *No child with red hair read any book on the list.*

Tovena (1998) notes that the effect can be weakened if the second N-word is replaced by an element that is not morphologically negative, such as *alcun* 'some/no':[21]

(76) I ?Nessun bambino coi capelli rossi ha letto alcun libro sulla lista.
No child with red hair read any book on the list.

3.2 Interpretation of the Combinations

The phenomenon referred to as 'negative concord' involves a sentence that contains several potentially negative elements, but whose semantic representation contains just one negation. For the interpretation of the structures described in this section, the situation is varied.

On the one hand, we have French, which has the weakest form of negative concord and allows interpretations with double logical negation relatively freely. We will use the term 'double negation' for cases where a simple sentence contains several N-words, or N-words and the negator, and its semantic representation contains two negation symbols, as in the following example.

(77) F Personne n'a rien payé. (co-occurrence of two N-words)
For: *There is no one who paid nothing.*
$\neg\exists x \neg\exists y$ pay(x,y)

On the other hand, we have Romanian, which systematically requires negative concord readings and does not allow double negation. In the other three languages, double negation is possible, but with great difficulty.

We distinguish three cases. First, if a simple sentence contains just a negator, or just one N-word, it is represented as a negative sentence with a single negation. This configuration is possible in all of the languages except Romanian, where N-words always co-occur with the negator; recall example (59a) above.

[21] The opposite order is not possible because *alcun* is not an N-word, but an NPI, cf. (76) and (i).

(i) I *Alcun bambino coi capelli rossi ha letto nessun libro sulla lista.

(78) F Pierre ne vient pas.
$\neg$come(Pierre)
I Nessuno parla.
$\neg\exists x$ speak(x)

Second, if a simple sentence contains several negative elements of the same type (that is, at least two N-words, and no negator), it can be interpreted in two ways. This is possible in French, impossible in Romanian, and very difficult in the other languages.

1. An interpretation with a single negation (negative concord reading), represented as a negation taking scope over the variables corresponding to each of the N-words in the sentence:

[...N-word$_x$...N-word$_y$...N-word$_z$...]
$\neg\exists$xyz V(x,y,z): a world without V

(79) F Personne n'aime personne. (with flat intonation)
Nobody loves anybody.

2. A double negation interpretation:

[...N-word$_x$...N-word$_y$...N-word$_z$...]
$\neg\exists x \neg\exists yz$ V(x,y,z) : 'for all x, there exists at least one y and one z such that V(x,y,z)' (equivalent to $\forall x\ \exists yz$ V(x,y,z))

(80) F PERSONNE n'aime personne. (emphasis on the first *personne*)
Nobody loves nobody.

Third, if a simple sentence contains several negative elements of different types (that is, one or more N-words and the negator), it allows two interpretations, with one or two negations. This is possible in all of the languages under consideration, with varying degrees of acceptability and different restrictions.

(81) I Non viene nessuno.
$\neg\exists x$ come(x): *No one is coming.*

(82) I NESSUNO non viene.
$\neg\exists x\ \neg$come(x): *NO ONE is not coming.*

Romanian allows only the single negation reading, while in French, the sentence is interpreted as a double negation, regardless of the relative order of the N-word and *pas*.

(83) F RIEN ne va pas. = 'Everything is fine.'

(84) F Pierre n'a PAS rien dit. = 'Pierre said something.'

In short, for French, it is possible to account for negative concord phenomena by saying that the co-negator *ne* contributes nothing to the interpretation, except marking scope. The situation is more complicated in the other languages. In Spanish, Italian, and Portuguese, a simple sentence with a single N-word is interpreted as negative.

(85) P Nenhum turista protestou.
$\neg\exists x\ V(x)$: *No tourist protested.*

If a simple sentence contains at least two N-words (and no negator), it allows a negative concord reading if one of them is preverbal. Otherwise, the sentence is not interpretable.

(86) P Nenhum turista visitou nenhum museu.
$\neg\exists x \exists y\ V(x,y)$: *No tourist visited any museum.*

(87) P O Pedro não indicou nenhum museu a nenhuma turista.
$\neg\exists x \exists y\ V(p,x,y)$: *Pedro did not indicate any museum to any tourist.*

The sequence [negator + N-word] receives a negative concord reading:

(88) P O Pedro não visitou nenhum museu.
$\neg\exists x\ V(p,x)$: *Pedro did not visit any museum.*

If the order is [N-word + negator], either we have a double negation reading, or the sentence is unacceptable.

(89) P NENHUM não visitou aquele museu.
NOBODY didn't visit this museum.

This interpretation is difficult to obtain in sentences that contain only N-words. Examples like (90) are practically fixed, and the pattern is not very productive. Their interpretation requires a break in the intonation contour between the preverbal N-word and the rest, as indicated in (91).

(90) I ?Nessuno ama nessuno.
$\forall x\ \exists y\ V(x,y)$: *Nobody loves nobody.*

(91) S Nadie | quiere a nadie.
$\forall x\ \exists y\ V(x,y)$

Some speakers also allow double negation readings in sentences of this type with N-word determiners (Tovena 1998), as observed above for (75), but these examples remain marginal.

On the other hand, the three languages pattern together, and with French, in that the double negation reading is the only possible one if the N-word is a short answer to a negative question, cf. (92) and (25) above.[22]

(92) I a. A: Chi non ha risposto? B: Nessuno.
A: Who didn't answer? B: No one.
b. A: Cosa non hai visto? B: Niente.
A: What didn't you see? B: Nothing.

In Romanian, the double negation reading is still unavailable in this case, according to the majority of our informants:

(93) R A: Cine n-a mâncat? B: Nimeni
A: Who didn't eat? B: Nobody ate.

The data discussed in this section are summarized in Table 3.

<table>
<tr><th></th><th>Syntactic constraints on co-occurrence</th><th>Constraints on interpretation</th></tr>
<tr><td>R</td><td>Preverbal negator nu always present</td><td>single negation</td></tr>
<tr><td rowspan="4">I
P
S</td><td>negator + V + N-word(s)</td><td>single logical negation</td></tr>
<tr><td>N-word + V + zero or more N-words</td><td>single logical negation</td></tr>
<tr><td>(N)EVER + N-word + V + zero or more N-words</td><td>single logical negation</td></tr>
<tr><td>N-word + negator</td><td>unnatural, strong prosodic and discourse conditions on double negation interpretation</td></tr>
<tr><td rowspan="3">F</td><td>co-negator ne present before the verb in high register</td><td>ne blocks all interpretation of N-words as NPIs</td></tr>
<tr><td>negator and one or more N-words</td><td>2 logical negations</td></tr>
<tr><td>several N-words</td><td>Ambiguous, 1 or 2 logical negations</td></tr>
</table>

Table 3 – Negative sentences with several negations

4 Analyses Proposed in the Literature

In this section we present a (non-exhaustive) panorama of the analyses of negative concord proposed in the literature in recent years, in order to give an idea of the variety of approaches and solutions adopted for the Romance

[22] Some of our informants do not agree with this judgment for Spanish. For them, the answer *Nadie* induces the negative interpretation: 'Nobody saw anything'.

languages. The analyses are grouped according to whether or not they postulate an ambiguity for N-words.

4.1 Analyses with Ambiguous N-words

We begin with analyses that assume a lexical ambiguity for N-words.

Bosque (1980) and Rizzi (1982) Bosque and Rizzi favor a double classification for Spanish and Italian, respectively. The basic idea is that only the first occurrence of a negative form (an N-word or the negative marker) expresses negation.

Bosque refers simply to word order, and claims that the N-words appearing after the verb are polarity items (Bosque 1980: 21), whereas those in preverbal position incorporate the sentential negation *no* (a restatement of the analysis of Rivero 1970).

According to Rizzi, the occurrences of N-words in Italian are either negative quantifiers (in preverbal position), or existential quantifiers subject to specific polarity constraints (in postverbal position). A negative incorporation rule, based on the one proposed by Klima (1964), assigns a negative feature provided that the item in question occupies a position c-commanded by a VP. Rizzi does not specify where in the representation the negative feature to be incorporated comes from.

These analyses run into three kinds of problems. First, the negative incorporation rule is optional, but it must apply in declarative sentences; this has to be stipulated. Second, under this approach, a single reading (double negation) is predicted for example (94), but this is incorrect. In (94), *nessuno* is not in the local context of a licenser and therefore should not have an NPI reading—a necessary condition for negative concord according to this analysis. Because it is in a configuration where negative incorporation can apply, it has a negative interpretation.

(94) I Non pretendo che nessuno ti arresti.
I don't demand that no one arrest you.
I don't demand that someone arrest you.

Finally, contrary to facts, the analysis predicts that example (95) should be unacceptable, because the N-word cannot incorporate the negative feature in its surface position, and there is no other position in the scope of a licensing element for it to move to.

(95) I Hai parlato per niente. *You spoke for nothing.*

Richter and Sailer (1999) Richter and Sailer propose a double classification for N-words in French within a lexicalist framework (HPSG); in their analysis most of the constraints that govern negative concord are encoded in the lexical entries. N-words are analyzed as negated existential quantifiers or as variables that must be bound with narrow scope and whose occurrence must be licensed in collocation with an affective operator, in the sense of Klima (1964). The treatment in terms of collocation leads to a multiplication of entries for all the elements, and a specification of the contextual conditions for each individual case.

Technically, the solution amounts to making part of the surrounding structure (to which the lexical conditions apply) available locally in lexical entries. This is achieved by means of a special attribute in the lexical description of words. In a sense, N-words become collocations. Moreover, the constraints specify where in the 'syntactic domain' (that is, the surrounding structure) the licensing material must be located. In the case of negative concord, the logical form that licenses an N-word corresponds to a type of sentence called a 'minimal complete sentence'.

van der Wouden and Zwarts (1993) Van der Wouden and Zwarts offer a semantic version of the ambiguity analysis. These authors adopt the classification of concord phenomena proposed by den Besten (1986), in which the following two cases are distinguished.

(i) Negative spread: The negative feature propagates onto every indefinite expression in its scope.

(ii) Negative doubling: Every sentence containing a negative expression (and no indefinites of the preceding type) must contain a particular negative element.

Negative concord is analyzed in terms of the ambiguity of N-words and / or the negator: N-words are interpreted as positive existential quantifiers when they appear in a monotone decreasing context, and otherwise as negative universal quantifiers. This amounts to saying that these lexical items denote $\exists$ and $\neg\exists$. In the case of negative doubling, a particular item must be ambiguous. It is realized by a morphologically negative form, but it expresses the identity function and is thus an expletive when it is in the scope of a trigger, with the exception of French *ne*, which always denotes the identity function.

It follows that in Italian, a sentence like (96), in which the comparative licenses an occurrence of so-called 'expletive *non*', must be classified as an instance of a negative concord sentence. This is not the generally accepted view.

(96) I Maria è più intelligente di quanto non sia Carlo.
Maria is more intelligent than Carlo (is).

The authors claim that the ambiguity effects appear only in monotone decreasing contexts, but they have to add that this is only true for a subset of these contexts, because F *peu* for example does not trigger this effect. Here again, their typology of decreasing contexts does not seem relevant, and we can account for the facts more adequately by saying that the presence of a negative item (negator or N-word) is a necessary but not sufficient condition for the realization of the phenomenon in question.

4.2 Analyses that do not assume an ambiguity for N-words

In this section we consider analyses that postulate a single status for N-words. Two dimensions of classification are possible. The proposals can be classified according to the status they attribute to N-words or according to their hypotheses about the number of negations in the representation. These two approaches are not independent. The option of characterizing N-words as negative polarity items permits a local resolution of the question of compositional interpretation of the sentence with a single logical negation in its representation. But in that case the source of the negation has to be explained. On the other hand, the option of characterizing N-words as items associated with a semantic negation means that the question of compositionality has to be resolved at the sentence level.

Although Laka Mugarza (1990) and Zanuttini (1991) say that they favor a unique classification of N-words, their uniform lexical entries allow several options for interpretation, defined by different rules, at the level of syntactic representation called Logical Form. It is therefore debatable whether their proposals belong in this group of analyses that do not assume ambiguity.

N-words as polarity items Laka Mugarza claims that N-words are negative polarity items. When they are preverbal, they occupy Spec/ΣP. This projection, which is higher than IP, can be interpreted as a syntactic locus for information about the utterance, because it hosts the operators that affect truth values, including the abstract negative morpheme.[23] In this position, the N-word can acquire a negative interpretation via Spec-head agreement with the head of ΣP. Instead of the existential interpretation considered to be typical of polarity items, the N-word receives the force of a universal quantifier. It must be noted, however, that the possibility of occupying Spec/ΣP is disallowed for other polarity items like *any*. Note also that, on the one hand, the ΣP projection licenses the occurrence of an N-word by means of the empty negative morpheme in its head position, and on the

[23] This projection brings to mind the 'judgement operator' proposed by Bierwisch (1980).

other hand, ΣP is itself licensed by the presence of the N-word in its specifier position. This circularity is also found in Ladusaw (1992).

N-words as negative quantifiers Zanuttini argues that N-words are negative quantifiers. The main elements of her analysis are the following. First of all, the Italian negative marker *non* is the head of a negative functional projection NegP-1 located above the tense projection, whereas the French marker *pas* is the specifier of a negative functional projection NegP-2, which is lower than the tense projection. In other words, typological variation is accounted for by hypothesizing multiple negative projections. Next, postverbal N-words acquire sentential scope by raising to Spec/NegP-1 in Logical Form, where their negative component is licensed by Spec-head agreement. This is the case for examples like (99a). On the other hand, in (99b), which does not contain a negative marker, the N-word raises to Spec/CP in Logical Form, where it is licensed via Spec-head agreement with the complementizer. Note that (99b) is not fully acceptable, as Zanuttini suggests.

(99) I a. Dubito che non venga nessuno.
I doubt that nobody is coming.
b. ??Dubito che venga nessuno.
I doubt that anyone is coming.

Finally, multiple occurrences of N-words are subject to resumptive quantification, so that they fuse and create a single negation. The process is subdivided into two operations. There is 'absorption', by which two or more instances of unary quantifiers combine and give rise to an *n*-ary quantifier. Then there is 'factorization', by which the negation is 'extracted'—as opposed to creating several successive instances of the sequence $\forall\neg$, corresponding to a negative quantifier[24]—and represented just once after the quantifier, which in turn has undergone absorption. Finally, non-negative contexts like questions include a yes/no operator in Comp that can license the N-word.

Zanuttini nevertheless does not explain why the N-word in (100) does not have a negative interpretation.

(100) I Ha telefonato nessuno? *Did anybody call?*

The Neg head selects TP and, when it is realized lexically (that is, when *non* is there), it is capable of 'lexically marking' TP. This marking makes N-word raising possible. But in (100) we have raising without *non*. Further-

---

[24] Her choice of the representation $\forall\neg$ rather than $\neg\exists$ is primarily motivated by the hypothesis that *presque* modifies universal quantifiers.

more, it is unclear why tense should be a barrier for negative quantifier raising, given that this is not the case for other kinds of quantifiers. For example F *Tous les étudiants aiment deux livres* 'All of the students like two books' allows a reading in which *deux livres* has wide scope. Moreover, in the case of N-words in preverbal position, we could say that lexical marking of TP is unnecessary because there is no raising in LF. But Zanuttini does not explain why this is prohibited in the case of negative concord, or why the presence of marking would lead to a double negation reading. Finally, Zanuttini states that an N-word can appear postverbally without *non*, as long as it does not have sentential scope. But this does not explain the variation observed in the constituent negation data, discussed in Tovena (1998).

Two operations for negative quantifiers: iteration and resumption De Swart (1999) proposes an analysis within the framework of Generalized Quantifier Theory that is presented as an extension of ideas of May (1989) and van Benthem (1989). The hypothesis consists of supposing that N-words are monadic negative quantifiers that allow two kinds of composition: (1) composition by 'iteration', leading to a double negation; (2) composition by 'resumption' leading to the construction of a polyadic quantifier (a single negation binding the occurrences of several variables). De Swart's reason for preferring this analysis over Zanuttini's 'factorization' (which yields the same results) is that factorization is an *ad hoc* operation that must be postulated specifically for negative concord, whereas the construction of a polyadic quantifier from repeated occurrences of a monadic quantifier is a phenomenon attested elsewhere in the grammar. This supposed similarity between negative concord and other cases of polyadic quantification does not appear to be so striking. De Swart cites two well-known cases:

(101) F a. Cinq linguistes ont écrit sept articles.
Five linguists wrote seven articles.
b. Quel étudiant aime quel livre ?
Which student likes which book?

Example (101a) has two interpretations, one 'distributive' (involving a total of 35 articles), and one 'cumulative' (seven is the total number of articles produced by authors belonging to a group of five linguists). The second interpretation is the one that cannot be handled by simple composition (reiteration), and can be used to justify an analysis involving a polyadic quantifier. Example (101b) is also often said to be ambiguous, with one reading corresponding to 'Give me all ordered student-book pairs such that the first element likes the second', which has a polyadic flavor, at least superficially (quantification over pairs). In fact, it is highly doubtful that (101a) and (101b) illustrate the same phenomenon, and in particular it is unclear whether anything more than monadic quantification is needed for (101b).[25] If the two examples are not analogous, then most of the force of the argument must come from (101a), which does not involve the reuse of an identical quantifier in any obvious way. In fact, the same kind of interpretation can be observed any time two plural entities are involved.

(102) F Cinq linguistes ont écrit tous les articles.
Five linguists wrote all of the articles.

There are many other dissimilarities between (101a) and cases of negative concord: (101a) may be ambiguous, but the cumulative quantification is not the more salient reading. Furthermore, there do not appear to be any situations where cumulative quantification is obligatory. On the other hand, there are many languages in which negative concord is obligatory, and in the other languages where it exists, it is always strongly preferred. In short, de Swart does propose a mechanism capable of producing the existing interpretations, but there are no decisive arguments for her claim that concord derives from the same mechanisms as (101a,b). Such a hypothesis would also leave the most remarkable properties of the phenomenon unexplained, and consequently, many additional stipulations would be required in order to achieve an acceptable degree of empirical adequacy. For example, in the English expression in (103a), interpreted as in (103b), there is no semantic similarity that could justify polyadic fusion.

(103) a. hardly no time
b. hardly any time

Negation as a propositional semantic feature Ladusaw (1991) proposes an analysis inspired by the notion of 'foot feature' in Gazdar et al. (1985). This analysis is based on the following ingredients:

(i) Negation is realized by a unique morphosyntactic feature [NEG]. This feature is associated with negators and negative quantifiers.
(ii) As a foot feature, it is inherited by the categories that dominate it, all the way to the level of the proposition, which is where negation can be semantically active.

Aside from the insights taken from Generalized Phrase Structure Grammar, Ladusaw's theory seems to be built upon two principles: that

[25] We could treat the dual interpretation in terms of exhaustive vs. non-exhaustive response to the question and rely on monadic quantification alone. In other words: 'Q x (student) like y (book). Instantiate x et y.' This is an important point, in particular because de Swart's treatment applies to the 'reprise d'une série de k occurrences du même quantifier monadique Q' and because *quel* is a perfect illustration of the identical repetition of a quantifier.

negation is a semantic feature of propositions (so there can be one and only one per propositional nucleus), and that it can be expressed by various constituents of the proposition. It is clear that the first principle cannot be accepted as it is if the language under consideration has sentences that are ambiguous between a negative concord reading and a double negation reading. But this is typical in many languages, in particular in many Romance languages. Ladusaw (1991) does not, in fact, consider any dialects with ambiguity. There is another question that his approach leaves unanswered: If negation is necessarily unique in a proposition, why is it marked on several constituents? A slightly different analysis is presented in Ladusaw (1992). Here, Ladusaw suggests that N-words are indefinites, more precisely NPIs without quantificational force. The NPI analysis also applies to the negative marker. The objectif is to eliminate the need for an absorption rule *à la* Zanuttini to solve globally the problem of a compositional treatment.

Ladusaw claims that it is not necessary for negation to be expressed by an element visible in the surface syntactic structure. The notion of concord is reformulated in terms of negative chains. In logical form, there is an abstract operator, triggered by syntactic rules (and not by any particular morpheme), which closes the chain formed by the N-words. The main difficulty with this proposal is its circularity, because N-words are a kind of variable (*à la* Kamp/Heim) that require closure by an operator of a certain type, whose presence is in turn triggered precisely by the N-words in the right configuration.

N-words as indefinites Acquaviva (1993) claims that N-words are variables that correspond to indefinites that must be interpreted *in situ* and closed by a negative operator. Sentential negation always involves this operation of variable binding, because it is the negative operator that provides the sentential scope. This also applies to sentences that do not contain an N-word, because in this case the variable corresponding to the event is bound.

We can say that this analysis is inspired, on the one hand, by Ladusaw (1992), and his idea of postulating a closure of each occurrence of an N-word by a negative element. On the other hand, it contrasts with Zanuttini (1991), in that it argues against the quantificational nature of N-words and their movement in logical form.

Negation as a constrained feature in the proposition Corblin (1996) analyzes N-words in French as complex negative quantifiers (a combination of a negation and a variable in its scope). Grammatically, these expressions instantiate arguments of the verb and can in principle saturate more than one argument of the same verb:

(104) F Personne n'a rien offert à Marie.
No one offered anything to Marie.

(105) F Personne n'a présenté Marie à personne.
No one introduced Marie to anybody.

Empirically, the interpretations attested in French are negative concord and double negation, with the first negative quantifier taking scope over the second. Double negation, while not impossible in ordinary sentences (pronounced with unmarked intonation), is clearly favored in situations where one of the terms carries a strong accent. The doubly negative interpretation is moreover the only possible one in question-answer sequences of the type in (106). The relevant point here is that the answer in (106) can only be interpreted as 'Everyone gave something to Marie'.

(106) F A: Qui n'a rien offert à Marie ? B: Personne.
A: Who gave nothing to Marie? B: Nobody.

More than two negations (negator or N-word) can be expressed without giving rise to anything more than double negation semantically. Given this observation, Corblin argues that the empirical facts can be derived by postulating a limit on complexity. The axiom 'one negation per proposition' is essentially a default interpretation of sentences with multiple negative words, because the recursive interpretation of a variable-binding negation is a complex operation corresponding in fact to the maximal complexity that the human processor can handle (no recursive structure of this type involving three negations can be calculated in the predicate-argument domain). To account for the attested interpretations, Corblin assumes that a negative quantifier 'naturally' tends to reduce to a negative indefinite if it is interpreted in the scope of a negative quantifier, and this must happen whenever it would otherwise introduce a third negation into the representation. Like Ladusaw's analysis, this proposal does not address the question of why natural languages typically use a negative quantifier to mark argument positions, if its negative value is generally not retained in the interpretation.

Negating an event through its (non-)participants Tovena (1996, 1998) aims to explain the nature of concord as a sentence-level phenomenon sensitive to the structure of the event described by the sentence, and at the same time clarify the differences between N-words and NPIs. Three salient points of her proposal are the following. (i) An N-word can be used to mark the fact that a participant position in a certain kind of event must not be instantiated. Broadly speaking, a participant corresponds to a position identified by one of the thematic roles of an event, including the spatial and temporal dimensions. Italian takes the option of overtly marking all participants that cannot be instantiated. (ii) If the presence of a participant is negated, we can infer that the event is also negated, but the inverse is not always true. The contribution of N-words is thus highlighted (in comparison to that of the negative marker, if present). (iii) A language can choose to mark as negated: the participants that cannot be instantiated, the predicate, or both (as in Italian). Negation is therefore calculated at several levels, in particular at the level of the entities that are potentially involved and at the level of the event they would be involved in. Italian makes use of the nature of the assertion, thetic or categorical (see Kuroda 1972, Sasse 1987), and word order considerations, to determine the strongest stable negative scope that can be calculated from the information that a particular participant is being negated, and it marks this scope overtly. In English the strongest scope is not necessarily marked, but it is calculated in a similar way. In (107) below, the negative quantifier *no* is in a prepositional phrase in both examples, but only (107a) contains an instance of sentential negation, because instruments as in (107b) are rarely participants. But the hierarchy of thematic roles is not totally fixed; it can be modified to account for certain discourse constraints. Recall for example the absence of concord in (95) and also the acceptability of (108), which varies according to context.

(107) E a. He took that stand on no occasions.
b. He ate an orange with no knife.

(108) I ?L'assassino non ha ucciso il giardiniere con nessun tagliacarte.
The murderer didn't kill the gardener with any paperknife.

Using the thetic/categorical distinction, Tovena also accounts for the fact that (i) in yes-no questions, where the truth of the event is under discussion, an N-word always has a negative interpretation if it is in the predicative base of a categorical sentence; but (ii) in the predication of a categorical sentence or in a thetic sentence, a negative interpretation depends on whether or not the predicate/sentence is negated, cf. (100) and (109). The indeterminacy of the truth value in a question does not imply, however, that an N-word can appear with an existential/indefinite interpretation. Instead, we expect that it should be unacceptable.

(109) I Non ha detto niente? *She didn't say anything?*

N-words as universal quantifiers dependent on negation Giannakidou (2000) proposes an analysis of concord in Greek whose extension to Romance should be examined. Her approach involves a universal quantifier that has to be licensed by a negation in the same verbal domain; Giannakidou emphasizes (correctly, in our opinion) the local nature of concord. The advantage of this analysis is that it directly resolves the question of compositionality, since no N-word contains a negation. But it is doubtful that this can be extended to the Romance languages. In Greek, the negative marker is always present, and it can therefore be considered to contribute the negative meaning. With the possible exception of Romanian, none of the Romance languages considered here has this property, because an N-word alone can express a negation, and there is concord between two N-words in a clause that contain no negator.

4.3 Summary of existing analyses

In spite of intense efforts focused on the subject, and the variety of hypotheses considered, it appears to us that no existing analysis can claim to offer a general account with a plausible explanation of the existence, the extent, and the nature of the phenomenon. Each solution proposed starts with a simple, unified approach, but then complicates it with *ad hoc* additions.

Let us summarize the aspects of concord that no analysis has been able to handle in a unified way. (1) Concord is a basic and 'natural' phenomenon, widely attested in typologically different languages, and appearing in particular as a natural tendency in many creoles. (2) It is 'local', most often restricted to one proposition (verb plus arguments). (3) It is manifested in the use of N-words, which are typically formed by the composition of the negative marker with an indicator of the type of variable involved. (4) N-words occupy variable slots that depend on the verbal negation. In concord readings, they play the role of variable symbols that depend on negation. (5) It is difficult to find convincing examples of similar phenomena elsewhere in the grammar.

As far as the Romance languages are concerned, several specific questions emerge: (1) The status of the negative marker clearly distinguishes Romanian (where the marker is obligatory in all negative sentences) from Italian, Spanish, and Portuguese (where the marker is obligatory present or absent depending on the position of the N-word) and from French (where the negative marker *pas* is not used for concord). (2) This partition is also reflected in the possibility of double negation, maximal for French, practically non-existent for Romanian, and very limited for Italian-Spanish-Portuguese. Here again, the challenge is finding an approach that links these properties, and explains them, or at least gives them a common formulation. This will be our objective in the following section.

5 A Principled Account of Multiple Expression of Negation

In this section we develop an analysis of the expression of negation in the Romance languages based on the interaction of three principles: two principles that we present as generalizations valid for most languages, and one that applies to a large set of languages, including almost all of the Romance languages.[26] The principles that we formulate are non-technical. We simply aim to provide a plausible account of the existence of the phenomenon as the result of distinct constraints associated with the expression of negation. We believe that the principles are of different types. Two of them concern the expression of negation: Principle 1 and Principle 3 have to do with the options and strategies for the lexical marking of negation and its dependent variables. Principle 1 is general, and Principle 3 constitutes a particular realization of Principle 1, common to almost all of the Romance languages, and allowing a characterization of the typological division outlined above. Principle 2 is a hypothesis about the very strict limits on the calculation of embedded negations in the predicate-argument domain. It allows us to explain why the incorporation of the negative marker in the lexical realization of negative variables is a possible option for satisfying Principle 1, and why it is a viable solution, even though it is superficially non-compositional.

Using these principles we address several of the questions raised in the previous sections: (1) Why is the negative marker incorporated (often morphologically) into the expression of arguments in many languages? (2) Why is it that multiple N-words are so often used as arguments of a predicate without giving rise to an equal number of negations in the interpretation?

Let us begin with the semantics of negation, which we treat in the classical way as an operator related to logical complement. If a semantic representation contains predicates in the scope of a negation, the corresponding sentence is verified by models that do not satisfy the conditions in the scope of the negation. Things are more complicated if we take into account the arguments of the predicate. If the argument is a constant, it is outside of the scope of the negation:

(110) F Pierre n'est pas venu. *Pierre did not come.*

The meaning of this sentence is that all models that include at least one instance of Pierre satisfying the predicate 'come' must be removed from the class of models that make the sentence true. From the point of view of the expression of negation, it is therefore plausible to suppose that every language has what we have been calling a 'negative marker' or 'negator', that

[26] The analysis developed in this section is largely based on Corblin and Tovena (2001).

is an expression whose presence in the syntactic scope of a verb means that the predicate expressed by the verb must be removed from the class of possible models. Such an expression can be used with verbs with no arguments (if they exist) and for arguments realized as constants. In the preceding example, the semantics consists of removing all models that contain at least one 'coming' event realized by Pierre, in the time and place relevant for the interpretation of the sentence, from the set of models that satisfy the discourse.

In most theories of natural language, verbal predicates are defined as 'eventualities' associated with thematic roles, and with spatio-temporal locations by means of meaning postulates. Meaning postulates link the existence of an eventuality of type V and the existence of entities filling the roles associated with the eventuality: if we have an eventuality of type *meet*, for example, there must exist at least two protagonists and a time and place where these protagonists meet. The set of roles invoked by universal meaning postulates of this type could be called the set of 'obligatory arguments' of the predicate. Obligatory arguments are identified by the following test:

(111) Identifying obligatory (semantic) arguments
If X is an obligatory argument, then a sentence in which X is left unrealized but referred to by the corresponding N-word preceded by *et* or *mais* is ungrammatical.

This test is inspired by Corblin and Derzhanski (1997) and illustrated by the examples in (112).

(112) F a. *J'ai mangé, mais / et rien. *I ate, but / and nothing.*
b. *J'ai mangé, mais / et nulle part. *I ate, but / and nowhere.*

It is difficult to propose an analysis of the underlying phenomenon insofar as this presupposes certain elements that are under discussion here. We will simply use the test as a descriptive tool. One point should be noted: This test identifies spatio-temporal locations as obligatory arguments of the verb, something that would not be accepted in all theories.

If the obligatory arguments of a negated verbal predicate are not constants, then they are variables that must be bound in order for the sentence to have denotational content. Consider the following example:

(113) F Pierre n'a pas mangé. *Pierre did not eat.*

To interpret this sentence, we have to subtract 'eating' eventualities where Paul is the agent, but which ones precisely? Since an 'eating' eventuality also supposes a theme (object) and a spatio-temporal reference, we can only calculate the semantics of the sentence if we know which values for these variables require the elimination of an eventuality from the model. In principle, semantically, a variable can be interpreted in the domain of the negation, in the domain of a higher quantifier, or identified with a contextually accessible individual (anaphor). Linguistically, the marking of these different variable interpretations can fall under one of the following cases:

(i) non-realization: The variable does not correspond to any surface lexical item.
(ii) realization: The realization of the argument by a lexical item can restrain the domain of the variable (to one sort of individual or another) and perhaps specify the scope relation of the variable in an unambiguous way.

5.1 Principle 1. The Marking of Negative Variables by Incorporation of the Negative Marker

We formulate the following hypothesis:

(114) Principle 1: Lexical Expression of negative arguments
Natural languages have a way of marking linguistically that the variable of an obligatory argument must be interpreted in the domain of the verbal negation.

In principle, the lexical marking can be specific (negative indefinite) or limited to a family of contexts (polarity item).

5.1.1 Non-realization and realization of obligatory arguments

The explicit realization of obligatory arguments is not strictly required in positive or in negative sentences. In general, in positive sentences, if non-realization is syntactically possible, the unrealized argument can be interpreted in two ways: anaphorically or existentially.

Consider (115). The unrealized argument is most often interpreted by existential closure ('Pierre ate something'). This can be seen as a direct consequence of the meaning postulates concerning 'eat'. The unrealized object argument can also be identified with a contextually salient entity (*On lui a proposé un pain. Pierre a mangé.* 'He was offered a piece of bread. Pierre ate')—in general not the most plausible option.

(115) F Pierre a mangé. *Pierre ate.*

Now let us consider the case of negative sentences, like (113), and the way the unrealized theme-object argument is interpreted. The existential closure interpretation is not available. Out of context, this sentence cannot mean 'There was something that Pierre did not eat'. The only accessible interpretations are: (1) with the variable in the scope of the negation, or the 'universal' interpretation, corresponding to 'Pierre didn't eat anything';

(2) the less plausible identification of the variable with a salient object in the context (*On lui a proposé un pain. Pierre n'a pas mangé,* 'He was offered a piece of bread. Pierre did not eat').

The first interpretation can to some extent be derived from more general principles. This seems to be what we observe for other explicit quantifiers like *si*.

(116) F Si Pierre a bu, il n'a plus soif.
If Pierre drank, he is no longer thirsty.

In (116), the unrealized theme-object argument is interpreted in the restriction of the quantifier introduced by *si*, and there is no accessible interpretation by existential closure. It is perhaps necessary to postulate a general principle that interprets uninstantiated obligatory arguments as variables in the domain of an adjacent explicit quantifier, and by existential closure only if there is no such explicit quantifier. In this case, the non-realization of an argument variable in a negative sentence would naturally be interpreted as involving a variable in the scope of the negation.

5.1.2 The limitations of non-realization

The non-realization of arguments is limited as a matter of principle: it is not possible to eliminate the ambiguity between the interpretation in the scope of an adjacent quantifier and the interpretation by identification with a salient element of the context. This point is particularly important for spatio-temporal locations, for which zero-anaphora is generally very accessible, as illustrated by (117). In principle, the sequence in (117) is ambiguous between the interpretation 'At 8 o'clock, Pierre is not smoking', and the interpretation 'Pierre never smokes'.

(117) F A huit heures, Pierre sort. Il ne fume pas.
At 8 o'clock, Pierre goes out. He does not smoke.

Non-realization of arguments also has extrinsic limitations: syntactically, certain arguments must be realized (for example the subject in some languages, and the complements of some verbs), and sometimes the non-realization of an argument is associated with a specific interpretation of the verb: in French, for instance, *manger* without a complement means 'eat a meal', *boire* without complement means 'regularly consume alcohol', and so on.

These limitations can explain why languages are very likely to have forms for marking when an argument variable is to be interpreted in the scope of the verbal negation.

5.1.3 Marking of negative variables

Lexical marking of negative variables can only be achieved by three kinds of expressions:

1. Indefinites: also used to mark a variable to which existential closure applies.
2. Polarity items: licensed only in a family of monotone decreasing contexts (or non truth conditional contexts, depending on the analysis), including negation.
3. Negative indefinites: licensed only in negative sentences.

With regard to the first case, remember that certain indefinites, called PPIs (recall fn. 13), are disallowed in negative sentences if they are interpreted in the scope of the negation, but they are possible in other monotone decreasing contexts and can be interpreted very naturally in the scope of these operators. Negation is the only anti-licenser. Consider for example:

(118) F Je n'ai pas vu quelqu'un. *I didn't see someone.*

(118) has only one interpretation, namely: 'There is someone that I didn't see'. It cannot be interpreted to mean 'I saw no one'. In contrast, (119) is perfectly acceptable with *quelqu'un* taken as a variable in the scope of *si*.

(119) F Si vous avez vu quelqu'un, dites-le-moi.
If you saw someone/anyone, tell me.

The option of using negative polarity items is clearly illustrated by the standard English example: *I don't see anybody*. Note that this strategy also has intrinsic limitations, because NPIs must be licensed by a preceding trigger. The subject, for example, cannot be marked as a negative variable by a polarity item. The most widespread solution in natural languages for realizing a negative variable is incorporating the negative marker into the expression that occupies the variable position. *Nobody* is the prototypical example. Standard English uses this option once per sentence, and incorporation is not accompanied by repetition of the negative marker in its canonical position: *Nobody came*. In this language, the unmarked option, generally available for identifying negative variables, is to realize them as polarity items.

We can also consider a non-morphological version of incorporation. In contemporary vernacular French, for example, the terms *personne, rien* obviously have negative content, given that their presence alone is enough to force the negative interpretation of a sentence (in the absence of the negative marker). This can be generalized to modern French usage, where these terms induce a negative representation of the sentence when they are in the scope of *ne*.

In principle, incorporation (morphological or otherwise) presents several advantages: it is unambiguous, economical (no extra lexical items), and possible in all syntactic positions, not subject to the licensing constraints characteristic of polarity items.

Would it then be possible to apply incorporation of the negative marker (or its meaning) systematically to all variables to be interpreted in the domain of negation? A priori, this generalization runs into just one obstacle: if negative meaning is expressed both on the verb (negative marker) and on the variable (or on more than one variable), it should be possible to obtain a compositional interpretation that takes both negations into account and leads to a double negation. But this hypothesis seems to be excluded for other reasons, captured by Principle 2, and we believe that this is why languages resort to incorporation so frequently to mark negative variables.

5.2 A Single Negation per Verb and At Most Two Negations

(120) Principle 2: At most two negations per verb

Within the domain of the verbal predicate and its arguments, normally only a single negation can be calculated. One additional embedded negation is the maximum level of complexity allowed in this domain.

Ladusaw's (1991) formulations in fact go in the same direction. For him, negation is a sentence-level feature, in other words a feature that is only 'semantically active' at the level of the proposition, although it can be expressed in multiple positions in the proposition. It is very difficult to find a simple proposition containing more than one negation in its semantic representation, and it is altogether impossible to find one with more than two. This observation was made in Corblin (1994, 1996), and in Corblin and Derzhanski (1997), and it is independent of any particular analysis of the lexical items that make up the sentence and of any hypothesis concerning the lexical marking of variables. The restriction clearly applies to the treatment of the relationship of a verb to its arguments, because embedded structures involving two verbs do not obey this constraint. As we saw above, the preferred interpretation of (121) is the single negation interpretation, $\neg\exists xy$ believe(x,y).

(121) F Personne ne croit personne. *Nobody believes anybody.*

(122) F Il n'y a personne qui ne croit personne.
There is nobody that believes nobody.

In contrast, sentence (122) only has a double negation interpretation, $\neg\exists x\neg\exists y$ believe(x,y). This seems to confirm that double negation is dispreferred within a single simple proposition.

This restriction to two negations is not trivial. It is very easy to find examples with three embedded negations: *Je ne dis pas qu'il ne croit pas qu'elle ne soit pas honnête* 'I'm not saying that he doesn't believe that she's not honest' (with different verbs), and for a computer program, or even a speaker with some experience with logical formulae, it is not at all difficult to determine what the (putative) triple negation reading of *Personne ne confie rien à personne* would be.[27] For more details, see Corblin (1994).

We will not go into a detailed examination of the nature of this constraint here. The observation itself is enough to clear away the only obstacle to marking negative variables by incorporation. A general constraint limiting the number of negations in a simple proposition to one simply makes the compositional calculation of negative meaning impossible.

Among the Romance languages presented here, the case that poses the most problems for this constraint is the obligatory double negation interpretation in French (as spoken in France, vernacular or standard) of sentences involving *pas*.

(123) F Il (n') a pas rien mangé.
He didn't eat nothing.

We have no hypothesis for these examples. We simply note that the French system has been more profoundly modified than that of the other Romance languages, by the invention of the new negative marker *pas*, which replaced *ne*, now merely an optional co-negator. Furthermore, it is well known that this obligatory double negation does not exist in many varieties of French (e.g. Quebecois), or in French-based creoles (Déprez 1999).

With these two principles, we can easily explain the existence of the phenomenon of negative concord, and why it is so widespread. If the compositional calculation of the potentially negative expressions in a proposition is impossible, then marking negative variables by incorporation is the most natural and economical solution. We concede that we have not established conclusively that words like *personne* and *rien* are expressions incorporating negative meaning (they could also be polarity items), but our hypotheses allow us to consider treating them as negative quantifiers. There are genuine negative quantifiers (for example *nobody* in Black American English), which are not interpreted as contributing multiple negations when repeated in a simple sentence. How can we characterize the case of standard English within this approach? We find words that look superficially like

---

[27] This reading would be equivalent to *Pour chacun, il y a au moins une personne à qui il confie tout* 'For each person, there is at least one person to whom he tells everything'.

instances of incorporation[28] (*nobody*), but no manifestations of negative concord. We could suggest the following: in standard English, the general strategy adopted for the realization of negative variables calls for polarity items in co-occurrence with the negative marker. Incorporation of a negative marker in the expression of a variable (*nobody, nothing*) is not used for the lexical realization of a negative variable, but to express a negation scoping over this variable. In other words, whenever a negative marker co-occurs with another negative marker, in isolation or incorporated into another negative quantifier, the result is a marked double negation structure. In short, standard English does have expressions that incorporate the negative marker, but these forms are not used for marking negative variables. This creates synonymous pairs (*I see nothing / I do not see anything*),[29] and makes co-occurrence the marked case, corresponding to double negation: *I do not see nothing*.

And how is that non-standard varieties of English, with exactly the same lexical material, have negative concord? They have simply lost the constraint that stipulates that negative variables are realized as polarity items. In Black English, for example, terms that incorporate negation become the normal way of realizing negative variables, as in many other languages.

5.3 Principle 3: *Neg-first*

As indicated above, Principle 3 applies less generally, although it covers a set of languages that goes well beyond the Romance family (see Jespersen 1917 / 1962, Dahl 1979).

(124) Principle 3: Neg First (general version)
A clause with a negated verb (a verb that is to be represented in the domain of a logical negation) must contain a preverbal negation (the negative marker or an N-word).

Let us quickly illustrate this principle for Italian. A sentence can only be negative if it contains at least one negation. Principle 3 stipulates that such a

---

[28] *Nobody* can no doubt be characterized as the incorporation of the negative marker *no* into an element represented as a variable term. This does not differentiate standard English from non-standard English. Should we still analyze *nobody* as an N-word? Assuming a definition based on the morpho-semantic composition of the term, it must be an N-word in both varieties of English. If we add an additional 'functional' condition requiring that an N-word must provide the basic solution for the expression of negative variables, *nobody* is an N-word in non-standard English, but not in standard English.

[29] Note that the sentence with negation of the variable is the one that is judged to be emphatic.

sentence must contain a preverbal negation. It thus makes the following predictions:

> **X V nessuno* (if X does not contain a negation)
> *Nessuno V*
> *Non V nessuno*

We will see below that this principle has to be slightly modified in order to account for the awkwardness of *Nessuno non V*.

We take the term *Neg-first* from Jespersen (1917 / 1962: 5):

> ... there is a natural tendency, also for the sake of clearness, to place the negative first, or at any rate as soon as possible, very often immediately before the particular word to be negativized (generally the verb).

Following Horn (1989), we can interpret this regularity as a general tendency for negation to precede its domain, rather than follow it, in nominal combinations also (e.g., F *non-retour* 'no return'). As we pointed out previously, negation applies to the predicate argument structure that represents the eventuality described in the sentence, and in this sense we can say that the verb is the domain of negation.

We now consider the different variants of the principle as illustrated by the Romance languages examined here.

5.4 The Case of Romanian

In Romanian the negative marker is *nu*. The Neg-first Principle is instantiated as follows:

(125) Neg-first Principle (Romanian):

> A simple negative sentence must contain the preverbal negative marker *nu*.

As the examples in section 2.2 showed, every negative sentence in Romanian, whether of not it involves negative variables, must contain the marker *nu* in preverbal position (126). In contrast, sentences (127)–(128) violate the Romanian version of Neg-first and are unacceptable:

(126) R Petre nu a mîncat nimic. *Petre did not eat anything.*

(127) R *Nimeni a venit. *Nobody came.*

(128) R *Petre a mîncat nimic. *Petre has eaten nothing.*

N-words in Romanian are originally derived from morphological incorporation of the negative marker, as we saw in section 2.2, but the incorporated negative element is not capable of satisfying Neg-first. Only *nu* counts for this principle. Romanian instantiates as many negative variables as necessary.

(129) R Nimeni nu a zis nimic. *Nobody said anything.*

The data concerning the possibility of double negation in Romanian motivate the following remark: the marker *nu*, which satisfies Neg-first, never gives rise to a double negation interpretation, regardless of intonation and discourse context.[30] We can therefore venture the following empirical generalization.

(130) A negative marker that satisfies Neg-first cannot give rise to double negation.

5.5 The Case of French

5.5.1 Historical perspective

It is difficult to talk about French without considering its diachronic evolution. In the earliest stages of French, the negative marker was *ne*. The Neg-first Principle in effect was the same as for Romanian:

(131) Neg-first (French, stage 1):
A simple negative sentence must contain the preverbal negative marker *ne*.

Ne thus fell under the definition of negative marker that we have adopted throughout this chapter. Consider the Old French example in (132):

(132) OF Jeo ne di. *I do not say.*

The language then underwent a series of transformations, often referred to as the 'Jespersen cycle'. The negative marker *ne*, derived from Latin *non*, often appeared with postverbal minimizers with adverbial status (Bolinger 1972), including *pas, point, mie, goutte*, whose occurrence gradually became obligatory. The set of minimizers eventually reduced to two (*pas*, *point*), then to *pas* alone. *Pas* systematically accompanied the original negative marker *ne*, until it was itself reanalyzed as the negative marker. The lexical marking of negative variables underwent a similar change: a certain number of indefinites became the typical markers of variables to be interpreted in the scope of the verbal negation expressed by *ne*, most notably *rien*, *personne*, *aucun N*. In fact, up until at least the 19th century, these

---

[30] In Romanian, more generally, our informants' judgments indicate that the double negation interpretation is very difficult to obtain. For example, for all speakers, sentence (i) allows the simple negation reading ('a world without love') but only some informants accept double negation, given a particular intonation and special contextual conditions.

(i) Nimeni nu iubeste pe nimeni. *Nobody loves anybody / nobody.*

If this interpretation exists in Romanian, it can only be expressed by two N-words, never by a pair of negations where one member is the marker *nu*.

indefinites had very widespread use as polarity items. In (133) we give a series of illustrative examples, taken from a single novel, *Corinne ou l'Italie*, by Madame de Staël, published in 1807. Compare these uses of N-words with the data summarized in Table 2.

(133) F a. Et je ne croyais pas que personne pût jamais répondre à l'idée du caractère et de l'esprit d'un homme.
And I didn't believe that anyone could ever live up to the idea of the character and mind of a man.

b. Ai-je jamais fait de mal ?
Have I ever done wrong?

c. Comment vous rien taire dans cette solitude !
How is it possible to keep anything from you in this solitude!

d. Je n'aime pas qu'on fasse rien par calcul.
I don't like for anything to be done by calculation.

e. Il ne se peut pas que vous ayez rien à m'apprendre qui refroidisse et ma tendresse et mon admiration.
It is not possible that you can tell me anything that will cool my affection and my admiration.

f. Mon régiment part pour les îles, et il n'est pas permis à aucun officier d'emmener sa femme avec lui.
My regiment is leaving for the islands, and it is not permitted for any officer to take his wife with him.

g. On devient incapable d'aucun mouvement spontané.
We are becoming incapable of any spontaneous action.

We can offer at least two arguments to show that these words have become negative. When used alone as answers to a question, they constitute a negative response. And a combination of two of these elements as arguments of the same verb can produce a double negation interpretation, as discussed in section 3.2.

In the history of French, the elements under consideration show two broad tendencies:

1. The use of N-words (*personne*, *rien*, *aucun N*) as polarity items is very rare in contemporary French. The examples cited above are felt to be old-fashioned or literary by today's speakers. More commonly, these terms seem to be reserved for marking negative variables, and so they can only appear as arguments of a verb preceded by *ne* (optionally, see below).
2. Preverbal negative *ne* tends to disappear in common spoken French. Speakers use *ne* systematically in writing (formal French). They judge

sentences with *ne* as acceptable, but they produce such examples quite rarely, especially in conversation.

5.5.2 The modern language

Assuming that *ne* is no longer the negative marker in modern French, we can reformulate Neg-first in the following way:

(134) Neg-first (French, stage 2):
A simple negative sentence in French can contain the preverbal co-negator *ne*.

This formulation in fact implies that contemporary French is not subject to Neg-first. This is true for spoken French, since we find simple negative sentences in which the verb is not preceded by any lexical material associated with negation, and partially true for formal French, since the element *ne* is no longer an autonomous negative marker. But it is perhaps possible to explain the survival of *ne* with no semantic content in formal written French as the trace of an older version of Neg-first (135), which gave a special status to the negative marker *ne*.[31]

In comparison with Romanian, French is distinguished above all by the semantic, rather than morphological, nature of the negative incorporation in variable markers. The analysis proposed here treats the contemporary French expressions *personne, rien, aucun N* as markers of negative variables by semantic incorporation of the verbal negation when they are used as arguments (verbal negation + variable interpreted in the scope of negation). Consequently, they are not treated like the earlier homophonous polarity items, which still exist in some old-fashioned uses. In short, we treat these negative expressions as negative quantifiers / variables when they are in the syntactic scope of *ne* (present or potentially present), and as polarity items in cases that reflect an earlier stage of the language (and these are all cases where *ne* cannot appear).

5.5.2 The status of N-words

It may be useful to say something more about the phrase 'negative quantifiers/variables'. In accordance with the analysis presented here, these N-words can be identified lexically as negative quantifiers as their content consists of a negation and a variable in the scope of this negation. But by Principle 2, if two of these terms co-occur in the domain of the same verb,

---

[31] Furthermore, we would expect that the presence of an N-word before the verb should favor the omission of *ne*, and that conversely, *ne* should be more likely to be preserved if the N-word comes after the verb. These predictions are difficult to confirm, given that the most frequent preverbal N-words (*personne, rien*) tend to mask preverbal *ne* phonetically, see Coveney (1998).

the second one is interpreted by default as a negative variable. Our analysis is therefore close to approaches that postulate an ambiguity for N-words in the syntactic domain of *ne*. But for us, none of the occurrences in the domain of *ne* can be identified with the NPI occurrences illustrated in (137). Under the present hypothesis, *personne* is ambiguous in *Personne n'aime personne*, in the same way that *nobody* is ambiguous in *Nobody loves nobody*, which is said to allow an additional negative concord interpretation. This ambiguity is thus totally unrelated to the existence of a use of *personne* as an NPI. The use of these words as polarity items became impossible in negative sentences (in the domain of *ne*) once they became negations themselves. However, there remains a limited possibility to find them as NPIs. Such a use now has two characteristics: It is limited to non-negative sentences, and it is perceived as old-fashioned.

This analysis is not the only imaginable one, as these expressions could also be treated as polarity items whenever possible, that is whenever the licensing conditions are satisfied. For example in (135), the first expression would be a negative quantifier, and the second could be a polarity item (see the licensing conditions for *le moindre*, which can be taken as representative of NPIs in French).

(135) F Personne n'a rien prévu. *Nobody foresaw anything.*

(136) F Personne n'a prévu la moindre chose.
Nobody foresaw the slightest thing.

There is at least one argument that shows that N-words cannot be analyzed as polarity items in the scope of *ne*. In French, polarity items cannot be modified by *presque* 'almost', see (137).

(137) F Je n'aime pas qu'on fasse *presque rien par calcul.
I don't like for almost anything to be done by calculation.

On the other hand, N-words in the scope of *ne* are perfectly compatible with *presque* (138). We take this as evidence that in the scope of *ne*, these expressions are not polarity items, but true negations.

(138) F a. Presque personne ne fait rien.
Almost nobody does anything.
b. Personne ne fait presque rien.
Nobody does practically anything.

The situation in French can therefore be presented as follows:

(139) Uses of *rien, personne, aucun N*:
(i) In the scope of *ne*, they are negations.

(ii) In non-negative NPI contexts, they are polarity items (old-fashioned in contemporary French).

In effect, we have a case of specialization, because in contexts where these terms carry negative meaning, their use as NPIs is disallowed. This can also explain why NPI use in other contexts is disappearing in French: These words have become exclusively negative, and their positive use as NPIs evokes an older stage of the language. This idea leads us to suggest a hypothesis about the contrast *Je n'ai pas rien dit* 'I didn't say nothing' vs. *Je n'ai pas dit le moindre mot* 'I didn't say the smallest word'. If we were to suppose that *rien* could be used freely as an NPI in contemporary French, it would be surprising that the NPI reading is impossible in this context, where *le moindre*, a typical NPI, is licensed (Corblin 1996). However, if we postulate a generalized locality constraint, one that prohibits the use of these expressions as NPIs in the scope of *ne*, then we derive the fact that *rien* has to be a negative quantifier in this example.

This does not explain why *rien* in combination with *pas* is not affected by Principle 2, which reduces multiple virtual negations to one. In this respect, the context of *sans* brings up some interesting difficulties. In many ways, *sans* and *sans que* have the same syntactic and semantic properties as *ne pas*; in particular, they both license an object marked by *de* (see section 2.1).

(140) F Je n'ai pas mangé de pain. *I didn't eat any bread.*

(141) F Il est resté huit jours sans manger de pain.
He went 8 days without eating any bread.

(142) F Il est resté huit jours sans que son fils mange de pain.
He went 8 days without his son eating any bread.

French N-words and NPIs are licensed after *sans*:

(143) F Il est resté huit jours sans rien dire à personne.
He went 8 days without saying anything to anybody.

(144) F Il est resté huit jours sans dire le moindre mot à personne.
He went 8 days without saying a single word to anyone.

In this context, French N-words can be modified by *presque*.[32]

(145) F Il est resté huit jours sans presque rien manger.
He went 8 days without eating practically anything.

[32] This is not always the case; see (i), suggested by a reviewer.

(i) F *Il est resté huit jours sans manger presque rien. ('without eating almost anything/nothing').

All of these observations motivate an analysis of the expressions appearing after *sans* as negative quantifiers, and not as NPIs.[33]

We conclude by giving the version of Neg-first appropriate for contemporary French in (145). It represents a significant weakening, because the principle is now an optional constraint. The other important points are the fact that N-words have acquired a status of full negation (see section 2.2.2), and this is their only possible treatment in negative sentences, and the fact that the occurrences of these elements as NPIs reflect an earlier stage of the language.

(146) Neg-first (contemporary French):
A simple negative sentence can contain the preverbal marker *ne*.

Finally, it should be noted that the interpretation of combinations of *pas* with N-words does not follow directly from the three principles that we have formulated. These principles predict the solution adopted in Quebec French (QF).

(147) QF Je n'ai pas vu personne. = 'I didn't see anyone.'

5.6 The Case of Italian

Contrary to French and Romanian, for which the Neg-first principle refers specifically to the (co-)negator, the principle for Italian seems to be satisfied by any negative expression that appears before the verb.

(148) I Non mangia. *She is not eating.*

(149) I Nessuno mangia. *Nobody is eating.*

We propose the following version of the principle for Italian:

(150) Neg-first (Italian):
A simple negative sentence must contain one and only one preverbal negation. Negations include: the negative marker (*non*) and any morphological incorporation of this marker with a negative variable (*nessuno*, etc.)

In the pair of sentences in (148)–(149), we take *non* in the first sentence and *nessuno* in the second to be the preverbal element that satisfies Neg-first. The ungrammaticality of (151) outside denial echo contexts, which have a double negation interpretation, as in (69), is explained by the specification that only a single preverbal marker is allowed. This restriction may be too strong for speakers that accept (151), but the point is that these are

[33] We leave many problems undiscussed here, notably the status of expletive *ne* following *sans que*.

exactly the sentences that are not accepted by all speakers, even in denial contexts.

(151) I *Nessuno non mangia. *Nobody does not eat.*

We saw in section 2.2.2 that Italian forms almost all of its N-words by prefixation of the negative marker. The particular formulation of the principle for Italian embodies a generalization: Instead of requiring the negative marker to appear independently before the verb, it can also be morphologically incorporated into an N-word to satisfy the constraint. Posner (1984) observes that 'the examination of popular and dialectal texts reveals no evidence of the use of [the negative marker] after [an N-word] in Central and Southern Italy or in Sardinia, and informants claim that even illiterate speakers do not make this "mistake".'(1984: 16).

The violation of Neg-first in Italian gives rise either to ungrammaticality or to double negation, see (152).

(152) I NESSUNO non ha visto questo cartello.
NOBODY didn't see this sign.

We interpret this in the following way: Once Neg-first is satisfied by a negative expression, the occurrence of a second negative is treated either as a violation of the rule, or as the establishment of a new domain where a new negation must be calculated. Given this formulation of Neg-first, we can also predict which double negation reading will be available: it must be the one that presents the configuration N-word + *non V* with a prosodic break in between.[34] This is because in this case, *non* cannot be the negative expression that satisfies Neg-first. The hearer either rejects the sentence, or he divides it into two negative parts, producing a double negation. In contrast, in the configuration *non* V + N-word, *non* satisfies Neg-first, and by virtue of the generalization proposed in (134), it cannot be involved in a double negation.

We conclude this section by presenting a number of problematic cases. Sentences (153)–(155) confirm that the satisfaction of Neg-first by N-words in Italian is only possible for morphologically negative N-words. *Mai* 'never' has a negative meaning but it is derived from a positive form (Latin *magis*). Its exceptional status was already mentioned in the discussion of (65).[35]

---

[34] For the possibility of a double negation reading with heavy negative phrases, see Tovena (1998: 264).

[35] Posner (1984:13) observes that *mai* only picked up a negative meaning after the 14th century, whereas *nessuno* and *niente* were firmly established in their negative function in the literary texts of Dante and Boccaccio.

(153) I ?*Mai accetta questa decisione.
Never does she accept this decision.

(154) I *Ha mai parlato. 'has never spoken'

(155) I Mai nessuno non guarda la partita.
Nobody never watches the match.

5.7 Spanish and Portuguese

We do not provide a detailed analysis here, but we can confirm that the principles proposed above can account for these two languages, with some differences.

Spanish and Portuguese require a version of Neg-first that is similar to Italian (disallowing two preverbal negatives). However, unlike Italian, Neg-first for these languages does not seem to differentiate between etymologically negative N-words and other N-words.

For Spanish and Portuguese, we observe a tendency (also noted for French) to restrict the use of negative quantifiers/variables as NPIs.

In conclusion, the three languages Italian, Spanish, and Portuguese appear to be constrained by quite similar versions of Neg-first, while Romanian and French constitute distinct cases.

6 Conclusion

In this chapter, we have primarily examined the phenomenon of negative concord in a representative selection of the Romance languages. We have studied the lexical elements involved, their possible syntactic combinations, and the interpretations associated with these combinations.

Several analyses have been proposed in the literature to account for the syntactic and semantic aspects of negative concord. In our opinion, however, none of them can really claim to provide an overall solution offering

---

The behavior of *mai* should be examined in more detail in order to understand better how negative elements work in emphatic function sentence-initially. For example, the emphatic sentence (i), with future tense, is acceptable, while (153) and (ii) are not.

(i) I MAI leggerò questo libro. *NEVER will I read this book.*

(ii) I *MAI leggerò nessun libro. *NEVER will I read any book.*

These data suggest that in (i) *mai* functions as an operator over the entire sentence, given that it has a negative interpretation in isolation, but it cannot license other N-words.

The case of emphatic sentences characterized by strong emotion, as in (iii), which requires a particular prosody with no pause, also deserves closer attention.

(iii) Sono tutti degli ingrati. Nessuno non è venuto.
They are all ingrates. Not a single one came.

plausible explanations for the existence, extent, and nature of the phenomenon. These questions underlie the analysis that we have proposed.

Our approach is based on the interaction of three principles, to be understood as generalizations. The first principle captures the fact that, in a large number of languages, there is an unambiguous way to mark argument variables that have to be interpreted in the scope of the verbal negation. Lexical marking by incorporation of the marker of verbal negation is a simple strategy, because the dependency of the variable is expressed by repetition of the quantifier. This explains why negative concord emerges as a basic and very widespread phenomenon, built upon the use of N-words that are often formed by composition of the negative marker with an indicator of the type of variable involved.

The second principle restricts recursion of negation in the verb-argument domain. By default, there is one negation per verbal domain, and there is a strict upper limit of two negations. This explains why the strategy of repeating the lexeme that marks negation does not lead to ambiguity (except in very exceptional cases). The fact that double negation is a marked interpretation is explained in our analysis by the fact that this reading corresponds to the maximum complexity allowed for embedding of negation in the verbal domain. As the constraint refers to the verb-argument domain, we can also explain the strongly local character of negative concord.

Finally, our analysis has shown that the distribution of negative expressions in a number of Romance languages can be accounted for with a series of constraints that are all variants of a single cross-linguistic tendency: to realize negative expressions in preverbal position.

8

Subject Inversion and Discourse in Romance

JEAN-MARIE MARANDIN

1 Introduction[1]

The subject NP can appear to the left or to the right of the verb in the Romance languages. Throughout this study, I will use the term 'inversion' as a descriptive term to refer to the postverbal placement of the first argument of the finite verb, in particular the NP that is, syntactically speaking, the subject. It is generally assumed that the pre- or postverbal placement of the first argument of the verb (usually its subject), is the result of syntactic and discourse constraints. In this study, I leave aside syntactic considerations in order to focus on the pragmatic conditions governing the felicity of inversion. Within the generative tradition, the focus-ground partition is taken to be the crucial dimension for treating subject placement, with postverbal placement reserved for focused subject NPs. In pragmatic approaches, inversion is seen as a multi-faceted phenomenon, and the focus-ground partition is just one factor among others that explains the placement of the subject NP. I will show, based on an analysis of inversion in root and subordinate clauses, in question-answer pairs, and in narrative discourse, that the focus-ground partition is not the relevant factor for the analysis of inversion. Instead, I claim that two other factors are involved: inversion is felicitous either (i) when the predicate is given, or (ii) when it describes a 'disposition' of the referent of

[1] I thank Claire Beyssade, Olivier Bonami, Elisabeth Delais-Roussarie, Danièle Godard, Alain Kihm, and Isabelle Simatos, for reading, discussing, and commenting on the many earlier versions of this analysis. All errors remain, of course, my own.

Fundamental Issues in the Romance Languages
Danièle Godard (ed.).

the subject. In the former case, inversion is related to how the utterance locally elaborates on the current discourse topic (DT). In the latter, it depends on an element of the speaker's knowledge. The two factors are distinct in nature: one belongs to the discourse-local context and the other to the speaker's general knowledge. Consequently, two felicity conditions must be posited: the Given Predicate Condition and the Presupposed Disposition Predicate. Crucially, there is no strict correlation between these two felicity conditions and the constructions that syntactically license the different types of inversion. This means, for example, that instances of stylistic inversion in French or instances of unaccusative inversion in Italian may be pragmatically licensed by either of the two conditions.

The paper proceeds as follows. In section 2, I briefly present the empirical basis of this study: a set of constructions where inversion is syntactically licensed in five Western Romance languages (Catalan, Spanish, French, Italian, Portuguese). The data pertaining to the felicity of inversion in context were obtained from several informants in the course of three surveys.[2] In section 3, I discuss the information structure approach to inversion and I introduce the main counterexamples. The Given Predicate Condition (GPC) is defined and illustrated in section 4, the Presupposed Disposition Predicate (PDC) in section 5. I review the properties of inversion in discourse in section 6.

2 Domain of the Study

The domain of the study consists of instances of inversion occurring in root and subordinate clauses in three discourse configurations: (i) in answers to questions, (ii) in 'out of the blue' statements, and (iii) in narrative discourses. Methodologically, question-answer (QA) pairs provide the context for analyzing the focus-ground structure of utterances and modeling the dynamics of the discourse topic (Büring 1997). Looking at narrative discourse allows a generalization of the results obtained from dialogue contexts to monologue discourse.[3] Finally, it is crucial to include subordinate clauses when examining

---

[2] The survey took the form of questionnaires, sent by e-mail, in which informants had to evaluate the felicity of inversion in short dialogues, given a context that was described verbally. I thank the informants who participated in the various surveys: Luis Alonso-Ovalle, Annie Delaveau, Teresa Espinal, Bernard Fradin, Danièle Godard, Rodrigo Gutiérrez-Bravo, Françoise Kerleroux, Alain Kihm, Brenda Laca, Nicola Munaro, Josep Quer, Lucia Tovena, Graciela Vasquez. For their patience and helpfulness, I thank in particular: Joaquim Brandão de Carvalho, Patricia Cabredo-Hofherr, Anna Gavarró, Nicola Grandi, Alda and Luigi Mari. Marta Donazzan provided additional Italian data used in this revised version. All examples (unless otherwise noted) are taken from these surveys.

[3] Moreover, the distribution and use of constructions licensing inversion may be different in dialogue and in narrative discourse. For example, the unaccusative inversion of French in root clauses is never used in dialogue.

the link between information structure and inversion, since subordinate clauses are not associated with an independent focus-ground structure.

In fact, the descriptive notion of inversion is imprecise and should be used with caution. The term 'inversion' (in the singular) misleadingly suggests a uniform syntactic phenomenon. First of all, the term includes not only constructions where the postverbal NP exhibits the properties of a subject NP, but also unaccusative constructions, where the postverbal NP has the properties of a direct object. Furthermore, there are several kinds of postverbal placement for the subject NP. For example, in addition to the unaccusative construction ((1a) below), French allows two types of subject inversion: stylistic inversion (1b) and elaborative inversion (1c).[4] The main properties that distinguish these two types of inversion are the following: (a) stylistic inversion is only grammatical in extraction contexts, while elaborative inversion is licensed in all types of clauses; (b) The subject does not have a fixed position in stylistic inversion, whereas it appears obligatorily at the right edge of the clause in elaborative inversion; (c) The object cannot be realized as a (referential) NP in stylistic inversion, whereas there is no constraint on the object in elaborative inversion.[5]

(1) F a. Unaccusative construction:
i. Je voudrais que vienne Marie.
I would like for Marie to come.
ii. Alors sont arrivés trois hommes en armes.
Then three armed men arrived.
iii. Quand sont arrivés les enfants, Pierre travaillait.
When the kids arrived, Pierre was working.

---

[4] Elaborative inversion is not simply a case of heavy NP shift. Heavy, semantically singular subject NPs do not give rise to such inversion (see (ia) below); some sort of semantic plurality is involved in licensing (ib).

(i) F a. *Passera devant le conseil de discipline l'élève de troisième C qui a été surpris en train de fumer un joint dans les toilettes hier.
come-fut before the disciplinary council the pupil of 3rd grade who has been caught smoking pot in the toilets yesterday
The 3rd grade student who was caught smoking pot in the toilet yesterday will appear before the disciplinary council.
b. Passeront devant le conseil de discipline les élèves de troisième C qui ont été surpris en train de fumer un joint dans les toiletes hier.
The 3rd grade students who were caught ...

[5] Stylistic inversion has been studied extensively in the generative framework since Kayne (1973), who coined the term and established the distinction between subject NP inversion and subject clitic inversion in French. The reader is referred to Kayne (1986), Kayne and Pollock (1978), Korzen (1983; 1992) and, for more recent overviews, Hulk and Pollock (2001), Bonami and Godard (2001) and Bonami, Godard and Marandin (2001). See also Kampers-Manhe (1998) and Marandin (2001) for discussion of the unaccusative construction in French.

b. Stylistic inversion:
   i. (Je me demande) à qui a parlé Paul ?
      I wonder to whom Paul spoke.
   ii. Voici le livre qu'a rédigé le fils de Marie.
      Here is the book that Mary's son wrote.
   iii. Sur la place (Paul savait que) se dressait une cathédrale gothique.
      On the square, (Paul knew that) a Gothic cathedral towered.

c. Elaborative inversion:
   (Paul pense que) devront repasser l'examen tous les étudiants qui ont raté le contrôle continu.
   (Paul thinks that) must-fut take-again the exam all the students who failed the continuous assessment
   (Paul thinks that) all the students who failed the continuous assessment will have to take the exam again.

I make a sharp distinction between argument position (first, second, etc., argument in the verbal valence) and grammatical function (subject, object, etc.). I use the term 'inversion' to refer to the postverbal placement of the first argument of the verb.[6] When the functional status of the constituent that realizes the first argument is relevant, I will be careful to distinguish between 'postverbal placement of the subject NP' and 'postverbal placement of the first argument realized as an object NP'.

I now present the inventory of the constructions considered in this study, in addition to the three French constructions illustrated in (1):

1. Free inversion in root clauses.[7] The characteristic properties of this type of inversion are the following: (i) It is said to be obligatory in a response to a question if the subject NP is in focus; (ii) The subject NP appears obligatorily at the right periphery of the utterance; (iii) There is no lexical constraint imposed on the main verb:

(2) [Who ate the apple?]
    C Se l'ha menjat la Maria.
    S Se la comió María.
    I L'ha mangiata Maria. / Se l'è mangiata Maria.
    P Comeu-a a Maria.
    Mary ate it.

---

[6] My notion of argument ordering (allowing us to identify the first argument) is taken from Head driven Phrase Structure Grammar (Pollard and Sag 1994).

[7] The label 'free inversion' is misleading. 'Free' should be interpreted as 'not subject to a syntactic licensing condition' (unlike stylistic inversion in French, for example).

Free inversion is not syntactically homogeneous in the four languages that allow it: see Zubizarreta (1998) for a comparative analysis of Italian and Spanish;[8] Ambar (1988, 1999); Costa (1998) for Portuguese; Vallduví (1991; 1993) for Catalan. French does not have free inversion; nevertheless, elaborative inversion does have a family resemblance with free inversion as it shares certain features of free inversion: (i) It is possible with a focused NP, (ii) It imposes no lexical restrictions on the verb or VP, and (iii) It requires the placement of the subject NP at the right edge of the clause.

(3) [Who ate apples?]
F a. Ont mangé des pommes [tous ceux qui étaient dans le pré].
have eaten apples all those who were in the meadow
b. *Ont mangé [tous ceux qui étaient dans le pré] des pommes.

2. Presentational inversion, which is found in root and subordinate clauses.[9] Its characteristic properties are the following: (i) It is appropriate in wide-focus utterances; (ii) It imposes a double constraint on the verb: it is possible only with intransitive verbs, and more specifically, only with so-called 'presentational' verbs (Hatcher 1956).

(4) [What's happening?]
C Toquen les campanes.
S Están tocando las campanas.
P Estão a tocar os sinos.
I Suonano le campane.
Bells are ringing.

This type of inversion raises two questions: (i) How should we define the family of verbs that license it, and (ii) What is the appropriate syntactic analysis? In a nutshell, is it an unaccusative construction, or does it subsume several syntactic constructions (unaccusative or unaccusative-like) depending on the verb or the particular language involved?

Pinto (1997:20) addresses both questions in Italian and concludes that presentational inversion does not pattern with the unaccusative construction.[10] I will not attempt to address the question for the other languages

---

[8] See also Burzio (1986), Longobardi (2000), Renzi (1988), Rizzi (1982; 1997), and Suñer (2003).

[9] There is no generally accepted term for this type of inversion. The term *presentational* (F. *présentatif*) is taken from Hetzron (1975: 374), cited in Lambrecht (1994:177).

[10] More precisely, she shows that the family of verbs that license presentational inversion does not coincide with the family of lexically unaccusative verbs. *Entrare* is reputedly unaccusative, but not *telefonare*, and nevertheless both license this type of inversion. *Impallidire* and *stufarsi* are reputedly unaccusative, yet they do not license inversion.

(i) I Che cosa è successo ? *What happened?*

here.[11] This is why I use the descriptive term 'presentational inversion' to sidestep the question of the precise syntactic analysis of this type of inversion in each language.

As for the verbs that license it, according to Hatcher (1956) (still one of the most complete surveys, based on Spanish), the verbs that occur with this type of inversion can be grouped into seven semantically defined subclasses: verbs of existence/presence, absence, commencement, continuation, production, occurrence, appearance, movement towards a point.[12] As we will see below in section 5, this account is not satisfactory.

3. The construction called 'emphatic order' by Contreras (1976:89ff) in Spanish. Its characteristic features are the following: (i) It is only possible in root clauses (*ibid*.:89); (ii) It co-occurs with a narrow focus constituent realized in a preverbal position (distinct from the position of left-dislocated elements) carrying a specific accent (contrastive accent according to Contreras, contrastive or emphatic according to Zubizarreta (*ibid*.:118)); (iii) The postverbal subject NP does not have a fixed position (see (5b.i) and (5b.ii)).

---

a. È entrata Beatrice. (= ex. 12, *ibid*.: 20) 'entered Beatrice'
b. Ha telefonato Dante. (= ex. 17, *ibid*: 22) 'phoned Dante'
c. # È impallidito Berlusconi.(= ex. 13, *ibid*: 20) 'went-pale Berlusconi'
d. # Si è stufata Penelope. (ibid.) 'got-bored Penelope'

[11] See among others Aronovich (2003) for Spanish.

[12] For a similar classification for Italian, see Sornicola (1994), Bernini (1995: 55) or Wandruszka (1982), cited in Bernini (*ibid*:57). Note that the same types of verbs are found in the unaccusative construction in French, particularly in subjunctive sentential complements (Marandin 2001):

(i) F a. Je voudrais que fonde la glace entre eux.
I wish that melt-subj the ice between them
I wish things would cool down between them.
b. Je voudrais qu'explose la vérité.
I wish that explode-subj the truth
I wish the truth would break out.
c. Je voudrais que vienne Marie.
I wish that come-subj Marie.
I wish Mary would come.
d. Je voudrais qu'existent de réels obstacles à la mondialisation.
I wish that exist-subj real obstacles to globalization
I wish there were real obstacles to globalization.
e. Je voudrais que cesse la guerre.
I wish that stop-subj the war.
I wish wars would come to an end.

(5) a. [What did you do?]
S Eso MISMO hice yo. (Contreras 1976:90, ex. 10.9)
this same did I
I did the very same thing.

b. [Where did Don Fermín take his spurs from?]
S i. De la SALA sacó don Fermín sus espuelas.
from the room took out don Fermín his spurs
ii. De la SALA sacó sus espuelas don Fermín. (Contreras 1976: 90, ex. 10.12)
Don Fermín took his spurs from the room.

The subject can appear preverbally in this construction when it is in narrow focus; it should then carry the so-called 'contrastive' or 'emphatic' accent (indicated by capitals):

(6) [Who took his spurs from the room?]
S Don FERMÍN sacó sus espuelas de la sala. (Contreras 1976: 91, ex. 10.20)

I will say nothing about the syntactic aspects of inversion in subordinate clauses. The only point that matters for this study is that it is syntactically licensed in such clauses: in restrictive relative clauses (7), in the coda of cleft constructions (8), and in temporal subordinate clauses (9).[13,14]

(7) C La poma que li ha donat en Pau és sobre la taula.
S La manzana que le dió Pablo está sobre la mesa.
F La pomme que lui a donné Paul est sur la table.
I La mela che gli ha dato Paolo è sulla tavola.
P A maçã que lhe deu o Pedro está em cima da mesa.
The apple Paul gave him is on the table

(8) C Són granades el que llancen els policies contra els manifestants.
S Son granadas lo que lanzan los policías contra los manifestantes.
F Ce sont des grenades que lancent les policiers contre les manifestants.
I Sono granate quelle che lanciano i poliziotti contro i manifestanti.
P São granadas que lançam os policias contra os manifestantes.
It is grenades that the policemen throw at demonstrators.

---

[13] The French versions in (7)-(9) present instances of stylistic inversion.

[14] The agreement between past participle and preverbal object in French does not apply when the subject is postverbal, for most speakers who still apply the agreement rule 'the past participle agrees with the object if cliticized or extracted' (Abeillé and Godard 2000). Contemporary normative grammars hesitate (Isabelle Simatos, p.c.), while this was a well-know exception for classical grammarians (e.g. Vaugelas).

(9) C desprès que van haver menjat el pastís els nens
S después de que comieran el pastel los niños
F [a cake] après que l'eurent mangé les enfants
I [a cake] dopo che l'ebbero mangiato i bambini
P depois de terem as crianças comido o bolo
after the kids ate the cake

Note that the presentational inversion also is grammatical in subordinate clauses:[15]

(10) C quan surti el sol
S cuando salga el sol
F dès que se lève le soleil
I non appena sorge il sole
P assim que se levante o sol
as soon as the sun rises

3 Inversion and Focus-Ground Structure

It is commonly accepted that the placement of the subject NP is determined by the focus-ground structure of the utterance. Usually, the focus-ground structure is assumed to reflect the division between new and old information in the utterance. Two major types of division are distinguished, illustrated below using the usual method based on the contrast between constituent questions (inducing narrow focus) and questions of the type *What's happening*? (inducing wide focus), illustrated in (11) and (12), respectively:[16]

(11) [Who came?] Marie est venue. *Marie came*
Old information = Background: $\exists x$ came(x)
New information = Focus: x = Marie

(12) [What happened?] Marie est venue. *Marie came*
New information = Focus: came(Marie)

3.1 Inversion in Utterances with Narrow Focus Subjects

The generalization commonly formulated to describe the constraint on inversion in the Romance languages other than French is the following:

(13) Inversion is obligatory if the subject is in narrow focus.

---

[15] (10F) is an instance of unaccusative inversion in French.

[16] For the analysis of the new information in (11), represented as an equation, see Lambrecht (1994) and Beyssade *et al.* (2003).

Typically, inversion occurs in answers to subject-constituent questions (e.g. *Who came? Who ate the apple?*). This has been illustrated with instances of free inversion in (2) above. Yet, the limitations of generalization (13) are immediately obvious. It only applies to root clauses and therefore cannot explain cases of inversion in subordinate clauses (see (7)-(9) above), which are usually considered to contribute information belonging to the background. Moreover, even for free inversion in root clauses, (13) does not adequately capture the appropriate felicity condition.

3.1.1 Inversion and the narrow focus status of the subject

Several cases have been reported in the literature, in which narrow focus subject NPs should not be postverbal in answers to Subject Constituent Questions.

1. In Portuguese, according to Ambar (1999:27), focused subject NPs should be preverbal when they are non-exhaustive foci (using Ambar's terminology). The answer in (a.i) is complete and the one in (b.ii) is incomplete; subject NPs in incomplete answers are obligatorily preverbal. To account for the contrast, Ambar introduces a distinction between exhaustive focus and non-exhaustive focus.[17]

(14) *Who ate the cake?*
P a. i. (A tarte) comeu a Joana.
ii. # A Joana comeu (a tarte).
b. i. # (A tarte) comeu a Joana (*about the others I do not know*).
ii. A Joana comeu (*about the others I do not know*).
Joana ate (the cake).

2. In Spanish, focused subject NPs are preverbal in the emphatic order (Contreras, 1976:91) or when they are emphatic or contrastive foci (Zubizarreta 1998). See (6) above repeated below as (15).

(15) [Who took his spurs from the room?]
S Don FERMÍN sacó sus espuelas de la sala.

3. In Italian, according to Kiss (1998:269), contrastive focused NPs can be preverbal. She relates this possible preverbal placement to her notion of identificational focus: identificational foci denote discourse referents belonging to a closed set of known alternatives.

[17] I repeat Ambar's examples, in particular the parenthetical remark indicating the effect associated with (14b.ii) (I will come back to this remark in section 4.3), except that I replace the ungrammaticality mark '*' used by Ambar with the symbol for inappropriateness '#'.

(16) I Chi di voi due ha rotto il vaso ?
Which of you two broke the vase?
a. Maria ha rotto il vaso.
b. L'ha rotto Maria, il vaso.

Hence, the generalization (13) should at least be reformulated as in (17):

(17) Subject NP in answers to Subject Constituent Questions are postverbal when
(i) they are narrow foci; and
(ii) noncontrastive or nonemphatic or nonexhaustive (...)

Moreover, generalization (13)/(17) only applies to root clauses and it excludes French. Even if we agree to leave French out of the picture, we would still like to understand what exactly is meant by the notions of contrast and exhaustivity.

3.1.2 More data

I bring up another piece of data that I have tested several times in the surveys.[18] The QA pairs in (18) are made up of a Subject Constituent Question, and a partial answer. The answer partially resolves the Subject Constituent Question by identifying a particular aspect of the issue raised by the question. Such answers prototypically encourage the continuation of the dialogue about the same issue. Postverbal subjects are forbidden in such answers, as (18) shows.

(18) [Who repainted the table?]
C a. La Maria l'ha esmerilat (...)
b. # L'ha esmerilat la Maria.
S a. María la preparó (...)
b. # La preparó Maria.
I a. Maria l'ha scrostato (...)
b. # L'ha scrostato Maria.
P a. A Maria lixou-a (...)
b. # Lixou-a a Maria.
Maria sanded it (...)

The question now is whether the infelicity of inversion in (14)-(16) has the same cause as in (18). Remember that Ambar reports that answers with a preverbal subject in Portuguese (14) trigger an incompleteness effect: the answer does not bring the issue under discussion to an end. If we could show that cases (14) and (18) are both instances of the same discourse configuration, we

[18] These data have never before been discussed, to my knowledge.

would at least understand the obligatory preverbal placement of the subject.[19] It would only remain for us to account for the cases described in terms of contrast in Spanish (15) and Italian (16). As we shall see, this will require a drastic change of perspective that shifts the explanation from the informational status of the subject NP considered in isolation to the discourse status of the VP.

3.2 Inversion in Wide-Focus Utterances

Inversion is infelicitous (see (19) below) or felicitous (see (20) below) in answers to questions of the type *What's happening?* (see also (4) above). At first blush, then, the placement of the first argument (possibly the subject) does not seem to be fixed in wide focus utterances.

(19) [What's happening?]
S a. #Ha comido la manzana María.
b. María ha comido la manzana.
María ate the apple.

(20) [And what about Marie, any news?]
C a. El seu marit s'ha mort aquest matí.
b. Aquest matí ha mort el seu marit
S a. Su marido murió esta mañana.
b. Esta mañana murió su marido.
I a. Suo marito è morto questa mattina.
b. È morto suo marito questa mattina.
P Morreu-lhe o marido esta manhã.
Her husband died this morning.

The infelicity of inversion in (19) is readily explained when one accepts (13) or (17): the subject is not in narrow focus. On the other hand, (20) is problematic: Inversion should never be felicitous in such answers. In order to save (13) and to maintain a unified approach to subject inversion, a new kind of focus has been proposed: presentational focus. According to such proposals, the NP *her husband* is in presentational focus: It provides an item of new information by virtue of the fact that it introduces a new discourse referent (henceforth DR). Notice that the answer in (20) features a verb (*die*) that allows presentational inversion, unlike (19). I will elaborate on this observation in section 3.3.2, after first considering an explanation in terms of presentational focus.

The solution of positing a new kind of focus runs into several difficulties. The first is general: presentational inversion is appropriate in subordinate

[19] Note that in both cases, the notion of topic appears to offer no help.

clauses (see (10) above), which do not have their own focus-ground structure.[20] The second difficulty is empirical. Sasse (1987) has shown that utterances with presentational inversion do not systematically introduce a new DR: they can also introduce a new eventuality (see Sasse's opposition between 'event-centered' *vs* 'entity-centered' utterances). This is generally the case in narrative discourse or in temporal subordinate clauses. This might be the case for (20) in context: The answers report a new event (the death of Mary's husband). Note that the preverbal or postverbal placement of the first argument does not correlate with the dialogue status of the DR it corresponds to ; it may be more or less activated (depending on whether or not the questioner formulates the question about Mary to ask indirectly for news about her husband), but in any case it is highly accessible considering the forms of the questions and the answers. As for (10) above, it is hard to imagine that the sun would need to be introduced as an independent DR for narrative purposes, whereas it makes sense to refer to the rising of the sun as a temporal reference point in the course of narrated events. Since event-centered utterances may have postverbal subjects, the notion of presentational focus loses all explanatory force, as does any other explanation that relies on a specific status for the subject NP. The third difficulty is theoretical: how can the different definitions of focus be unified? For ordinary informational focus, we can represent the new information by instantiating a variable (corresponding to a DR whose status in the overall universe of discourse is irrelevant) introduced in the old content (see (11) above). For presentational focus, the new information has to be represented by introducing a new DR in an utterance whose content is in fact totally new.[21] It has been proposed that the entire utterance contributes little information other than the introduction of a DR corresponding to the subject, because the verb is 'informationally light' (Birner 1994, 1995, Zubizarreta 1998). For this to work, light information should be seen as analogous to old information in the utterance content. This solution is counter-intuitive: the ringing of bells (4) can be just as crucial a piece of information as the death of an acquaintance in a context (20). I conclude, therefore, that the notion of presentational focus causes more problems than it solves.

---

[20] In order to save the explanation in terms of presentational focus, Lambrecht (1994:126) suggests that subordinate clauses *can* establish a focus-ground division independent of, and analogous to, the 'real' one that characterizes the utterance as a whole.

[21] I refer to Lambrecht (1994) for the analysis of the problems caused by the failure to distinguish the old or new status of a piece of content and the activation status of the DRs in the universe of discourse (i.e., collapsing together inactive and new DRs on the one hand, and active and old DRs on the other).

3.3 Discussion

The link between inversion and information structure is a kind of dogma for many theories in contemporary linguistics. And yet, such a line of explanation is dangerously insufficient. The idea that postverbal subjects in wide focus utterances are postverbal because they are in presentational focus, and that this behaves like information focus, just seems an *ad hoc* construct forged to save observation (13). But in any case, (13) fails to account for the placement of narrow focus subjects since there are contexts in which such subjects just cannot be postverbal. I conclude that we must reconsider the relationships between inversion and focus-ground structure.

3.3.1 Inversion and the discourse status of VP

Observation (13), reformulated in (17), only considers the informational status of the subject NP. I change perspective and focus on the discourse status of the VP. Instead of (13)/(17), I propose the observation in (21).[22]

(21) Inversion is felicitous if the VP is repeated.

The observation in (21) adequately describes the context licensing the prototypical examples of free inversion (2). In these contexts, the VP can be omitted (22b), which is characteristic of repeated material:[23]

(22) S ¿Quién comió la manzana ? *Who ate the apple?*
 a. Ha comido la manzana María.
 b. María.

Moreover, it directly accounts for the obligatory preverbal placement of subject in (18) above. For the moment, I leave aside the preverbal placement in (14)–(16).

The thrust of (21) is that it is not restricted to free inversion and that it is not linked to focus-ground structure. For example, it applies to emphatic order in Spanish, which is appropriate with a postverbal subject only if the VP is repeated. This is shown by the contrast between (23a) and (23b.i). In (23b.i), the finite verb in the answer (*prestar*, 'to lend') is different from the verb in the question (*dar*, 'to give'); in this case, the postverbal placement of the subject is strongly dispreferred.

(23) S ¿A quién le dió su carro María ? *Who did Mary give her car to?*
 a. A PABLO se lo dió (la probrecita).
 She / the poor thing gave it to Pablo.

[22] I will return to the obligatoriness of this inversion in section 4.1.2 below.

[23] In order to save space, I will only give examples from one language. The extension to the other languages should be assumed, unless the examples are explicitly said to illustrate a specific feature of a particular language.

b. i. ??A PABLO se lo prestó (la pobrecita).
   ii. (La pobrecita) se lo prestó a Pablo.
   She / the poor thing lent it to Pablo.

For French, (21) applies to elaborative inversion (24) and to stylistic inversion, as seen in the relative clause in (25). Contrasts in (25) are crucial, because they show that (21) is not limited to root clauses.[24] In (24a), the verb in the answer (*être reçu*, 'to pass') repeats that of the question, whereas it is different in (24b) (*échouer* ('to fail') vs. *être reçu*).

(24) Qui est reçu ? *Who passed the exam?*
F a. Sont reçus Pierre, Paul et Bernadette.
   Pierre, Paul, and Bernadette passed.
  b. #Ont échoué les deux élèves que présentait Paul.
   The two students presented by Paul failed.
  c. Les deux élèves que présentait Paul ont échoué [, sont reçus Pierre, Paul et Bernadette].
   The two students presented by Paul failed, [Pierre, Paul, and Bernadette passed it].

In (25), the placement of the subject in the relative clauses in the answer directly depends on whether it is repeated from the relative clause in the question (*s'occuper*, 'to be responsible') or not (*s'occuper vs entraîner*, 'to train').

(25) Que sont devenus les étudiants dont Bernard s'est occupé ?
What became of the students that Bernard was responsible for?
F a. i. Les étudiants dont s'est occupé Bernard ont tous brillamment réussi.
   The students who Bernard was responsible for all have brillantly succeeded.
  ii. Les étudiants dont Bernard s'est occupé ont tous brillamment réussi.
  b. i. Les étudiants que Bernard a entraînés ont réussi aux Olympiades, ceux qu'il a soignés sont devenus prof de gym.
   The students that Bernard trained won at the Olympics, those that he treated became gym teachers.

[24] It applies also to subjunctive complement clauses in French for those speakers who use the unaccusative construction productively:

(i) Qui veux-tu qui vienne ? *Who do you want to come?*
F a. Je veux que vienne Paul. *I want Paul to come.*
  a'. Je veux que Paul vienne.
  b. #Je veux que parte Paul *I want Paul to leave*
  c. Je veux que Paul parte (et que vienne Marie).
  I want Paul to leave (and Marie to come).

ii. #Les étudiants qu'a entraîné Bernard ont tous réussi aux Olympiades, ceux de Jean-Marie ont repris un cursus normal.
The students that Bernard trained won at the Olympics, Jean-Marie's went back to a normal program.

In summary, the observation (21) is more general than (13): it is not limited to answers to Subject Constituent Questions. For the moment, it relies on the notion of repetition, which is defined and generalized in section 4 by appealing to the notion of 'given content'. This notion is defined independently of the focus-ground structure, which furthermore paves the way for a unified analysis of inversion in root and subordinate clauses.

3.3.2 Inversion in wide focus utterances

Observation (21) readily explains (19) above, but has nothing to say about the felicity of inversion in wide focus utterances in (20). We should now take seriously the observation that inversions observed in answers to questions of the type *What's happening?* are all instances of presentational inversion. Remember that presentational inversion is considered to be licensed by particular classes of verbs (section 2). Such an account is not accurate enough, though. In fact, it depends on the verbs and, for each verb, on the choice of the referential type of the subject. For example, the verb *cinguettare* 'twitter' in Italian allows the postverbal placement of its first argument when it corresponds to birds but not to women (26).

(26) I a. Piero entrò. *Piero walked in.*
i. Le donne cinguettavano in un angolo del salone.
ii. #Cinguettavano in un angolo del salone le donne.
The women were twittering in a corner of the lounge.
b. Piero uscì in giardino. *Piero walked in the garden.*
i. Cinguettavano gli uccellini.
ii. ?Gli uccellini cinguettavano.
The birds were twittering

In the same way, *alzarsi* 'stand up' licenses subject inversion when the subject NP denotes the wind (27b), but not when it denotes an animate referent (a child in (27a)).

(27) I a. La mamma entrò nella camera.
The mother came in the room.
i. Il bambino si alzò.
ii. *Si alzò il bambino.
The child got up.

b. Gli invitati uscirono in giardino.
The guests walked in the garden.
i. Si alzò il vento.
ii. ?Il vento si alzò.
The wind picked up.

Crucially, the same condition is observed in root clauses and in subordinate clauses.

(28) I a. quando cinguettavano gli uccellini, / quando gli uccellini cinguettavano, ...
a'. #quando cinguettavano le donne, / quando le donne cinguettavano, ...
b. quando si alzò il vento, / quando il vento si alzò, ...
b'. #quando si alzò il bambino, / quando il bambino si alzò, ...

Of course, inversion will be felicitous when the VP is repeated as we observed with run-of-the mill verbs in section 3.1.1. In (29), the postverbal placement of the subject occurs independently of the class of the verb or the relationship between verb and subject.[25]

(29) I. a. A: Quando si è alzato il vento?
B: Alle otto si è alzata una grossa tempesta.
At 8 o'clock a huge storm arose.
b. A: Quando si è alzato Gianni?
B: Si è alzato alle dieci quel pigrone!
He got up at 10, the lazybones!

But, inversion that depends on the choice of verbs and subject is felicitous independently of the discourse status of the VP. The question then is whether presentational inversion is subject to the same felicity conditions as the inversion we observed in answers to Subject Constituent Questions. I will come to this in section 5.

3.4 Conclusion

Analyzing inversion only in terms of focus-ground structure would mean treating inversion in root and in subordinate clauses differently, treating French separately from the other Romance languages (by projecting purely

---

25 The observation should be refined. Informants report that they prefer the preverbal placement of the subject when it is repeated from the question:

(29') I. a. A: Quando si è alzato il vento?
B: Il vento si è alzato alle otto.
b. A: Quando si è alzato Gianni?
B: Gianni si è alzato alle dieci.

syntactic aspects of each language into pragmatic analysis), and complicating the focus-ground structure by adding more and more subtypes of focus. Dissociating the analysis of inversion from this level of structure allows a unified and descriptively more adequate approach. This is the route I take from now on. The analysis I propose involves two felicity conditions. The former builds upon generalization (21) and extends it. It primarily involves the discourse within which the utterance is situated (section 4). The latter is proposed to cater for the characteristics of the presentational inversion in (20) (a particular lexical restriction and the presentational effect) although it is not limited to the presentational type, as we shall see. This second condition primarily involves the speaker's knowledge (section 5).

4 The Given Predicate Condition

First, I modify the observation in (15) by replacing the intuitive concept of 'repeated material' with the construct concept 'given content'. This concept will be crucial for the formulation of the first felicity condition for inversion: the Given Predicate Condition (GPC). The notion of given content is defined within the model of discourse topic dynamics (Büring 1997); it is independent of the focus-ground partition (section 4.1). This is why the GPC is insensitive to the syntactic type of the sentence where inversion occurs (root *vs* subordinate clause). Next, I extend the empirical foundations of the analysis and show different ways in which 'given content is given' (section 4.2). The semantic definition of given content allows us to account for inversion in discourse contexts that are apparently very different. Finally I return to the analysis of cases of obligatory preverbal placement, up to now described in terms of non-exhaustive focus (Portuguese) or contrastive focus (Spanish or Italian) (section 4.3). I show how the GPC accounts for these cases without resorting to any extra categories.

4.1 The Notion of Given Content

The notion of given content is introduced in analyses of prosody.[26] I adopt the definition of Beyssade *et al.* (2003), which links the notion of given content to that of discourse topic (henceforth DT):

(30) Given content is the content of the open proposition that expresses the core content of the discourse topic, its 'common denominator'.

I assume here that the DT is defined by a question (the question under debate) and that the analysis of the <question, answer> pair reveals the structure and

[26] It plays a crucial role in analyses of intonation; see Schwarzschild (1999) and Büring (1998), who demonstrate that it is the crucial factor in Focus-marking intonation.

the dynamics of the DT (Büring 1997). I also assume an analysis of questions along the lines of Hamblin (1973): the denotation of a question is the set of propositions that resolve it. From this perspective, an answer conveys a proposition that is a member of this set. By hypothesis, an utterance develops the DT when it resolves the question under debate at the moment of utterance; that is, it conveys a proposition that belongs to the denotation of this question. I illustrate the model directly by means of two QA pairs that show a contrast in subject placement.[27]

4.1.1 The notion of given content

I compare two dialogue configurations that show two different ways of elaborating the same discourse topic. First, I take the QA pair in which free inversion is felicitous: example (2), repeated in (31) below.

(31) S ¿Quién comió la manzana? *Who ate the apple?*
  a. Ha comido la manzana María.
  b. #María ha comido la manzana.
  Maria ate the apple.

We can identify the DT defined by the question in (31) as the set of propositions capable of resolving it (32a); the open proposition (32b) represents the given content, i.e. the common content of the DT:[28]

(32) a. DT: {Marie ate the apple, Pierre ate the apple, ...}
  b. Given content: *x* **ate the-apple**

Note that in this case, the given content overlaps with the content that makes up the ground. A single variable is introduced that corresponds to the object of the question. The predicate *ha comido la manzana* belongs to the given content in (31).

Now, consider the QA pair (18), partly repeated in (33), in which inversion is infelicitous:

(33) I Chi ha ridipinto il tavolo? *Who repainted the table?*
  a. Maria l'ha scrostato, ...
  b. #L'ha scrostato Maria, ...
  Maria sanded it, ...

In (33), the answer (33a) does not address the question directly; nevertheless, it does contribute some information for the resolution of the question. This

27 This presentation is informal; see Büring (1997) or Beyssade *et al.* (2003; 2004) for the formal details and empirical arguments.

28 For the sake of readability, I adopt an informal notation. Propositions are represented by the utterances that express them. Open propositions are represented as English sentences with variables in italics and constants in bold.

answering strategy (often attested in conversation) is interpreted by Büring as a special strategy for developing the DT: the speaker introduces an intermediate question (*Who sanded the table?*) that defines a sub-topic within the global topic corresponding to the original question (33a).[29] Intuitively, the speaker considers different aspects of the overall painting process. In terms of the model adopted here, the DT can be defined as a set of sets of propositions (corresponding to the denotations of the original question and of the intermediate question), as shown in (34a). The common content of the DT is represented in (34b):

(34) a. DT: {{Marie sanded the table, Pierre sanded la table, ...}, {Marie repainted the table, Paul repainted the table, ...}, ...}
b. Given: x P **the-table**

In this case, the verb is not part of the given content. The open proposition (34b) introduces two variables: the individual variable x, which restricts the focal content of the answer, and the predicate variable P. In a way, the instantiation of P (by the predicate *scrostare* in (33)) constitutes new information; it is interesting to note that in certain languages, it is not realized prosodically in the same way as focused content: in German and French, it carries an accent similar to the English B accent (see Büring 1997, 1998 for German, Marandin *et al.* 2002 for French).

4.1.2 The Given Predicate Condition

I abandon the notion of repetition and propose that the felicity condition for inversion should be formulated in terms of the notion of given content (35). This amounts to adopting a pragmatic definition of the condition.

(35) Given Predicate Condition (GPC):
Inversion is felicitous if the predicate is given.

The GPC readily accounts for the felicity of free inversion and its infelicity in answers that do not repeat the VP because they change the ongoing DT, as in (18) analyzed in (34) above. Since it does not mention the status of the subject in the focus-ground structure, the GPC can apply to emphatic order of Spanish (see (23) above) or to the different syntactic types of inversion of French, in particular in the relative clauses of (25) above. I will elaborate on these two cases below.

4.1.3 Obligatory postverbal placement of the subject in free inversion

I return briefly to the obligatoriness of inversion when the subject NP is in narrow focus in the Romance languages that allow free inversion (the contrast

---

[29] Technically, the intermediate question is accommodated. For a critical evaluation of this model, see Marandin (2005).

between (31a) and (31b) above), in order to highlight the fundamental difference between generalization (13) and the GPC (35).

It is generally assumed that the Romance languages have an accentuation rule analogous to the English Nuclear Stress Rule (NSR): The constituent that is most deeply embedded or furthest to the right carries the most salient accent. It is also agreed that the constituent that contributes focal information is prosodically distinguished in the Romance languages. We can suppose, then, that the focal constituent can be prosodically distinguished by being assigned the most salient accent when on the right edge of the utterance.[30]

The GPC is neutral with respect to this hypothesis: It merely establishes a condition on the licensing of inversion. If the condition is satisfied contextually, inversion is possible, and (supposing that the prosodic organization proposed for the Romance languages is correct) we can assume that it is obligatory because it gives rise to a direct alignment of prosody and constituent order. In other words, such an alignment targets the subject NP if and only if the GPC licenses postverbal placement. It should be made clear what this implies for the pragmatic or information-structural analysis of the contrast between pre- and postverbal placement of the subject. Subject placement is not *per se* a focus marker, a 'Focus-Marking' device (Büring 1998), but it may create a configuration in which a prosodic marking strategy for focal content applies to the subject NP, as it applies to other constituents.

4.2 Empirical Diversity of Given Content

For the sake of clarity, up to now I have used QA pairs in which the given content corresponds to the repeated content. The definition of given content in (30) does not mention the lexical material that expresses the DT content. In other words, one might expect that the same content could be expressed by propositions with different lexical material, and conversely, that the repeated content might not count as given content. I illustrate the two cases in the following subsections.

4.2.1 Given content is not necessarily repeated

I present two typical examples where inversion is felicitous even though the predicate is realized lexically in different ways in the question and in the answer. The QA pair (36) was constructed on the basis of the attested example (86) below; the QA pair (37) is taken from a film by Pedro Almodóvar.[31]

---

[30] A particularly clear presentation of this hypothesis can be found in Zubizarreta (1998). Beyssade *et al.* (2004) show that this hypothesis is not correct for French; the prosodic organization of French is clearly distinct from that of English.

[31] I owe (37) to Lambrecht who analyzes it in (2004, ex. 21).

(36) [Who assassinated Kennedy?]
C El va matar l'Oswald.
S Lo mató Oswald.
I L'ha ucciso Oswald.
P Matou-o o Oswald.
Oswald killed him.

(37) [How do you know?]
S Me lo ha contado Huma.
Huma told me.

In these two pairs, the respondant reformulates the question without modifying the issue under discussion. From the perspective of topic development, the two pairs are analogous to pair (31). In pair (36), the speaker treats *to kill* and *to assassinate* as synonymous verbs for the issue under discussion. In pair (37), the question *Who told you?* is treated as equivalent to *How do you know?* In the first case, the reformulation exploits a lexical near synonymy (the speaker neutralizes the difference in meaning of the two verbs for the definition of the DT), and in the second, a near synonymy of a pragmatic nature: One can choose to answer either question (*How do you know?* or *Who told you?*) in a situation where knowing something (concerning someone's private life) necessarily means having been told about it.

Speakers recognize this situation. Thus, informants answer the question in (38) by using either a preverbal or a postverbal subject:[32]

(38) [Who was responsible for the racers?]
C a. Els ha entrenat en Pau.
b. En Pau els ha entrenat.
S a. Los entrenó Pablo.
b. Pablo los entrenó.
I a. Li ha allenati Paul.
b. Paul li ha allenati.

[32] Below, I give another example of the same type, taken from the survey:

(i) [Who prepared the baked apples?]
C La Maria les ha pelat.
S María las peló.
I Maria le ha sbucciate. / Le ha sbucciate Maria.
P A Maria descascou-as. / Descascou-as a Maria.
Marie peeled them.

The two possibilities (not equally natural, according to informants, as one might expect) reflect the fact that in this situation the question *Who prepared the baked apples?* can be treated as pragmatically equivalent or not to *Who peeled the apples?* with regard to the amount of work required for this dish: once the apples are peeled, very little remains to be done to finish the recipe.

P a. Treinou-os o Paulo.
b. O Paulo treinou-os.
Paul trained them.

They do, however, observe a difference in meaning between the answer with the postverbal subject (version a) and the preverbal version (version b). In the (a) versions, Paul trained all the racers under consideration in the question. In the (b) versions, he trained some of them, which implies that he is not solely responsible for all the racers under consideration. This holds in a context where Paul is a trainer and where there are several categories of people who are responsible for the racers (trainers, doctors, coaches, etc.) This difference explains the effect of incompleteness that characterizes the (b) versions: they do not exhaust the issue, considering the set of all racers in the situation.

In the (a) versions, the speaker treats the verbs *to be responsible for* and *to train* as synonymous; consequently, the content of the VP *trained the racers* counts as given content:

(39) a. DT: {Paul was responsible for the racers, Marie was responsible for the racers, ...}
b. Given: [to be responsible for ≡ to train] *x* **trained the-racers**

In the (b) versions, we have a context analogous to the one triggering obligatory preverbal placement of the subject in (33). The speaker distinguishes several aspects of the issue defined by the question.

(40) a. DT: { {Paul was responsible for the racers, Marie was responsible for the racers, ...}, {Marie trained the racers, Pierre trained the racers, ...}}
b. Given: *x P* **the-racers**

The condition for inversion is not satisfied: The verb is not given, and so the predicate does not belong to the given content in the discourse context.

It is interesting that an identical distinction turns up in the comments of French informants concerning the pre- or postverbal placement of the subject in the relative clauses in (25), repeated below in (41):

(41) Que sont devenus les étudiants dont Bernard s'est occupé ?
What became of the students that Bernard was responsible for?
F a. Les étudiants que Bernard a entraînés ont tous réussi aux Olympiades universitaires.
b. Les étudiants qu'a entraîné Bernard ont tous réussi aux Olympiades universitaires.
The students that Bernard trained were all successful at the university Olympiads.

The answer in (41b) refers to the same set of students as introduced by the question. The answer in (41a) strongly implies that the set of students that Bernard trained is a subset of those he was responsible for. As such, (41a) is perceived as a partial response that calls for the discourse to be continued to mention the other students (25b.i): *Les étudiants que Bernard a entraînés ont réussi aux Olympiades, ceux qu'il a soignés sont devenus prof de gym.* (The students that Bernard trained won at the Olympiads, those that he treated became gym teachers.) For speakers who produce (41a), the given content in the thematic context can be represented as in (42); the predicate is not given in the relative clause:

(42) Given: **the-students (Bernard *P* the-students) became** *x*

French informants are quite firm about the interpretation of the contrast between pre- and postverbal subject placement in the relative clauses in (41). I take this as a strong indication that the GPC is operative in licensing French stylistic inversion in subordinate clauses. By the same token, the GPC is a condition that applies independently of the syntactic realization of the inversion, which is why it can apply cross-linguistically.

4.2.2 Repeated material is not necessarily given

The survey included a context in which informants judged an answer with a preverbal subject to be just as felicitous as an answer with a postverbal subject, even though the verb from the question is repeated and the NP *Pierre* is syntactically focused in the question:[33]

(43) [Was it Pierre who ate the cake?]

C	a.	Sí, en Pere se l'ha menjat.	b. Sí, se l'ha menjat en Pere.
S	a.	Sí, Pedro se la comió.	b. Sí, se la comió Pedro.
I	a.	Si, Pietro l'ha mangiato.	b. Si, l'ha mangiato Pietro.
P	a.	Sim, comeu-o o Pedro.	b. Sim, o Pedro comeu-o.
		Yes, Pierre ate it.	

All of the material from the question can be omitted in this kind of QA pair (with an answer reduced to *Yes*), which signals that the entire content of the VP can be considered as given.[34] In the same context, answers that confirm Pierre's role in the disappearance of the cake, but modify the question, do not allow inversion:

---

[33] In the survey, the context was defined in the following manner: 'A mother speaks to a group of children. The birthday cake has disappeared. [Answer without using a cleft].' Unfortunately I do not have reliable data concerning the prosody of these utterances in Spanish and Portuguese.

[34] Beyssade *et al.* (2003) explicitly propose that ellipsis targets given material. A similar analysis is found in Ginzburg and Sag (2000).

(44) [Was it Pierre who ate the cake?]

C	a. En Pere l'ha amagat.	b. #L'ha amagat en Pere.
S	a. No, Pedro la escondió.	b. #No, la escondió Pedro.
I	a. Pietro l'ha nascosto.	b. #L'ha nascosto Pietro.
P	a. Não, o Pedro escondeu-o.	b. #Não, escondeu-o o Pedro.
	Pierre hid it.	

Thus, the inversion in the answers in (43b) does seem to fall under the GPC. Why then do informants judge preverbal placement to be just as felicitous? One clue is the difference in meaning that informants report. In this context, the answers with a preverbal subject (43a) do not trigger an effect of incompleteness; on the contrary, they are felt to be complete statements with a strong effect of confirmation.

Such a difference in meaning suggests the following explanation in the present framework. The speaker treats the content of the VP as not given, and repeats it in his/her answer. By doing so, the speaker presents the content of the answer as his/her own contribution to the ongoing interaction. She takes responsibility for and asserts the entire propositional content.

If the explanation of the contrast between the (a) and (b) answers in (43) is on the right track, it must be admitted that the pre- or postverbal placement of the subject is not uniformly linked to a single effect in discourse. Preverbal placement of the subject either occurs in a move that results in the splitting of the DT into several related subtopics or in a move that strongly marks the commitment of the speaker to the propositional content conveyed by his/her utterance.[35]

4.2.3 Given situational content

The analysis of inversion in announcements is a recurring problem in the literature; an 'announcement' is a short discourse that is not part of a conversation. Announcements can have pre- or postverbal subjects. Most cases exhibit the features of presentational inversion (section 5.6 below). But some others have the features of inversion licensed by the GPC (35):

(45) C Es crema el pastís!
S ¡Se está quemando la torta!
I Brucia il dolce!
P Está-se a queimar o bolo!
The cake is burning!

[35] Büring (1997) lists three different ways of splitting the DT: partial, contrastive, and purely implicational (1997:56). My proposal predicts that inversion should not be felicitous in utterances executing any of these three thematic moves.

In this case, the VP can be omitted, and the utterances are pragmatically equivalent to utterances comprising a single NP:[36]

(46) F a. i. Le bébé pleure ! *The baby is crying!*
ii. Le bébé ! *The baby!*
b. i. La tarte brûle ! *The pie is burning!*
ii. La tarte ! *The pie!*

The possibility of omitting the VP is an indication that its content is given. But it is not given in the thematic progression (since announcements do not follow a preceding discourse). The informants observe that announcements of the type exemplified in (45) are not felicitous unless the speakers hear the baby crying or smell the burning cake (or see a clock indicating that the intended cooking time has been exceeded, etc.) We can therefore hypothesize that the VP content is given in the situation. Assuming that the utterance situation can play the same role as the DT (47a), we can characterize the contextual configuration for inversion as satisfying the GPC. The predicate is given (47b):[37]

(47) a. Situation: {the cake is-burning, ...} or {something is-burning, ...}
b. Given: **The-cake is-burning** or x **is-burning**

I will go no further into the analysis of this type of announcement: One would have to construct a notion of DT capable of integrating the utterance situation, and this would take us well beyond the domain of this study of the Romance languages.

4.3 Recalcitrant Cases

We still need an explanation for the cases of obligatory preverbal subject placement presented in section 3.1.1 to show the inadequacy of generalization (13) (as a felicity condition for inversion). An NP that has been analyzed as a non-exhaustive focus in Portuguese (14) or as a contrastive (or emphatic) focus in Spanish (15) or Italian (16) appears preverbally. I take these in turn in the following subsections.

4.3.1 Non-exhaustive focus in Portuguese

I come back to example (14), repeated as (48) below. I show that the analysis that I develop here is capable of handling this case without multiplying the

[36] This observation is due to Claire Beyssade. I also thank Alda Mari, whose comments on announcements in Italian suggested this analysis to me.

[37] There is no constraint on the DR corresponding to the subject: it can either be identified or not.

types of focus. Preverbal placement is required because the GPC is not satisfied contextually, even though the predicate is repeated.

(48) [Who ate the cake?]
P a. i. (A tarte) comeu a Joana.
ii. #A Joana comeu (a tarte).
b. i. #(A tarte) comeu a Joana (*about the others I do not know*).
ii. A Joana comeu (*about the others I do not know*).
Joana ate the cake.

The comment indicating the incompleteness effect associated with (48b.ii) (*about the others I do not know*) is ambiguous. It can mean: (i) 'The others (Pierre, Paul, ...) did not eat the cake, they refused it, they ate something else, etc.' or else (ii) 'Joana ate the whole cake, almost all of the cake, Pierre ate the crumbs, etc.' Given these two discourse configurations, preverbal placement is expected, since the GPC is not satisfied.

In the former configuration (i), the speaker considers several people and their actions. The DT is therefore complex and involves several interrelated intermediate questions, according to our hypothesis. The situation is analogous to that of (33) above.[38] The DT has no fixed common content.[39]

(49) a. DT: { {Joana ate the cake, Pierre ate the cake, ...}, {Pierre ate a fruit, Paul ate a fruit, ...}, {Pierre refused the cake, Paul refused the cake , ...} }
b. Given: $x\ P\ y$

As in (33), in the (b) answers in (38) or (41) above, the preverbal subject triggers an incompleteness effect, and this effect cannot simply be reduced to the effect associated with non-exhaustive focus. The notion of non-exhaustive focus merely reflects the fact that an utterance does not give all the instantiations of the focal variable introduced by the question (here *Who ate the cake?*). In the case considered here, the incompleteness effect is not confined to the resolution of the question *Who ate the cake?* It is more global and relates to the thematic development. The speaker considers several instantiations of the focal variable, along with several instantiations of the variable (or variables) introduced in the collection of questions that define the discourse

---

[38] The informants produced answers with a preverbal subject in response to the question *Who repainted the table?* when the answers go on to mention different stages of the table-painting process, but also when the answers mention other activities related to this process within the same situation, i. e. in situations that were described as in (i) below.
(i) a. [Who repainted the table?] Marie sanded it, Pierre painted the top, ...
b. [Who repainted the table?] Marie sanded it, Pierre prepared the dinner, ...

[39] Such an explanation of the contrasts in (48) crucially relies on the distinction between the construct concept *given* and the descriptive notion of *repeated*.

topic (*P*, *y* in (49b)). The opposition exhaustive vs. non-exhaustive focus only partially characterizes the effect associated with this type of utterance and leads to an inadequate explanation. After all, the answer may be complete with regard to the question (treated as an intermediate question by the respondant) since in the context, Joana may be the only one who ate the cake. It remains incomplete with regard to the DT initiated by the question: The respondant has more to say about the cake or the eating of the cake or the persons related to the cake and its eating.

In the latter configuration, which I reconstruct explicitly in (50), the content of the verb is part of the common content, but the content of the predicate is not, as (51b) shows:[40]

(50) P Quem comeu a tarte? *Who ate the tart?*
A Maria comeu metade e as crianças o resto.
Maria ate half of it and the kids the rest.

(51) a. DT: {Maria ate half of the cake, Pierre ate a quarter of the cake, the kids ate the rest of the cake, ... }
b. Given: *x* **ate a-portion-of-cake** *y*

Once again, the GPC is not satisfied; hence, inversion is not felicitous. Then, I conclude that the GPC succeeds in explaining away the obligatory preverbal placement of subjects observed by Ambar in answers to Subject Constituent Questions in Portuguese. In fact, the explanation is not specific to Portuguese: Inversion is never felicitous in answers that correspond to a partial elaboration of the DT initiated by the question.

4.3.2 Contrastive or emphatic foci

The notions of contrast or emphasis have an impressive range of meanings in the literature.[41] Hence, the characterization of a use or a construction in terms of contrast or emphasis is simply useless as long as precise definitions are not given. More data is needed to understand what is going on with the emphatic order of Spanish (15) and Kiss' data in Italian (16). In particular, we need to know more about the prosodic realization of the fronted subject XP in both cases and about the impact of such utterances on their contexts. Thus, this section must be considered tentative.

The obligatory preverbal placement of the subject in Emphatic Order when the VP is not repeated is an indication that the GPC applies to emphatic order. See (23) above or (52) below.

---

[40] Inversion is infelicitous in this context in all of the languages under consideration.

[41] I refer the reader to Umbach (2004) (among others) for an overview of the different meanings.

(52) S ¿Dónde trabajan Pierre y Paul? *Where do Pierre and Paul work?*
a. i. Los pobres desgraciados trabajan en Jussieu.
ii. En JUSSIEU trabajan los pobres desgraciados.
The poor things work at Jussieu
b. i. ??#EN JUSSIEU pierden el tiempo (los pobres desgraciados).
ii. (Los pobres desgraciados) pierden el tiempo en Jussieu.
They / the poor things waste their time at Jussieu.

In what discourse configuration does it occur? The current proposal predicts two possible discourse configurations. Either utterances with Emphatic Order and preverbal subject are dialogue moves changing the DT initiated by the question, in particular partial answers that partially elaborate the current DT as in (18) or (48b) above. Or, they are reinforced statements like the answers (a) in (43) above: The speaker signals his/her strong commitment to the propositional content by treating the whole content of his/her utterance as non given.

As for (16) in Italian, repeated below as (53), Kiss does not give details about the prosodic realization of the preverbal subject NP. According to informants, it strongly resembles the one that is observed in utterances analyzed with contrastive XPs by Rizzi (1997) and illustrated in (54).[42] Contrary to Rizzi's claim, the notion of contrastive is not relevant here: the fronted XP, that is a negative expression, cannot be analyzed as denoting an element in a set of alternatives.[43]

(53) I Chi di voi due ha rotto il vaso? *Which of you two broke the vase?*
a. Maria ha rotto il vaso.
b. L'ha rotto Maria il vaso.

(54) I A: Suo fratello e suo cugino sono appena arrivati. Sai chi inviterà?
Her brother and her cousin have just arrived. Do you know whom she will invite?

[42] Notice that such utterances may license a reinforced form of negation (preverbal n-word with sentential *non*) for some speakers of Italian.

[43] In the examples below, provided by Godard and Marandin (2006), the fronted XPs are not contrastive.

(i) I A. Allora sono arrivati i pacchi?
So, have the packets arrived?
B. No, NESSUNO (non) è ancora partito!
No, none has even gone yet!

(ii) I A chi ha parlato Maria per tutta la serata?
To whom did Maria speak the whole evening?
Al suo ex-RAGAZZO ha parlato (Maria).
She spoke to her ex-boy friend.

B: a. Nessuno dei DUE la stupida (non) inviterà.
b. Nessuno dei DUE (non) inviterà la stupida.

According to Godard and Marandin (2006), the answers in (53) and (54) are instances of a construction that conveys proposition deferment or proposition denial—i. e., moves that object to contextually activated propositions. In both instances, they object to a proposition inferable from the question (*either you or Maria has broken the vase*, *Maria (the stupid one) will invite her brother and / or her cousin*) and may result in questioning the very relevance of the question. For example, an informant reports that (53a) strongly evokes the proposition 'I haven't done it'. This is a clue that utterances featuring such a construction belong to moves that modify the DT initiated by the question. The question is then why they seem to allow relatively easily the postverbal placement of the subject NP? I am not yet in a position to answer this question, which deserves a specific survey. But, a comment can be safely made here: the notion of contrastive, or identificational, focus is of no use in accounting for it, since it requires a propositional antecedent and not a set of individual alternatives.

4.4 Conclusion

The GPC relies crucially on the notion of given content, defined independently of the focus-ground partition. It is meant to be a unified principle to account for the obligatory preverbal placement of the subject NP and for the possibility of inversion in languages that impose distinct syntactic licensing conditions on inversion. In addition, the GPC allows an explanation of the contexts where pre- and postverbal placement are both felicitous, with a difference in meaning recognized by informants. Two cases must be distinguished. In the first (illustrated by (38), (41), (43) with the configuration (44)), the lexical material taken from the context (by the answer to the question) can be considered either to convey given content, or not. In either case, the utterance with preverbal subject is associated with a thematic incompleteness effect. In the second case (illustrated by (43)), the lexical material taken from the context (by the answer to the question) is not considered to convey given content: The speaker chooses to take over the content and to present it as the informative contribution of his own utterance to the context. In this case, the utterance has the effect of a reinforced assertion. The analysis therefore accounts for not only the felicity condition for inversion, but also paves the way for a characterization of the effects of inversion in discourse.

5 The presupposed disposition condition

I turn now to inversions that occur independently of the discourse status of the VP. We have already seen some examples in utterances involving presentational inversion in section 3.2. In this section, I make explicit the claim that it involves another felicity condition. This type of inversion has two characteristic features: (a) The referent of the subject and the property described by the VP stand in a relation traditionally called 'semantic solidarity'[44] and (b) The inversion has a presentational effect. The utterance introduces an eventuality and/or a participant in this eventuality into the universe of discourse. I propose analyzing the idea of solidarity with the help of the notion of disposition (Bourdieu 1995) and deriving the presentational effect from the thetic nature of the proposition conveyed by the utterance (see among others Kuroda 1973). This kind of inversion presupposes (in a pragmatic sense) the attribution of the disposition described by the predicate to the referent of the subject. The thetic effect follows from this presupposition. The utterance does not attribute a disposition, rather it describes a manifestation of a disposition that is treated as a commonly shared characteristic of the referent of the subject. The notions of disposition and pragmatic presupposition are thus at the heart of the second felicity condition, the Presupposed Disposition Condition (PDC). There are at least three modes of disposition presupposition. It can be part of the encyclopedic knowledge that the speaker has about the referent of the subject (section 5.2) or part of the contextually accessible knowledge about the referent of the subject (section 5.3). Finally, I make the hypothesis that the presupposition can be part of the narrative code, in order to handle a recalcitrant type of presentational inversion (section 5.5). The appeal to the notion of theticity is motivated in section 5.4. I will claim that the PDC is always what makes presentational inversion felicitous;[45] but it is not restricted to this type of inversion. For example, locative inversion, which is arguably an instance of stylistic inversion in French, obeys the PDC. Thus, the PDC is a condition on inversion in general and it appears under several guises that are linked to different modes of disposition presupposition.

5.1 Preliminaries

5.1.1 Utterances with presentational inversion

I make a broad distinction between two types of utterances involving presentational inversion: utterances where the verb describes a stereotypical property of the referent of the subject (55) and utterances where the verb describes

---

[44] The term and the observation are apparently due to Coseriu (1967); see also to Bernini (1995:56), who mentions other work.

[45] Except in contexts in which the GPC applies, such as (29) above.

the presence, appearance, or disappearance of the referent of the subject in a given place (56).[46]

(55) I a. Suonavano le campane. *Bells were ringing.*
b. Abbaiavano i cani. *Dogs were barking.*

(56) I È entrato il marito. *The husband entered.*
E Llega el tren. *The train arrives.*

The same distinction can be made for utterances involving locative inversion.[47] The term 'locative inversion' is a descriptive label refering to the surface configuration [$PP_{locative}$ V NP_{theme}]; it suggests nothing about the syntactic analysis of the configuration in the different languages.

(57) F a. Dans le salon papotait un groupe de femmes.
In the living room was chattering a group of women.
b. Sur la place poussait un grand figuier.
On the square grew a big fig tree.
I a. In questo palazzo ha vissuto un poeta. (Pinto, 1997:68, ex 43c)
In this palace lived a poet.
b. In questa università hanno studiato molti linguisti. (Pinto, 1997: 68, ex. 43e)
In this university studied many linguists.

(58) F De la maison sortit un groupe d'hommes cagoulés.
Out of the house walked a group of masked men.
I a. Dalla commissione vengono due commenti. (Bernini,1995:63, ex. 39) *From the committee come two comments.*
b. Sul palato artificiale vengono fissati 62 elettrodi d'argento. (Sornicola, 1994:39, ex. 11)
On the artifical palate are fixed 62 silver electrodes.

[46] It is intriguing that attempts at characterizing the family of verbs compatible with presentational inversion fail to dissociate the meaning of the verbs themselves from the overall presentational effect of the entire utterance. For example, Wehr (1984:53), quoting Hatcher (1956:7), claims that in presentational inversion, 'the verbs [...] tell us only or mainly that the subject exists or is present; is absent, begins, continues, is produced, occurs, appears, arrives.' This results in a confusion of lexical meaning and sentential meaning and prevents one from factoring out what is common to these verbs. Lambrecht (1994:181) does dissociate the meaning of the verbs and the function of the utterance. He recognizes the lack of agentivity as the relevant feature for a verb to be used presentationally: 'there is an upper limit to the degree of agentivity a predicate can have to be exploitable as presentational and thus to be able to appear with presentational syntax or prosody.' Yet, the problem is that the presentational function he postulates does not correspond to a homogeneous and unified set of syntactic or prosodic constructions.

[47] Out of caution, I restrict myself to locative inversion in French and in Italian.

Note the lexico-syntactic heterogeneity of the examples above: The sentences in (55) and (57) contain verbs that are said to be unergative, while the verbs in (56) or (58) are said to be unaccusative.[48]

5.1.2 The notion of disposition

Attributing a disposition to an individual means expecting that he will behave in a certain way when the conditions for the manifestation of this disposition are met. To say that Jean is jealous is to say that Jean will behave in a way typical of a jealous person if he should find himself in a situation that can trigger this type of behavior. Thus the predicate *jealous* is said to describe a disposition. Philosophical analyses distinguish two kinds of disposition: strong disposition (or tendency) and weak disposition (or capacity) (Ryle 1949).

> Attributing a tendency to an individual amounts to predicting that he will behave according to this tendency when certain conditions are met, while attributing a capacity amounts to denying that if he has the opportunity of behaving according to this capacity, he will not do it necessarily (adapted from Bourdieu, 1995:65).

For example, bells have a tendency to ring (bells ring when the circumstances allow them to ring) or Pierre has the capacity to play tennis (Pierre plays tennis when the circumstances allow it and nothing stands in the way of it). In one case we predict an eventuality, in the other we predict the possibility of an eventuality.

The notion of tendency (strong disposition) will allow us to capture more precisely the stereotype effect observed in the cases of inversion illustrated in (55) and (57). For example, an utterance such as *Bells ring* describes a crucial property that one must be familiar with to use the noun *bell* appropriately, in the same way that the use of the term *lemon* requires that the speaker is familiar with the propositions 'lemons are yellow, lemons are tart, lemon juice is good to quench one's thirst, etc.' (Putnam 1975). The notion of capacity (weak disposition) will allow us to account for another case of inversion that I illustrate using French stylistic inversion in section 5.3. For the time being, I leave aside the characterization of utterances involving verbs of presence, appearance, or disappearance, as illustrated in (56) and (58); I will come back to them in section 5.5.

Bourdieu emphasizes the conditional character of the disposition attribution: A disposition only manifests itself if certain specific circumstances obtain. He makes this explicit in definition (59), where '>' stands for the modal conditional (1995:107). In every possible world sufficiently similar to the

[48] Locative inversion in French is an ordinary case of stylistic inversion (with topicalization of PP) (Bonami *et al.* 1998).

present world, where the individual *i* finds himself in a situation *o* where he has the opportunity to act according to behavior *c*, *i* acts according to *c*.

(59) disposed (i,c) ⇔ (∃o (be-in (i,o) & be-an-appropriate-situation-for (o,c)) > behaves-according-to (i,c))

I illustrate definition (59) (which I have simplified for readability) by taking the example of the strong disposition associated with bells (60) and I introduce the contrast between a dispositional utterance (61a) and an utterance that describes the manifestation of a disposition (61b). In dispositional utterances, the tendency is attributed to the referent of the subject (the utterance expresses a categorical proposition), whereas in utterances describing a manifestation of the tendency, the tendency can be presupposed. The utterances with postverbal subject (55) are exactly the ones in which the attribution of the tendency is presupposed (the utterance expresses a thetic proposition):

(60) ∀*x* ((bell (*x*) & be-in-a-situation-of ringing (*x*) > ring (*x*))

(61) a. Les cloches sonnent.
Bells ring.
b. A sept heures, les cloches sonnaient.
At seven o'clock, bells were ringing.

I propose that the general form of the presupposed disposition condition should be as in (62). The term 'presupposed' is used in its pragmatic (and not logical) sense, meaning 'present in the cognitive state of the speaker at the time of utterance':

(62) Presupposed Disposition Condition (PDC):
Inversion is felicitous if the disposition *d* described by the predicate is characteristic of the referent of the subject and presupposed by the speaker.

The PDC is completely independent of focus-ground structure, which explains why it licenses inversion in both root and subordinate clauses (see (10) above for example). Moreover, it is independent of the discourse status of the VP, which explains its independence with respect to the local topic development. The only discourse constraint that applies to such an inversion is linked to the conditional nature of disposition attribution: the situation that is described should be one that gives rise to the manifestation of the disposition of the particular referent denoted by the subject.

5.2 Strong Disposition in Encyclopedic Knowledge

5.2.1 The condition

The first type of inversion licensed by the PDC is exemplified in the short discourse in (63). It involves a strong disposition in the encyclopedic knowledge of the speaker:

(63) I [Alle sette di sera rientrò al villaggio.] Suonavano le campane. [Abbaiavano i cani. Si diresse verso la chiesa.]
At seven o'clock, he returned to the village. Bells were ringing. Dogs were barking. He went to the church.

Two factors contribute to the felicity of the inversion: (a) The speaker knows (60), and (b) The situation described in the context is one in which the disposition can manifest itself. In (63), the world described is that of a village at the hour of the angelus.[49]

The particular form of the PDC in this case is given in (64): (64a) is a condition on the knowledge of the speaker (which in this case is nearly indistinguishable from his lexical knowledge) and (64b) is a condition on the discourse environment.[50]

(64) Presupposed strong disposition condition:
  a. The speaker knows of a strong disposition that is typical of the referent of the subject: [$\forall x$ (D(x) & be-in-the-situation-of D > D(x))]
  b. The context describes a situation appropriate for the manifestation of D(x).

Condition (64b) explains why utterances featuring such an inversion do not occur at the beginning of a narrative. They require a situation that is already introduced, such that it makes possible the manifestation of the disposition of the DR corresponding to the first argument of the verb.[51]

---

[49] The same analysis applies to *Abbaiavano i cani*.

[50] The subject can be a proper noun. In this case, P is implicit (Olivier Bonami, p.c.):

(i) F Le silence se fit. Alors commença à sonner Big Ben.
Silence fell. Then Big Ben began ringing.

[51] This fact has been noted in traditional grammatical descriptions. For example, Le Bidois (1950) writes: 'This type of inversion ['absolute inversion', in Le Bidois's taxonomy] only occurs within a narrative. Indeed, it should be recognized that absolute inversions usually occur in the course of a narrative, for the simple reason that it is hard to speak of an event happening before the circumstances in which it occurs have been introduced' (1950:21). The utterance situation can play this role, which explains why there are announcements where inversion is licensed by the PDC (see section 5.4.2).

5.2.2 The Presupposed strong Disposition Condition in French

The Presupposed strong Disposition Condition is operative in French and licenses several types of inversion with distinct syntactic properties. First, it licenses the inversion that is found in root clauses of narrative discourse.[52] Such an inversion has an additional constraint that explains why (63) cannot be translated as (65): The eventuality must be a transition, which is enforced in (66b): [53]

(65) F *[Pierre rentra au village à sept heures.] Sonnaient les cloches, aboyaient les chiens.

(66) F a. # On éteignit les lumières. Aussitôt aboyèrent les chiens.
The lights were switched off. Immediately barked the dogs
b. On éteignit les lumières. Aussitôt se mirent à aboyer les chiens.
The lights were switched off. Immediately the dogs started barking.

The Presupposed strong Disposition Condition (64) applies to locative inversion. According to (64a), the state or activity described by the verb must denote a disposition of the referent of the subject. This is what the contrasts in (67) and (68) below illustrate. In (67), *papoter* ('to chit-chat') might be considered to be a tendency of women (they chit-chat whenever they have the chance) but not *crier* ('to shout'):[54]

---

[52] It is analyzed as an instance of unaccusative construction in Marandin (2001). Note that it is constructionally restricted to narrative discourse, it is not used in oral discourse (compare this with (4) above):

(i) F a. [What happened then?] *Sonnèrent les cloches. 'rang the bells'
b. [What happened then?] *Se mirent à sonner les cloches. 'started to ring the bells'

[53] This constraint is only valid for root clauses, as (i) shows:

(i) F Je voudrais bien que n'aboient plus les chiens.
I really wish that dogs would no longer bark.

See Zaenen (1993) for the link between this kind of aspectual restriction and the unaccusative construction. In contemporary French root clauses, the sentence must also contain a temporal connective (*alors, aussitôt, auparavant,* etc.) that is not necessarily sentence-initial (which calls into question any analysis that appeals to focal preposing of the temporal adverb):

(ii) F On éteignit les lumières. Se mit aussitôt à aboyer une meute de chiens.
One switched off the lights. Started immediately to bark a pack of dogs
The lights were switched off. Immediately a pack of dogs started barking.

[54] Disposition attribution is a favored device in discriminatory discourse! There are other constructional constraints on locative inversion in French:

(i) the location described by the PP must denote a typical location for the manifestation of the tendency;
(ii) the DR corresponding to the locative NP cannot be less identifiable than that corresponding to the theme NP (Marandin 1997).

(67) F a. Il entra dans le château. Dans le salon papotait un groupe de femmes.
He came into the palace. In the lounge were chit-chatting a group of women.
b. #Il entra dans le château. Dans le salon criait un groupe de femmes.
He came into the palace. In the lounge were shouting a group of women.

In (68), *se dresser* ('to rise up') is a tendency of cathedrals, but not *s'écrouler* ('to collapse'); however, the latter is a proven tendency of sand castles:

(68) F a. Il entra dans la ville. Sur la place se dressait une cathédrale.
He entered the city. On the square towered a cathedral.
a'. #Il entra dans la ville. Sur la place s'écroulait une cathédrale.
He entered the city. On the square was collapsing a cathedral.
b. Sur la plage s'écroulait un château de sable.
On the beach was collapsing a sand castle.

5.3 Weak disposition in background knowledge

The second sort of inversion involves a weak disposition (capacity) of the referent of the subject in background knowledge. This is illustrated by the contrast in (69), with relative clauses considered out of context.[55] Inversion is possible in the relative clauses in (69a), but not in (69b); what differentiates the two relative clauses is the property denoted by the VP: *lire*, *écrire*, *acheter des livres* as opposed to *brûler des livres*.

(69) F a. La liste des livres qu'a lu / acheté / écrit Proust à l'automne 1917 ne nous est pas parvenue.
The list of the books that Proust read / bought / wrote in the fall 1917 is not known to us.
a'. La liste des livres que Proust a lus / achetés / écrits) à l'automne 1917 ne nous est pas parvenue.

---

[55] Instances of this mode of presupposition were not systemtically included in the survey; therefore I cannot present examples from the other Romance languages. I can simply mention the following Italian data in which the two properties 'wear a dress' and 'nervously rumple a dress' stand in contrast:

(i) I [Callas was depressed]
a. Il vestito nero che la diva portava / che portava la diva era macchiato di lacrime.
The black dress that the diva was wearing was stained with tears.
b. Il vestito nero che la diva stropicciava (nervosamente) / #che stropicciava la diva era macchiato di lacrime.
The black dress that the diva was rumpling nervously was stained with tears.

b. ?La liste des livres qu'a brûlé Proust à l'automne 1917 ne nous est pas parvenue.

b'. La liste des livres que Proust a brûlés à l'automne 1917 ne nous est pas parvenue.
The list of the books that Proust burned in the fall 1917 is not known to us.

Note that inversion becomes possible with *brûler des livres* ('to burn books') if the utterance appears in a discourse in which one has introduced the fact that Proust really did burn books, as illustrated by the short (fictitious) discourse in (70):[56]

(70) F Proust et Mallarmé étaient très déprimés par leurs échecs, ils détruisaient manuscrit sur manuscrit. On ne connaîtra jamais la liste des livres qu'a brûlé Proust à l'automne 1917.
Proust and Mallarmé were depressed by their failures, they kept destroying one manuscript after another. We shall never know the list of books Proust burned in the fall 1917.

The possibility of inversion in (70) proves that inversion is sensitive to information accessible in the universe of discourse. The contrast between *lire*, *écrire*, *acheter*, and *brûler (des livres)* still needs to be characterized. I propose doing this in terms of weak tendency: we expect that Proust (a writer) should read, write, and buy books, but not destroy them by burning. It is not necessary to have any particular familiarity with Proust to construct the identifying property of one or more books based on a weak disposition. Constructing a property based on an unexpected capacity is only possible if it has been introduced into the universe of discourse. A generic capacity (writers write books) licenses inversion without having to be evoked in the context, while an exceptional capacity must be introduced explicitly in the immediate context.

I will not give an explicit formulation of the PDC for this case. This would require the construction of a model of the epistemic state of the speaker, which would be too much of a digression for this study, devoted to the Romance languages (but see, for example, Ginzburg (to appear), and Marandin 2005).

We can see now why it is impossible to give a lexical characterization of inversion licensed by the PDC in general. Presentational inversion, locative inversion, and the unaccusative construction in French are restricted to intransitive verbs, but this is not the case for stylistic inversion licensed by the PDC

[56] Inversion is equally felicitous if the subject referent is changed:

(i) F On ne connaîtra jamais le nombre des livres qu'ont brûlé les nazis dans les années 30.
We shall never know the number of books the Nazis burned in the thirties.

(*écrire, acheter* are transitive). Although it is true that presentational inversion and the unaccusative construction in French are restricted to non-agentive verbs (illustrated in (71) for example), this is not the case for stylistic inversion (the subject remains agentive in the relative clauses of (69) and (70)).

(71) F a. Pierre se leva. Aussitôt se réveilla une douleur ancienne. (Atkinson 1973)
Pierre got up. Immediately woke up an ancient pain
Pierre got up. Immediately an old pain started up again.
b. *Pierre se leva. Aussitôt se réveilla Marie.
Pierre got up. Immediately Marie woke up.

5.4 Theticity

Utterances involving an inversion licensed by the PDC are thetic. The distinction between categorical and thetic propositions is based on the nature of the predication involved. In categorical propositions, a property is attributed to the referent of the subject (the subject is categorical, or else a predicatum). No property is attributed to the subject in thetic propositions. The subject denotes a participant in the eventuality in the same way as the other constituents of the utterance.

I claim that the thetic effect of inversion licensed by the PDC is related to the fact that the disposition described by the predicate is not attributed in the utterance, but presupposed by the speaker. This intuition is supported by comparing the short discourses in (72) and (73): informants clearly prefer preverbal placement of the subject in (72), and postverbal placement in (73). In (72), the utterance is situated in a context where bells have lost their disposition to ring; the utterance reestablishes this disposition, whereas in (73), the utterance describes the ringing of a bell in a completely prototypical context (a village, at the hour of the angelus, etc.):

(72) C L'església havia estat reconstruïda desprès del terratrèmol. Les campanes tornaven a tocar. La porta era completament nova.
S Después del terremoto habían reconstruido la iglesia. Las campanas volvieron a tocar, la puerta era nuevecita.
I La chiesa era stata ricostruita dopo il terremoto. Le campane suonavano di nuovo. La porta era nuova fiammante.
P A igreja fora reconstruída após o terramoto. Os sinos badalavam novamente. A porta estava novinha em folha.
The church had been rebuilt after the earthquake. Bells rang again. The door was brand new.

(73) C Va tornar al poble a les set del vespre. Tocaven les campanes, els gossos bordaven. Es va dirigir cap a l'església.
S Regresó al pueblo a las siete de la noche. Estaban tocando las campanas, ladraban los perros. Se dirigió hacia la iglesia.
I Alle sette di sera rientró al villaggio. Suonavano le campane. Abbaiavano i cani. Si diresse verso la chiesa.
P Voltou à aldeia pelas sete horas da tarde. Badalavam os sinos, ladravam os cães. Dirigiu-se à igreja.
He came back to the village at seven in the evening. Bells were ringing, dogs were barking. He went to the church.

The link between inversion and theticity in the Romance languages has been investigated in detail in Matras and Sasse (1995). The survey convincingly concludes that inversion is not always correlated with theticity. This conclusion is correct, since utterances containing an inversion licensed by the first condition, the GPC, generally convey a categorical proposition. In contrast, I claim that inversion licensed by the second condition, the PDC, has always a thetic effect.[57]

5.4.1 Empirical underpinnings

Two facts can be adduced to support this claim. First of all, a dispositional utterance (61a) can never show inversion of the subject:

(74) [What sound do dogs make?]
I a. I cani abbaiano.
b. #Abbaiano i cani.
Dogs bark.

Second, inverted subjects licensed by the PDC are strongly dispreferred as anaphoric antecedents. This is illustrated in (75) and (76) below where inversion occurs in a preposed temporal adverbial clause or in a relative clause within a preposed PP. This is in keeping with the lack of saliency of the discourse referents introduced by thetic subjects.[58]

(75) I a. Quando [i cani]$_i$ abbaiano, [e]$_i$ fanno paura a tutto il vicinato.
b. Quando abbaiano [i cani]$_i$, [e]$_{\#i}$ fanno paura a tutto il vicinato.

[57] It is generally assumed that the subject NP in utterances expressing a thetic proposition cannot be definite, which is correlated to the widely held assumption that the DR it introduces should not be identified and active. This is even considered a criterion for identifying thetic propositions. This is generally true, but not always, as we will see below.

[58] An inverted subject can be the antecedent of a pronoun in discourse, which is expected given the prevalence of accommodation in discourse (Kamp and Reyle 1973):

(i) F Le silence se fit. Aussitôt entra [un soldat en armes]$_i$. [Il]$_i$ avait fière allure.
Silence fell. Immediately an armed soldier came in. He had style.

S a. Cuando [mis perros]$_i$ ladran, [e]$_i$ asustan a todo el vecindario.
b. Cuando ladran [mis perros]$_i$, [e]$_{\#i}$ asustan a todo el vecindario.
When my dogs bark, they frighten the whole neighborhood.

(76) F a. Dans les pages que [Proust]$_i$ rédigea vers la fin de sa vie, [il]$_i$ mit toute sa haine de l'aristocratie.
a'. Dans les pages que rédigea [Proust]$_i$ vers la fin de sa vie,[il]$_{\#i}$ mit toute sa haine de l'aristocratie.
In the pages Proust wrote toward the end of his life, he put all his hatred of the gentry.

5.4.2 The presentational effect

The notion of theticity allows an account of the presentational effect found with this type of inversion. Sasse 1987 identifies two possibilities for thetic utterances in discourse: They introduce either an eventuality or a participant in the eventuality.[59] In fact, the two are not truly in opposition: The second effect is subordinate to the first, as established by Ladusaw's 1994 analysis, which I adopt.

> In a thetic judgment [a / the cat is sleeping there],[60] only the existence of the eventuality is affirmed, but commitment to that description will indirectly, obliquely […] commit the judger to the existence of the cat. […] The cat has a much fuzzier existence in the thetic judgment than it does in the categorical version, where it is presented and affirmed directly first of all, before moving on the predication. In this way, Brentano's view of the thetic mode of judgment nicely represents the effects of unselective existential closure over the description, giving priority to one object [the eventuality] while obliquely entailing the existence of subparts of the complex object. (Ladusaw, 1994: 255; underlining and comments in brackets added).

A thetic utterance describes an eventuality and the assertion of the proposition describing this eventuality implies the existence of its participants. The use of a thetic utterance therefore allows the indirect (cf. Ladusaw's 'oblique') introduction of a discourse referent by introducing an eventuality into the universe of discourse. This is what explains the discursive function usually observed for these utterances in discourse: they are used to introduce a protagonist or a circumstance relevant for the succeeding narrative. Conse-

---

59 The same opposition is found in Wehr (1984), who contrasts *Topik-Introduktion* and *neutrale Beschreibung* (1984:95).

60 Ladusaw cites Kuroda's Japanese example: *neko ga asoko de nemutte iru* ('A / the cat is sleeping there').

quently they have a meta-narrative flavor that has been noted in corpus studies of real discourse.[61]

The analysis accounts for an observation that is made frequently in studies of attested discourse concerning the contextual status of the discourse referent (DR) corresponding to the subject NP: It is not an active referent, something that is frequently illustrated with the short discourse in (77):[62]

(77) I a. #Maria mi ha scritto una lettera. È arrivata la lettera ieri.
b. Maria mi ha scritto una lettera. La lettera è arrivata ieri.
S a. #María me escribió una carta. Llegó la carta ayer.
b. María me escribió una carta. La carta llegó ayer.
Maria wrote me a letter. It arrived yesterday.

In narrative terms, the DR associated with the postverbal NP does not correspond to a protagonist of the narrative realized in the immediately preceding discourse segment. There would be a kind of pragmatic contradiction in indirectly introducing a protagonist that is already 'on stage' in the discourse.[63]

It should be noted, however, that there is no general constraint on this type of inversion prohibiting the subject from being associated with an active DR. The utterance can be used, for example, to reintroduce an active DR in a new discourse segment. This is illustrated by the contrast in (78). In (78a), the DR 'a letter' is reintroduced in the same narrative space, hence the oddness of the discourse segment (which has been confused with agrammaticality). On the other hand, in (78b), the DR is reintroduced in another spatio-temporal frame; the passage from one frame to the other is explicitly marked by the temporal phrases (*six months ago* vs *yesterday*). The discourse segment is then coherent.[64]

---

[61] For instance Bernini (1995:69) observes for the corpus he studies: 'In non-initial clauses, VS order [...] is employed only if the clause does not describe one of the subevents constituting the main line of the news item.'

[62] The contrast in (77) in Italian is due to Vanelli (1981), cited in Calabrese (1992) and since then, in countless transformational studies; the Spanish example is due to L. Martí (p.c.).

[63] This was noted by Wehr (1984:16): 'The DR that is introduced using this construction is not yet active. The utterance is used to establish it as an active DR'. I translate using my terminology. In particular, I use *active DR* instead of *Topik* since *Topik* can lead to confusion: the DR introduced does not have to be at the center of the upcoming thematic development. As Wehr herself notes, it is simply a DR that is relevant for the following discourse. I will come back to this point in section 6.

[64] I thank Luigi Mari for the contrast in (78). Here we have an example of a thetic sentence where the DR is active and identified, proving that theticity can be indifferent to the discursive status of the subject's DR. We can make the same observation in sentences with locative inversion. This is illustrated in the short discourses in (i) below, which involve a transition from a narrative segment to a descriptive segment:

(78) I a. #Maria mi ha scritto una lettera. È arrivata la lettera ieri. (= 77-Ia)
b. Maria mi ha scritto una lettera sei mesi fa. Ieri, finalmente, è arrivata la lettera.
Maria wrote me a letter six months ago. Yesterday, at last, it arrived.

5.5 Narrative Disposition

We still need to account for the examples in (56) and (58), which involve verbs of presence, appearance, and disappearance ('to come in', 'to arrive', 'to walk out', 'to die', etc.) At first sight, an analysis in terms of disposition is unavailable, even though these utterances bear a strong family resemblance to those in which inversion is licensed by the two variants of the PDC presented above. I propose a third variant of the PDC that provides an explanation for this resemblance: inversion is licensed by the attribution of a weak disposition (capacity) characteristic not of the referent of the subject, but of the protagonist of the narrative.

5.5.1 Resemblance

The utterances in (56) and (58) have the same meta-narrative flavor in discourse as the ones in (55) and (57). They describe an eventuality, so they can introduce a participant in this eventuality. They have the same distribution in discourse as the utterances licensed by variant (64) of the PDC: they cannot appear in absolute discourse-initial position. And the reason for this is apparently the same: the protagonist must appear or disappear in a situation that has already been introduced. Finally, these utterances have the same pattern concerning anaphora:[65]

(79) C a. Quan [la Maria]$_i$ va arribar, [e]$_i$ estava furiosa.
b. Quan va arribar [la Maria]$_i$, [e]$_{\#i}$ estava furiosa.
S a. Cuando [María]$_i$ llegó, [e]$_i$ estaba furiosa.
b. Cuando llegó [María]$_i$, [e]$_{\#i}$ estaba furiosa.

(i) F Pierre entra dans le salon où la Callas rencontrait Picasso pour la première fois. A la droite du piano se trouvait la diva, à gauche se tenait le maître.
Pierre came into the lounge where Callas was meeting Picasso for the first time. To the right of the piano was standing the diva, to the left the master.
I Celebravano gli ottant'anni di Picasso. Nel salone troneggiava il maestro attorniato da una folla di ammiratori.
Picasso's 80th birthday was celebrated. In the lounge was sitting enthroned the master surrounded with a throng of admirers.

[65] This pattern cannot be the mere result of the postverbal placement of the subject NP. In elaborative inversion, the postverbal subject NP is a possible antecedent in French:

(i) F Après qu'eurent parlé [les députés et les sénateurs]$_i$, [ils]$_i$ se dirigèrent vers le buffet.
After the MPs and the senators spoke, they made their way to the buffet.

I a. Quando [Maria]$_i$ arrivò, [e]$_i$ era in collera.
b. Quando arrivò [Maria]$_i$, [e]$_{\#i}$ era in collera.
P a. Quando [a Maria]$_i$ chegou, [e]$_i$ estava zangada.
b. Quando chegou [a Maria]$_i$, [e]$_{\#i}$ estava zangada.
When Mary arrived, she was furious.
F a. Quand [les enfants]$_i$ sont arrivés, [ils]$_i$ étaient en pleurs.
b. Quand sont arrivés [les enfants]$_i$, [ils]$_{\#i}$ étaient en pleurs.
When the children arrived, they were in tears.

I conclude therefore that these utterances express a thetic proposition in the same way as the examples in (55) and (57).

5.5.2 Narrative disposition

To handle these cases, I assume the concept of 'narrative disposition'. Any narrative or discourse protagonist, as an object of the discourse or narrative, has the capacity to appear in or disappear from the discourse as long as the circumstances (intrinsically bound to the discourse itself) do not preclude it. This capacity is not associated with the referent *per se*, but to the referent as a narrated object. This can be formulated as in (80):

(80) $\forall x$ ((narrative-participant (x) & be-in-a-situation-of Q) > Q(x)), where Q $\in$ {verbs of presence, appearance, or disappearance}

I also assume that the disposition of (80) is part of the narrative competence of the speaker. We can then propose that the variant of the PDC that licenses inversion is completely parallel to the one in (64):

(81) Narrative Disposition Condition:
a. The speaker is aware of the weak disposition characteristic of all discourse and narrative protagonists:
$\forall x$ ((narrative-participant (x) & be-in-a-situation of Q) > Q(x)), where Q $\in$ {verbs of presence, appearance, or disappearance}
b. The context describes a situation compatible with the manifestation of Q(x).

The parallelism between (64) and (81) is no accident. It reflects the similarity of these utterances as to their discursive use. A verb of presence, appearance, or disappearance can be used in place of a stereotypical verb in all cases where it would not be relevant to mention a dispositional property of the referent of the subject in the context of the narrative, or in cases where no such property exists (which is overwhelmingly the case for human protagonists).

Condition (81) has a strong conventional character which manifests itself in the choice of verbs that give rise to this use. I give a single example: *telefonare* in Italian, a verb that cannot be described in isolation as a verb of appearance. I adopt Lambrecht's (1994) analysis:

(82) I Ha telefonato Giovanni. *Giovanni phoned.*

> This sentence could be uttered for example to inform an addressee that in her absence the person named Giovanni tried to reach her. The utterance is a way of introducing "Giovanni" into the universe of discourse by way of mentioning the fact that he called (Lambrecht, 1994:181).

In other words, *telefonare* can act like a verb of appearance with respect to DR introduction conventions. This goes beyond the limits of a lexical approach: Referentially, *telefonare* is not a verb of appearance or of movement. This verb allows the description of a prototypical eventuality (in the modern world) in which a person makes his presence felt; this is what makes inversion of the subject possible.

5.6 Announcements

The contrast between pre- and postverbal placement of the subject in announcements (83) is completely parallel to the contrast that Schmerling (1976) points out for English (84). In English, the contrast involves the placement of the salient accent (accent A in the usual terminology, represented here by capitals). It must also be related to (20) above, a context initiated by an open question calling for a globally informative utterance: In that context, we observed that the answer can have either a pre- or a postverbal subject.

(83) I a. Truman è morto !
b. È morto Johnson !

(84) E a. Truman DIED!
b. JOHNson died!

I repeat Schmerling's description of the two situations determining the production of the utterances in (84). In the first situation, the death of Truman was expected (the media had been reporting day after day the evolution of his illness); in the second situation, Johnson's death was not foreseen. The same two situations are typical for the announcements in (83).

We saw in section 4.2.3 that inversion can be licensed by the GPC in an announcement if the predicate is given by the situation. This is not the case in the first situation: Truman was sick, not dead. The announcement of his death is therefore expected to take the form of an utterance with a preverbal subject: The predicate is not given in the situation. In the second case, Johnson's death and Johnson himself were absent from the universe of discourse (media reports); the speaker in (83b) makes use of a meta-narrative utterance that allows him to introduce Johnson's death and Johnson himself and to make them the object of the narration. The same verb 'to die' is used in both utterances (with the same semantic content). In (83a) it is treated as an ordinary predicate, and in (83b) it is used with the narrative goal of constructing a discourse object.[66] The same explanation is valid for the contrast between the pre- and postverbal subjects in the answers in (20). In other words, inversion in announcements can be analyzed along the same lines as inversion in answers. The possibility of inversion is not conditioned by the genre of discourse.

In the discussion of inversion in the answers in (20), I mentioned that it has been proposed that the content of certain verbs can be 'informationally light' in order to relegate their content to old information.[67] It is easy to see why it has been proposed, based on the analysis developed in this section. It results from a confusion of the informative content of the utterance, the felicity condition for inversion, and the use of the utterance in discourse. The utterances in (83b)-(84b) are fully informative; they modify the context by providing new information. On the other hand, they differ from utterances with preverbal subjects in that they are associated with presupposed knowledge on the part of the speaker. But this presupposition does not characterize the content of the utterance; it characterizes the use of the utterance in discourse. Along the same lines, note that the knowledge presupposed about the referent of the subject in utterances licensed by the narrative variant (81) of the PDC is basically nil, since the disposition has to do with the generic object of discourse rather than with the referent in particular. Finally, root clauses with inversion licensed by the PDC occur prototypically in meta-narrative utterances used for discourse management; this ancillary character of utterances must be dealt with separately, without being confused with the characterization of utterance content.

The similarity of Italian and English suggested by the parallelism between (83) and (84) indicates that the PDC is not specific to the Romance languages, and that phenomena other than subject NP placement may be sensitive to it.[68] I cannot develop this point here, but it is of great importance: It suggests that the PDC is not linked to a particular level of grammar and can have an impact in different structural dimensions (syntax, word order, or prosody) depending on the language.

---

[66] The verb 'to die', in spite of its lexical content, can therefore be a discourse protagonist introducing verb.

[67] For example, Zubizarreta (1998) discussing contrasts analogous to (84) proposes: 'It could very well be that the unavailability of a prosodic structure with Nuclear Stress on the predicate is due to the "pragmatic lightness" of the predicate involved. The subject being more noteworthy or relevant than the predicate, stress on the subject is preferred. (Note that the fact that pragmatically based notions such as "noteworthy" or "relevant" are difficult to define rigorously does not mean that they are not real)' (1998:69).

[68] This similarity is all the more significant given that English allows locative inversion, with discourse properties completely analogous to those found in French and Italian (but most likely a different syntactic structure, see Bresnan 1994, Marandin 1997).

6 Inversion in Discourse

Studies of inversion in real discourse tend to give up when they try to isolate the factor or factors licensing inversion by examining the syntactic or semantic class of the verb, the information structural status of the subject NP (topic, focus, etc.), or even the discursive status of the DR corresponding to the subject NP (active, inactive, accessible, etc.)[69] Sometimes they conclude that inversion is not amenable to any general explanation and that it is simply a stylistic device. The analyses that I have presented explain how this negative result might come about while also showing that inversion is not an erratic phenomenon.

Inversion is not a pragmatically unified phenomenon. It involves two distinct factors, which require the formulation of two felicity conditions. The first condition, the Given Predicate Condition (GPC), depends crucially on a discourse-based factor. The model, within Büring's framework, shows that the given nature of the predicate is inseparable from the thematic development in the discourse. It is to be expected, then, that this factor should be totally insensitive to the syntactic or semantic properties of the constituents of the utterance where inversion occurs. It is furthermore independent of the focus-ground structure of the utterance. We expect therefore to find inversion in sentences that only provide background information (e.g. subordinate clauses) and in sentences whose content is partitioned, whether the subject NP is in focus or not. The only generalization that holds from this point of view is that we never find inversion licensed by the Given Predicate Condition in wide focus utterances because there, the predicate is never given. Only inversion licensed by the Presupposed Disposition Condition (PDC) is possible in those sentences.

The second condition, the Presupposed Disposition Condition, depends crucially on an epistemic factor: the knowledge of the speaker about the DR corresponding to the subject. This knowledge has a different source in each of the three variants of the condition identified in the previous section: encyclopedic, contextual, or narrative. We do not expect the fine-grained properties of the lexical material to be specified. And in fact we have seen that it is impossible to find a lexical characterization for all the variants of the PDC, or even for each variant individually: the unergative/unaccusative distinction is irrelevant in the first case, the distinction transitive/intransitive in the second case, and distinctions in lexical content in the third (see the use of the verb *telefonare* to introduce a DR). Moreover, the restrictions on distribution in discourse associated with the Presupposed Disposition Condition are of a

69 See Atkinson (1973), Bernini (1995), Fuchs (1997), Hatcher (1956), Jonare (1976), Le Bidois (1950), Ocampo (1995), Sornicola (1994; 1995), Wall (1980), Wehr (1984).

completely different order from the restriction imposed by the Given Predicate Condition: for the latter, the constraint has to do with the content of the discourse topic, while the constraints imposed by the variants of the former have to do with the situation described.

One final remark is in order. It is impossible to consider inversion as a clue for thematic (dis)continuity, contrary to claims in the pragmatic literature such as the two generalizations in (85):

(85) a. Preverbal placement of the subject marks thematic continuity in extended discourse.
b. Postverbal placement of the subject marks thematic discontinuity in extended discourse.

It is false to say that inversion marks a thematic rupture. This is never the case with an inversion licensed by the GPC, precisely because the utterance picks up the stable content of the DT in these cases. This is illustrated in the short discourse in (86), where we observe the same phenomenon as in (36) above:

(86) I A Parigi è stato assassinato R.B. Lo ha ucciso uno squilibrato. (Bernini, 1995: 64, ex. 40)
R.B. was assassinated in Paris. He was killed by a madman.

The analysis in terms of the GPC predicts exactly the opposite of (85a). In a thematic development, preverbal placement is required when there is a modification of the DT under discussion.

It is not true that an inversion licensed by the PDC marks a thematic discontinuity, because the PDC is not tailored for the introduction of discourse topics. This can be the case, but not necessarily. For example, the attested short oral discourse in (87) illustrates a discursive transition in which the inverted utterance permits a recentering (from the female protagonist to the husband). On the other hand, the short discourse in (88) shows an inverted utterance that merely introduces a circumstance in the development of the current DT without changing the centering on Pierre, which preserves the topic chaining character of the discourse segment.

(87) I [ha detto lei / eh può darsi che è successo così / comunque ci siamo chiariti / alla fine ho capito / vabbè / alla fine ti sei confusa /] è entrato il marito / ha detto / no / è stato meglio così (Sornicola, 1994: 47, ex. 26)
she said / maybe it went like that / anyway we talked the matter / at last I got it / at last you get confused / her husband came in / he said / no / it's better like that

(88) F Pierre entra dans la ville. Sur la place se pressait une foule en colère. Il se dirigea vers le palais.
Pierre came into the city. On the square were crowding angry people. He went to the palace.

How is it that the generalizations in (85) have been proposed, if careful observation reveals so many counterexamples? The answer is that they assume that in discourse (as in simple sentences) the topic obligatorily appears preverbally. We saw in section 5.4 that this assumption is false. There is no direct correlation between the placement of the subject and the categorical (predicatum) vs thetic subject distinction. If such an assumption is already false for simple sentences, it is all the more invalid for discourse. More precisely, it holds only in the case of a segment structured by centering on a participant (illustrated in (88) above). But in this case, an explanation in terms of the notion of topic is superfluous. Utterances involved in this kind of textual organization are among those that never allow inversion, since they have a given content of the form in (89), a discourse configuration that does not permit inversion since the VP is never given.

(89) **Pierre** *P*

Inversion therefore cannot be taken as a marker for signaling how the discourse topic is developed. This is never the case for inversion licensed by the PDC. An utterance showing this kind of inversion can just as easily introduce a new thematic development as it can pursue the development of the current theme. Inversion licensed by the GPC, on the other hand, is always associated with the development of the current discourse topic.

7 Conclusion

We have isolated two felicity conditions for subject inversion that are linked neither to a specific syntactic construction nor to a particular focus-ground configuration. This result has major consequences for the grammar. First of all, we cannot use inversion as a motivation for focus-ground structure as a level of representation (information structure), whether it is conceived syntactically (hierarchy of functional projections, Rizzi 1997) or semantically (partition of the content, Vallduví and Engdahl 1995). Second, it is not possible to postulate a simple association linking a construction and a felicity condition, or a position and a felicity condition (assuming that a unique hierarchy of positions can be established). Inversion defines a broad topological organization of utterances, consisting of the field before the verb and the field after the verb. In other words, inversion plays a part in the linearization of constituents and not in their hierarchical organization. This is why all of the languages considered here are subject to the same two conditions, although they have distinct syntactic constraints on the placement of the subject. Since the two conditions specify no lexical or structural constraints, we expect that they can apply in other language families whose effects are not limited to the topological order of constituents. This seems to be the case for the Presupposed Disposition Condition (PDC): it is active in English in locative inversion and in the prosodic structure of some utterances (illustrated in (84)). The question remains open for the Given Predicate Condition (CPD). Büring (1998) and Schwarzschild (1999) show that the given status of constituents is an essential factor in the prosody of Germanic languages.

References

I Grammars and Presentations of Romance Languages

Catalan

Solà, J., M-R. Lloret, J. Mascaró and M. Pérez Saldanya (eds). 2002. *Gramàtica del Català Contemporani*. Barcelona: Editorial Empúries. (3vol.)

Wheeler, M. W., A. Yates and N. Dols. 1999. *Catalan: A Comprehensive Grammar*. London: Routledge.

Yates, A. 1975. *Catalan*. Teach yourself books, London: Hodder and Stoughton.

French

Abeillé, A., A. Delaveau and D. Godard (eds). (in prep). *Grande Grammaire du français*. Paris: Bayard Presse (to appear in 2010).

Damourette, J. and E. Pichon. 1911–1933. *Des Mots à la pensée. Essai de grammaire de la langue française. Tome III: Morphologie du verbe, structure de la phrase verbale, infinitif.* Paris: J. L. L. d'Artrey.

Hawkins, R. and R. Towell. 2001. *French Grammar and Usage*. London: Arnold. (2nd ed.)

Fagyal, Z. , D. Kibbee and F. Jenkins. 2006. *French: A Linguistic Introduction*. Cambridge: Cambridge University Press.

Grevisse, M. and A. Goose. 2007. *Le Bon usage*. Bruxelles: De Boeck-Duculot. (first pub. M. Grevisse, 1936).

Hollervach, W. 1994. *The Syntax of contemporary French*. Lanham: University Press of America.

Jones, M. A. 2005. *Foundations of French Syntax*. Cambridge: Cambridge University Press.

Martinon, P. 1927. *Comment on parle en français*. Paris: Larousse.

Riegel, M., J.-C. Pellat, and R. Rioul. *Grammaire Méthodique du français*. Paris: PUF.

Togeby, K. 1982–85. *Grammaire française*. Copenhague: Akademisk Forlag. (5 vols.)

Italian

Lepschy, A.L. and G.C. Lepschy. 1977. *The Italian Language Today*. London: Hutchinson.

Regula, M., and J. Jernej. 1975. *Grammatica italiana descrittiva*. Berne / Munich: Francke Verlag.

Renzi, L., G. Salvi, and A. Cardinaletti (eds). 2001. *Grande Grammatica Italiana di Consultazione*. Bologna: il Mulino (first ed. 1988, 3 vol.)

Salvi, G. and L. Vanelli. 1992. *Grammatica essenziale di riferimento della lingua italiana*. Firenze: Le Monnier.

Schwarze, C. 1995. *Grammatik der Italienischen Sprache*. Tübingen: Niemeyer.

Portuguese

Câmara, J. M.. 1972. *The Portuguese Language*, transl. by A. J. Naro, Chicago: the University of Chicago Press.

Cunha, C. and L.F.L. Cintra. 1984. *Nova Gramática do português contemporâneo*. Lisbon: Joãn Sá da Costa.

Da Silva Neto, S. 1977. *Introdução ao estudo da língua portuguesa no Brasil*. 4ᵉ éd. Rio de Janeiro: Presença.

Hutchinson, A. P. and J. Lloyd. 1996. *Portuguese; an essential grammar*. London: Routledge.

Mateus, M.H. M., A.M. Brito, I. Duarte and I.H. Faria (eds). 2003. *Gramática da Língua Potuguesa*. Lisbon: Caminho.

Teyssier, P. 1992. *Manuel de langue portugaise. Portugal-Brésil*. Paris: Klincksieck.

Romanian

Avram, M. 2001. *Gramatica pentru toţi*. Bucharest: Humanitas.

Augerot, J.E. and F. D. Popescu. 1983. *Modern Romanian*. Columbus, Ohio : Slavica, 1983.

Dobrovie-Sorin, C. and G. Pană Dindelegan (eds). in prep. *The Essential Grammar of the Romanian Language*. (3 vol.; vol 1, *Nominal Projections*, expected 2007).

Gramatica Limbii Române. Academia Română. Bucharest: Editura Academiei Române. 2005. (2 vol.)

Lombard, A. 1974. *La Langue Roumaine, une présentation*. Paris: Klincksieck.

Mallinson, G. 1986. *Rumanian*. London : Croom Helm.

Tasmowski, L. 2001. *Cours de grammaire roumaine*. 2e édition corrigée. Gent: C&C and Bucarest: Ed. Fundaţia Culturală Română.

Spanish

Butt, J. and C. Benjamín (1990), *A new Reference Grammar of Modern Spanish*. London: Edward Arnold.

Bosque, I., and V. Demonte (eds). 1999. *Gramática Descriptiva de la Lengua Española*. Madrid: Espasa Calpe. (3 vol., 2380 p.)

Coste, J., and M. Baqué. 1993. *Grammaire de l'espagnol moderne*. Paris: SEDES.

Presentations of Romance Languages

Agard, F. B. 1984. *A Course in Romance Linguistics*, Vol. 1: A synchronic view. Washington, DC: Georgetown University Press.

Bourciez, E. 1967. *Eléments de linguistique romane*. Paris: Klincksieck.

Harris, M., and N. Vincent (eds). 1988. *The Romance Languages*. Oxford: Oxford University Press.

Lausberg, H. 1969–72. *Romanische Sprachwissenschaft*. 3 vols. Berlin: de Gruyter.

Posner, R. 1996. *The Romance Languages*. Cambridge: Cambridge University Press.

Reinheimer, S., and L. Tasmowski. 1997. *Pratique des Langues Romanes*. Paris / Montréal: L'Harmattan.

Reinheimer, S. and L. Tasmowski. 2005. *Pratique des Langues Romanes ; les pronoms personnels*. Paris: L'Harmattan.

Teyssier, P. 2004. *Comprendre les Langues Romanes*. Paris: Chandeigne.

II References

Abeillé, A. 1997. Fonction ou position Objet ? *Le Gré des langues* 12: 8–33.

Abeillé, A., and D. Godard. 1994. The Complementation of Tense Auxiliaries in French. R. Aranovich, W. Byrne, S. Preuss and M. Senturia (eds), *WCCFL 13: The Proceedings of the Thirteenth West Coast Conference on Formal Linguistics*, 157–172. Stanford: CSLI Publications.

Abeillé, A., and D. Godard. 1996. La Complémentation des auxiliaires français. *Langages* 122, 32–61.

Abeillé, A. and D. Godard. 1997. The Syntax of French Negative Adverbs. D. Forget, P. Hirschbühler, F. Martineau and M.-L. Rivero (eds), *Negation and Polarity*, 1–27. Amsterdam: J. Benjamins.

Abeillé, A. and D. Godard. 1998. A Lexical Approach to Quantifier Floating in French. A. Kathol, J.-P. Koenig and G. Webelhuth (eds), *Lexical and Constructional Aspects of Linguistic Explanations*, 81–96. Stanford: CSLI Publications.

Abeillé, A. and D. Godard. 2000a. French Word Order and Lexical Weight. R. Borsley (ed), *The nature and function of syntactic categories*. Syntax and Semantics 32, 325–360. New York: Academic Press.

Abeillé, A. and D. Godard. 2000b. Varieties of ESSE in Romance Languages. D. Flickinger and A. Kathol (eds), *Proceedings HPSG 00 Conference*, 2–22. Stanford: CSLI on-line Publications.

Abeillé, A. and D. Godard. 2001. A Class of 'lite' adverbs in French. J. Camps and C. R. Wiltshire (eds), *Syntax, Semantics and L2 acquisition in Romance*, 9–25. Amsterdam: J. Benjamins.

Abeillé, A. and D. Godard. 2002. The Syntactic Structures of French Auxiliaries. *Language* 78: 404–452.

Abeillé, A. and D. Godard. 2004. De la Légèreté en syntaxe, *Bulletin de la Société Linguistique de Paris*, Tome XCIX-1: 69-106

Abeillé, A., D. Godard and I. A. Sag. 1998. Two Kinds of Composition in French Complex Predicates. E. Hinrichs *et al.* (eds), 1–41.

Abeillé, A., D. Godard, and P. Miller. 1997. Les Causatives en français: un cas de compétition syntaxique. *Langue Française* 115: 62–74.

Abeillé, A., D. Godard, and P. Miller and I. A. Sag. 1998. Bounded Dependencies in French. S. Balari and L. Dini (eds), *Romance in HPSG*, 1–54. Stanford: CSLI Publications.

Acquaviva, P. 1993. *The Logical Form of Negation*. PhD dissertation, Scuola Normale Superiore, Pisa.

Aissen, J., and D. Perlmutter. 1976. Clause Reduction in Spanish. *Berkeley Linguistics Society* 2: 1–30. (also1983, D. Perlmutter (ed), 360–403).

Aissen, J. 2001. Markedness and subject choice in Optimality Theory. G. Legendre, J. Grimshaw and S. Vikner (eds), *Optimality-Theoretic Syntax*, 61–96. Cambridge, MA: MIT Press.

Alsina, A. 1991. On the Argument Structure of Causatives. *Linguistic Inquiry* 23. 517–555.

Alsina, A. 1996. *The Role of Argument Structure in Grammar: Evidence from Romance*. Stanford: CSLI Publications.

Alsina, A. 2002. L'infinitiu. J. Solà *et al.* (eds), 2389-2454.

Amastae, J., G. Goodall, M. Montalbetti and M. Phinney (eds). 1995. *Contemporary research in Romance linguistics: papers from LSRL XXII*. Amsterdam: J. Benjamins.

Ambar, M. 1992. *Para uma Sintaxe da Inversão Sujeito-Verbo em Português*. Lisboa: Colibri.

Ambar, M. 1999. Aspects of the Syntax of Focus in Portuguese. G. Rebuschi and L. Tuller (eds), *The Grammar of Focus*, 23-54. Amsterdam / Philadelphie: J. Benjamins.

Anderson, S. 1992. *A-morphous Morphology*. Cambridge: Cambridge University Press.

Andrews, A., and C. Manning. 1999. *Complex Predicates and the Flow of Information*. Stanford: CSLI Publications.

Arad, M. 1998a. *VP-Structure and the Syntax-Lexicon Interface*. PhD dissertation, University College London.

Arad, M. 1998b. Are unaccusatives aspectually characterized? (and other related questions). *MIT Working Papers in Linguistics* 32: 1-20.

Aranovich, R. 2003a. The Semantics of Auxiliary Selection in Old Spanish. *Studies in Language* 27: 1-37.

Aranovich, R. 2003b. Two Types of Postverbal Subjects in Spanish Evidence from Binding. C. Beyssade *et al.*, *Empirical Issues in Syntax and Semantics 4*, 227-242. Paris: Presses universitaires de la Sorbonne.

Aranovich, R. 2006. *Split Auxiliary Systems; a cross linguistic perspective*. Amsterdam: J. Benjamins.

Ashby, W. J. 1981. The Loss of the Negative Particle *ne* in French: a syntactic change in progress. *Language* 56: 674–687.

Ashby, W. J. 1988. The syntax, pragmatics, and sociolinguistics of left- and right-dislocations in French. *Lingua* 75: 203–229.

Ashby, W. J. 1991. When does variation indicate linguistic change in progress? *French Language Studies* 1: 1–19.

Ashby, W. J. 2001. Un Nouveau Regard sur la chute du *ne* en français parlé tourangeau. *French Language Studies* 11: 1–22.

Atkinson, J. C. 1973. *The two forms of subject inversion in French*. The Hague: Mouton.

Attal, P. 1976. A Propos de l'indéfini *des*: problèmes de représentation sémantique. *Le français moderne* 44: 126–142.

Auger, J. 1994. *Pronominal Clitics in Québec Colloquial French: A Morphological Analysis*. PhD dissertation, University of Pennsylvania. IRCS Report 94-29.

Auger, J. 1995. Les Clitiques pronominaux en français parlé informel: une approche morphologique. *Revue québécoise de linguistique* 24.1: 21–60.

Augerot, J. E. 1974. *Romanian Phonology*. Moscow, Idaho: Idaho Research Foundation, University of Idaho.

Avram, L. 1999a. To have or to be? M. Coene *et al.* (eds), 373–391.

Avram, L. 1999b. *Auxiliaries and the Structure of Language*. Editura Universaţii din Bucureşti.

Bafile, L. 1993. *Fonologia prosodica e teoria metrica: accento, clitizzazione e innalzamento vocalico in napoletano*. PhD dissertation, Università di Firenze.

Baker, C. L. 1970. Double negatives. *Linguistic Inquiry* 1: 169–186.

Baker, M. C. 1988. *Incorporation: A Theory of Grammatical Function Changing*. Chicago: Chicago University Press.

Barbosa, P. 1996. Clitic placement in European Portuguese and the position of subjects. A. L. Halpern and A. M. Zwicky (eds), 1–40.

Barbu, A.-M. 1999. Complexul verbal. *Studii si cercetari Lingvistice* L(1), 39–84.

Bard, E. G., D. Robertson and A. Sorace. 1996. Magnitude Estimation of Linguistic Acceptability. *Language* 71: 32–68.

Bartholomew, K. M. 1979. *Problems in Italian Morphophonology*. Seattle: University of Washington Press.

Barwise, J. and R. Cooper. 1981. Generalized quantifiers and natural language. *Linguistics and Philosophy* 4: 159–219.

Bäuerle, R., C. Schwarze and A. von Stechow (eds). 1983. *Meaning, Use and Interpretation of Language*. Berlin: de Gruyter.

Belletti, A., and L. Rizzi. 1981. The syntax of *ne*: some theoretical implications. *The Linguistic Review* 1: 117–154.

Bendjaballah, S. 2002. Clitics in Berber. Paper presented at the morphology seminar, University of Leiden.

Benincà, P., and G. Cinque. 1991. Frasi subordinate al participio: 2. Participio presente. L. Renzi and G. Salvi (eds), Vol. 2, 604–609.

Benincà, P., and G. Cinque. 1993. Su Alcune Differenze fra enclisi e proclisi. *Omaggio a Gianfranco Folena*. Vol. 3, 2314–2326. Padova: Editoriale Programma.

Benincà, P. 1988. L'Ordine degli elementi della frase e le costruzioni marcate: 2. Fenomenologia della dislocazione a sinistra. L. Renzi (ed), Vol. 1, 153–194.

Benthem, J. van. 1989. Polyadic quantifiers. *Linguistics and Philosophy* 12: 437–464.

Bentley, D. 2006. *Split Intransitivity in Italian*. Berlin: Mouton de Gruyter.

Bentley, D., and T. Eythórsson. 2004. Auxiliary Selection and the Semantics of Unaccusativity. *Lingua* 14: 447-471.

Benveniste , E. 1965. L'Antonyme et le pronom en français moderne. *Bulletin de la Société de Linguistique de Paris* 60.1: 71–87. (also 1974, *Problèmes de linguistique générale*. Vol. 2, 197–214. Paris: Gallimard).

Benzing, J. 1931. Zur Geschichte von *ser* als Hilfszeitwort bei den Intransitiven Verben im Spanischen. *Zeitschrift für romanische Philologie* 51: 385–460.

Bernini, G. and P. Ramat 1992. *La frase negativa nelle lingue d'Europa*. Bologna: Il Mulino.

Bernini, G. 1995. Verb-subject Order in Italian; an investigation of short annoucements and telecast news. Y. Matras and H-J. Sasse (eds), 44–71.

Berruto, G. 1987. *Sociolinguistica dell'italiano contemporaneo*. Firenze: La Scuola.

den Besten, H. 1986. Double Negation and the Genesis of Afrikaans. P. Muysken and N. Smith (eds), *Substrata versus Universalis in Creole Genesis*, 185–230. Amsterdam: J. Benjamins.

Beyssade, C., E. Delais-Roussarie, J. Doetjes, J-M. Marandin and A. Rialland. 2004. Prosody and information in French. F. Corblin and H. de Swart (eds), 477-499.

Beyssade, C., J-M. Marandin, and A. Rialland. 2003. Ground/Focus revisited; a perspective from French. R. Núñez-Cedeño, L. López-Carretero, and R. Cameron (eds), *Language Knowledge and Use: a Romance Perspective*, 83-98. Amsterdam: J. Benjamins.

Bierwisch, M. 1980. Semantic Structure and Illocutionary Force. J. R. Searle, F. Kiefer, and M. Bierwisch (eds), *Speech Act Theory and Pragmatics*, 1–37. Dordrecht: Reidel.

Birner, B. 1994. Information Status and Word Order: an analysis of English inversion. *Language* 70: 233–259.

Birner, B. 1995. Pragmatic Constraints on the Verb in English Inversion. *Lingua* 97: 233–256.

Bolinger, D. 1961. Contrastive Accent and Contrastive Stress. *Language* 37: 83–96.

Bolinger, D. 1972. *Degree Words*. The Hague: Mouton.

Bonami, O. and D. Godard. 2001. Inversion du sujet, constituance et ordre des mots. Jean-Marie Marandin (ed), *Cahier Jean-Claude Milner*, 117–174. Paris: Éditions Verdier.

Bonami, O., D. Godard and B. Kampers-Manhe. 2004. Adverb Classification. F. Corblin and H. de Swart (eds), 143-184.

Bonami, O., D. Godard and J-M. Marandin. 1998. French Subject Inversion in Extraction Contexts. G. Bouma, G-J. M. Kruijff and R. T. Oehrle (eds), *Proceedings of the Joint Conference on Formal Grammar, Head-Driven Phrase Structure Grammar, and Categorial Grammar*, 101–112. Sarrebrück: University of Sarre.

Bonami, O., D. Godard and J-M. Marandin. 2001. Constituency and Word Order in French Subject Inversion. G. Bouma *et al.* (eds), 21–40. Stanford: CSLI Publications.

Bonet, E. 1991. *Morphology after Syntax: Pronominal Clitics in Romance*. PhD dissertation, MIT.

Bonet, E. 1995. Feature Structures of Romance Clitics. *Natural Language and Linguistic Theory* 13.4: 607–647.

Bordelois, I. 1988. Causatives: from Lexicon to Syntax. *Natural Language and Linguistic Theory* 6: 57–94.

Borer, H. (ed). 1986. *The Syntax of Pronominal Clitics*. Syntax and Semantics 19. Orlando: Academic Press.

Borer, H. 1994. The Projection of Arguments. E. Benedicto and J. Runner (eds), *Functional Projections*. University of Massachusetts Occasional Papers in Linguistics 17: 19–47. Amherst.

Borer, H. 1998. Deriving passive without theta roles. S. Lapointe, D. Brentari and P. Farrell (eds), *Morphology and its Relation to Phonology and Syntax*, 60–99. Stanford: CSLI Publications.

Borer, H. 2005. *Structuring Sense; volume II: The Normal Course of Events*. Oxford: Oxford University Press.

Borthen, K. 2003. *Norwegian Bare Singulars*. PhD thesis. Working Papers in Linguistics 32, Norwegian University of Science and Technology, Trondheim.

Bosque, I. 1980. *Sobre la negación*. Madrid: Cátedra.

Bosque, I. 1996. Por qué determinados sustantivos no son sustantivos determinados. Repaso y balance. I. Bosque (ed), 3-119.

Bosque, I. (ed). 1996. *El Sustantivo sin determinación. Presencia y ausencia de determinante en la lengua española*. Madrid: Visor.

Bosque, I. 1999. El Sintagma adjetival. Modificadores y complementos del adjetivo. Adjectivo y participio. I. Bosque and V. Demonte (eds), Vol. I, 217–310.

Bosveld-de Smet, L. 1997. *On Mass and Plural Quantification: The Case of French des-du NPs*. PhD dissertation, University of Groningen.

Bouchard, D. 1995. *The Semantics of Syntax*. Chicago: University of Chicago Press.

Bouma, G., R. Malouf and I. A. Sag. 2001. Satisfying Constraints on Extraction and Adjunction. *Natural Language and Linguistic Theory* 19: 1–65.

Bouma, G., E. Hinrichs, G-Jan M. Kruiff and R. Oehrle (eds). 2001. *Constraints and Resources in Natural Language Syntax and Semantics*. Stanford: CSLI Publications.

Bourdieu, E. 1995. *Dispositions et croyances dans la tradition pragmatiste*. Thèse de doctorat, EHESS. (published 1998, *Savoir faire*, Paris: Le Seuil).

Bresnan, J. W., and S. A. Mchombo. 1987. Topic, Pronoun and Agreement in Chichewa. *Language* 63: 741–782.

Bresnan, J. (ed). 1982. *The Mental Representation of Grammatical Relations*. Cambridge, MA: MIT Press.

Bresnan, J. 1994a. Locative Inversion and the Architecture of Universal Grammar. *Language* 70: 72–131.

Bresnan, J. 1994b. Linear Order vs. Syntactic Rank: Evidence from weak crossover. K. Beals, J. Denton, B. Knippen, L. Melnar, H. Suzuki and E. Zeinfeld (eds), *Papers from the Thirtieth Regional Meeting of the Chicago Linguistic Society*, 57–89.

Bresnan, J. 2001. *Lexical Functional Syntax*. Oxford: Blackwell.

Brugè, L., and G. Brugger. 1994. On the Accusative 'a' in Spanish. *University of Venice Working Papers in Linguistics* 4: 13–43.

Büring, D. 1997. *The Meaning of Topic and Focus: the 59th Street Bridge accent*. London: Routledge.

Büring, D. 1998. Focus and Topic in a Complex Model of Discourse. Ms., University of Cologne.

Burzio, L. 1986. *Italian Syntax: a Government-Binding approach*. Dordecht: Reidel.

Calabrese, A. 1992. Some remarks on Focus and Logical Form in Italian. *Harvard Working Papers in Linguistics* 1: 91–127.

Cardinaletti, A., and M. Starke. 1999. The typology of structural deficiency: A case study of the three classes of pronouns. Henk van Riemsdijk (ed), 145–233.

Carlson, G. N. 1977. *Reference to kinds in English*. PhD dissertation, University of Massachusetts, Amherst.

Carlson, G. N., and F. J. Pelletier (eds). 1995. *The Generic Book*. Chicago: University of Chicago Press.

Carvalho, J. Brandão de. 1989. Phonological Conditions on Portuguese clitic-Placement: on syntactic evidence for stress and rhythmical patterns. *Linguistics* 27: 405–436.

Cennamo, M. 1999. Late Latin Pleonastic Reflexives and the Unaccusative Hypothesis. *Transactions of the Philological Society* 97: 103–150.

Centineo, G. 1996. A Lexical Theory of Auxiliary Selection in Italian. *Probus* 8: 223–271.

Chenal, A. 1986. *Le franco-provençal valdôtain*. Aoste: Musumeci.

Chierchia, G. 1998a. Plurality of Mass Nouns and the Notion of 'Semantic Parameter'. S. Rothstein (ed), *Events and Grammar*, 53–103. Dordrecht: Kluwer.

Chierchia, G. 1998b. Reference to kinds across Languages. *Natural Language Semantics* 6: 339–405.

Chomsky, N. 1981. *Lectures on Government and Binding*. Dordrecht: Foris.

Chung, C. 1998. Argument Composition and Long-distance Scrambling in Korean: an extension of the complex predicate hypothesis. E. Hinrichs *et al.* (eds), 159–200.

Chung, S. and W. Ladusaw, W. 2003. *Restriction and Saturation*. Cambridge, Mass.: MIT Press.

Cinque, G. 1977. « *Mica* ». *Annali della Facoltà di Lettere e Filosofia*. Vol. 1 (1976), 101–112. Firenze: Leo S. Olschki editore.

Cinque, G. 1990. Ergative Adjectives and the Lexicalist Hypothesis. *Natural Language and Linguistic Theory* 8: 1–39.

Cinque, G. 2001. "Restructuring" and Functional Structure. L. Brugè (ed.), *University of Venice Working Papers in Linguistics 11*, 45-127. University of Venice, Department of Linguistics.

Cinque, G. 2002. A Note on "Restructuring" and Quantifier Climbing in French. *Linguitic Inquiry 33*: 617-636.

Cinque, G. 2005. Restructuring and functional structure. *Restructuring and Functional Heads: The cartography of syntactic structures*, vol 4. Oxford: Oxford University Press.

Coene, M., W. de Mulder, P. Dendale and Y. D'Hulst (eds). 1999. *Studia linguistica in honorem Liliane Tasmowski*. Padova: Unipress.

Cohen, A., and N. Erteschik-Shir. 2002. Topic, Focus, and the Interpretation of Bare Plurals. *Natural Language Semantics* 10: 125–165.

Condoravdi, C. 1994. *Descriptions in Context*. PhD dissertation, Yale University.

Contreras, H. 1976. *A Theory of Word Order with special reference to Spanish*. Amsterdam: North-Holland.

Contreras, H. 1986. Spanish Bare NPs and the ECP. I. Bordelois, H. Contreras and K. Zagona (eds), *Generative Studies in Spanish Syntax,* 25–49. Dordrecht: Foris.

Contreras, H. 1996. Sobre la distribución de los sintagmas nominales no predicativos sin determinante. I. Bosque (ed), 141–168.

Corblin, F. 1994. *Multiple Negation Processing*. HCRC Research Paper 62.

Corblin, F. 1996. Multiple Negation processing in Natural Language. *Theoria* 17: 214–259.

Corblin, F. 2005. De *pas davantage* à *non plus*. F. Lambert and H. Nølk (eds.), *La syntaxe au coeur de la grammaire*, 65–74. Rennes: Presses Universitaires de Rennes.

Corblin, F., and H. de Swart. 2004. *Handbook of French Semantics*. Stanford: CSLI Publications.

Corblin, F., and I. Derzhanski. 1997. Multiple Negation, Optional arguments and the Reification of Eventualities. F. Corblin, D. Godard and J.-M. Marandin (eds), *Empirical issues in Formal Syntax and Semantics I,* 219-242. Berne: Peter Lang.

Corblin, F., and L. Tovena. 2001. On the Multiple Expression of Negation in Romance. Y. D'Hulst, J. Rooryck, and J. Schroten (eds), *Romance Languages and Linguistic Theory 1999*, 87–115. Amsterdam: J. Benjamins.

Cordin, P., and A. Calabrese. 1988. Il pronome. L. Renzi (ed), Vol. 1, 535–641.

Cortés, C. and A. Gavarró. 1997. Subject-object Asymmetries and the clitic *en*. J. R. Black and V. Motapanyane (eds), *Clitics, Pronoun and Movement*, 39–62. Amsterdam: J. Benjamins.

Coseriu, E. 1967. Lexikalische Solidaritäten. *Poetica* 1: 293–303.

Costa, J. 1998. *Word Order Variation*. Tha Hague: Holland Academic Graphics.

Couquaux, D. 1979. Sur la Syntaxe des phrases prédicatives en français. *Linguisticae Investigationes* III: 245–284.

Coveney, A. 1998. Awareness of linguistic constraints on variable *ne* omission. *Journal of French Language Studies* 8: 159–187.

Craddock, W. (ms.) *Morfología del verbo español*. University of California at Berkeley.

Creissels, D. 2001. A Typology of Subject Marker and Object Marker Systems in African Languages. Paper presented at the International colloquium 'Typology of African Languages', Cologne, 2001.

Croft, W. 1990. *Typology and Universals*. Cambridge: Cambridge University Press.

Crysmann, B. 1999. Licensing Proclisis in European Portuguese. F. Corblin, C. Dobrovie-Sorin, J.-M. Marandin (eds), *Empirical Issues in Formal Syntax and Semantics 2*, 255–277. The Hague: Holland Academic Graphics.

Crysmann, B. 2000a. Syntactic transparency of pronominal clitics. R. Cann, C. Grover and P. Miller (eds), *Grammatical Interfaces in Head-Driven Phrase Structure Grammar*, 77–96. Stanford: CSLI Publications.

Crysmann, B. 2000b. Clitics and coordination in linear structure. B. Gerlach and J. Grijzenhout (eds), 121–160.

Crysmann, B. 2002. *Constraint-based coanalysis: Portuguese cliticisation and morphology-syntax interaction in HPSG*. PhD dissertation, University of Sarreland.

Cummins, S., and Y. Roberge. 1994. Romance Inflectional Morphology in and out of Syntax. H. Harley and C. Phillips (eds), *MIT Working Papers in Linguistics* 22: 53–70.

Cummins, S. 1996. *Meaning and Mapping*. PhD dissertation, University of Toronto.

Dahl, Ö. 1975. On Generics. E. Keenan (ed), *Formal Semantics of Natural Languages*, 99–112. Cambridge: Cambridge University Press.

Dahl, Ö. 1979. Typology of Sentence Negation. *Linguistics* 17: 79–106.

Dardel, R. de. 1958. *Le Parfait fort en roman commun*. Genève / Paris: Droz-Minard.

Davies, M. 1995. Evolution of Causative Constructions in Spanish and Catalan. J. Amastae *et al.* (eds), 105–122.

Davies, W. and C. Rosen. 1988. Union as Multipredicate Clauses. *Language* 64: 52–88.

Davis, S. and D. J. Napoli. 1995. On Root Structure and the Destiny of the Latin Second Conjugation. *Folia linguistica historica* 16: 97–113.

Dayal, V. 2003. A Semantics for Pseudo-incorporation. Ms. Rutgers University (online).

Delais-Roussarie, E. 1999. Accentuation et réalisation des clitiques en français. *Cahiers de Grammaire* 24: 17–37.

Delais-Roussarie, E. 2000. Vers une Nouvelle Approche de la structure prosodique. *Langue française* 126: 92–112.

Delfitto, D. 2002. *Genericity in Language; Issues of syntax, logical form and interpretation*. Alessandria: Dell'Orso.

Delfitto, D. and J. Schroten. 1991. Bare Plurals and the Number Affix in DP. *Probus* 3: 155–185.

Dell, F. 1973. *Les Règles et les sons*. Paris: Hermann.

Densusianu, O. 1938. *Histoire de la langue roumaine. Le seizième siècle*. Paris: E. Leroux.

Déprez, V. 1999. The Roots of Negative Concord in French and French Based Creoles. M. DeGraff. (ed.), *Language Creation and Language Change: Creole, Diachrony and Development*, 375-428. Cambridge, MA: MIT Press.

Diesing, M. 1992. *Indefinites*. Cambridge, MA: MIT Press.

Dobrovie-Sorin, C. 1990. Clitic Doubling, Wh-movement, and Quantification in Romanian. *Linguistic Inquiry* 21: 351–397.

Dobrovie-Sorin, C. 1994. *The Syntax of Romanian: comparative studies in Romance*. Berlin: Mouton de Gruyter.

Dobrovie-Sorin, C. 1995. On the Representation of Existential Readings. Ms., Univ. Paris 7.

Dobrovie-Sorin, C. 1997a. Existential arguments and existential predicates. A. Lawson (ed), *Proceedings of SALT VII*. Ithaca, NY: CLC Publications.

Dobrovie-Sorin, C. 1997b. Classes de prédicats, distribution des indéfinis et la distinction thétique-catégorique. *Le Gré des Langues* 20: 58–97.

Dobrovie-Sorin, C. 2000. Le(s) Thème(s) entre la syntaxe et la structure de l'information. C. Guimier (ed), *La Thématisation dans les langues*, 169–184. Actes du colloque de Caen sur la Thématisation. Berne: Peter Lang.

Dobrovie-Sorin, C. 2002. Generic Plural Indefinites and (Un)selective Binding. F. Corblin and H. de Swart (eds), 55-70.

Dobrovie-Sorin, C. (ed.). 2005. *Noms Nus et Généricité*. Paris: Presses Universitaires de Vincennes

Dobrovie-Sorin, C. 2007. Existential Bare Plurals: from Properties back to Entities, paper presented at the conference 'Noun Incorporation and its Kind', Ottawa 2006. MS, University Paris 7.

Dobrovie-Sorin, C., and C. Galves. 2000. Proclisis, Enclisis and Head to Head Merge. *Bucharest working papers in linguistics* II(1): 35–50.

Dobrovie-Sorin, C. and B. Laca. 1996. Generic BNP. Ms., Universités Paris 7 et Strasbourg 2.

Dobrovie-Sorin, C. and B. Laca. 1998. La Génericité entre la référence à l'espèce et la quantification générique. P. Sauzet (ed), *Actes de Langues et Grammaires III*, 163–177. Saint-Denis: Université Paris 8.

Dobrovie-Sorin, C., T. Bleam and M-T. Espinal. 2006. Bare nouns, Number and Guises of incorporation. S. Vogeleer and L. Tasmowski (eds) *Non-Definiteness and Plurality*, 51-79. Amsterdam: Benjamins.

Dobrovie-Sorin, C., T. Bleam and M-T. Espinal. 2005. Noms nus, nombre et types d'incorporation. C. Dobrovie-Sorin (ed.) *Généricité et détermination nominale*, 128-157. Paris: PUV.

Dowty, D. 1979. *Word Meaning and Montague Grammar: The Semantics of Verbs and Times in Generative Semantics and in Montague's PTQ*. Dordrecht: Reidel.

Dowty, D. 1991. Thematic Proto-roles and Argument Selection. *Language* 67: 547–619.

Duarte, I. and G. Matos. 2000. Romance Clitics and the Minimalist Program. J. Costa (ed), *Portuguese Syntax: New Comparative Studies*, 116–142. Oxford: Oxford University Press.

Dworkin, S. N., and D. Wanner (eds). 2000. *New Approaches to Old Problems. Issues in Romance Historical Linguistics*. Amsterdam: J. Benjamins.

Emonds, J. 1978. The verbal complex V' V in French. *Linguistic Inquiry* 9, 151–175.

Enrique-Arias, Andrés. 2000. Spanish Object Agreement Markers and the Typology of Object Agreement Morphology. S. N. Dworkin and D. Wanner (eds), *New Approaches to Old Problems. Issues in Romance Historical Linguistics*, 149–164. Amsterdam: J. Benjamins.

Farkas, D. 1978. Direct and indirect object reduplication in Romanian. D. Farkas, W. M. Jacobsen and K. W. Todrys (eds), *Papers from the Fourteenth Regional Meeting of the Chicago Linguistic Society*, 88–97.

Farkas, D. 1985. *Intensional descriptions and the Romance subjunctive mood*. New York: Garland.

Farkas, D. 1997a. Dependent Indefinites. F. Corblin, D. Godard and J.-M. Marandin (eds), *Empirical Issues in Formal Syntax and Semantics*, 243–268. Bern: Peter Lang.

Farkas, D. 1997b. Evaluation Indices and Scope. A. Szabolcsi (ed.), *Ways of Scope-Taking*, 183–215. Dordrecht: Kluwer.

Frakas, D. 2001. Dependent Indefinites and Direct Scope. C. Condoravdi and Renardel de Lavalette (eds), *Logical Perspectives on Language and Information*, 41-72. Stanford: CSLI Publications.

Farkas, D. and Y. Sugioka. 1983. Restrictive if / when-Clauses. *Linguistics and Philosophy* 6: 225–258.

Farkas, D. and H. de Swart. 2003. *The Semantics of Incorporation*. Stanford: CSLI Publications.

Fauconnier, G. 1975. Pragmatic Scales and Logical Structure. *Linguistic Inquiry* 6: 353–375.

Fellbaum, C. and A. Zribi-Hertz. 1989. La Construction moyenne en français et en anglais : étude de syntaxe et de sémantique comparées. *Recherches Linguistiques de Vincennes* 18: 59–79.

Fernández Soriano, O. 1999. El Pronombre personal. Formas y distribuciones. Pronombres átonos y tónicos. I. Bosque and V. Demonte (eds), Vol. 1, 1209–1273.

Fiengo, R., and M. R. Gitterman. 1978. Remarks on French Clitic Order. *Linguistic Analysis* 4: 115–147.

Fontana, J. 1996. On the Source of Variations in Clause Reduction Phenomena. Communication at the workshop 'The Syntax of Romance languages', ESSLLI, Prague.

Fontana, J. M. 1993. *Phrase Structure and the Syntax of Clitics in the History of Spanish*. PhD dissertation, University of Pennsylvania.

Fontana, J. M. 1996. Phonology and syntax in the interpretation of the Tobler-Mussafia law. A. L. Halpern and A. M. Zwicky (eds), 41–83.

Fouché, P. 1969. *Phonétique historique du français. Le verbe.* 3 vols. Paris: Klincksieck.

Fouché, P. 1981. *Morphologie historique du français. Le verbe.* Paris: Klincksieck.

Franco, J., and A. Landa. 1995. Conditions after SPELL OUT: the Case of Spanish Clitic Climbing. A. Dainora, R. Hemphill, B. Luka, B. Need and S. Pargman (eds). *CLS 31*, 105–117. Chicago: Chicago Linguistic Society.

Franco, J. 2000. Agreement as a Continuum: The Case of Spanish pronominal clitics. F. Beukema and M. den Dikken (eds), *Clitic Phenomena in European Languages*, 147–189. Amsterdam: J. Benjamins.

Fuchs, C. (ed). 1997. *La place du sujet en français contemporain.* Louvain-la-Neuve: Duculot.

Gaatone, D. 1971. *Etude descriptive du système de la négation en français contemporain.* Geneva: Droz.

Galves, C. 1997. La Syntaxe pronominale du portugais brésilien et la typologie des pronoms. Anne Zribi-Hertz (ed), 11–34.

Gavarró, A., and B. Laca. 2002. Les Perífrasis temporals, aspectuals i modals. J. Solà *et al.* (eds), 2663–2726.

Gazdar, G., E. Klein, G. Pullum and I. A. Sag 1985. *Generalised Phrase Structure Grammar.* Cambridge, MA: Harvard University Press.

Gerlach, B. and J. Grijzenhout (eds). 2000. *Clitics in Phonology, Morphology and Syntax.* Amsterdam: J. Benjamins.

Gerlach, B. 2002. *Clitics Between Syntax and Lexicon.* Amsterdam: J. Benjamins.

Giannakidou, A. 2000. 'Negative...Concord?' *Natural Language and Linguistic Theory* 18, 457-523.

Ginzburg, J., and I. A. Sag. 2000. Interrogative Investigations: The Form, Meaning and Use of English Interrogatives. Stanford: CSLI Publications.

Ginzburg, J. (to appear) *A Semantics for Interactions in Dialogue.* Stanford: CSLI and Chicago: the University of Chicago Press.

Givón, T. 1976. Topic, Pronoun and Grammatical Agreement. C. N. Li (ed), *Subject and Topic*, 149–188. New York: Academic Press.

Glasbey, S. 1997. I-level predicates that allow existential readings for BPs. A. Lawson (ed), *Proceedings of SALT VII*, 169–179. Ithaca, NY: CLC Publications.

Godard, D. and J. Jayez. 1993. Towards a Proper Treatment of Coercion Phenomena. *Proceedings of the 6th Conference of the European Chapter of the ACL*, 168–177.

Godard, D. 2004. French Negative Dependency. F. Corblin and H. de Swart (eds), *Handbook of French Semantics*, 351-389.

Godard, D. and J-M. Marandin. 2006, Reinforcing Negation: the Case of Italian. S. Müller, (ed.), Proceedings of the HPSG 06 Conference, 174–194. Stanford: CSLI on line Publications.

Gómez Torrego, L. 1999. Los Verbos auxiliares. Las perífrasis verbales de infinitivo. I. Bosque and V. Demonte (eds), Vol. 2, 3322–3389.

Gonçalvès, A. 1999. *Predicados Complexos Verbais, em contextos de infinitivo não preposicionado do portuguès europeu*. PhD dissertation, University of Lisboa.

Gonçalvès, A. 1996. Aspectos da sintaxe dos verbos auxiliares do português europeu. A. Gonçalvès *et al.* (eds), *Quatro estudos em sintaxe do português*, 7–50. Lisboa: Colibri.

Gregor, U. 1988. Brazil. U. Ammon, N. Dittmar and K. J. Mattheier (eds), *Sociolinguistics/Soziolinguistik,* 1263–1264. Berlin: de Gruyter.

Greimas, A. 1989. *Dictionnaire de l'ancien français*. Paris: Editions Larousse.

Grimshaw, J. 1982. On the Lexical Representation of Romance Reflexive Clitics. J. Bresnan (ed), 87–148.

Grimshaw, J. 1990. *Argument Structure*. Cambridge, MA: MIT Press.

Grimshaw, J. 1997. Projection, Heads, and Optimality. *Linguistic Inquiry* 28: 373–422.

Grimshaw, J. 1997. The Best Clitic: constraint conflict in morphosyntax. L. Haegeman (ed), 169–196.

Grupo di Padova. 1974. L'Ordine dei sintagmi nella frase. M. Medici and A. Sangregorio (eds), *Fenomeni morfologici e sintattici nell'italiano contemporaneo.* Atti del sesto congresso internazionale di studi, 147–61. Rome: Bulzoni.

Guasti, M. 1994. *Causatives and perception verbs*. Turin: Rosenberg et Sellier.

Gutiérrez-Bravo, R. 2000. Subjects, Left Periphery and Word order in Mexican Spanish. Paper presented at the 'Second Joint Stanford-UCSC Workshop on Optimal Typology'.

Gutiérrez-Rexach, J. The Formal Semantics of Clitic Doubling. *Journal of Semantics* 16: 315-380.

Haase, A. 1930. *Syntaxe française du XVII*[e] *siècle*. New edition, revised by M. Obert. Paris: Delagrave (first pub. 1898).

Haegeman, L. 1991. *Introduction to Government and Binding Theory*. Oxford: Blackwell.

Haegeman, L. (ed). 1997. *Elements of Grammar: Handbook of Generative Syntax*. Dordrecht: Kluwer.

Hale, K. and S. J. Keyser. 1986. *Some transitivity alternations in English*. Lexicon Project Working Papers 7. Cambridge, MA: Centre for Cognitive Science, MIT.

Hall-Partee, B. 1965. *Subject and Object in Modern English*. PhD dissertation, MIT.

Halpern, A. L. 1995. *On the placement and morphology of clitics*. Stanford: CSLI Publications.

Halpern, A. L. and A. M. Zwicky (eds). 1996. *Approaching Second: Second Position Clitics and Related Phenomena*. Stanford: CSLI Publications.

Hamblin, C. L. 1973. Questions in Montague Grammar. *Foundations of Language* 10: 41–53.

Harley, H. and R. Noyer. 1999. State-of-the-Article: Distributed Morphology. *Glot International* 4: 3–9.

Harris, J. 1997a. Why *n'ho* is pronounced [li] in Barceloní Catalan: Morphological Impoverishment, Merger, Fusion and Fission. B. Bruening, Y. Kang and M. McGinnis (eds), *PF: Papers at the Interface. MIT Working Papers in Linguistics* 30: 451–479.

Harris, J. 1997b. Morphologie autonome et pronoms clitiques en catalan et en espagnol. Anne Zribi-Hertz (ed), 35–55.

Haspelmath, M. 2004. Explaining the Ditransitive Person-Role Constraint: A usage-based account. *Constructions* 2004-2 (on-line journal, University of Düsseldorf).

Hatcher, A. 1956. *Theme and Underlying Question; two studies of Spanish word order*. Supplement to Word 12, Monograph 3. New York: Linguistic Circle of New York.

Haverkort, M. 1999. Prepositional Clitics as Hybrid Categories. Henk van Riemsdijk (ed), 391–398.

Hay, J. C. Kennedy and B. Levin. 1999. Scalar Structure underlies Telicity in Degree Achievements. T. Matthews and D. L. Strolowitch (eds), *Proceedings of SALT 9*, 127–144. Ithaca, NY: CLC Publications.

Hayes, B. 1990. Precompiled Phrasal Phonology. S. Inkelas and D. Zec (eds). *The Phonology-Syntax Connection*, 85–108. Chicago: University of Chicago Press.

Heim, I. 1982. *The Semantics of Definite and Indefinite Noun Phrases*. PhD dissertation, University of Massachusetts, Amherst. (published 1988, New York: Garland).

Hériau, M. 1980. *Le Verbe impersonnel en français moderne*. Atelier de reproduction de thèses, Université Lille III.

Hernanz, M. L. 1999. El Infinitivo. I. Bosque and V. Demonte (eds), Vol. 2, 2197–2356.

Herslund, M. 1988. *Le Datif en français*. Louvain: Éditions Peeters.

Hetzron, R. 1975. The Presentative Movement or why the Ideal Word Order is V.S.O.P. C. N. Li (ed), *Word order and word order change*, 345–388. Austin: University of Texas Press.

Higginbotham, J. 1985. On Semantics. *Linguistic Inquiry* 16: 547–593.

Higginbotham, J. 1987. Indefiniteness and Predication. E. Reuland and A. ter Meulen (eds), *The Representation of (In)definiteness*, 43–70. Cambridge, MA: MIT Press.

Hinrichs, E., A. Kathol and T. Nakazawa (eds). 1998. *Complex Predicates in Nonderivational Syntax*. New York: Academic Press.

Hirschbühler, P. and M. Labelle. 2000. Evolving Tobler-Mussafia Effects in the Placement of French Clitics. S. N. Dworkin and D. Wanner (eds), 165–182.

Hirschbühler, P. and M. Labelle. 2001a. La Position des clitiques par rapport au verbe à l'impératif dans l'évolution du français. *Recherches Linguistiques de Vincennes* 30: 13–37.

Hirschbühler, P. and M. Labelle. 2001b. Les 'clitiques' arguments en serbo-croate et dans l'histoire du français. Claude Muller (ed), 109–132.

de Hoop, H. 1992. *Case Configuration and Noun Phrase Interpretation*, PhD dissertation, University of Groningen (Grodil 4).

Horn, L. R. 1989. *The Natural History of Negation*. Chicago: Chicago University Press.

van Hout, A. 1996. *Event Semantics of Verb Frame Alternations. A Case Study of Dutch and Its Acquisition*. PhD dissertation, University of Tilburg.

van Hout, A. 2000. Event Semantics in the Lexicon-syntax Interface; Verb frame alternations in Dutch and their acquisition. C. Tenny and J. Pustejovsky (eds), *Events as Grammatical Objects*, 239-282. Stanford: CSLI Publications.

Hulk, A., and J-Y. Pollock. 2001. *Subject Inversion in Romance and the Theory of Universal Grammar*. Oxford: Oxford University Press.

Hyman, L. M. and S. Mchombo. 1992. Morphotactic Constraints in the Chichewa verb stem. L. A. Buszard-Welcher, L. Wee and W. Weigel (eds), *Proceedings of the Eighteenth Annual Meeting of the Berkeley Linguistics Society*, 350–364. Berkeley: Berkeley Linguistics Society.

Iliescu, M., and L. Mourin. 1991. *Typologie de la morphologie verbale romane. Vue synchronique*. Innsbrucker Beiträge zur Kulturwissenschaft, Sonderheft 80. Innsbruck: AMŒ.

Inkelas, S. and D. Zec (eds). 1990. *The Phonology-Syntax Connection*. Chicago: University of Chicago Press.

Ionescu, E. 1996. Accusative 'Clitic Climbing' in Romanian. A Case of Argument Composition. *Cahiers de linguistique théorique et appliquée* 32/33: 74–87.

Ionescu, E. (ed). 2004. *Understanding Romanian Negation ; Syntactic and semantic approaches in a declarative perspective*. Bucharest: Editura Universităţii Bucureşti.

Jaeggli, O. 1982. *Topics in Romance Syntax*. Dordrecht: Foris.

Jaeggli, O. 1986. Three Issues in the Theory of Clitics: case, doubled NPs and extraction. H. Borer (ed), 15–42.

Jakobson, R. 1995. Quest for the Essence of Language. L. Waugh and M. Monville-Burston (eds), *On Language: Roman Jacobson*, 407-421. Cambridge, MA: Harvard University Press.

Jespersen, O. 1962. Negation in English and Other Languages. *Selected Writings of Otto Jespersen*, 3–151. London: Allen and Unwin. (first publ. 1917)

Johnson, W. 1987. Lexical Levels in French Phonology. *Linguistics* 25: 889–913.

Jonare, B. 1976. *L'Inversion dans la principale non interrogative en français contemporain*. Studia Romanica Upsaliensia 16. University of Uppsala.

Kaisse, E. M. 1985. *Connected Speech: The Interaction of Syntax and Phonology*. 0rlando: Academic Press.

Kalluli, D. 1999. *The Comparative Syntax of Albanian. On the Contribution of Syntactic Types to Propositional Interpretation*. PhD thesis. University of Durham.

Kamp, H. and U. Reyle. 1993. *From Discourse to Logic*. Dordrecht: Kluwer.

Kampers-Manhe, B. 1998. *Je veux que parte Paul*: a neglected construction. A. Schwegler, B. Tranel and Myriam Uribe-Etxebarria (eds), *Romance Linguistics: theoretical perspectives. Selected papers from LSRL XVII*, 129–141. Amsterdam: J. Benjamins.

Kathol, A. 1998. Constituency and Linearization of Verbal Complexes. E. Hinrichs *et al.* (eds), 221–270.

Kayne, R. S. 1973. L'Inversion du sujet en français dans les propositions interrogatives (partie 1). *Le français moderne* 40: 10–42.

Kayne, R. S. 1975. *French Syntax: The Transformational Cycle*. Cambridge, MA: MIT Press.

Kayne, R. S. 1986. Connexité et inversion du sujet. M. Ronat and D. Couquaux (eds), *Grammaire modulaire*, 127–147. Paris: Editions de Minuit.

Kayne, R. S. 1991. Romance Clitics, Verb Movement, and PRO. *Linguistic Inquiry* 22: 647–686.

Kayne, R. S. and J-Y. Pollock. 1978. Stylistic Inversion, Successive Cylicity and Move NP in French. *Linguistic Inquiry* 9: 595–621.

Keenan, E. and B. Comrie. 1977. Noun Phrase Accessibility and Universal Grammar, *Linguistic Inquiry* 8: 63–99.

Kim, J.-B. and I. A. Sag. 2002. Negation without Movement. *Natural Language and Linguistic Theory* 20:339-412.

Kiparsky, P. 1982. Lexical Morphology and Phonology. Linguistic Society of Korea (ed), *Linguistics in the Morning Calm: selected papers from SICOL-1981*, 3–91. Séoul: Hanshin Publishing Co.

Kiss, K. 1998. Identificational Focus versus Information Focus. *Language* 74: 245-273.

Klavans, J. L. 1985. The Independence of Syntax and Phonology in Cliticization. *Language* 61: 95–120.

Kleiber, G., B. Laca and L. Tasmowski (eds). 2001. *Typologie des groupes nominaux*. Rennes: Presses Universitaires de Rennes.

Kleiber, G. 2001. Indéfinis : lecture existentielle et lecture partitive. G. Kleiber *et al.* (eds), 47–97.

Klima, E. S. 1964. Negation in English. J. Fodor and J. Katz (eds), *The structure of language*, 246–323. New Jersey: Prentice Hall.

Koenig, J-P. 1994. *Lexical Underspecification and the Syntax-Semantics Interface*. PhD dissertation, University of California at Berkeley.

König, E. 1991. The Meaning of Focus Particles – A Comparative Perspective. London: Routledge.

Korzen, H. 1983. Réflexions sur l'inversion dans les propositions interrogatives en français. M. Herslund, O. Mørdrup and F. Sørensen (eds), *Analyses grammaticales du français : études publiées à l'occasion du 50e anniversaire de Carl Vikner*. Etudes romanes de l'Université de Copenhague 24, 50–85.

Korzen, H. 1992. The Predicative Unit and Subject-verb Inversion in Modern French. M. Herslund (ed), *Word Order: two studies on central issues in the syntax of Danish and French*. Copenhagen Studies in Language 15, 65–124. Copenhagen: Handelshøjskolens Forlag.

Kratzer, A. 1995. Stage-level and individual-level predicates. G. N. Carlson and F. J. Pelletier (eds), 125–175.

Krifka, M., J. Pelletier, G. Carlson, G. Chierchia, G. Link, and A. ter Meulen. 1995. Genericity: an introduction. G. N. Carlson and F. J. Pelletier (eds), 1–124.

Krifka, M. (ed). 1988. *Genericity in Natural Language*. Proceedings of the 1988 Tübingen Conference. SNS-Bericht 88-42. University of Tübingen.

Kupferman, L. 1995. La Construction passive en *se faire*. *Journal of French Language Studies* 5: 57–83.

Kuroda, S. 1972. The Categorical and the Thetic Judgement. *Foundations of Language* 9: 153–185.

Kuroda, S. 1973. Le Jugement catégorique et le jugement thétique. Exemples tirés de la syntaxe japonaise. *Langages* 30: 81–110.

Labelle, M. 1985. Caractère post-lexical de la cliticisation française. *Linguisticae Investigationes* 9: 83–96.

Labelle, M. 1992. Change of State and Valency. *Journal of Linguistics* 28: 375–414.

Labov, W. 1972. Negative Attraction and Negative Concord in English Grammar. *Language* 48: 773–818.

Laca, B. 1990. Generic Objects: some more pieces of the puzzle. *Lingua* 81: 25–46.

Laca, B. 1996a. Acerca de la semántica de los plurales escuetos en español. I. Bosque (ed), 241–268.

Laca, B. 1999. Presencia y ausencia de determinante. I. Bosque and V. Demonte (eds), Vol. 1, 891–928.

Laca, B., and L. Tasmowski. 1994. Le Pluriel indéfini de l'attribut métaphorique. *Linguisticae Investigationes* 18: 27–48.

Ladusaw, W. A. 1979. *Polarity Sensitivity as Inherent Scope Relations*. PhD dissertation, University of Texas at Austin. (Published 1980, New York: Garland).

Ladusaw, W. A. 1991. Interpreting Negative Concord Structures. Paper presented at the Annual Meeting of the Linguistic Society of America.

Ladusaw, W. A. 1992. Expressing Negation. C. Barker and D. Dowty (eds), *SALT II: Proceedings of the Second Conference on Semantics and Linguistic Theory*. Ohio State University Working Papers in Linguistics 40, 237–260. Columbus: Ohio State University.

Ladusaw, W. A. 1994. Thetic and Categoric, Stage and Individual, Weak and Strong. M. Harvey and L. Santelmann (eds), *SALT IV: Proceedings from Semantics and Linguistics Theory IV*, 220–229. Ithaca, NY: CLC Publications.

Laenzlinger, C. 1993. A Syntactic View of Romance Pronominal Sequences. *Probus* 5: 241–270.

Laka Mugarza, I. 1990. *Negation in Syntax: On the Nature of Functional Categories and Projections*. PhD dissertation, MIT.

Lambrecht, K. 1987. The Status of SVO Sentences in French Discourse. R. S. Tomlin (ed), *Coherence and Grounding in Discourse*. Typological Studies in Language 11, 217–261. Amsterdam: J. Benjamins.

Lambrecht, K. 1988. Presentational Cleft Constructions in Spoken French. J. Haiman and S. A. Thompson (eds), *Clause Combining in Grammar and Discourse*, 136–179. Amsterdam: J. Benjamins.

Lambrecht, K. 1994. *Information structure and sentence form*. Cambridge: Cambridge University Press.

Lambrecht, K. 2004. Un Système pour l'analyse de la structure informationnelle des phrases. L'exemple des constructions clivées. J. Fernandez-Vest and S. Carter-Thomas (eds). *Structure informationnelle et particules énonciatives. Essai de typologie*, 21-62. Paris: L'Harmattan.

Landman, F. 1989. Groups I and Groups II. *Linguistics and Philosophy* 12: 559–605, 723–744.

Landman, F. 1996. Plurality. S. Lappin (ed), *The Handbook of Contemporary Semantic Theory,* 425–457. Oxford: Blackwell.

Lanly, A. 1977. *Morphologie historique des verbes français. Notions générales, conjugaisons régulières, verbes irréguliers*. Paris: Bordas.

Lapointe, S. G. 1980. *A Theory of Grammatical Agreement*. PhD dissertation, University of Massachusetts, Amherst. (Published 1985, New York: Garland).

Le Bidois, R. 1952. *L'Inversion du sujet dans la prose contemporaine*. Paris: Editions d'Artrey.

Leclère, C. 1976. Datifs syntaxiques et datifs éthiques. J-C. Chevalier and M. Gross (eds), *Méthodes en grammaire française*, 73–95. Paris: Klincksieck.

van der Leeuw, F. 1997. *Clitics: Prosodic Studies*. The Hague: Holland Academic Graphics.

Legaré, L. and J. Rollin. 1976. Syntaxe de l'auxiliaire en français. A. Ford, J. Reighard and R. Singh (eds), *Proceedings of NELS VI*. Montreal Working Papers in Linguistics 6, 187–195.

Legendre, G. 1987. *Topics in French syntax*. PhD dissertation, University of California at San Diego. (Published 1994, New York: Garland).

Legendre, G. 1989. Unaccusativity in French. *Lingua* 79: 95–164.

Legendre, G. 2000. Positioning Romanian verbal clitics at PF: An Optimality-Theoretic analysis. B. Gerlach and J. Grijzenhout (eds), 219–254.

Legendre, G. 2006. Optimizing auxiliary selection in Romance. In R. Aranovich (ed.), 145-180.

Legendre, G. 2007. On the Typology of Auxiliary selection. *Lingua*.

Legendre, G., J. Grimshaw and S. Vikner (eds). 2001. *Optimality-Theoretic Syntax*. Cambridge, MA: MIT Press.

Legendre, G., Y. Miyata and P. Smolensky. 1991. Unifying Syntactic and Semantic Approaches to Unaccusativity: a connectionist approach. L.A. Sutton, C. Johnson and R. Shields (eds), *Proceeedings of the 17th Annual Meeting of the Berkeley Linguistic Society. General Session & Parasession on the Grammar of Event Structure*, 156–167. Berkeley: Berkeley Linguistic Society.

Legendre, G. and P. Smolensky. To appear. French Inchoatives and Bi-directional Optimality Theory. D. Geerts, J. Moore and M. Polinsky (eds.), *Hypothesis A / Hypothesis B: Linguistics explorations in honor of David Perlmutter*. Cambridge, MA: MIT Press.

Legendre, G., A. Sorace and Smolensky, P. 2006. The Optimality Theory-Harmonic Grammar Connection. P. Smolensky and G. Legendre (eds). *Toward a Calculus of the Mind/Brain: Neural Network Theory, Optimality, and Universal Grammar,* 339-402. Cambridge, MA: MIT Press.

Legendre, G., P. Smolensky and C. Wilson. 1998. When is Less More? Faithfulness and Minimal Links in Wh-Chains. P. Barbosa, D. Fox, P. Hagstrom, M. McGinnis and D. Pesetsky (eds), *Is the Best Good Enough? Optimality and Competition in Syntax*, 249–289. Cambridge, MA: MIT Press.

Legendre, G, A. Vainikka, P. Hagstrom and M. Todorova. 2002. Partial Constraint Ordering in Child French Syntax. *Language Acquisition* 10.3: 189-228.

Lema, J., and M.-L. Rivero. 1992. Inverted Conjugations and V-second Effects in Romance. C. Laeufer and T. Morgan (eds), *Theoretical Analysis in Contemporary Romance Linguistics,* 311–328. Amsterdam: J. Benjamins.

Levin, B. and M. Rappaport Hovav. 1992. The Lexical Semantics of verbs of Motion: The perspective from unaccusativity. I. Roca (ed), *Thematic Structure: Its Role in Grammar*, 247–269. Dordrecht: Foris.

Levin, B., and M. Rappaport Hovav. 1994. A Preliminary Analysis of Causative Verbs in English. *Lingua* 92: 35–77.

Levin, B., and M. Rappaport, 1995. *Unaccusativity: At the Syntax-Semantics Interface*. Cambridge, MA: MIT Press.

Levin, B. and M. Rappaport Hovav. 2005. *Argument Realization*. Cambridge: Cambridge University Press.

Link, G. 1983. The Logical Analysis of Plurals and Mass Terms: A Lattice-Theoretic Approach. R. Bäuerle *et al.* (eds), 302–323.

Lloyd, P. M. 1993. *Del latín al español.* Vol. I, *Fonología y morfología históricas de la lengua española.* Madrid: Gredos.

Lois, X. 1996. Los Grupos nominales sin determinante y el paralelismo entre la oración y la frase nominal. I. Bosque (ed), 201–238.

Lombard A., and C. Gâdei. 1981. *Dictionnaire morphologique de la langue roumaine.* Bucarest: Editura Academiei.

Lombard, A. 1954–1955. *Le Verbe roumain. Etude morphologique.* 2 vols. Lund: Gleerup.

Longobardi, G. 1994. Reference and Proper Names: a theory of N-movement in syntax and logical form. *Linguistic Inquiry* 25: 609–669.

Longobardi, G. 2002. How Comparative is Semantics? A unified parametric theory of bare nouns and proper names. *Natural Language Semantics* 9, 335–369.

Longobardi, G. 2000. Postverbal Subjects and the Mapping Hypothesis. *Linguistic Inquiry* 31: 691–702.

Loporcaro, M. 2003. The Unaccusative Hypothesis and Participial Absolutes in Romance. Perlmutter's Generalization revisited. *Rivista di Linguistica / Italian Journal of Linguistics* 15-2: 199-203.

MacWhinney, B., and C. Snow. 1985. The Child Language Data Exchange System: An update. *Journal of Child Language* 17: 457–472.

Maiden, M. 1995. *A Linguistic History of Italian.* London / New York: Longman.

Malkiel, Y. 1969. Deux Problèmes de linguistique générale illustrés par le parfait fort de l'ancien hispano-roman. F. Dethier *et al.* (eds), *Mélanges offerts à Rita Lejeune, professeur à l'Université de Liège.* Vol. I, 471–483. Gembloux: J. Duculot.

Marandin, J-M. 1997. *Dans le Titre se trouve le sujet.* Mémoire d'habilitation, Université Paris 7.

Marandin, J-M. 2001. Unaccusative Inversion in French. Y. D'Hulst, J. Rooryck and J. Schroten (eds), *Romance Languages and Linguistic Theory 1999: Selected papers from Going Romance 1999*, 195–222. Amsterdam: J. Benjamins.

Marandin, J-M. 2005. Formattage de l'information : focus et contexte. F. Corblin and C. Gardent (eds), *Interpréter en contexte, 31-79.* Paris : Lavoisier.

Marandin, J-M., C. Beyssade, E. Delais-Roussarie and A. Rialland. 2002. Discourse marking in French: C accents and discourse moves. B. Bel and I. Marlien (eds), *Proceedings of the Speech Prosody 2002 Conference*, 471–474. Aix-en-Provence: Laboratoire Parole et Langage.

Mathesius, V. 1937. Double negation and grammatical concord. *Mélanges de linguistique et de philologie offerts à Jacq. van Ginneken* à l'occasion du soixantième anniversaire de sa naissance, 79-83. Paris: Klincksiek.

Matras, Y., and H-J. Sasse (eds). 1995. *Verb-subject Order and Theticity in European Languages. Sprachtypologie und Universalien Forschung* 48.1–2. Berlin: Akademie Verlag GmbH.

May, R. 1989, Interpreting Logical Form. *Linguistics and Philosophy* 12: 387–435.

McClure, W. 1995. *Syntactic Projections of the Semantics of Aspect*. Tokyo: Hitsujishobo.

McNally, L. 1992. *An Interpretation for the English Existential Construction*. PhD dissertation, University of California at Santa Cruz.

McNally, L. 1995. Bare plurals in Spanish are interpreted as properties. G. Morill and R. Oehrle (eds), *Formal Grammar, Proceedings of the 1995 ESSLLI Summer School*, 1997, 197-212.

McNally, L. 1998a. Existential Sentences Without Existential Quantification. *Linguistics and Philosophy* 31: 353–392.

McNally, L. 1998b. Stativity and Theticity. S. Rothstein (ed), *Events and Grammar*, 293–309. Dordrecht: Kluwer.

Mendikoetxea, A. 1999. Construcciones inacusativas y pasivas. I. Bosque and V. Demonte (eds), Vol. 2, 1574–1629.

Mélis, L., L. Tasmowski, P. Verluyten and D. Willems. 1985. *Les Constructions de la phrase française. Invitation à la réflexion sur le passif, le pronominal, l'impersonnel et le causatif.* Gent: Communication & Cognition.

Mélis, L. 1985. Les Tours pronominaux du français. L. Mélis *et al.*, 91–166.

Miller, P. H. 1992. *Clitics and Constituent in Phrase Structure Grammar*. New York: Garland.

Miller, P. H., and I. A. Sag. 1997. French Clitic Movement without Clitics or Movement. *Natural Language and Linguistic Theory* 15: 573–639.

Miller, P. H., G. K. Pullum, and A. M. Zwicky. 1997. The Principle of Phonology-Free Syntax: Four Apparent Counter-examples in French. *Journal of Linguistics* 33: 67–90.

Milner, J-C. 1978. *De la Syntaxe à l'interprétation : quantités, insultes, exclamations*. Paris: Le Seuil.

Milner, J-C. 1979. Le Système de la négation en français et l'opacité du sujet. *Langue Française* 44: 80–105.

Milner, J-C. 1982. *Ordres et raisons de langue*. Paris: Le Seuil.

Milner, J-C. 1986. *Introduction à un traitement du passif.* Publications de l'ERA 642, UFRL, Université Paris 7.

Monachesi, P. 1998. Italian Restructuring Verbs: A lexical analysis. E. Hinrichs *et al.* (eds), 313–368.

Monachesi, P. 1998. The Morphosyntax of Romanian Cliticization. P. Coppen, H. van Halteren and L. Teunissen (eds), *Proceedings of Computational Linguistics in The Netherlands 1997*, 99–118. Amsterdam: Rodopi.

Monachesi, P. 1999a. *A Lexical Approach to Italian Cliticization*. Stanford: CSLI Publications.

Monachesi, P. 1999b. The Syntactic Structure of Romanian Auxiliary and Modal Verbs. G. Bouma *et al.* (eds), 101–118.

Monachesi, P. 2000. Clitic Placement in the Romanian Verbal Complex. B. Gerlach and J. Grijzenhout (eds), 255–293.

Monachesi, P. 2005. *The Verbal Complex in Romance; a case study in grammatical interfaces*. Oxford: Oxford University Press.

Moore, J. 1990a. *Reduced Constructions in Spanish*. PhD dissertation, University of California at Santa Cruz.

Moore, J. 1990b. Spanish Clause Reduction with Downstairs Cliticization. K. Dziwirek, P. Farrell, and E. Mejias-Bikandi (eds), *Grammatical Relations*, 319–334. Stanford: CSLI Publications.

Moravcsik, E. A. 1974. Object-verb Agreement. *Working papers in language universals* 15: 25–140.

Morin, Y-C. 1978. Une Théorie interprétative des causatives en français. *Linguisticae Investigationes* 2: 363–417.

Morin, Y-C. 1979a. More Remarks on French Clitic Order. *Linguistic Analysis* 5: 293–312.

Morin, Y-C. 1979b. La Morphophonologie des pronoms clitiques en français populaire. *Cahiers de linguistique* 9: 1–36.

Morin, Y-C. 1981. Some Myths About Pronominal Clitics in French. *Linguistic Analysis* 8: 95–109.

Morin, Y-C. 1984. De Quelques lacunes dans la distribution réfléchis / réciproques. *Le français moderne* 52: 61–65.

Mouret, F. 2006. A Phrase Structure Approach to Argument Cluster Coordination, *Proceedings of the HPSG 06 Conference*, 247-267. Stanford: CSLI on-line Publications.

Mourin, L. 1974. Rejets et analogies dans la structuration des radicaux des parfaits irréguliers romans. *Revue roumaine de linguistique* 19: 191–217.

Mourin, L. 1975. Les Analogies dans les radicaux irréguliers des participes passés romans. *Revue roumaine de linguistique* 20: 115–138.

Muller, C. 1991. *La Négation en français*. Geneva: Droz.

Muller, C. (ed). 2001. *Clitiques et cliticisation*. Paris: Champion.

Napoli, D. J. 1981. Semantic Interpretation vs. Lexical Governance: clitic climbing in Italian. *Language* 57: 841–887.

Nespor, M. and I. Vogel. 1986. *Prosodic Phonology*. Dordrecht: Foris.

Nordhal, H. 1977. *Assez avez alé* : *ester* et *avoir* comme auxiliaries du verbe *aller* en ancien français. *Revue Romane* 12.1: 54–66.

Noyer, R. 1994. Mobile Affixes in Huave: optimality and morphological well-formedness. E. Duncan, D. Farkas and P. Spaelti (eds), *Proceedings of the Twelfth West Coast Conference on Formal Linguistics*, 67–82. Stanford: CSLI Publications.

Ocampo, F. 1995. The Word Order of Constructions with a Verb, a Subject and a Direct Object in spoken Spanish. Jon Amastae *et al.* (eds), 291–305.

Partee, B. H. and M. Rooth. 1983. Generalized Conjunction and Type Ambiguity. R. Bäuerle *et al.* (eds), 115–143.

Penny, R. 1991. *A History of the Spanish Language*. Cambridge: Cambridge University Press.

Peperkamp, S. 1997. *Prosodic Words*. PhD dissertation, University of Amsterdam. The Hague: Holland Academic Graphics.

Perlmutter, D. M. 1970. Surface Structure Constraints in Syntax. *Linguistic Inquiry* 1: 187–255.

Perlmutter, D. 1978. Impersonal passives and the Unaccusative Hypothesis. J. Jaeger and A. Woodbury (eds), *Proceedings of the Fourth Annual Meeting of the Berkeley Linguistic Society*, 157–189. Berkeley: University of California.

Perlmutter, D. (ed). 1983. *Studies in Relational Grammar 1*. Chicago: University of Chicago Press.

Perlmutter, D. 1989. Mutiattachment and the Unaccusative Hypothesis: The perfect auxiliary in Italian. *Probus* 1: 63–120.

Pesetsky, D. 1995. *Zero Syntax. Experiencers and Cascades*. Cambridge, MA: MIT Press.

Picallo, M. 1990. Modal Verbs in Catalan. *Natural Language and Linguistic Theory* 8: 285–312.

Pinchon, J. 1972. *Les Pronoms adverbiaux* en *et* y. *Problèmes généraux de la représentation pronominale*. Genève: Droz.

Pinto, M. 1997. *Licensing and interpretation of inverted subjects in Italian*. Utrecht: LED.

Plénat, M. 1981. *L''autre' Conjugaison ou la régularité des verbes irréguliers*. *Cahiers de grammaire* 3.

Poletto, C. 1999. The Internal Structure of AgrS and Subject Clitics in the Northern Italian Dialects. Henk van Riemsdijk (ed), 581–620.

Pollard, C. and I. A. Sag. 1994. *Head-driven Phrase Structure Grammar*. Chicago: University of Chicago Press and Stanford: CSLI Publications.

Pollock, J.-Y. 1986. Sur la Syntaxe de *en* et le paramètre du sujet nul. M. Ronat and D. Couquaux (eds), *La Grammaire Modulaire*, 211–246. Paris: Editions de Minuit.

Pollock, J.-Y. 1989. Verb Movement, Universal Grammar and the Structure of IP. *Linguistic Inquiry* 20: 365–424.

Popescu, A. 2000. The Morphophonology of the Romanian Clitic Sequence. *Lingua* 110: 773–799.

Posner, R. 1984. Double Negatives, Negative Polarity and Negative Incorporation in Romance: a historical and comparative view. *Transactions of the Philological Society* 1984: 1–26.

Postal, P. 1963. *Some Syntactic Rules in Mohawk*. PhD dissertation, Yale University.

Price, G. 1993. *Pas (point)* without *ne* in interrogative clauses. *Journal of French Language Studies* 3: 191–195.

Prince A., and P. Smolensky. 1993/2004. *Optimality Theory: Constraint Interaction in Generative Grammar*. Oxford: Blackwell (Revised version of Rutgers University Center for Cognitive Science and the University of Colorado at Boulder, Technical Report 2).

Pullum, G. K. 1988. Citation Etiquette Beyond Thunderdome. *Natural Language and Linguistic Theory* 6: 579–588.

Pustejovsky, J. and F. Busa. 1995. Unaccusativity and Event Composition. P. M. Bertinetto, V. Bianchi, J. Higginbotham and M. Squartini (eds), *Temporal Reference, Aspect and Actionality*, 159–178. Turin: Roserberg and Sellier.

Putnam, H. 1975. The 'meaning' of meaning. *Mind, Language and Reality. Philosophical papers II*, 215–271. Cambridge: Cambridge University Press.

Quicoli, A. C. 1976. Conditions on Clitic Movement in Portuguese. *Linguistic Analysis* 2: 199–223.

Radford, A. 1977. *Italian Syntax. Transformational and Relational Grammar*. Cambridge: Cambridge University Press.

Rappaport H., and B. Levin. 1998. Building verb meanings. M. Butt and W. Geuder (eds), *The Projection of Arguments: Lexical and Compositional Factors*, 97–134. Stanford: CSLI Publications.

Reinhart, T. 1995. *Interface Strategies*. OTS Working Papers in Linguistics.

Reinheimer, S. and L. Tasmowski. 1999. Les Verbes italiens à prétérit sigmatique. R. Brusegan and M. A. Cortelazzo (eds), *Il Tempo, i tempi. Omaggio a Lorenzo Renzi*, 211–225. Padoue: Unipress.

Reinheimer, S. and L. Tasmowski. 1999. Verbes réguliers, pseudo-réguliers et irréguliers dans les langues romanes. Actes du Colloque *Grammaire et lexique comparés des langues romanes*, 181-190. Leuven / Louvain-la-Neuve: CLLL.

Reinheimer, S. and L. Tasmowski. 2000. La Systématisation des verbes forts dans les langues romanes. Proceedings of the *XXIIe Congrès International de linguistique et de philologie romanes* VI, 437-448. Tübingen: Niemeyer.

Renzi, L. 1988. L'articolo. L. Renzi (ed), Vol. I, 357–423.

Richter, F. and M. Sailer. 1999. A Lexicalist Collocation Analysis of Sentential Negation and Negative Concord in French. V. Kordoni (ed), *Tübingen Studies in Head-Driven Phrase Structure Grammar*. Arbeitspapiere des SFB 340, Bericht Nr. 132, 231–300. University of Tübingen.

van Riemsdijk, H. (ed). 1999. *Clitics in the Languages of Europe*. Berlin: Mouton de Gruyter.

Rivas, A. M. 1977. *A Theory of Clitics*. PhD dissertation, MIT.

Rivero, M.-L. 1970. A Surface Structure Constraint on Negation in Spanish. *Language* 46: 650–666.

Rivière, N. 1981. *La Construction impersonelle en français contemporain.* Paris: Jean-Favard.

Rizzi, L. 1978. A Restructuring Rule in Italian Syntax. S. J. Keyser (ed), *Recent transformational studies in European languages*, 113–158. Cambridge, MA: MIT Press.

Rizzi, L. 1982. *Issues in Italian Syntax.* Dordrecht: Foris.

Rizzi, L. 1986. On the Status of Subject Clitics in Romance. O. Jaeggli and C. Silva-Corvalán (eds), *Studies in Romance Linguistics*, 391–419. Dordrecht: Foris.

Rizzi, L. 1991. *Residual Verb Second and the Wh-Criterion.* Technical Reports in Formal and Computational Linguistics 2. Faculté des Lettres, University of Geneva.

Rizzi, L. 1997. The Fine Structure of the Left Periphery. L. Haegeman (ed), 281–304.

Rochette, A. 1990. Restructuring Classes of Verbs in Romance. A.-M. di Sciullio and A. Rochette (eds), *Binding in Romance: essays in honour of Judith McA'Nulty*, 96–128. Ottawa: Canadian Linguistic Association.

Rohlfs, G. 1969. *Grammatica storica della lingua italiana e dei suoi dialetti.* Torino: Einaudi.

Rohlfs, G. 1972. *Historische Grammatik der italienischen Sprache und ihrer Mundarten, II. Formenlehre und Syntax.* Berne / Munich: Francke Verlag.

Rosen, C. 1981. *The Relational Structure of Reflexive Clauses: Evidence from Italian.* PhD dissertation, Harvard University. (Published 1988, New York: Garland).

Rosen, C. 1984. The Interface between Semantic roles and Initial Grammatical Relations. D. Perlmutter and C. Rosen (eds), *Studies in Relational Grammar 2*, 38–77. Chicago: Chicago University Press.

Rosen, S. 1989. *Argument structure and complex predicates.* PhD dissertation, Brandeis University.

Rouveret, A. 1991. Cliticisation et temps en portugais européen. J. Guéron, and J.-Y. Pollock (eds), *Grammaire générative et syntaxe comparée*, 147–170. Paris: CNRS Éditions.

Rouveret, A. 1999. Clitics, Subjects and Tense in European Portuguese. H. van Riemsdijk (ed), 639–677.

Rouveret, A. and J.-R. Vergnaud. 1980. Specifying Reference to the Subject: French causatives and conditions on representations. *Linguistic Inquiry* 11: 97–202.

Ruwet, N. 1972. *Théorie syntaxique et syntaxe du français.* Paris: Le Seuil.

Ruwet, N. 1988. Les Verbes météorologiques et l'hypothèse inaccusative. C. Blanche-Benveniste, A. Chervel and M. Gross (eds), *Hommage à la mémoire de Jean Stéfanini*, 383–402. Aix-en-Provence: Publications de l'Université de Provence.

Ruwet, N. 1990. *En* et *y* : deux clitiques pronominaux antilogophoriques. *Langages* 97: 51–81.

Ryle, G. 1949. *The Concept of Mind.* New York: Barnes and Noble.

Saccon, G. 1995. *Ne*-cliticization does not support the Unaccusative / Intransitive Split. G. V. Morril and R. T. Oehrle (eds), *Formal Grammar, Proceedings of the European Summer School in logic, language and information*, 227-238. Barcelona.

Sag, Ivan A., T. Wasow and E. Bender. 2003. Syntactic Theory, a formal introduction. Stanford: CSLI Publications.

Salvi, G. 1980. Gli Ausiliari 'essere' e 'avere' in italiano. *Acta Linguistica Academiae Scientiarum Hungaricae* 30: 137–162.

Sánchez-Rei, X. M. 1999. Repercusións gramaticais do uso da interpolación pronominal en galego. *Cadernos de Lingua* 19: 85–110.

Sandfeld, K. 1970. *Syntaxe du français contemporain. Les pronoms.* Paris: Droz.

Sasse, H-J. 1987. The Thetic / Categorical Distinction Revisited. *Linguistics* 25: 511–580.

Schmerling, S. 1976. *Aspects of English Sentence Stress.* Austin: University of Texas Press.

Schmitt, C. and A. Munn. 1999. Against the Nominal Mapping Parameter. Bare Nouns in Brazilian Portuguese. N. Hall, M. Hirotani and P. Tamanji (eds), *Proceedings of the Northeast Linguistics Society* 29: 339–353.

Schwarzschild, R. 1991. *On the meaning of Definite Plural NPs.* PhD dissertation, University of Massachussetts, Amherst.

Schwarzschild, R. 1999. GIVENness, avoid F and other Constraints on the Placement of Accent. *Natural Language Semantics* 7: 141–177.

Schwegler, A. 1983. Predicate Negation and Word Order Change: a problem of multiple causation. *Lingua* 61: 297–334.

Siewierska, A. 1988. *Word Order Rules.* London: Croom Helm.

Silverstein, M. 1976. Hierarchy of Features and Ergativity. R. M. W. Dixon (ed.), *Grammatical Categories in Australian Languages*, 112–171. Canberra: Australian Institute of Aboriginal Studies.

Simpson, J. and M. Withgott. 1986. Pronominal Clitic Clusters and Templates. H. Borer (ed), 149–174.

Skytte, G., G. Salvi and M. R. Manzini. 1991. Frasi subordinate all'infinito. L. Renzi *et al.* (eds), Vol. 2, 483–569.

Smolensky, P. 2006. Optimality in Phonology II: Harmonic Completeness, local Constraint Conjunction, and Feature Domain Markedness. In P. Smolensky and G. Legendre, *The Harmonic Mind: from neural computation to optimality-theoretic grammar*, vol 2, 27-160. Cambridge, MA: MIT Press.

Sorace, A. 1993a. Incomplete vs. Divergent Representations of Unaccusativity in non-native Grammars of Italian. *Second Language Research* 9: 22–47.

Sorace, A. 1993b. Unaccusativity and Auxiliary Choice in non-native Grammars of Italian and French: asymmetries and predictable indeterminacy. *Journal of French Language Studies* 3: 71–93.

Sorace, A. 1995a. Contraintes sémantiques sur la syntaxe : l'acquisition de l'inaccusativité en italien L2. *Acquisition et Interaction en Langue Etrangère* 5: 79–113.

Sorace, A. 1995b. Acquiring Argument Structures in a Second Language: the unaccusative/unergative distinction. L. Eubank, L. Selinker and M. Sharwood Smith (eds), *The Current State of Interlanguage*, 153–175. Amsterdam: J. Benjamins.

Sorace, A. 2000. Gradients in Auxiliary Selection with Intransitive Verbs. *Language* 76: 859–890.

Sorace, A. 2004. Gradience at the Lexicon-Syntax Interface: evidence from auxiliary selection and implications for unaccusativity. A. Alexiadou, E. Anagnostopoulou and M. Everaert (eds), *The Unaccusative Puzzle,* 243-268. Oxford: Oxford University Press.

Sorace, A. and M. Cennamo. 2006. Unaccusativity ate the syntax-lexicon interface: evidence form Paduan. R. Aranovich (ed), 65-100.

Sornicola, R. 1994. On Word Order Variability: a study from a corpus of Italian. *Lingua et stile* 29: 25–58.

Sornicola, R. 1995. Theticity, VS Order and the Interplay of Syntax, Semantics and Pragmatics. Y. Matras and H-J. Sasse (eds), 72–83.

Strawson, P. F. 1950. On Referring. *Mind* 59: 320–344.

Steedman, M. 2006. Surface-compositional scope-alternation without existential quantifiers, MS, University of Edimburg (on-line).

Suñer, M. 1982. *The Syntax and Semantics of Spanish Presentational Sentence-Types*. Washington, DC: Georgetown University Press.

Suñer, M. 1987. *Haber* + past participle. *Linguistic Inquiry* 18: 683–690.

Suñer, M. 1988. The Role of Agreement in Clitic Doubled Constructions. *Natural Language and Linguistic Theory* 6: 391–434.

Suñer, M. 2003. The Lexical Preverbal Subject in a Romance Null Subject Language: where are thou? R. Nuñez-Cedeno, L. López and R. Cameron (eds), *A Romance Perspective on Language Knowledge and Use*, 341-358. Amsterdam: J. Benjamins.

de Swart, H. 1994. Indéfini et généricité. *Faits de Langues* 4: 139–146.

de Swart, H. 1996. (In)definites and Genericity. M. Kanazawa, C. J. Piñón and H. de Swart (eds), *Quantifiers, Deduction, and Context,* 171–194. Stanford: CSLI Publications.

de Swart, H. 1999. Négation et concordance négative en français. *Recherches de linguistique française et romane d'Utrecht*. (also 2001, Indéfinis négatifs et concordance négative en français, G. Kleiber *et al.* (eds), 167–187).

de Swart, H. and I. A. Sag. 2002. Negation and Negative Concord in Romance. *Linguistics and Philosophy* 25: 373-417.

Tasmowski, L. 1980. Troncation, épenthèse et morphologie verbale. *Studii şi Cercetări Lingvistice* 31: 620–630.

Tasmowski, L. 1984. ?*Lui faire téléphoner quelqu'un d'autre : une stratégie ? *Linguisticae Investigationes* 8: 403–427.

Tasmowski, Liliane. 1985. Faire Infinitif. L. Mélis *et al.*, 223–365.

Tasmowski, Liliane. 1990. ...En semble... ou ...semble en... *Le français moderne* 58: 28–42.

Tasmowski, L., and H. van Oevelem. 1987. Le Causatif pronominal. *Revue Romane* 22: 40–58.

Tekavčić, P. 1972. *Grammatica storica dell'italiano, II. Morfosintassi*. Bologna: il Mulino.

Torrego, E. 1989. Unergative-Unaccusative Alternations in Spanish. I. Laka and A. Mahajan (eds), *Functional Heads and Clause Structure*. MIT Working Papers in Linguistics 10: 253–272.

Tortora, C. 2000. Object Clitic Placement in Romance: the case of an Italian dialect. Paper presented at LRSL 30, University of Florida, Gainesville.

Tovena, L. M. 1996. Negative Concord, Events and Negative Chains. *Proceedings of ESCOL '96*, 313–322. Ithaca, NY: CLC Publications.

Tovena, L. M. 1998. *The Fine Structure of Polarity Sensitivity*. New York: Garland.

Tovena, L. M. 2000. Neg-raising: Negation as Failure? J. Hoeksema, H. Rullmann, V. Sánchez Valencia and T. van der Wouden (eds), *Perspectives on Negation and polarity items*, 331–356. Amsterdam: J. Benjamins.

Tovena, L. M. 2001. Between Mass and Count. K. Megerdoomian and L. A. Bar-el (eds), *Proceedings of WCCFL 20*, 565–578. Somerville, MA: Cascadilla Press.

Tovena, L. M. 2002. Distributional Restrictions on Negative Determiners. K. Jaszczolt and K. Turner (eds), *Meanings in Contrast: The Cambridge Papers*, 3–28. Amsterdam: J. Benjamins.

Tovena, L. M. 2003. Determiners and weakly discretised domains. J. Quer, J. Schroten, P. Sleeman and E. Verheugd (eds.), *Romance Languages and Linguistic Theory 2001*, 333—348. Amsterdam: John Benjamins.

Tovena, L. M. 2004. Negative Quantification and Existential Sentences. To appear in K. Heusinger and I. Comorovski (eds.) *Existence: Syntax and Semantics*, Dordrecht: Springer.

Tovena, L. M. 2005. Discourse and Addition. *Proceedings of Workshop on Discourse domains and information structure*, European Summer School on Language Logic and Information, 47–56. Edinburgh.

Tovena, L. M. 2006. Dealing with Alternatives, in *Proceedings of the 10th Sinn und Bedeutung*, 373–387, Berlin.

Tuttle, E. 1986. The Spread of *esse* as Universal Auxiliary in Central Italo-Romance. *Medioevo Romanzo* 11: 229–287.

Umbach, C. 2004. On the Notion of Contrast in Information Structure and Discourse Structure. *Journal of Semantics* 21: 155-176.

Uriagereka, J. 1995. Aspects of the Syntax of Clitic Placement in Western Romance. *Linguistic Inquiry* 26: 79–123.

Vallduví, E. 1991. *The Informational Component*. New York: Garland.

Vallduví, E. 1993. Catalan as VOS: Evidence from Information Packaging. W. J. Ashby, M. Mithun, G. Perisinotto and E. Raposo (eds), *Linguistic Perspectives on the Romance Languages: selected papers from LSRL XXI*, 335–350. Amsterdam: J. Benjamins.

Vallduví, E. 2001. La Dislocació del verb en català. A. Bover, M-R. Lloret and M. Vidal-Tibbits (eds), *Actes del Novè Colloqui d'Estudis Catalans a Nord-Amèrica*, 467–494. Barcelona: Abadia de Montserrat.

Vallduví, E. and E. Engdahl. 1995. Information Packaging and Grammar Architecture. J. Beckman (ed), *Proceedings of NELS 25*, 519–533. UMass Graduate Linguistic Students' Association.

Vallduví, E. and M. Vilkuna. 1998. On Rheme and Kontrast. P. Culicover and L. McNally (eds), *The Limits of Syntax*. Syntax and Semantics 29, 79–108. New York: Academic Press.

van den Eynde, K. and C. Blanche-Benveniste. 1970. Essai d'analyse de la morphologie du verbe français. *Orbis* 19: 404–429.

van Geenhoven, V. 1996. *Semantic Incorporation and Indefinite Descriptions: semantic and syntactic aspects of noun incorporation in West Greenlandic*. PhD dissertation, University of Tübingen.

van der Wouden, T. and F. Zwarts 1993. A Semantic Analysis of Negative Concord. U. Lahiri and A. Z. Wyner (eds), *SALT III: Proceedings of the Third Conference on Semantics and Linguistic Theory*, 202–219. Ithaca, NY: CLC Publications.

Vanelli, L. 1981. Il Mecanismo dittico. *Studi di Grammatica Italiana* 10: 293–311.

Van Valin, R. D. 1990. Semantic Parameters of Split Intransitivity. *Language* 66: 221–260.

Vanvolsem, L. 1999. La Position des pronoms personnels avec les verbes modaux en italien. M. Coene *et al.* (eds), 169–182.

Vendler, Z. 1967. *Linguistics in Philosophy*. Ithaca, NY: Cornell University Press.

Vigário, M. 1999. Pronominal Cliticization in European Portuguese: a postlexical operation. *Catalan Working Papers in Linguistics* 7: 219–237.

Vigário, M. 2003. *The Prosodic Word in European Portuguese*. Berlin: Mouton de Gruyter.

Villada M. 2001. *Status of Clitics in Galician and Spanish*. Mémoire de MSc in Computational Linguistics, University of Essex.

Villalta, E. 1995. Plural Indefinites in Spanish and Distributivity, paper given at-Going Romance 1994.

Vogel, I. and D. J. Napoli. 1995. The Verbal Component in Italian Compounds. J. Amastae *et al.* (eds), 367–381.

Wall, K. 1980. *L'Inversion dans la subordonnée en français contemporain.* Studia Romanica Upsaliensia 30. Université d'Uppsala.

Wandruszka, U. 1982. Studien zur Italienischen Wortstellung. Tübingen: Gunter Narr Verlag.

Watson, K. 1997. French Complement Clitic Sequences: a template approach. *French Language Studies* 7: 69–89.

Wehr, B. 1984. *Diskusstrategien im Romanischen.* Tübingen: Gunter Narr Verlag.

Wilkinson, K. 1991. *Studies in the Semantics of Generic Noun Phrases.* PhD dissertation, University of Massachussetts, Amherst.

Wilkinson, K. 1995. The Semantics of the Common Noun Kind. G. N. Carlson and F. J. Pelletier (eds), 383–397.

Williams, E. B. 1962. *From Latin to Portuguese. Historical Phonology and Morphology of the Portuguese Language.* Philadelphia: University of Pennsylvania Press.

Yllera, A. 1999. Las Perífrasis verbales de gerundio y participio. I. Bosque and V. Demonte (eds), Vol. 2, 3391–3441.

Yvon, H. 1948. *Pas* et *point* dans les propositions négatives. *Le français moderne* 16: 19–35.

Zaenen, A. 1993. Unaccusativity in Dutch: integrating syntax and lexical semantics. J. Pustejovsky (ed), *Semantics and the lexicon*, 129–161. Dordrecht: Kluwer.

Zagona, K. 1988. *Verb Phrase Syntax: A parametric study of English and Spanish.* Cambridge, MA: MIT Press.

Zanuttini, R. 1991. *Syntactic Properties of Sentential Negation. A comparative study of Romance languages.* PhD dissertation, University of Pennsylvania.

Zanuttini, R. 1997. *Negation and Clausal Structure; a comparative study of Romance languages.* Oxford: Oxford University Press.

Zimmer, R. 1992. Die Morphologie des Italienischen, Spanischen und Portugiesischen Verbs. Einzelsprachlich und im Vergleich. Tübingen: Niemeyer.

Zribi-Hertz, A. (ed). 1997. *Les Pronoms : morphologie, syntaxe et typologie.* Saint-Denis: Presses Universitaires de Vincennes.

Zribi-Hertz, A. 1982. La Construction SE-moyen du français et son statut dans le triangle: moyen-passif-réfléchi. *Linguisticae Investigationes* 6: 345–401.

Zribi-Hertz, A. 1987. La Réflexivité ergative en français moderne. *Le français moderne* 55: 23–54.

Zribi-Hertz, A. 1994. La Syntaxe des clitiques nominatifs en français standard et en français avancé. *Travaux de linguistique et de philologie* 32: 131–147.

Zubizarreta, M-L. 1985. The Relation between Morphophonology and Morphosyntax, the case of Romance causatives. *Linguistic Inquiry* 16: 247–289.

Zubizarreta, M-L. 1987. *Levels of Representation in the Lexicon and in the Syntax*. Dordrecht: Foris.

Zubizarreta, M-L. 1998. *Prosody, Focus and Word Order*. Cambridge, MA: MIT Press.

Zwicky, A. M. 1977. *On Clitics*. Bloomington: Indiana University Linguistics Club.

Zwicky, A. M. 1987. Suppressing the Zs. *Journal of Linguistics* 23: 133–148.

Zwicky, A. M. and G. K Pullum. 1983. Cliticization vs. Inflection: English n't. *Language* 59: 502–513.

Subject Index

Name index